The Necessity of Anti-Semitism

Frederic Raphael

THE NECESSITY OF ANTI-SEMITISM

CARCANET

First published in Great Britain in 1997 by
Carcanet Press Limited
4th Floor, Conavon Court
12–16 Blackfriars Street
Manchester M3 5BQ

A CIP catalogue record for this book
is available from the British Library

ISBN 1 85754 324 6

The publisher acknowledges financial
assistance from the Arts Coucil of England.

Set in Sabon by Ensystems, Saffron Walden
Printed and bound in England by SRP Ltd, Exeter

FOR MY GRANDCHILDREN

Contents

Introduction

Since we all abuse journalists and – when criticised – critics for their affectations of durability, it is hard to find good reasons why one's own ephemera should be exempt from wrapping the fish they deserve. However, not all publications are equally perishable and some with modest circulations are more hospitable to unfashionable opinions, or longer arguments, than their more successful rivals. Since a number of these essays and reviews appeared first in the *Times Literary Supplement*, the *Jewish Quarterly*, *Poetry Nation Review* and *Prospect*, it is unlikely that they have been read so widely that reprinting them amounts to no more than a bang on the same old drum.

My main defence for collecting them, however, is that they do constitute a kind of whole. Of course, there is bound to be a ragbag aspect to any such volume, but the fact that they cannot have been *intended* to present a consciously coherent argument or to maintain a consistent theme gives them, I should like to think, a sort of involuntary integrity. It is only in slightly surprised, occasionally embarrassed, retrospect that I perceive the regular lines of my assumptions and, yes, my prejudices. Essays and book reviews involve a process of self-discovery and that self is, to a degree, created by the need to be as honest, truthful and amusing as may be. 'Amusing' seems a give-away here, but if brevity does not always entail wit, the confines of a review insist on enough sharpness to arrest and, if possible, both provoke and entertain the skimming reader.

A large number of my reviews have been written for a

succession of literary editors of the *Sunday Times*, of whom the first was Jack Lambert. I was recruited, if that is the word for so eager a volunteer, by Pat Murphy, with whom, in the 1960s, I used to play bridge occasionally at Crockford's. He was an amiable, anxious Irish Catholic who, so I have been promised, believed that the Jews had been, and continued to be, properly stigmatised for their deicide. This did not in the least prevent him from recommending me to Jack Lambert, nor from being a keen admirer of both Peter Shaffer and Brian Glanville. Pat may have been a theoretical anti-Semite, of a traditional 'Christian' kind, but in practice he neither discriminated against nor, it seems, was able to recognise the fiendishness of individual Jews.

Jack Lambert was a fastidious literary editor from whom I learned many lessons; he was vigilant, but rarely caustic, and saved me from any number of naivetés and inelegances. To some tastes, he was the epitome of the middlebrow (I suspect that he preferred C.P. Snow to Marcel Proust), but he was a genuine lover of the arts and he had the one crucial skill for a literary editor: he knew how to match the right book with the right critic in order to give his pages both authority and lightness. He preferred that one like rather than dislike a book and he wasted no large space on venom or personalities. Jack had had a good war in small boats. If he had suffered considerably, he rarely spoke of it except in terms of comedy: he recalled a petty officer who, on watch in the North Sea, reported 'Heavy breathing on the port bow'; a walrus had broken surface and was frowning balefully at H.M.'s ship. Jack's Distinguished Service Cross reminded one that there were greater dangers than that of being cut for length. Thanks to him, I graduated from being a reviewer of fiction to the general books from which I have derived much pleasure and education. If I have spent more time than I should have on anatomising what was of little account, even dull books can require the kind of peripheral reading which leads to instructive, perhaps chastening, discoveries.

There is, I confess, an element of provocation in the title of this collection and there are, I suppose (and perhaps hope), people who will be unamused by it. The reference to Shelley's notorious pamphlet, *The Necessity of Atheism*, is obvious enough, but I am perhaps a little more in earnest than he was. The 'necessity' to which I draw attention is not, depend upon it, prescriptive. Percy Bysshe may have thought that the repudiation of God was a necessary preliminary to the kind of virtuous world in which he would have liked to live; anti-Semitism, on the other hand, seems to me to be an ineradicable and, in that sense, 'necessary' part of the world in which we have to live. Its 'necessity' is that Judophobia is part of the whole 'argument' – the plot – of the great fiction which used to be called Christendom and is now 'Europe'.

Since my texts develop this theme, with a variety of arguments and instances which the reader can judge (or supplement), there is no need to insist on it here. What honestly surprises and slightly disconcerts me, as I read the mass of journalism and essays which I have accumulated, is how frequently – obsessively, it might be said – I have reverted to the theme of Jews and anti-Semitism. In this respect at least, I feel a certain affinity with Wittgenstein who, having imagined in his youth that 'metaphysics' could be shown to be definitively unspeakable and thenceforth no longer his subject, spent most of his life examining and refining responses to its manifold and, it seems, unavoidable instances.

Two books were the illuminating gospels of my time at Cambridge: Wittgenstein's *Philosophical Investigations* and Karl Popper's *The Open Society and its Enemies*. Wittgenstein died soon after I went up to St John's, but his aura was still evident, especially among the Moral Scientists (as we then called ourselves, in happily arcane reference to David Hume). His posthumous publication of *Philosophical Investigations*, in 1953, seemed to give us access to a resurrected discourse which, unlike the gnomically intractable *Tractatus Logico-Philosophicus*, was vivid, clear and, apparently, open-ended and open-minded. Its answers often came in the form of questions and its inconclusive conclusions offered exemplary instances of discussion without dogma. As for Popper, he advocated a systematic lack of system: his 'war work', as he called *The Open Society*, was a passionate argument for tolerance and the confession of fallibility. We were not merely likely to be wrong, we could only be right if we *tried*, as it were, to see if we were wrong: only by testing our ideas in practice, and against other possibilities, could we hope to call our society civilised. To seek to falsify one's own arguments was the sign of an honourable intelligence; the best defence against bad faith is to point out the chinks in one's own armour. In England, it would be nice to believe, this is sometimes known as having a sense of humour.

It is hardly a secret now that Wittgenstein, like Popper, was – to say the least – not an easy man. In both of them, tolerance was more recommended than practised. There is comedy here, but also irrelevance. We were perhaps lucky, in those discreet years, not to know too much about the private lives of those we admired; after all, the vanities of philosophers are one thing and their arguments another (unless, of course, they are not). Wittgenstein's human failings, if that is what they were, are a comfort to those who care nothing for the problems of philosophy, but they are of small interest to anyone who turns to him for what was uniquely important in his work. Popper's notorious irascibility and intolerance of contradiction made the wits say that *The Open Society* was written by its enemy, but the character of the messenger does not invalidate his message.

As for Wittgenstein, however jealous he may have been of his own ideas (he anathematised old friends for suspected plagiarism), the long and generous lesson of *Philosophical Investigations* is that there is no systematic way of simplifying the complexities of language and no Alexandrian solution to the multiplicity of Gordian knots in which it ties us. The whole history of man's thinking, erroneous or not, self-contradictory or not, is synthesised in language. Those who accuse 'modern philosophy' of reducing everything, including God, to a 'mere matter of words' fail to see that matters of words are rarely mere. A French philosopher called Brice-Parrin (of whom I know nothing else) said 'Words are loaded pistols'; a Nazi once told Popper, who was inviting him to be reasonable, that his gun was his argument. When we talk about ideas, we are also dealing with licences to kill.

One must not exaggerate. The great good fortune of the British and the Americans in this murderous century is that they have known triumph without enduring humiliation. Both nations suffered appalling casualties in the wars they fought, but they have not known defeat or invasion. My good fortune is a function of having been born in the United States and having grown up in England. Through no merit of my own, and without having raised a rifle except as a cadet at Charterhouse, I have known about many terrible things but experienced few.

During my first term at Public School, Oration Quarter 1945, a very skinny boy (whose name was Maxwell, C.J.M.), was nicknamed 'Belsen' by witty members of our house. I was a timid new boy, very reluctant to be known as a Jew, and I can remember the alarm, tinged with despicable glee (what struck another could not strike me), with which I witnessed 'Belsen's' casual persecution. C.J.M. Maxwell was not a Jew and no necessary malice was involved; Belsen, like Bedlam, was a source of derision, not a place of horrors. There is still something so remote from English experience about the Holocaust (as we have now largely agreed to call it, despite Christopher Ricks' fastidious objections, not least to its self-important appropriation of a capital letter) that to harp on it can seem immodest. Not so long ago, while writing amiably about a novel of mine, a reviewer accused me of being 'unashamedly Jewish'. Little did he know of how often, during miserable, cowardly times at school, I wished to be a Christian soldier.

My experience of anti-Semitism has never been life-threatening; it has sometimes been painful, since I have a thin skin, but it has been limited to brief periods of verbal abuse and sly harassment, nearly all of them several decades ago. Boys will be boys, and so will men, at times. I cannot deny that some of my books and other work have paid back old scores, not all of them on my own behalf. If they are lucky, writers have long memories and I have taken unworthy pleasure in using the names of my ancient enemies whenever I needed to christen a fool or nominate a boor. On the whole, however, when I have dealt with anti-Semitism in print, it has not been from any personal motive, still less from any monotonous loyalty to Judaism or to 'the Jews'.

I am not religious, although – out of a certain piety (respect for my hardly more observant father's wishes) – my wife and I pay our subscription to the Liberal Synagogue which we never attend. I do not belong to a 'community'. Writers, in my view, should 'get alone', as Adam Morris puts it. My obsession with anti-Semitism has persisted only because anti-Semitism has. As any Wittgensteinian might expect, Jew hatred does not take a single form and, like metaphysics, it is not to be repressed by a simple interdiction. Since 1945, few intelligent men or women have proclaimed their anti-Semitism (which was far from the case before the war), but fewer are wholly immune to its sly temptations. Even Jews can become dispassionate to the point of connivance with their enemies. My great aunt Minnie, who converted to Christianity, told my mother that she had not been a lady until she ceased to be Jewish. The pettiest kinds of provocation do not deserve solemn response; when our local

MP, Alan Clark, announces his qualified admiration for the Führer, we can offer him a brief heil and leave it at that. The fantasy of outlawing *feelings*, merely because they are puerile or squalid, will lead to greater injustices and absurdities than it could ever remedy. No one can be obliged to like Jews, or even to give them the time of day; it is enough if they, like everyone else, can be citizens of an open society where everyone is equal before the law and the ballot box. The comedy of anti-Semitism in England lies in the fact that its most urgent advocates – Eliot, Pound, Wyndham-Lewis, Belloc, William Joyce, W.B. Yeats – were metics (men of foreign origins) or self-important World Figures like Mosley or H.G. Wells or petty *provocateurs* like Evelyn Waugh.

Anti-Semitism is a not a serious issue because certain people are, or used to be, excluded from golf clubs. In more solemn form, however, it belongs to a persistent way of conceiving of the world, and even of imagining the universe, which is at once unjust and absurd. What then is to be done? Anti-Semitism cannot be banned and yet, it seems, it would be grotesque not to challenge it. It *is* grotesque and it can be challenged, but not by proscription. Neither the virtues of the Jews nor the barbarities of their persecutors will render anti-Semitism unthinkable or even, to perverted minds, delectable. If we insist on Jewish virtues, we are soon obliged to deny Jewish vices; if we list atrocities, we invite charges – deicide, International Finance, etc. – to justify them. There is, of course, a place for anti-defamatory legislation, but it must be the same legislation which protects all the citizens of a civilised, non-theocratic society.

Nothing has contributed more to the mystification of the Holocaust than the search for some great, overriding 'reason' for it. It is possible to read the murder of about six million people – of whom at least a quarter were children – as having its place in some (peculiar) 'metaphysical' scheme, but the same might be true, as Dostoyevsky pointed out, of the death of a single child.

We need not scan the stars to divine why men are shits, bullies, murderers and thieves. To talk of the 'silence of God' does more to lend dignity to the inquest than to bring the guilty to account. The notion that behind a great crime there must lie a great motive is seductive to those who, in the style of the doomy German philosophers they choose to admire (if only because they can read them in the original), want to garb their discourse in polysyllabic pretentiousness. The failure to punish those who took part in the Holocaust was not due to the inscrutable or unprecedented nature or scale of their crimes. Existing laws, concerning murder, theft, unlawful imprisonment and a number of other felonies, were always available in the countries where the Holocaust was carried out. The failure to apply those laws thoroughly is what makes Europe a haunted continent where the high hope of 'unity' is founded on basic assumptions of forgiving and, more pressingly, forgetting.

Even in Germany, I believe, it was never explicitly stated that killing or robbing Jews was permitted. The notion of 'war crimes' was a convenience alike for the criminals and for those (Lord Annan is their vicar on earth) who had better things to do than to prosecute them. To encourage young Spartiates to learn the art of killing, the Spartans used each year to declare war on the Helots who were their slaves. Probationary warriors could harden their hearts and their muscles by slaughtering them with impunity. For us to speak only of 'war crimes' when we mean mass murder of civilians far from the war zones was, and remains, a distortion of the facts. What it does, of course, is to disparage those (sc. Jews) who 'so many years after the event want to keep old wounds open'. We all know the humbug and what noble lords and forgiving divines give utterance to it. The truth, which is emerging so neatly as the statute of limitations disarms it, is that even the victors often connived with, and profited from, the thefts which they chose not to rectify. Anti-Semitism was not a prejudice; it was also a profitable business. Ask the Swiss.

These essays and articles do, I fear, return again and again to the impossible question 'why?'. It might well be that were I not a Jew, whatever that means, I should be more interested in topically urgent things such as ethnicity, the female condition, morality in public life and the state of English cricket, but even the worst of losers must play the cards he is dealt and not wonder too much what he has done to deserve them. I live a privileged life (I and my wife and my children and my grandchildren, Jews or not, are free to pursue our own purposes) and the comedy of my grievances is that I have little to complain about. To that extent at least, I am innocent of special pleading.

After all the seriousness with which I have, from time to time, sought to confront the horrors of the century, I have to confess that probably the most unanswerable work of art, when it came to 'refuting' Hitler (and Mussolini), was Chaplin's *The Great Dictator*, in which a naïve accuracy and condign derision were matched. The next best medicine was concocted by Mel Brooks, in *The Producers*: 'don't be stupid, be a smarty/ Come and join the Nazi party' tells us more about the seductions of Fascism than a dozen sociological analyses or self-pitying tosh like *Heimat*.

It is, of course, impossible in practice to discountenance torturers by laughing at them, as Vladimir Nabokov recommended in *Invitation to a Beheading*, but to take them unremittingly seriously is to pay them much too much honour. Those fortunate enough to have been exempt from unspeakable cruelties should have the petty courage neither to forget its victims nor to solemnise their torturers by taking them more seriously than they deserve. Rebecca West once said that moral problems arose not from not knowing what one ought to do, but from the effort to find plausible reasons not to do it. The same applies to telling the truth.

Frederic Raphael

An ABC of Modern Cant

AID   Payments to Third World countries in order to give their rulers something to fall back on, usually in Geneva or Zurich, should the tiny proportion of our money they devote to the betterment of their peoples (e.g. by building airports named after themselves) fail to appease the populace or buy off the next generation of generals and politicians who, once corruption has been swept aside, will demand that such payments be increased. It is alleged in some quarters that if all aid to Third World Countries were to be stopped, Switzerland would become a Third World country. How would we then be able to hold up our heads?

BANGLADESH   We all bear a heavy weight of responsibility when natural disasters strike Bangladesh and hence have no right to deplore its treatment of women, writers or other negligible people of that kind. *Cujus regio, ejus religio* is a slogan we (and a number of other people) might do well to ponder.

CEASE-FIRE   The time taken by, e.g., Balkan militias to reload or, in the case of 'prolonged c-f', to re-supply their artillery.

DIALOGUE   Any shouting match at which the louder mouth dictates demands to opponents to whose arguments it has no intention of listening. We need much, much more of it in the present perilous state of the world. Under the auspices of the

President of the United States, it removes the guns from the hands of thugs and bullies and puts money into them instead; it also requires them to shake hands (q.v.) with people they would like to murder, thus proving that, if the price is right, man is essentially a moral being. Yet there are those who carp.

EUROPE   It has put its divisions behind it and, with all faults, has set an example to the world which it will ignore at its peril. That the Germans are now our friends, regardless of their past behaviour, is yet another proof that man is a moral being. We should not rest until everyone has a right and a duty to pay VAT in the common interest. If, as we should, we believe every word Ted Heath says, we shall soon export more than we import and salvation will follow. Anyone who disagrees can almost certainly not spell his own name.

FUTURE, THE   We must all look to it. It is so much more important than the past. Our children and our grandchildren will almost certainly have to live in it and they will blame us if their cultural heritage is not preserved despite everything that governments are trying to do in order to destroy education, public services and the fabric of civilisation. Paul Johnson wonders if it will come at all, yet he goes on writing. What a man!

HAND-SHAKE   The proof that everyone can be friendly if there is a photographer present. There is no one in the world to whom John Major has been seen to refuse a hand-shake; this is known as global statesmanship. If both hands are pressed into service, the restultant hand-shake is guaranteed to bind the partners in mutual trust (q.v.) for up to fifteen seconds. True statesmen always look at the camera when shaking hands, never at their companions. No one should shake hands for a living without seeing his dentist regularly.

IDEAL WORLD   Something unlikely to be achieved overnight, but still worth working for and believing in if we are not to fall into cynicism. Without ideals, man is a beast or, in vexed cases, a conceptual artist. In an ideal world, Paul Johnson would be king and Mrs Thatcher would be his Prime Minister. Sadly, it is not so.

JEWS Nobody in the world now has any prejudice against Jews, not even the Arabs, who would like them all to be dead.

KURDS This ancient people excites a wide measure of sympathy and loathing. No Western statesman ever promised them anything, but they are still not going to get anything. Since they do not constitute a serious threat to their neighbours (who constitute a very serious threat to them), it is generally agreed they do not have a leg to stand on. There are no famous Kurds. Edward Said holds the West to blame for this.

LAST CHANCE As in 'last chance for peace'; a phrase invented by Lord (Christopher) Mayhew, when grovelling in front of the late President Nasser. It then described Israel's golden opportunity to disappear voluntarily before being annihilated by the Good and the Beautiful President. We all know the consequences of its failure to do what Mayhew so altruistically proposed.

MONEY There is no place for it in the settlement of international disputes. No British government has ever offered or hoped to receive any in return for its countless services to the betterment of the world. No one in the tax-free Common Market secretariat has ever been remotely interested in it, not even for a moment. It is easily recognisable by the strings which are attached to it. When duly alerted, the police will remove it.

NEVER A word never used by negotiators. We will never negotiate with the gunmen until we have to.

OBSERVERS People in lightweight clothing who take free trips to disagreeable places where they see whatever their own governments have primed them to see, either 'widespread intimidation' or 'a lack of widespread intimidation'. Such people often become Lords and Ladies and are always cautiously hopeful about the future of democracy in emergent countries. They will visit TV studios at short notice and for a frankly derisory fee.

PEACE PROCESS A magic wand which transforms terrorists, criminals and their irreconcilable enemies into amenable and reasonable human beings with a surprising measure of common interests. It never (q.v.) involves the promise of money (q.v.) or the threat of force or the withdrawal of 'aid' (q.v.). Participants can be recognised by the long journeys they make to pose for photographs, on either side of a table lined with fruit and soft drinks. Their appearance together on the White House lawn establishes that they have become irreversibly committed to hand-outs. It is now time (which is rarely on our side) for President Asad of Syria to see the wisdom of drinking mineral water. We can but work and hope.

QUESTIONABLE PRACTICES   Practices about which no questions are ever asked. It is, for instance, a q.p. to suggest that market forces could ever for a moment have influenced the decisions of those who believe in their universal validity. Hence no one can ever ask what relationship existed between Mrs Thatcher's selfless promotion of British armaments manufacturers in Third World Countries – so that they can defend themselves against their poorer neighbours – and her son's business interests.

RELIGION   Everyone should be free to worship his or her God in his or her own way. We must respect the beliefs and doctrines of others, especially when they are fatuous, cruel, superstitious or dotty and held by people with facial hair who might threaten our dividends or the universal right to motoring. We should, on the other hand, be properly suspicious of those who advocate the use of reason, which was invented by the French for their own purposes. Those who suppose that we might be better off without God-given doctrines or spiritual leaders should probably have their hands cut off. They should certainly never be permitted to publish books.

SELF-DETERMINATION   Who, apart from the Kurds, is to be denied this universal human right? The Nagas are a special case. Kashmir is part of India and always will be, thanks to the sagacity of the British. The inhabitants of East Timor are mostly dead, so the case does not arise.

TRUST   Without it, where would we be? Luckily, Britain is still the most widely trusted country in the world. This unique state of affairs is a miracle, not least since, for instance, Mr Callaghan made solemn promises to the Cypriots which he very wisely did nothing to honour. Thanks to him, Cyprus is now two places instead of one and, once the holiday season is behind us, no one can remember where it is. Men fought and died to achieve this.

UNIVERSAL HUMAN RIGHTS   The birthright of every man and woman in which, like Tinkerbell, we must all believe. Would you have a brave little light go out for all humanity?

VICTORY FOR COMMONSENSE   Rare.

WEST, THE   The source of all human wisdom and all human evil. Since the abolition of the East, Japan is now part of the West. Men fought and died to achieve this.

X   The universal symbol of the progress of democracy. Where X marks the ballot paper, truth, honour and justice are bound to prevail. We need no longer worry about South Africa. Once Haiti is a democracy, Americans will once again go there for cheap holidays, cock-fights and money-laundering. This will represent a Victory for Common Sense (q.v.).

YOUTH   Their voices must be heard; their opinions must be endorsed; they are our future (q.v.). It is inconceivable that youth should ever be wrong. Their message for all of us is 'the louder the better'. We ignore this at our peril. Remember Pompeii.

ZIONISM   The sole form of self-determination unacceptable to the altruistic Lord Mayhew. Zionism is the only reason that the Arabs are not our friends. Lawrence of Arabia advised leaving the oil in the sand, but it is now too late for that. Enoch Powell holds the forerunners of the Zionists responsible for stoning Jesus. He was once a professor of Greek in Australia and hence is never wrong.

Alexander the Great

How great was Alexander? He is a mythical figure in almost all senses, except that he certainly existed. His conquests set a standard which, unfortunately for mankind, others have attempted to emulate though none has surpassed. As a leader, he was literally inspirational: his kiss alone was known to invigorate dispirited veterans. Recklessly courageous (leading from the front became, as they used to say, his trip), he was also a military genius, whose tactics continue to figure in the Sandhurst curriculum. He won set-piece battles against all-comers, and when they refused to come, he burst the bounds of the known world to seek them out: the Indian Porus gave him his toughest fight and was rewarded with Alexander's trust and friendship, which – unlike others – he did not betray.

Treachery, real or imagined, became an obsession. When he left Macedonia for Asia Minor, Alexander was at the head of a tightly bonded army, with an officer corps united behind its king. The immensity of his conquests both gave his companions access to wealth and power and engendered fractious ambitions which ruptured traditional loyalties. Before very long, Alexander decided (and deferential oracles confirmed) that he was the god whom his father, Philip of Macedon, had been about to proclaim himself when he was assassinated by Pausanias, one

Review of John Maxwell O'Brien, *Alexander the Great: the Invisible Enemy*, in the *Sunday Times*, 1992.

of his bodyguards, a beautiful favourite who felt that his grievances had been inadequately redressed by the king.

The assassin was promptly killed – too promptly, in the view of those who thought that torture might have revealed accomplices in high places. Whether or not Alexander or (more plausibly) his mother, the formidable Olympias, was implicated, the king's death was opportune for the prince, whose polygamous father had just remarried and whose new wife had given birth to a son. With Medean ruthlessness, Olympias had the infant tortured to death in front of the junior widow, who hanged herself shortly afterwards: so much for Macedonia's 'civilised' style.

Alexander always out-Hamleted Hamlet in tributes to his father, but was he involved in Philip's murder and did he fear that he deserved to go the same way? Or was his morbid apprehension of plots merely typical of autocrats whose enterprises prosper beyond their greediest dreams? As everything he touched turned to gold, he took to distributing largesse, as well as death sentences, with increasing lack of discrimination. His generosity was almost a gesture of contempt. At one late stage, he even threw handfuls of money to his horses, in sarcastic reproach to a subject king (subsequently executed) who provided cash rather than the fodder which had been promised.

Historians have offered us a choice of Alexanders, from the world's ideal head prefect and *Victor Ludorum* to an under-sexed over-achiever. W. W. Tarn, (*Alexander the Great*) in particular, touted him as an idealist, anxious to hellenise the barbarian Orient, first with the sword and then by wholesale subsidised marriages between Greek men and Asian women (never vice versa). In this, it was suggested, he anticipated Cecil Rhodes, who is alleged to have claimed that the problem of Africa's blackness could be solved by 'fucking it white'. This missionary vision of Alexander has yielded – largely as a result of Peter Green's puncturing accuracies (in his *Alexander the Great*) – to that of a virtually insane self-inflator. His wholesale sponsored marriages were intended less to homogenise the empire than to stock a glorified stud-farm which would create a kind of a prototypical SS, an élite corps that would owe all its loyalty, and all its prospects, to the king.

The Hitlerian reading of Alexander's adventure is excessive: he treated war as a savage sport, but he lacked any exterminatory or thousand-year fantasies. By failing to father a durable

heir, he created all the circumstances for the prolonged destabi-
lisation of the Middle East. It could be argued that the grovelling, the opportunism, the sycophancy, the bossism and the
callousness of the Levant are abiding aspects of the classical
education given to it by Alexander's hellenising vanity.

Like Hitler, however, and also like Napoleon, he belonged
only marginally to the nation he claimed to champion: Hitler
was Austrian, Napoleon came from Corsica and Alexander
from Macedon, which no Greek recognised as a proper part of
Greece, despite today's Greek government claiming him as a
national hero and Macedonia as a Greek province whose name
it means to deny to the ex-Yugoslavian region which corre-
sponds, in large measure, to the original Macedon.

Alexander was a genius of a kind, but he was also someone
who had to play the part of a genius. John Maxwell O'Brien
reads this paragon of the man of action in an interesting light.
Every schoolboy used to know that Aristotle was Alexander's
tutor and that the young prince slept with Homer under his
pillow. Far from discounting the philosopher's influence, Professor O'Brien argues that Alexander became an almost excessively
bookish young man, remarkably dependent on models like
Achilles and Herakles, whom he counted among his ancestors.
O'Brien adds another exemplar whom others have failed to
spot: Dionysos, the androgynous god of wine and ecstatic
blood-letting, whose travels were legendary enough to excite
Alexander's emulatory conceit.

O'Brien makes his point by larding his trim but otherwise
unexceptional account of Alexander's short life with pertinent
quotations from the *Iliad* – to underline the Achillean affectations (including the vicious rages) of the man – and, more
interestingly, with lines from Euripides' *Bacchae*, in order to
show how closely Alexander's behaviour mimicked that of the
peripatetic god of wine. If Dionysos was the least war-like of
gods and the most marginal (his mother was mortal, although
his father was Zeus), he was famed for inspiring an appetite not
only for orgiastic boozing but also for tearing animals – and
those who questioned his belated divinity – into bloody pieces.
He was, in short, as restless and as vindictive as Alexander who,
for all his aggressive style, was insecure enough to need a
literary warrant for his 'crusade'.

The Macedonians were renowned for their unphilosophical
symposia, the mammoth drinking bouts where manhood was

measured in the capacity to put away uncut wine and where tongues were loosened in fellowship which could turn, abruptly, to enmity. In one notorious instance, Alexander skewered 'black' Kleitus, the senior commander who had saved his life at the battle of the Granicus and who made the mistake of assuming that it gave him the right to question the king's policy of recruiting Persians to key posts in what had previously been a Macedonians-only command structure. The killing of Kleitus provoked one of those periods of sulky remorse from which Alexander's men learned to rouse him with pleading reproaches to resume the leadership he alone could supply. His own bad behaviour was used to elicit displays of indulgent affection which finally excused everything. Perhaps he killed Kleitus because he represented a debt due from a king who insisted that everyone owe everything to him.

O'Brien's choice of Dionysos as one of Alexander's role models is rendered particularly convincing in view of the king's destruction of Thebes, early in his martial career, after the mainland Greeks rose in rebellion. The sentimental side of Alexander (perhaps mindful of Aristotle, and of the tragedians he admired) spared Athens, but Thebes was literally levelled. In *The Bacchae* – written when Euripides was in exile in Macedon – Dionysos was said to have done the same thing, in the guise of an earthquake, when King Pentheus failed to honour his divinity. O'Brien suggests that, as usual, guilt followed Alexander's vindictive rage and that drink was the only palliative. Fearing no other mortal, Alexander became his own most dangerous enemy. All sorts of reasons have been given for his early death (he was not quite thirty-three), from malaria to a sort of 'doctors' plot', but it seems likely that he was a victim of acute alcoholic poisoning. Wine and blood were addictive tipples; he could never resist another round of either. He was one of the bravest and greatest generals who ever lived, but there is not a lot more to be said for him.

Teams and Dreams

How long is it since ex-US Secretary of State Dean Acheson forsook diplomacy for candour by observing that Great Britain had lost an empire and had yet to find a role? Sixties' London was outraged at the public assertion of what was obvious. The outrage was that an American should be both patronising and right. Thirty-four years later, Britain remains uncertain of its role and resentful of its lost supremacy. Some anti-Europeans fancy that they can restore an Anglo-Saxon hegemony with a North Atlantic super-league, and that Washington will welcome – if not be flattered by – their hullo-again knock at the door. Few English illusions are more enduring than the belief that America envies the wit and wisdom of The Old Country which many Americans dislike and to which most are indifferent.

In the early 1950s, Churchill's failure to enter (and domininate?) the Common Market at the outset, was due not only to continuing imperial dreams but also to a belief that our natural allies, and kissing cousins, were not dodgy continentals but ungarlicky Americans. Churchill's sentimental memories of his American mother probably primed his reluctance to become wedded to the Continent. Perhaps he was also punishing France for not jumping to accept the common citizenship which he had proposed to her as von Runstedt closed on Paris in 1940, but – as their 'secret' correspondence shows – Churchill revelled in his tepidly reciprocated infatuation with FDR. During the war, the interests of America and Britain, especially in the Far East, rarely coincided as closely as the PM's coy love-letters to

'Former Naval Person' maintained. America never wanted to save the British Empire; it preferred to acquire its assets and assume its kudos. Christopher Thorne's *Allies of a Kind* is the documented, unsentimental text here.

Some Americans have, of course, been genuinely Anglophile, at least in their choice of tailors or reading material: others recall without amusement how, in 1812, the Redcoats burned the White House. In the 1930s the Mayor of my birthplace, Chicago, who had a large Irish constituency, offered to 'punch King George in the nose' if he entered the city limits. George Bernard Shaw, with his facility for glib epigrams, remarked that Britain and America were two countries divided by the barrier of a common language. After the war, Churchill attempted to bind them together under common covers with his *History of the English-Speaking Peoples*, which proved to be a voluminous gospel with few apostles.

In decline, the British have varied in their feelings about America. At times, they toy with sulky divorce, as Churchill's successor did during Suez when surprised by Eisenhower's unsurprising America-first policy (Ike, it is said, did not relish Anthony Eden calling him 'my dear'); at others, the British affected privileged closeness, for instance during Macmillan's purported intimacy with Kennedy. What better typifies (or explodes) the cant of Anglo-American parity than the image of an aged Prime Ministerial cuckold giving paternal guidance to a young, adulterous President? The joke was always on the Greats Man, who persuaded himself that, *mutatis mutandis* (often a more tricky manoeuvre than supposed), the British could be to the Yanks what the civilised Greeks were said to be to the loutish Romans. Such antique affectations ignored the evidence that most Romans despised the fawning Levantines who peddled their phrases and, when selected, their persons to their imperial masters. *Suaviter in modo* may have been a plausible motto for the Edwardians, but it has become something of a strain, late in the second half of the American century, for the British to continue to condescend, from below.

Nevertheless, Mrs Thatcher in her (long) turn, persuaded herself that she and Ronnie Reagan were quite an item. Some pundits, still credulous about Britain's crypto-leadership, claim that she played Lady Macbeth to the President's more reluctant Thane. In less hot-lipped fact, although her toes may have twinkled, she regularly danced to American tunes. Karl Marx said that history repeats itself first as tragedy, then as farce; the Anglo-American alliance began as a partnership but it had already ended, long before Mrs T., under Denis Healey's chancellorship, as a buy-out.

Like Churchill in one petty respect, I was born to Anglo-American duplicity. In the 1930s, dual loyalties – British father, American mother – seemed unlikely to provoke schizophrenia. When I was a small boy in New York City, my father said tomahto and I said tomayto, but no one wanted to call the whole thing off. When we came to London, on brief 'leaves', I scorned the stunted buildings and the square, small, black automobiles. However, there was quaintness in the busbies of the guardsmen, in the red buses with outside staircases and in the taxis whose roofs could be folded down, on request, on sunny days. The fact that it took more than four dollars to buy a single pound indicated that the Bank of England remained the safest place in the world. The British still paraded the intimidating institutions which had seduced Henry James by their aesthetically enriching dignity. What could the US offer against the Crown, the Empire, the Peerage, the Public Schools, cricket and the ancient universities (complete with lawns)?

My English family seemed largely to be composed of elderly persons living in Mansion Flats. Uniformed maids wheeled in tea trolleys double-decked with starchy layers of bread and butter, scones (in hallmarked chafing dishes), pre-sliced Madeira and fruit cakes. English meals consisted of brown Windsor soup, blackened joints, leathered roast potatoes, vegetables that had been boiled colourless and suet pudding. Gimme a hamburger, OK? (No, I was told, the English *never* said okay). London was as full of ABC cafés and Lyons tea-shops as it now is of McDonalds and Burger Kings.

In London, my father ceased to be the man who wore seersucker suits in his air-conditioned Rockefeller Center office and who went dancing with my mother at the Cotton Club (he had been amateur champion of the world and admired the black men who 'trucked' down Harlem's Lennox Avenue). Here he became a bowler-hatted gentleman who disappeared on Saturday afternoons to North Foreland to play golf, in plus-fours, with a millionaire uncle after whom I had been named, in the hope of a legacy that did not materialise.

America was the place to which we returned, gladly, and for good, I assumed. In New York we could listen to Jack Benny and Eddie Cantor and Fred Allen, whose brand of radio comedy was unthinkable – too broad, too Jewish (though no one quite said *that*) – on Reith's BBC where the straight face, and the toffee nose, prevailed. I saw my first movie at the Museum of Modern Art. Oddly enough, it was a truncated version of Abel Gance's *Beethoven*. My mother thought me too sensitive to be exposed to the unsubtle terrors of *Snow White and the Seven Dwarfs*. In the Golden Age of Hollywood, film acting, despite the exquisite Myrna Loy and the suave Dick Powell, was still a vulgar activity compared with The Theatre, of which London remained the capital (one of my very distant cousins ran The Theatre Royal, Drury Lane, and one of my aunts was once told that she was the image of Marie Tempest; she sat bolt upright ever after).

Isolationism was still rampant in the US, but this lent the glamour of inaccessibility to European culture, especially if you lived on the East Coast. The bloodiness of politics in the Old Countries was synonymous with seriousness: Germany and Russia, with their ideological antagonism, were both menacing and exemplary (depending on which example you chose to honour). To intellectuals, there was something enviable in the force and violence of European politics and in the 'maturity' of its literature. Most Americans, however, wanted only to be rich and happy and left alone. They had no stomach for foreign adventures and only an acquisitive respect for foreign Art, which was often more investment than inspiration.

Until well into the war, England remained a faraway, almost entirely thatched country of which most Americans knew very little, except through films in which George Arliss impersonated Disraeli or Robert Taylor rowed faster than the rest of his stuck-up crew as a Yank at Oxford. When, in 1938, my father was transferred to the London office of Shell, supposedly for only a year, I began a tactful – all right, panicky – transition into an English schoolboy. One of my first friends was called Martin, but I was discouraged from his company lest his accent prove infectious. It was important that I did not drop my aitches as well as my short 'a's'. England, I discovered, was a small place in which minutiae loomed large. For the first time, I was instructed to call people 'Sir'.

My father was asked to stay in London and help organise oil supplies for the war effort. There was a debate about whether I should return alone to the US, but my Oxford-educated father decided that it was, after all, no marked misfortune to be an English gentleman rather than an American Jew. Yes, that was *exactly* how things were in those days. Unsurprisingly, my mother did not shed her American accent (she has not lost it to this day); as a result she was often reminded, not least by my vindictive grandmother, of the inferiority of American culture, despite the *parvenu* charmlessness of the surging dollar.

In his almost inaudible 1940 broadcasts – later mimicked with breathy accuracy by (Sir) Kingsley Amis (perhaps his best work?) – Roosevelt promised the beleaguered British that he was sending them . . . his prayers. Since the rest of the people in the ARP shelter were hoping for something with somewhat greater firepower, it was, for a while, quite an embarrassment to be a Yank. Although Churchill made out that Lend-Lease was an act of unparalleled generosity and solidarity, FDR had clearly closed a smart deal in chipping off bits of the Empire in return for clapped out, decommissioned destroyers. The business of America was, as usual, business. It needed all of Ed Murrow's manly empathy on the radio to make Americans care about the blitz and – in case anyone has forgotten – it was not until the Japanese attacked Pearl Harbour, and Hitler improbably (and imprudently) kept his word to his oriental 'Aryan' allies by declaring war on the US, that Britain and the USA become indissolubly bonded, for a few years anyway.

The Americanisation of Britain did not really begin until 1942. That was when North Devon, to which my school had been evacuated, was filled with over-here, overpaid, oversexed GI's whose uninhibited dialogue, overheard while they were on route marches, first taught me four-letter words. My mother's childhood friends arrived on our doorstep in London with PX boxes of Del Monte's Yellow Cling Peaches and Hershey Bars and tins of ham and comic books. I was now an English schoolboy, doing Latin and Greek and preparing for Public School and it was too late to turn back. My mother's kid cousin, Irvin, thrilled by England, said to her, 'For a Kansas City girl, you sure have come a long way.' All he saw of Europe proper was a field in Belgium. After crash-landing his glider and being taken prisoner at Arnhem, he was shot by the SS.

I intrude this autobiographical résumé only because it certifies, like a scrap of conscious litmus paper, how commandingly superior English culture remained, at least until mid-century. By the time I had my post-war chance to go back to America, I had been convinced – as a fourteen-year-old prig – that an English education was the best in the world and that, in the midst of the Old Continent's misfortunes, I had been fortunate. I was more than happy, in due course, to become a (very covert) Yank at Cambridge.

After the war, as Corelli Barnett and others have argued, the British misread the world. Victory vindicated their vanity without nerving them to take the spoils. Churchill, like Themistokles, first saved his country and was then rejected by it. The 1945 Labour government, whose Socialism appalled Washington, became dependent on American aid without having won American trust. In 1956, when the Tories imagined that dependence did not entail deference, Eden behaved like a great statesman while lacking the autonomy, or the treasure, of a great state. Britain's age of parody, in life and in art, began with the humiliation inflicted upon her (and her expedition to Egypt) by an American president who, as allied Commander-in-Chief, had led British armies to victory, even if he had, as official historians liked to believe, depended on the expertise of Field-Marshal Montgomery.

Within a few years of Suez, Britain had lost almost all its affectations of *gravitas*. Soon after it, Malcolm Muggeridge spoke with commissioned prescience, in an American magazine, of Britain's 'royal soap-opera'. When Macmillan went, rather sportingly, to see *Beyond The Fringe*, he was brutally abused by the now sainted Peter Cook in an improvised addendum to his usual drawling impersonation of the PM. In Carnaby Street, the Union Jack was available, Y-fronted, for any bum that chose to sport it.

In some ways, everything went on as before, but parody grew like elder in the English garden: what preserved the appearance of Britain's institutions and myths – honour, respect, reticence, fairplay – was an unending yearning to put them on the streets (cf. Pinter's *The Homecoming*). English roses went on the pill and were plucked by a new, civilian invasion of Americans on the make.

I once asked a Greek woman whether a certain icon in her shop was for sale. 'In Athens,' she answered, '*everything* is for sale.' By the end of the 1960s, the same was true of London. 'Satire' had become the dominant mode and satire – somewhat like Wittgenstein's idea of philosophy – leaves everything *almost* as it is. Swinging London glowed like rotten wood, as Sir Walter

Ralegh said of the first Elizabeth's court, and complacent politicians took the glow for a new dawn. The triumphs of the Beatles persuaded Sir Alec Douglas-Home that a quartet of endearingly dissolute irregulars – his 'secret weapon' – had reconquered America for the Crown. Harold Wilson was the first, but not the last, Prime Minister to take breakfast with David Frost, whose knighthood for opportunism is the emblematic instance of the way we live, and climb, now.

The rock'n'roll/country-and-western music which has, for thirty years, blared in European ears is the audible enforcer of a 'cultural' occupation which has transformed and subjugated the Old Continent. The French have complained more loudly than most, but they too have succumbed to *le* fast food, jeans, and Johnny Hallyday. An esperanto of bullshit and psycho-crap has splattered US kulchur like ketchup on a world which – here's the comedy – often denounces US influence. As elder statesmen winced at American *maladresses* and pseudo-hippies and as Ken Tynan demonstrated against the Vietnam War (and subsequent US interventions elsewhere), the world became more and more irrevocably American. At the same time as he marched on Grosvenor Square, Tynan was magnanimous enough to work for *The New Yorker*, just as Harold Pinter's loathing for today's America does not lead him to deny Broadway his plays or Hollywood his screenplays. Integrity must earn its buck.

The world of the Arts – European cinema, for sorry instance, whose talents supposedly had Hollywood in fee during the late 1950s and early 1960s – has been largely bought out and overwhelmed by the mindless moguls of the 1980s and 1990s. English talent was among the most easily, and eagerly, recruited: our best directors have become the millionaire *condottieri* of a strident 'culture' whose allure lies precisely in its ignorance of Henry James's Great Institutions. When Colin Welland, on the strength of one success, bragged to Hollywood that the British were coming, the locals were too polite to point out that they had already, and often, come; unlike Caesar, they had also been seen and as swiftly conquered by the home side.

Time was that American publishers were privileged to publish English literature: today, in most cases, they are damned if they will. Is it that Americans write better than British writers? No, they write more loudly, more confidently, more commandingly. In the arts, sad as it may be, there is a cruel correlation between authority and authorship. Great powers do not always produce great art (there is no rule here) but petty powers very rarely do. Imperial and then beleaguered Athens was the source of both sublime tragedy and matchless comedy. After its fall, into decadent civility, its arts withered, even if prize-winners' laurels continued to be distributed. H. G. Wells and Bernard Shaw and Bertrand Russell, albeit opposed to empire, depended on British imperial prestige in order to have their ideas, or persons, taken seriously (why else did Stalin accord Wells an interview?). Who would listen to Gore Vidal if the mock-mandarin voice which he raises against America's 'National Security State' did not have an American accent? American art and ideas have become intellectually masterful because of American economic and military mastery. Art follows the flag (economically, Jasper Johns makes them one and the same).

The open invasion of England by American capital now threatens to dismantle even those institutions which Henry James thought so valiant and irreplaceable. A small and horrible example is available in the – as they put it – 'always distinctive' 1997 catalogue which Century/Hutchinson have just sent me, with the kind suggestion that I ask for any books that I might like to review. Although I am an addictive (and eclectic) collector of books, I can report that – under their present American masters – a once literate English publishing house is not advertising a single volume, on any subject, which anyone with less than, say, a century to waste would want to pick up. Shall I be missing something if I fail to read *The Death and Life of Bobby Z* by Don Winslow, 'a brilliant thriller set on the American-Mexican borders'? Or *The Partner*, by John Grisham 'the most popular author writing in the world today'? Or Patrick Robinson's *Nimitz Class*, alleged to be 'the greatest novel of submarine warfare since *The Hunt for Red October*'? I can wait, I can wait, as I can for *Every Day* by Elizabeth Rogers. What would you do, they tease, if you were happily married with three children and got a card from the greatest love of your life asking if you could meet? 'And when you do, you see two things: you still love this man and he is dying . . .' I would say that I was in the wrong conundrum. Next case: *The Secrets of Nostradamus*. This is David Ovason's 'first book on Nostradamus'. My prediction is: there's going to be a sequel and there's nothing anyone can do about it, or about Lynne Franks' *Absolutely Now*, 'a Futurist's Journey to Her Inner Truth'. The kid travels alone as far as I'm concerned and not, I hope, on a return ticket. Paul Solotaroff's *Becoming Who You Are* is by a client of Dr Romero, its gurusome subject, and joined his group as a 'sad sack editor at the Village Voice', only to emerge eighteen months later to win two Pulitzer nominations. Now he's not sad, but I am. Anyone who wants to read all (or, OK, *any*) of these books needs Dr Romero more than he needs them.

The Americanisation of England (which I, at least, might once have regarded with equanimity, not to say glee) has reached the point where terrible movies – *Tin Cup, Lone Star, First Wives' Club* (how often do you want to walk out during a trailer?) – receive lengthy, cringing reviews, as do gross, fake novels like Philip Roth's latest. In imitation of American models, a plethora of prizes creates a parody of merit; sponsored award-winning is the only avenue to success or reputation. If England wishes to recover its artistic dignity, the simplest means would be to ban *all* awards; they are the hand-guns of the arts, always falling into the wrong hands.

When power fails, attendant ideas and icons lose their force. How else should we explain the way in which the 'charm' of Communism and the 'need' to take it seriously were dispelled overnight when Soviet power collapsed? Previous to 1989, the *New Statesman*'s archives contains boundless, creepy, crawling instances of the vice which La Boétie first diagnosed in 1576 in his posthumous *Discours de la servitude volontaire*. It was said, in the Greek world, that when Athens was vanquished, 'the summer went out of the year'. The bankruptcy of the Soviet Union seemed to take the winter out of the year, but it has not yet led to any convincing renaissance either in the arts or in politics. The Soviets, we now realise, resembled Cafavy's Barbarians, whose retreat dismayed the City where lethargy and timidity had been excused by their menace.

Today, we are left only with an America whose foreign policy is both muscular and unprincipled (even by coherent self-interest) and whose domestic philosophy is compounded of sentimental fraudulence and corporate greed. The Clinton style, in which unctuous effrontery alternates with uplifting hypocrisy, has been eagerly adopted by both political parties – big- and little-endians – in Britain's addictively mimetic Lilliputia. Elections are now determined not by a competition of articulate ideas, but by a popularity contest between toothy candidates whom the British must, with the help of rented spin-doctors, be gulled into *liking*. Following the cheery American example, politicians are not expected to think any more; they have, like Mickey Mouse and Donald Duck, only to wave and wave and wave until people love them. One dares to imagine that there could have been more scintillating new dawns than the one which, rising behind the vacuous fortresses of endless Disneylands, is vivid with superstars and candy-striped like all the best humbug.

De Amicitiis

How many genuine friends do you have? The question is calculated to disconcert; nearly everyone fears that he lacks a full team. Desmond Morris may promise that we are all likely to have roughly the same number of names in our address books, but who fails to fear that others have a more exhilarating roster? In fact, communication theory maintains that there is a natural limit to the scope of our acquaintance; intimacy is not boundlessly elastic. Robert Escarpit, a witty French scholar and Byron expert, argues that if Jesus had had a larger band of disciples than twelve, it would only have increased the number of possible traitors or the probability of an early schism. On this view, the unwieldiness of modern cabinets, rather than the vacillations of particular Prime Ministers, procures those splits between close friends and *mere* friends on which gossip seizes; enlarge the party and those who squeeze into the kitchen will always be accused of privileged access to the cookie jar.

It is reassuring to believe that, when it comes to friendship, intensity counts for more than statistics. Although we may envy the many clubs and pubs (and beds) which agile socialisers manage to frequent, gregariousness is a parody of friendship, just as promiscuity is a travesty of passion. Alberto Moravia made a typically Mediterranean distinction between desire and affection. Although the most rigid of heterosexuals, he recognised the ardour of male bonds and he was almost embarrassed by their tenacity. His need to *talk* to his current closest friend was so peremptory that he appears not to have left a voluminous private correspondence. Yet a telephone call, however prompt or effusive, is not a *present* in the way that a letter is: who takes *care* over a phone call, except in the sense of being careful that the world is not listening to it? Recent events may suggest that we shall soon be invited to read people's collected telecommunications, but prattle is no more a true form of correspondence than remarks, as Gertrude Stein observed, are literature. Except for the electronics buff, even the sweetest call cannot be retrieved, unlike those yellowing letters which touch or puzzle the memory when discovered in old files. (Not long ago, I found a bundle of manuscript sheets, signed 'Yours aye, Roger'. Who was this Roger and did I ever write to him with the same roguish assumption of comity?)

Cicero was Moravia's great Roman precursor. His letters to Atticus, his mundane banker friend, display a raciness rare in his public speeches. Who can fail to like the private face better than the public? Yet if Marcus Tullius had not been a grandiloquent actor on the political scene, would we be as touched and as amused by his backstage familiarities? Although we have none of his letters *from* Atticus, we have a sense of the uncritical affability of his old friend, which redeems him from the dust. Whatever his historical obscurity, a letter's recipient tints the text and spices the style. Is it not a different Philip Larkin who scribbles to Kingsley Amis from the one who writes to Barbara Pym? Byron's letters to his rakish chum Douglas Kinnaird are raunchier and more natural than the jocular, jingling jibes addressed to John Murray, his publisher. It is sometimes an effort to sustain old intimacies, though one hates to let them go. Byron's later letters to John Cam Hobhouse suggest a wilful determination to be as larky and as loyal as the undergraduate who first made John Cam's acquaintance. As a result, Byron left his autobiography in the hands of Murray and Hobhouse and the tractable Tom Moore who were better friends to their own reputations than to Byron's. Had his lordship sent the wicked pages to Kinnaird, who was a rake and an aristocrat, it is unlikely that they would have been committed to the flames in Albemarle Street.

Atticus, by contrast, had the uncensorious courtesy to conserve Cicero's letters and so kept a window open on a world which would seem infinitely less lively without them. The decline of letter-writing is a symptom of how much less trouble authors now take to amuse or beguile each other. Professionalism must be partly responsible: when I suggested to an amusing Californian screenwriting friend that we correspond, he said, 'Sorry, but I never write on spec.'

Friendship is an older emotion than love and, in the ancient world at least, nearly always a more reliable one. It was, said Empedocles, the alternate influence of *philotes* (affection) and *neikos* (strife) – not *eros* (sexual passion) – which made the world breathe in and out. Even Catullus, whose passion for Lesbia has been judged to be almost womanish in its romantic longings and rancours, reproached her most bitterly for betraying his *amicitia*, not his *amor*. Ovid was dry-eyed in love, which he advertised, in *Amores*, to be a game of callous deceit; he reserved his tears, in the *Tristia*, for the false friends who denounced his unwise reticence when privy to a plot against Augustus and so led to his exile.

In similar circumstances, we may assume that E. M. Forster would have kept his mouth shut: is he not best remembered for that (in)famous *boutade* in which he declared that he hoped he would betray his country before he betrayed his friend? Such fidelity is most dangerous when friendships become political: Montaigne, whose love for La Boétie was an unconditional *coup de foudre*, recalls a friend of Tiberius Gracchus, Caius Blosius, who was asked at his trial whether he would have set fire to the temples of the gods if Gracchus had required it. Blosius replied that Tiberius would never have asked such a thing (he would not have been Tiberius if he had), but that he would indeed have done it rather than fail his friend. Who is to decide whether, in the world of Anthony Blunt and Donald Maclean, such wholehearted allegiance is noble or indecent? Hugh Sykes-Davies, who was kind enough to procure me the grant which enabled me to start as a writer, earned scornful notoriety for saying that he would have greeted the disgraced Blunt 'as if nothing had happened', which is proof either of Cantabrigian ethical laxism or of apostolic staunchness; it all depends on the moral metrication you select.

The duration of our friendships seems to testify to the steadfastness of our character. Even the most mutable chameleon tends to treasure someone who will give longstanding evidence of his true colours. Polonius' traditional advice is to keep one's friendships in good repair, but need we go through life with a spiritual spanner tightening the nuts we first met when in juvenile circumstances? If it suggests constancy to have known people for many years, there is a tendency for dead wood to lean together and so give the illusion of steadiness to what has become fruitless proximity. Willie Maugham, hearing a maudlin New Year's Eve party singing 'Should Auld Acquaintance Be Forgot?', was heard to murmur, 'I d-d-d-o so wish it c-c-ould.' Maugham's cynicism was perhaps self-protective; his skin remained thin for all his Lacertian appearance. Certainly, he was more sentimental than he cared to broadcast: hearing that his old friend Norman Douglas was broke, he arranged for him to have a small annuity, but on the condition that he never discovered the name of his benefactor. 'Because,' Willie said to Rebecca West (who told me the story), 'you know what he r-r-read at Oxford, don't you? B-b-biting the hand that f-f-feeds you.'

How many people can cope as graciously with being poorer than their friends as that antique Roman who, having no fortune by which to make them remember him, bequeathed to two rich friends his wife and daughter, whom he asked them to support? It says much for their sense of humour, and the regard in which they held him, that his impudence was honoured by the legatees. In my experience, few friends take money more seriously than those who insist that they are immune to its lure. I once made the mistake of taking pity on a film director friend of mine who regarded my work in Hollywood as proof that I had, as he loudly put it, 'sold out'. Some years ago, after he had been protractedly out of work, I found myself with some spare cash, so I sent him a cheque, for a largish small amount, if only so that we might enjoy our own fat Christmas without a bad conscience. I hoped for nothing more than a word of gratitude. Instead, in one of the few letters I ever received from him, he informed me that his first instinct had been to return my cheque at once, but less excitable counsels (probably his wife's) had prevailed. Although offended, he had decided to put the money in a special bank account. It would there earn interest against its imminent repayment; he would touch it only if, as he did not in the least expect, he remained unemployed in the new year. It was a reasonable, if not a markedly effusive reaction, and I assumed that our friendship would continue as before. In the event, we became entirely estranged. Eventually, he changed métiers; I heard that he had become the head of an Approved School. If he has not had the need to spend what I sent him, it must by now have become quite a tidy sum. From time to time

I am told that he continues to speak ill of me and my work to mutual acquaintances, which suggests that he may still have a soft spot for me.

It is one of the ambiguous pleasures of authorship to receive unsolicited mail which is not always from charities or finance companies or sellers of discounted garden tools. Now and again, and sometimes again and again, I am the target of people who seek to ingratiate themselves by telling me, in single-spaced, marginless detail, how badly I have left myself down with this book or that script. The odd thing is that their economy-labelled, bio-degradable envelopes both alarm and excite me when I see them bulging in the letter-box (they often contain cuttings from my more particularly malevolent critics, as if to warn me, in Pablo Neruda's words, 'We are Many!'). Such people always contrast their brand of abusive honesty with the despicable geniality of fine-weather friends, of whom I am taken to have as many as Timon of Athens. It never occurs to a scold that it requires a certain talent to be a flatterer. The Duke de la Rochefoucauld remarked that it is easy to sympathise with our friends' misfortunes, not least because it gives us a chance to manifest our generosity in doing so. It demands subtler qualities to offer convincing congratulations on a man's success than it does to sit sadly with Job as he scans his sour notices. Lawrence Durrell used to say that, even if he were in the depths of the Amazonian jungle, he could always rely on certain friends to let him know how badly his latest novel had been received, but never how well. The worst of best friends are those who, having been sent an advance complimentary copy of a new book, signal its reception with I-know-you-expect-me-to-be-honest disappointment. Could they not bring themselves to tell a pretty lie or two? An unremitting diet of home truths may be wholesome, but it makes for a dull table.

Giuliano, the Sicilian bandit who fascinated both Gavin Maxwell and Mario Puzo, wore a belt buckle on which was inscribed: God Protect Me From My Friends. He was duly betrayed by Pisciotta, his cousin and trusted liegeman. That other outlaw, the artist, who lives a life uncrutched by tenure or pension funds, who lacks the easy solidarity of fellow-directors or work-mates, very easily falls victim to the company of those who reveal themselves to be mental *toreros*; their habit is to flourish their capes in preparation for the next moment of unwanted truth. Should you be goaded into goring them with equally pointed candour they will tell you, in a wounded voice, that you are not worthy of their attentions.

Philip Roth used to divide his friends between those who would hide him, when the Gestapo came to call, and those who would not. I am not sure that we should set such standards or imagine that we can tell a hero from a trimmer (can we be sure which we are ourselves?). It is enough, I think, to refrain from malice or delation. The other day, I heard that an old Cambridge friend of mine was gravely ill, halfway round the world. Thinking of John, I became aware, belatedly, that he was remarkable in never having expected anything of me, except friendliness. A professorial member of the Classical Club, in which I am an eternal probationer, he combines scholarship with tolerance. It is impossible to quarrel with him, though easy to disagree; rigorous with himself, he is easy with others. I shall always remember lounging in the swimming pool with him, conversing in the Roman style about the emperor Nero, during the coronation of Charles and Diana, while our wives watched the box. He inscribed his books to me, '*Amicitiae causa*'. Such men are rare, in anyone's life, and even more rarely deserved.

The Necessity of Anti-Semitism

I hope that it will not seem churlish if I take as my subject tonight a book which perhaps ought to be, but certainly is not, in the Parkes Library. It is with no reproachful impudence that I draw attention to its unavailability. Its absence reflects discredit neither on the great Doctor Parkes nor on those who cherish his example. I am as sensible of the honour of being tonight's lecturer, the twenty-fifth in a distinguished line, as I am of my thin credentials as a student of Judaism and its relations with Christianity. In my ignorant circumstances, it is perhaps prudent of me to have chosen for discussion a book which no one can have read, since no one has yet written it. My tactics are taken, of course, from Jorge Luis Borges, though my manoeuvres may lack his elegant skittishness. I shall treat the author of *The Necessity of Anti-Semitism* as if his book had been accessible at least to me and I will ask you to trust me to epitomise and gloss him fairly. He will concede, in his perambulatory remarks, that some of what he says is compounded with an earlier essay, entitled *The Holocaust and Modern Memory*, of which the present work is a plump precipitate.

The title is, of course, reminiscent of Shelley's notorious pamphlet, *The Necessity of Atheism*, which procured the poet's prompt eviction from Oxford. Had 'anti-Semitism' had any

The Parkes 25th Anniversary Lecture delivered at the University of Southampton, 1989.

large sense at the end of the 18th century, a book with the same title as *our* author's would have led to no such rustication, even if advertised more blatantly than Shelley's shocker, which was, in fact, not as insolent as its title. A modern philosopher would soon see that Percy Bysshe was simply one more undergraduate making a logical distinction between statements about God – of their nature unprovable – and statements about physical events, which were susceptible of tangible proof. In the sunny confidence of the Enlightenment, young Percy assumed that he need only draw attention to the questionable status of the deity for the whole social and moral superstructure postulated on scriptural authority and divine primacy to collapse in dusty shame. The young imagine that the obvious has never previously been observed. Shelley's faith in the power of radical argument was seconded by a guileless belief both in the virtue of truth and in the universal freedom from superstition and humbug consequent on its proclamation. The Oxford authorities – most of them men of the cloth – thought it easier to get rid of Shelley than of the enabling structure on which their cloistered comforts and intellectual complacencies reposed. In my own undergraduate days, an editor was sent down from Cambridge for publishing a blasphemous work which accused God, in the early 1950s, of being too old for omnipotence.

Our author will remark on the tragi-comedy of Shelley's personal fate when he attempted to live according to his principles. Without gloating or jeering, he will point out that the secondary characters suffered more tragically than comically. Shelley demonstrated that liberation could be as destructive as it might prove exhilarating. It rarely occurred to him that good-heartedness was not automatically followed by good-headedness; he assumed that right feeling would always procure right action. The shrillness of his tone and the shambles of his actions need not wholly disqualify him from our sympathy. Our author will remind us that *The Necessity of Atheism* drew unfoolish, if unoriginal, attention to the absurdity – to use another provocative but not inept term – of theological systems.

A. J. Ayer was no less intent on rectificatory mischief when he spoke, in *Language, Truth and Logic*, of metaphysics as 'literal nonsense'. Although his polemic was prudent enough to procure him preferment rather than expulsion from the academic world, Ayer, like Shelley, was insisting that statements about God, and morals, were of necessity – by their logical nature – pseudo-propositions: they had the form of scientific assertions but were void of empirical content. They could be neither true nor false but were literally nonsensical, since they concerned matters immune to sensible observation. Any scrutinising ascent to heaven in order to verify how many angels danced in the pin-headed discotheque in the sky was embargoed by ladders which must always lack the required steps and were inevitably made of mundane stuff. Ayer's middle initial did not, you will recall, stand for Jacob; he neither wrestled with, nor gave much credence to, angels. He did not deny that God existed, which would have been a logical indiscretion, but he gave us to understand that attempts to guess or interpret the divinity's wishes or purposes, let alone to claim dogmatic access to them, were philosophically disreputable. In this, he was putting modern, positivistic dress on a view of the gods which Epicurus had, with sage agnosticism, propounded more than two millennia earlier.

In a fascinating – if tendentious – footnote, our author speculates on the possible motive for Ayer's iconoclastic posture. He observes that his first book was written just before the outbreak of Hitler's war, when the forces of unreason were loud with murderous purposes. Ayer, an Oxford scholar with Jewish origins, illustrates – in an insular mutation – one of the strategies, neither dishonourable nor – I daresay – conscious, by which Jewish intellectuals sought to find a way out of isolation by devising and advocating universalising doctrines: those whose common characteristic was that they applied everywhere and to everyone. The word 'scientific' was a badge pinned by their adherents on Freudianism, Marxism and Positivism. Our author may be accused of mere speculation, and of being sidetracked before he begins, but I detect consistent purpose in his taking Ayer as an emblematic instance, just before the Holocaust, of a certain kind of intellectual response to impending disaster. Our author will scrupulously point out that the ideas of the Vienna circle are neither validated nor damaged by the motives which may be said to underlie them. Here he prefigures a general point which applies throughout *The Necessity of Anti-Semitism*: the ascription of causal links between psychological circumstance and intellectual or barbarous notions is a needless and metaphysical intrusion. All that we can hope to do, our author tells us, is to discern patterns. His constant idea, as his argument unfolds, is to draw our attention to configurations, not to seek to hammer out a causal chain.

When A. J. Ayer embraced, with all the fervour of a convert, the notion of philosophy as the hand-maiden of science, he was of course suggesting a radical change of employment for a discipline which had previously seen service with God. Science, in the late 1930s, was the new universal deity. Ayer's dismissive attitude to traditional pieties was of a piece with that of his German-speaking teachers in Vienna, although it was spiced with a puncturing wit which was rarely their style.

The Logical Positivists never, so far as we can tell, supposed themselves to be addressing the Jewish Question. They lacked Freud's self-probing fascination with motive. Their notions were systematically anti-personal: the value of what they had to say was independent of who was to say it, or why. 'Autobiography,' we were taught, 'is not a method in philosophy'. The Logical Positivists shared with Freud at least an impatience with any notion of exceptional cases. Their laws, like God's writ, applied without, so to speak, Andorran pockets where man was untaxed by the common rules. Freud never allowed that any male human being, under any social or moral circumstances, could escape the Oedipus Complex. One might as well imagine that by taking steroids a great sprinter could outrun his own shadow.

The Jewishness of the intellectuals who advocated these schemes of universal validity was, one might say, neither incidental nor determinant. It can be noticed; it is part of an undeniable pattern. What it 'means' need not detain us. 'Don't ask for the meaning, ask for the use,' Wittgenstein advised, which will hardly deter us from speculation but reminds us that it may be more fruitful to examine what useful place anti-Semitism has in the logic of Europe than to seek its essential meaning. The distinction between deep anti-Semitism, of the kind supposedly entertained by Céline, by Paul de Man, by Heidegger or by Ezra Pound, and the shallow prejudices of the *Français moyen* or of the Mosleyite bully-boy will, our author insists, turn out to be delusive, not because they all share the same taint or disease or delusion but because the whole idea of looking at each case as if it were more or less profound and so, in some way, more or less dignified is based on a medical or psychoanalytic model which misses the most important issue – the persistence, or necessity (if we accept our author's provocations), of anti-Semitism as a useful, perhaps ineradicable, element of what we shall call the language of civilisation. Here we can recall Paul Valéry's paradox, *'la profondeur de la surface'*. Deep down, we might gloss him, language is superficial.

The eagerness with which brilliant Jews initiated or participated in homogenising, renovatory schemes does not, I repeat, cast doubt on – nor necessarily lend lustre to – them, but there is an undoubted tendency for them to seek, at least at certain stages, to slough off 'innate' particularism in favour of a voluntary (but necessary – because truthful) allegiance. Contingency – the lack of an obligatory logic – nauseated Jean-Paul Sartre's hero, Roquentin; it was hardly less repugnant to those who felt themselves arbitrarily cornered in a logic foisted upon them by a God in Whom they did not believe. A footnote will remark on Sartre's extraordinary post-war essay in which the Jew, alone of men, is exhorted to embrace the essence which his enemies – rather than God – choose for him and to wear their repugnant stars as if they were decorations.

To resume: we need not postulate either cowardly purpose or covert treachery in the ambitions of those who – Jew or Gentile, Jew *and* Gentile – adopted a white-coated, impersonal posture. A. J. Ayer is an interesting local case for us, since he was under no great threat and cannot plausibly be accused of any fugitive purpose. He thought that he was enrolling himself in a truthful crusade to cleanse the world of windy dogma and obscurantist pretension. And wasn't he? Science was independent of personal opinions and advocated universal laws which incidentally rendered ridiculous those recently propounded at Nuremburg. Jewish intellectuals saw in the new economics, in the new physics, even in new music and art, universalising opportunities. By voluntarily relinquishing their particularism they would become united with all mankind; they would trade obsolete debentures for common shares in the future. Such ambitions may have been vain; were they ignoble? They combined immodesty (not always disreputable in men of genius) with humility (the discounting of personality, even in the arts, was programmatic). They hoped, one might say, to disappear in the public pool of humanity, although some of them wanted to do so with a bigger splash than others.

It is almost impossible for us to imagine ourselves in the situation of those who lived before the Holocaust. What was not avoided now reads as inevitable. The evasive efforts of statesmen and of intellectuals alike seem puny, perhaps fatuous; unforgiving condescensions are no less malapert. It is more useful to trace the patterns of response than to arraign individuals for their frailties. The fetish of biography has reached gross proportions in the contemporary world of books; I am disposed to read this as an indication of a regressive reluctance to examine history rather than the higher gossip. The Hellenistic Greeks, with categorical acumen, contrasted biography (worthless) with history (worthwhile). What interests our author is that the attempts to create a new class – of selfless scientific engineers – or to create a new classlessness – officered by initiates in dialectical materialism – were immensely seductive, if finally fruitless, to a variety of minds who thought, like Percy Bysshe, that faulty logics could be no sooner seen than undone. Every major intellectual and aesthetic movement of the twentieth century proposed to exchange old logics for new, imagining that such an alteration was self-evidently desirable and must – how man craves imperatives *and* freedom in the same breath! – *must* procure therapeutic consequences. Their prospectuses varied; their promises wore a singular uniformity: certain obstacles to truth had to be got rid of and the way to an undistinguishing millennium would then be open. Bargaining, whether commercial or diplomatic (had not the Bolsheviks made the diplomatic archives public?), would be replaced by true and unarguable standards. Rhetoric would yield to equations. Ayer's great precursor, Bertrand Russell, once said that if we had certified proof that the elimination of the Jews (he did specifically exemplify the Jews), if the elimination of the Jews could guarantee universal and eternal happiness for mankind, then there could be no sustainable reason for not doing away with them. Now it is no part of my purpose to put Russell among the anti-Semites, let alone among the fools, but I ask you to file this plausible folly in your minds, not in order to be armed against Russell but in order to notice the temptation, even in a great and, on the whole, right-thinking man, to embrace murderous possibilities, if the terms are good enough. How odd, to put no finer a point on it, for Russell to look for divine guarantors for a solution to earthly misfortune which, although offered in the form of a scandalous paradox, does not finally differ from the one proposed by Adolf Hitler! Let us not labour this point, but note it well: Russell could imagine without repugnance a God who offered those kinds of terms. The disappearance of the Jews, self-effacingly proposed by Positivists, Communists and other universalisers, was – I mean to remind you – a common feature both of benign and of malign blueprints for the future. It is impossible for me to believe that Russell could ever have accepted the small print of the diabolical contract offered by God, but his provisional agreement is there on the paper. This marginal episode serves to illustrate one simple, perhaps banal, point: even the cleverest men, and perhaps *particularly* the cleverest men, will endorse theories of elimination (either gleefully or, as in Russell's case, with reluctant unselfishness) without any serious consideration of what the bloody specifics of the matter will involve. If he goes on to ask what Russell's attitude would be to, say, a mere millennium of universal bliss on the same terms, our author may be accused of squeezing more juice from a freak fruit than one can well swallow, but is he not right to emphasise the 'eternal seductiveness', as he rather winsomely puts it, 'of Lady Macbeth'? Just one little death and the crown is on the right head! One sacrifice and utopia is our common address! Our author asks us to share the temptations of the prospect before we froth our indignation. Where Russell fell, we should not disdain at least to falter, although we may concede that this particular wedge has no thin end.

Before leaving the chestnut stall, we may recall George Bernard Shaw asking his neighbour at dinner whether, at 1920s prices, she would go to bed with a man for a hundred pounds. When she showed some interest in the deal, he asked whether she would do it for half a crown. Bridling, she said, 'What do you take me for?' Shaw replied, 'We've established what you are; it simply remains to discover your price.' Shall we be equally severe with Russell's lapse as with Julius Streicher's obscene rant? Do they both 'mean the same thing'? Is it merely a question of establishing their price? Yes? No? Yes *and* no? 'Say it if you like,' John Wisdom used to advise, 'but be careful'. Be *very* careful. How? Quite.

Our author's next chapter seems disjunctive from the foregoing. He proceeds to ask why it is that the *Shoah* has proved indigestible both in the history and in the literature of the postwar years. Theodor Adorno famously remarked that there could be 'no poetry after Auschwitz', but do our bookshops not bulge with slim volumes? Have birds ceased to sing or novelists to be short-listed? Our shelves may be ominous with silences, of which Paul Celan's, self-imposed, is not the least loud, but on any commonsensical reckoning, poetry rhymes on. We may revert to this apparent refutation of Adorno in due course. For the present our author elects to distinguish between what can be digested and what can be assimilated. Assimilation denies uniqueness; it denotes the likeness of one thing to another.

Here another notable intellectual figure becomes paradigmatic. Since I am not a German-speaker, I hope that I do not travesty him when I take Ernst Nolte to have argued, in a number of influential texts, for the assimilation of Hitler's war against the Jews with other campaigns, whether Stalinist or Hitlerian, in which populations of dubious loyalty were either transported or massacred. Nolte, if reports are to be trusted, recoils from endorsement of Hitler's methods, but does not find his policies devoid of prophylactic sense. Affecting dispassionately to repair a black hole in German history, Nolte can scarcely prevent himself from being dragged into it. The language of obscenity has hydratic muscles: cut, they come again.

There is a certain courage in the historian's determination to stitch regular words over an abyss more commonly stepped silently around. Nolte darns where others have preferred, often briefly, to damn. By using the old historical vocabulary to cover the *Shoah*, Nolte means no harm to the Jews. As a good German, we are assured, he means well to the Germans: he wants to give them a history *comme les autres*, with highs and lows, but without unfathomable lacunae. The lakes he wishes to drain are, it may be, full of blood, but it is old blood and perhaps can scarcely be distinguished, after all this time, from spilt milk. Such reclamation is now a sociable, even overdue, act of cultural ecology and patriotic renovation. The new Germany – with reunification in mind – needs a history which builds over the past. Being in the same place as other nations furnishes a curious alibi.

Nolte's arguments for the declassification of his fellow countrymen from eternally tainted demons to people with an unfortunate but un-unique history are neither stupid nor malevolent, though they are spiced with an aggressive self-pity which we should properly hesitate to ascribe to innate characteristics. I remarked of Nolte just now, 'He means well'; I hope I spoke unsarcastically, but I ask you to apply Wittgenstein's formula and ask not what he means but what the *use* of his protracted work turns out to be. Never mind the motive, what pattern is being woven? One of its elements is that Nolte and his faction are obliged to re-eliminate the Jews in the process of their sanitary engineering. This act of re-elimination has nothing in it of savage nostalgia; we need not question that the main intention is to bury Nazism and spoil it of the glamorous uniqueness which might inspire its resurrection or at least its cult. The irony is that Nolte's act of ponderous sepulture – of deep-sixing, to use a less fancy term – requires the banalisation of the *Shoah*, its down-grading from singularity to yet another great pity: in brief, its assimilation to other routinely regrettable procedures.

Our author will insist here on the indigestibility of the Jewish experience. He does so, he would like to believe, out of no desire to pre-empt forever the supreme tragic role for Jews alone. This kind of morbid vanity has its uses, as Mr Begin used embarrassingly to remind us, but it derives from a mystique rather than from history (but then what is history?). Our author's belief that he is not involved in special pleading may be a delusion, but the discerning of patterns is not necessarily rendered self-serving or misleading because a man may incidentally figure in them himself. Indigestibility is not a boast, but a fact, and – in our author's estimation – a significant one. It would, he is willing to agree, be no unquestionable misfortune for the Jews if their history could be assimilated to that of other victims of murderous malevolence. It just happens to be the case that this assimilation fudges the issue. Here he recalls Sir Lewis Namier's notorious remark when asked why he did not deal with Jewish history: 'The Jews do not have a history, they have a martyrology'. Namier did not deny his Jewishness, as we know, and was a fervent Zionist, but that fervour was, so he thought, independent of academic purposes.

A fat footnote (my favourite kind, as long as it is at the bottom of the pertinent page) will observe that the methodology of which Namier was a pioneer – his reductionist analysis of political parties in terms of the interests, social and economical, of their particular members – appears to be in direct opposition to the universalising (often determinist) schemes of the Marxists, the Logical Positivists and the Freudians, but it is of a piece with them in this at least: it deconstructs the antique model by unclotting group interests through the rigorous revelation of individual motivations. It may seem that this is counter to the homogenising strategies of others but it too has the consequence, *as if by chance*, of questioning existing categories: if groups are best and properly analysed in terms of their atomic rather than their molecular structure, so to say, then we are right to think that there is no typology of man which *necessarily* links him with any allegiance larger than the one to which his own interests – in either the genial or the mercenary sense – incline him. It requires no large effort, in our author's view, to see that Namier was dissolving old configurations and assimilating all men, at least those under his minute scrutiny, to a common model, however discrete its monistic manifestations. There is, you might say, lumping up and lumping down, but all lumping is assimilatory, systematic, universalising. When Namier exempted the Jews from history, he grudgingly, even charmlessly, relegated (or promoted) them into a special category, just as Arnold Toynbee, a constructionist of megalomaniac confidence, did when he referred to Judaism as a 'fossil religion'. As Hugh Trevor-Roper points out with mischievous accuracy, this procured Toynbee great prestige in Arab countries. Well, it would, wouldn't it? But the observation is not rendered void on that count. Vain men can still tell the truth; the modest too can be tendentious.

We may object here – and the paradox is central to our considerations – that the notion of anti-Semitism, so far from being 'necessary', appears largely irrelevant to the evaluation of the historians we have mentioned. Trevor-Roper, like Namier, is a Zionist, although unlike Namier he is not a Jew, but his attacks on Toynbee do not depend on any ascription of anti-Semitism to that polymath windbag, nor does Toynbee's estimation of the Jews greatly vary, in categorical terms, from Namier's. Jewish self-hatred – that boring charge, which can hardly be distinguished from Jewish intelligence or even, perhaps, from Jewish self-importance – cannot explain away Namier's irritated dismissal of what the cant calls 'his own people' as a historical topic. There was, he seems to be saying, – if not *with* Toynbee certainly not *against* him – something tiresomely unique about the Jews. They play, one might say, a monotonous character-part on the historical stage and cannot, with conviction or success, be enrolled for any other. With one bound, our author jumps back to indigestibility.

We are, as Brillat-Savarin gastronomically observed, what we eat. We are also, one might add, what we do *not* eat. The literal and the metaphorical run, at times, on parallel lines which meet and do not meet at mealtimes. The indigestible may be killed and even swallowed, but it fails to become us; our system refuses it. It is not a matter of appetite or personal preference when a cow refrains from *foie gras*. Such abstention is neither creditably humane nor discreditably puritanical. The herbivore's abstention is not a moral matter. With man, it is rather different. Killing and eating are, we are promised, natural to him. But – as Walter Burkert emphasises in *Homo Necans* – man knows he kills, just as he knows, to his disastrous and unique distress, that he dies. He has to eat; does he have to kill? He excuses himself and blinds himself to what happens in the abattoir by saying that what is digestible is natural; what does not come up again has, as they say, gone down all right. Nevertheless, as anthropologists note-takingly insist, menus vary; they are hot and cold, they include or exclude fish, fowl and red herring. Red herring is perhaps one of the most interesting dishes, much more commonly consumed and much more sustaining than the scornful proverb suggests. Man kills and eats; guilt and innocence sit constantly with us at table. We have blood on our knives, most of us, if not on our washed hands. The sacrificial and the utilitarian share facilities, though one or the other aspect may cloak the logic of our bloody consumption. Eating the evidence is often the best way of getting rid of it. You will remember the old joke about the secret so secret that its recipient was instructed 'Swallow before reading'. The act of swallowing is a form of obedient credulity no less than it can be one of solemn communion. We swallow stories as well as food; they too become part of us.

Our author suggests that the uniqueness of the Jews, which need hardly be attributed to innate qualities or divine selection, is due, at least in part, to their equivocal status, literally and metaphorically, in the routines of social consumption. Jews sometimes do and sometimes do not eat with others; they may approach the common table, but they often sit at it either uncomfortably or with uneasy showiness. It is not simply a matter of whether there is *jambon de Parme* in prospect, nor is it entirely a metaphorical matter. To put it shamelessly, the Jew takes the missionary position in the old *New Yorker* cartoons: he is not sure whether he is to eat or to be eaten. The grammatical slippage between the alternatives alerts us, as any first-year Freudian would notice, to the structural ambiguity of the supposed antithesis. The Jew is at home with the series of trick choices of which 'Heads I win, tails you lose' is the chestnuttiest. If assimilated, he becomes indistinguishable; if he insists on being indigestible, he sticks in the throat of the world, as George Steiner, *philosophe* and gastronome, has memorably put it. Can he expect a better fate than to be coughed into the dustbin? Words too are food; they have their dietary significance. Even the most ordinary phrase has its poisonous freight. Man kills; words – as Norman Cohn reminds us – give him his bloody warrant.

Our author points out how what is, in some sense, a fate determined by others is often rigged to be the consequence of a choice on the part of the victim. The sacrificial heifers at Athenian festivals were offered their favourite food as they reached the altar, in order that, in lowering their heads towards the delicacies, they might give the nod to their own slaughter. The condemned man's breakfast procures a not dissimilar acceptance of the sacrificial role. Nadezhda Mandelstam remarks on how rarely human victims scream and struggle in the face of death and injustice. If she rightly sees no necessary virtue in brave reticence, the choice of mute resignation, on the part of victims, is perhaps their last luxury, in that it is defiantly *chosen*. Mrs Mandelstam had the right, God knows, to suggest that it was at least as honourable to embarrass one's killers as to deny them the satisfaction of witnessing one's fear. It is a point on which those of us who have been spared the horror should perhaps have the modesty not to pontificate.

How does our author propose to illustrate the indigestibility of the *Shoah* in particular in the European or perhaps the world-scheme? How, in due course, can he link this with what he dares to call *'The Necessity of Anti-Semitism'*? He may begin with a dry example of how societies which either engendered or acquiesced in genocide both have and have not acknowledged the scandal. Before that, I might remark that a recent correspondent of mine was full of furious reproach when I used the word 'scandal' with regard to the *Shoah*. It made him think of Christine Keeler, he said. Well, we can only use the vocabulary available to us (the limits of our world are the limits of our language, which is why silence can recommend itself as a fitting figure for the unspeakable). 'Scandal' has been debased, like so much of our vocabulary, but its root meaning involves 'an affront to religion'. It is, one can argue, not inappropriate, once again bearing in mind the ambiguities available in the definition, to call the *Shoah* a scandal; not only, I mean to say, does mass murder cry out for a merciful God and, in the face of His helplessness, throw amiable notions of divinity into scandalous question, but – and this 'but' is scarcely adversative, as we shall see – but/and the fact of the *Shoah*, that it took place, jars so painfully with established notions of divinity no less than of humanity that, in order to save the logic by which, for better or worse, Western civilisation (in particular) proposes to continue living, it turns out to be necessary to mount a two-pronged operation which has as its secret and single purpose the *de-*scandalisation of the *Shoah*, its eviction from crucial centrality in the relations between man and his sacred machinery. The issue is crucial indeed: as the matter of the Carmel of Auschwitz implies, The Jew must, if nothing else, be denied a supplanting cross, a crueller, trumping Calvary.

The Irishman denies that he stole the bucket and adds, by way of further mitigation, that it had a hole in it anyway. On the secular as on the theological level, Europeans are driven, without malice or conscientious callousness, to deny that they had any responsibility for the Holocaust and, when goaded beyond patience, can suggest that the Jews are tiresomely vain, not to say cashing in, when they maintain that the *Shoah* was a unique and unredeemably scandalous event. The holes in the bucket, the seriously vexed suggest, were partly self-inflicted and go to show what kind of merchandise certain people are in the business of peddling.

We shall resist the urge to lampoon or to ascribe consciously blinkered motives to honourable men. We shall limit ourselves to taking vigilant note. In this context, observe that what happened to the Jews between 1941 and 1945 at first had no descriptive term in any public record. The Battle of Alamein was never merely 'something that happened in the desert'. Yet the survivors of the camps were long known to us, almost anonymously, as 'Displaced Persons'; no one asked what their place was, or would be: they could neither go back nor go forward. 'D. P.' might as well stand for Damned People. They continued to have numbers (which had to be reduced) but they had no names. Ernest Bevin, who is still touted as a Great Foreign Secretary, remarked that he was 'not 'aving the Jews push to the front of the queue'. In his lovable way, he was one of the first, as the Greeks used to say, *sozein ta phenomena*, to hold appearances together by cleaving to the concepts which had served the old order and could thus sustain those continuities on which recovery – covering up again – seemed to depend. Bevin's orderly vulgarity, in denying precedence to notorious queue-bargers, however desperate their case or loud their mouths, served early notice that no large homage would be available to those with hard-luck stories. *Vae victis* was a slogan that extended even to victims who declared themselves on the victorious side. 'How many divisions does the Pope have?' was Stalin's dismissive response to moral suasions. (It turns out that he has, to say the least, more than dialectical materialists cared to count.) 'How much clout do the Jews have?' was Bevin's loudly unspoken question, 'And how much does anyone want them to have?' was the equally brazen supplementary.

We may qualify our veneration for good old Ernie, but it would be foolish to sneer too promptly. Our author counsels us to try to imagine what could conceivably have been the right and appropriate response to what the Allies found in the heartland of civilised Europe. It is one of the uneasy oddities of the 1939–1945 war that the vast majority of the fighting forces, at least of the Western allies, discovered just what they had been fighting for or against, only when they were all but victorious. In this respect, the effect preceded the cause; here again, the pattern proves more evident than the motivation. I once had a tense evening with a decent man, who had gone right through the war in a Guards Regiment, no contemptible record, and who promised me that it had been fought on behalf of the Jews. This was, I felt, to do them too much honour. His remarks were made without rancour, perhaps with a sense of righteous purpose, but the ambiguity which irritated my oversensitive susceptibilities is surely undeniable. The Jews were, in the Guardee's decent blue eyes, both literally and figuratively the reason for Britain's involvement. Thus they were, albeit without any such intention, responsible for Britain's expenditure, in men and treasure, and – not quite the same thing – they were the sole beneficiaries of the allied effort. By the same token, they could hardly have any reproachful claim, could they, against their selfless saviours? An officer and a gentleman thus impersonated sentiments of a decidedly – what shall we say? – Jew-conscious order. We may hesitate here to speak of anti-Semitism, as if it were a clinical condition, with a regularly identifiable pathology, and our hesitation will be, in my view, wholly proper. And yet, can we deny that there was, in the Guardee's guileless candour, the symptoms of a defensive-accusatory bias – balance perhaps – at the centre of his perception of events in which he played a gallant part?

Our author, with his penchant for digressive procedure, will contrast the notion of a war fought 'to save the Jews' with the steady resistance which Winston Churchill encountered when he sought to honour certain Jews' desire to fight under their own flag, and in an exclusively Jewish regiment, against the Nazis. Here again, no charges of malice are necessary (although some are warranted) in order to see how the idea of Jewish soldiers was as alarming to their supposed champions as that of defenceless and incurably civilian Jews was contemptible. The 'Heads you lose' syndrome rears its ugly tail. (And what shall we say of Israel's fundamental reluctance to conscript its Arab citizens? Is that different? How different? Comfortably or uncomfortably? Should these questions not be put? Why?)

In academic circles, the indigestibility of the Jews finds an equally ambivalent crux in an apparently nominalist context. The extermination of six million Jews at first had no specific descriptive or denoting term at all. El Alamein, you will recall, was one thing, with a place in official history, but the camps and their lethal factories gave no opportunity for crossed swords on official maps. Martyrs have no battle-honours; the death of fossils is not honourable.

Already, in 1945, in my first quarter at Charterhouse, very thin boys were nicknamed 'Belsen'; but Belsen itself formed no part of the curriculum. When the term Holocaust began, thanks – I think – to Elie Wiesel, to be applied to the attempted genocide of the Jews, grammarians sought to limit the damage to the verbal stock by seeking at least to deny the term a capital letter when applied to the *Shoah*. Etymologists winced at the appropriation of what should, as they were prim enough to insist, have entailed a *wholly* burnt offering, to what was, at best or worst, only a partially successful operation. The Jews had to be warned off from the tactless appropriation of one of *our* words in order to describe, without proper linguistic certificate, *their* particular misfortune. We might note that 'holocaust' does not, in its etymology, imply that all the conceivable victims were burnt. A holocaust of oxen would scarcely have implied the simultaneous incineration of the entire bovine population. Shall we see any symptomatic significance in a pedantry which becomes so compulsive as to itself verge on a howler? Why not? I have, as you will notice, accepted the term publicised by Claude Lanzmann, in the title of his film, in order to designate the mass murder of the Jews. It may well be best to use the Hebrew term, but the reluctance of Europeans to delegate a term of their own vocabulary remains an indication of the duplicities involved and of the phenomena that had to be saved, or salvaged.

We are by now aware that our author trades – perhaps revels – in ambiguities. He sees the Jews as both like and unlike other men, both part of Europe and external to it, both assimilable and indigestible. He may still claim here that he is simply trying to clarify a situation, not to propose an aetiology, yet he will be disappointed if we have not picked up several clues as to what is to come. Surely we are supposed to recognise an attempt at least to indicate why anti-Semitism is not a sad contingency or even a disagreeable contagion, but a constant and essential working part of Europe's sombre and unreformed logic. The reluctance of philologists to concede a single stick of their linguistic furniture symbolises, without exaggeration, how reluctant are the lords of the word to lease or release a single item of their basic inventory. It is all, we begin to see, part of a set; this set has mythological significances which render it unbreakable, in every sense, although the myth itself cannot be disclosed. In the elevated charades of duplicity, we must know that there is a hidden term, said and unsaid, implicit and explicit, but we cannot – without rendering the world's game unplayable, without 'blowing it', or the whistle – be told what it is. We cannot be told because the other players, even those who rule the court and watch the lines, at best only half-know; they know and they do not know, just as Heracleitus' Supreme Being both wishes and does not wish to be called Zeus.

'Forgetting too is a kind of conservatism' is the cryptic quotation our author chooses to alert us to the tenacity with which men prefer the old language to any recognition of the new thing. 'Through a glass darkly' will always be preferable to seeing things face to face. The magic of words, of formulaic utterance, derives from their place in mythical procedures from which – and here our author presages a new theme – man again and again supposes himself able to emancipate himself, as Shelley exemplifies, only to find that the shadow is stronger than the substance; reality is systematically ignored in order that the myth remain intact, untouched like the Ark of the Covenant, any contact with which – however well-intentioned – was necessarily punished by death, not because the culprit had done anything wicked, but because he had done something unforgivable. Taboo has no appeal court. The *Shoah* has not *accidentally* suffered a double eviction; its discounting sustains continuities which no 'injustice' can be suffered to curtail. By double eviction, our author alludes to both assimilation – which seeks to disperse the Jewish clot by analogising their fate with that of other unfortunates, and so removes them from hermetic consideration – and, for egregious instance, to their literal transportation to Israel. The desire of Zionists to leave does not affect the larger, different logic of *why*, despite all the obstacles, their departure was part of a process which they themselves imagined they were decisive in ending forever. The Athenians, classicists will recall, having killed the sacrificial beasts, tried the executioner's axe for murder and then flung it into the multitudinous seas. The Europeans – so a hyperbolic argument might maintain – went through a supplementary routine, having disposed of some of the axe-men: they repudiated the surviving victims and flung them into Asia. It is a matter of mythic obligation, no less than of sorry contingency, that the resulting state, supposedly the realisation of a Jewish dream, was destined also to become a pariah altogether unlike the other *parvenu* post-war states, however shameless in their corruption or their murderous practices. We have all heard of the West Bank, but how many have heard of East Timor?

The reason that it is argued that studies of motivation, on the Namieresque model, cannot be decisive – although they may be sociologically of great interest – is that we are seeking to understand the unspeakable roots of a tragic enactment which can never be analysed without remainder through the articulation of any single logic, however subtle. Duplicity involves more than one variable. Certainly, we cannot atomise the issue by reducing it to a matter of the vile ambitions of a Gauleiter or the almost understandable reluctance of an Auschwitz guard to exchange his hellish office for a freezing billet on the Russian front. The sorry ironies parasitic on the *Shoah* go so far as to include the documented dilatoriness of certain mechanicals in the full implementation of the Final Solution, lest its success should lead to their assignation to a fighting unit. Poor unpardonable bastards! Among them are to be found those axes which Europe accused of unique bloodiness and threw away, the better to attain freedom from miasmal guilt and to procure that unity on which, with truly admirable hypocrisy (the Greek word involves dramatic performance), the new solidarity is based. All foundations have blood in them somewhere, as readers of René Girard will not need to be told.

In view of such men (there but for the grace of what is left of God go some at least of us!), we can see that the noblest tragedian – Aeschylus or Racine – could never begin, even with the equipment of genius, to encompass the gross muddle of tragic and comic ingredients which lead us, when taking the Nazis as seriously as their crimes, to flinch from recognising their grotesque and almost pitiful absurdity. The unspeakableness, which Adorno was honouring when he spoke of the death of poetry, has its shallow as well as it bottomless end. Can we even begin to conceive of a purging, a cathartic logic in which the *Shoah* could be disgraced as, for instance, slavery was disgraced – rendered indefensible – by Wilberforce? Has any new, disembarrassing formula begun to be given? What would it be for a new Shelley to find a way, however naive, of removing – by clearly describing – the strategies of malice and distinction by which Europe persists in conducting its morality? What new language could conceivably, conceptually, render the old charades unrepeatable, unplayable? What poet, to come to Adorno's point again, could displace, decentralise Ezra Pound and T. S. Eliot, the canonised good and baddish fairies of the modern Parnassus? Even now our author will dread being misunderstood; he will implore his readers once again not to suppose that he is blaming anyone or everyone for what is implicit in the language: the unlaughable comedy of the situation is that we cannot quickstep our way away from partnership with the shadows, which are also ourselves, and with whom we are sentenced to dance or limp through any conceivable future.

Here is the nature of the necessity which makes anti-Semitism Europe's elastic, agile, weightless companion, as necessary to its articulations as is the negative to its vocabulary. For modern Europe, our author will say, the Jew *is* 'not'. It is what Hitler wanted to be able to say; he was denied, but with no decisive denial: we shall be reminded that throughout the *Shoah* – even when it was no kind of a secret – not a single allied broadcasting

station, and not the Vatican either, ever uttered a single inexpen-
sive word of warning to those who were mounting the trains in
accordance with Eichmann's lethal timetable. The repetition of
the fact becomes, as they say in philosophy, a mere lament. Its
futility does not, however, imply that the sacrifice of the Jews,
whether or not they were wholly burnt, was not in accordance
with the logic of European thought and that their elimination –
their being thrust over the *limen* or threshold – was not part of
a mythically inspired scheme to be rid of their damnable witness,
their martyr role, to be done with impudent alternatives, with
the Pascalian witnesses who now, to Christianity's shame,
outranked God in the ghastliness of their suffering. It is here
that we see the rupture of those continuities which James Parkes,
in his industrious decency, wanted to emphasise. Fearing, yet
preceding, the *Shoah*, he can hardly be derided for failing to
take it into account. But we must now be conscious of being
and not being in the same tradition as Christianity, and it is
with this situation – in the centre of a once excluded middle –
that any plotting of our present moral chaos must seek to deal.
The Jews, our author will tell us, are marginal to Europe's
history and to its apparent confidence in its future, which will
be built over its past. There is unacknowledged but reinforcing
blood in the foundations of the old continent's new harmony,
just as Jimmy Hoffa's body, we are told, underlies certain steel
and concrete investments by the Mafia. The Jews, our author
insists, are the margin which runs down the middle of the page.
The caesura they announce is a loud blank, but it speaks and
will always speak louder than the words with which, in furtive
reasonableness or honest exculpation, in Christian apology or
its pragmatic shamelessness, historians and apologists of all
kinds will hope to drown it.

Losing It

In the Art Gallery of South Australia, in Adelaide, one of the modern rooms provides a text for the thinking tourist. In the centre of its smart parquet floor is one of Richard Long's acts of lapidary minimalism: a circle of Cornish stone. The placing of Long's imported slabs on the chamfered floor beneath them has an irony which trumps modish aesthetics: Australia is an ancient and astonishing country on which western 'civilisation' has laid deceptively familiar patterns. Its cities mimic Europe and America (and increasingly cater to Japan); its countryside, apparently limitless in resources and variety, has been no less wilfully – and irreparably – defaced by the descendants of the dressed apes who landed at Botany Bay just over two hundred years ago.

It was perhaps a kind of panic that took us to an Art Gallery: Cultural Check-Lists ease the shock of new worlds. It is, after all, mildly devastating to find that one knows almost nothing about the flora and fauna of a country which one has come, just a little patronisingly, to explore. The charm of the kangaroo and the cuddliness of the koala had been enough to seduce, though scarcely to prepare, us for what we found and what – more significantly – experts told us of the dangers which threaten even the most 'typical' Australian wildlife.

Vanishing (not to mention vanished) species are virtually beyond the scope of regret or remorse, although National Parks and private nature reserves are – the hand-outs claim – clawing back at least a fraction of Australia from the predatory invaders who have imposed their crushing stones and foisted their fatal, imported accomplices (animal and vegetable) on a once miraculously intact ecology. We learnt that the key word here is 'feral', whose Latin root means 'wild', but which, to ardent local naturalists, denounces anything of non-native origin, however 'harmless': they positively *snarl* the word 'sheep', whose countless hard hooves have pounded the shallow soil to dust.

You cannot understand today in Australia without some knowledge of her yesterdays. On another wall of the same Adelaide museum, Nikolaus Lang – a German artist – has a concave, shield-like work entitled 'Dedicated to the Vanished Adelaide Tribe Number 8'. This elegant, russet mixture of the penitential and the pretentious suggests a belated sense of shame at what 'civilisation' has brought to a continental island which, two centuries ago, knew neither fox nor rabbit, neither pine nor vine, neither dog nor trout, neither property nor genocide.

In the period since Darwin's travels in the *Beagle*, European man – *our* enlightened species – has usurped evolution's office and made unnatural selection his particular province. European man has rendered Australia a place of lost or endangered species of every kind, from the Aborigines – whose rights, still unreliably honoured, were not constitutionally guaranteed until the 1960s – to the pygmy perch, the easy target of the imported (hence nobler) trout. The seas, the streams, the land and the air are full of new emptinesses as the result of the white man in whose superior intelligence we continue, if furtively, to believe.

Many species – like the Tasmanian tiger or the pig-footed bandicoot – were taken to be either nuisances or expendable sources of fur. Botany Bay, the first landfall, was so called because of the plethora of plant life found on its shores: twice as many varieties as existed in the whole of Britain. Of the four thousand forms of flora tabulated by Joseph Banks and his colleagues, half are now lost.

And what do I care? Shame at the extinction of some exotic weed or of one breed of minute marsupial mouse has, I confess, rarely disturbed my rest. What is a 'monotreme', that I should weep for it? (It is, I can now tell you, a species which does not distinguish between its excretory and its sexual equipment: one size fits all.) Frankly, until our Australian excursion, I should willingly have signed the death warrant of the common-or-garden mole without a scruple. I cannot, even now, promise not to do my best to secure his eviction from my mown patch, but

my eyes are, I should like to think, open at last: the bell, I have
to come to realise, is tolling for more than Leadbetter's Possum.
The ingenuity and ingenuousness of Australian species cry out
for a greener God than the One whose dominion, after the
arrival of Captain Cook, extended literally over palm and pine.

The British imported their diseases (measles and smallpox
decimated the Aborigines) and their schisms to Australia: the
governing class was, of course, Protestant; the chained and
humiliated convicts whom they were commissioned to dump
were often Irish Catholics (Fenian garbage for whom no tip was
distant enough). Jailers and felons had only one thing in
common: they hated Australia. Who had time for a sense of
responsibility to such a bloody awful paradise? Indigenous wild
life, with its absurd anatomy, was there to be eaten, flayed and
got rid of before it ate all the precious crops. You can, for
instance, blame the disappearance of the succulent (and once
prolific) *Pterodoma Melanopus* on the English penal system:
starving convicts gobbled it to death.

My out-of-the-grey commission to leave autumn behind and
take a look at the still unsilent spring of South Australia found
me as unprepared as the smuggest colonial adventurer. Never
mind an inability to distinguish between wombats and potoroos,
or between wallabies and kangaroos, I had no idea even that
the term 'Pom' – the nickname for Englishman – was seldom
uttered with affectionate deference. Expecting to find hordes of
cuddly koalas on every tree and confident that my knowledge
of the Greek meaning of her name would bring a platypus
promptly to the surface of whatever pond I chose to visit, I
knew nothing of what was really at stake in the ecology of
Australia. Could I ever have guessed that the greatest single
service to the environment which one of my fervent instructors
could propose was that Australians should immediately kill all
their cats? Dead wood, I was to discover, was seriously to be
preferred to live felines: it was part of a food-and-shelter chain
which predatory pets (and the unspeakable fox) were busy
wrecking.

South Australia is bracketed by two great nature reserves.
The Flinders Ranges, to the north, are remote and vast enough
to provide scenic immunities from the urbanisation which
spreads south from Adelaide to the coast. The yellow-footed
wallaby, feared extinct, has been saved and is now fairly prolific
there. These spectacular peaks and teetering crests offer small

temptation to the developers who have turned the Adelaide Hills into a suburb where European spring, summer and autumn flowers bloom in the same sweet season, an apparent triumph for emigration.

Our environmental education began on Kangaroo Island, to the south. I imagined some conveniently populous outdoor zoo, but the Flinders Chase National Park contains some 74,000 hectares in which, if all goes well, endangered species can live in their uncurtailed, often covert natural habitat. 'Camera opportunities' depend on tact, stealth and good fortune.

Kangaroo Island (some 150 kilometres long) is not wholly consecrated to nature. The 'scrub' was largely cleared after the war, when veterans were rewarded with tracts of land. By their industry, they neatened most of the island into profitable pasture. The government allotted them so many (quick-growing) pine-trees each; the timber market encouraged the foreign wood (indigenous eucalyptus is less saleable) as well as sheep and cereals. (The rabbit, happily, made no landfall here.) Awareness of the tension between the interests of the farmers and of the conservationists was lesson one in local realities. It was delivered by Craig, the young ex-Ranger, now a freelance tour-guide, whose enthusiasm was to take us up and down the island, under clawing winds and dramatic skies, with genially relentless instructiveness.

We arrived to bad news: a forest fire had closed Flinders Chase Park and might forbid our seeing the koalas and even the kangaroos who lived there. Nature does not run a regular-hours business: one must have patience or restrict oneself to visiting prisoners in their zoos. Fortunately, the sea-lions lived in a non-smoking section of the island. As we four-wheel drove to their cove, we saw the usual sorry remains of crushed animal life: magpie, possum and what-was-*that*? Craig said it was an 'Anna'; a large lizard-like creature which, when alive, is called a Goanna. 'Being run over takes the "go" out of it.' Craig promised that anything that gets run over is never in short supply. Sure enough, we saw a goanna on the go soon afterwards.

Sentiment may play little part in the conservancy code, but the sea-lions, lolling wantonly on their easy sands put on a love-me-do show which suggested that this was never their first gig. Yet these grave, shark-scored senators and roly-poly youngsters, gourmandising on their milky mothers, were until recently clubbed to the verge of extinction by the bloody executioners acting on behalf of madame's furrier. Murder is a system as well as a sin.

As we discovered that sea-lions have no tear-ducts (and hence have difficulty cuffing sand from their lustrous round eyes), the smoke clouds were lumped against the horizon: the bush-fire, fanned by the wind, was threatening the whole park (and our selfish hopes of seeing koalas). Craig kept us busy mostly with birds that day: we splashed around Murray's lagoon where the water-legged tea-trees are said to shelter the rare Latham's Snipe (he was a no-show). Our obvious eyes enjoyed the cruising eagles and the stretching ibis and tried to see what Craig so effortlessly read in nature's busy text. The ash blew in from the National Park. Cinders have been known to fly eleven kilometres, mocking firebreaks with their hurdling menace. While we looked at our watches, the whole park was menaced with incineration.

Nature is rarely obliging, but during the night, when we were out spotting miniature penguins (and a rare, nocturnal Stone Curlew), the wind came about and drove the fire back on itself. The park was safe and we would be able to feed our kangaroos – a blanket name, of course, for an astonishing number of species – and wallow in wallabies. Craig promised us a grove where koalas found their favourite eucalyptus brand. Kangaroo Island, for all its furtive liveliness, might have seemed almost vacant without him. Having been a ranger, he knew it backwards and took a happy view of its prospects. Even the fire, whose black evidence still scorched the air, did not dent his optimism. The banksia bushes, he illustrated, had a sort of emergency survival kit: the heat triggered, but did not destroy, the seed-pods, thus procuring a replacement for the burnt parent. He showed us where the traces of earlier fires were already being repaired by first-year growth. Later, under other tutelage, we were to have a less sanguine reading of the situation.

With Craig, everything was great. We even had the luck to spot a koala and her baby on a tree right next to the road. We never had to go to the standard feeding place, but enjoyed madame's elegant condescensions by ourselves. Here was the ultimate, unblinking invitation to anthropomorphism: she was a character, neat, prudent but unafraid, crying out for her Beatrix Potter. She sat there, on her narrow rump, with unaggressive insolence, the baby in her firm, loose grasp, worth

14,000 miles of anyone's travels. At lunch, the galahs, with their erratic raucousness, put on a superb white-and-salmon show; according to Craig only the gulls – aggressive and idle – were despicable. We fed kangaroos (and saw a joey to drool over emerging from the pouch on cue), although we had the feeling that they were packet-roo-food-junkies. Later, in the bush, we sidled up to an old fellow, alone and huge, as he munched through his last set of teeth (he gets three and dies – of starvation – when the last are ground away). Despite a poolside vigil, we were denied the platypus. The only real place to see them was, we were told, the zoo.

What we were not told we were to learn, in very clear terms, from Dr John Wamsley, who runs the Warrawong Sanctuary in the Adelaide Hills whose prettification – like so many things – makes Wamsley wild. The complacencies of the governmental conservancy agencies neither impress nor placate the doctor, whose one-man crusade is based on ideas which are dismissed and denounced by the centrally-funded pundits. As for the platypus we might see in Adelaide or Sydney zoo, we had better know that on an average it had to be replaced, in captivity, every three *days*: the idea, Wamsley insisted, that they – or any endangered species – could be 'rescued' by isolation and by artificially stimulated breeding was fatuous. Put a male and a female in the same pool and wait for nature to take its course? Forget it! *He* had bred platypus precisely by putting males and females in *separate* pools and allowing them to make their own arrangements. In the event, one male did all the fertilising work (alas, we were never to see its improbable – and monotreme – progeny).

Zoo is not a nice word in Wamsley's vocabulary. He applies it, caustically, to all wildlife programmes except his own. His doctorate is in mathematics, but it lends his Noah-like character intimidating prestige. He was a wild child and he is something of a wild man, with his grizzled beard and long hair under a towelling hat (removed to disclose an abbatial baldness). Warrawong is a mere 35 acres, but it advertises Wamsley's ferocious resolve, as well as providing his living. When first he told his parents he wanted to work with animals, they offered to have him trained as a butcher or a taxidermist. He glories in surprising (as he has no difficulty in recruiting) his critics.

Wamsley has his groupies too, and deserves them. His ideas are uncompromising: whatever does not belong in Australia should be shown no mercy. The only import at which his eyes kindled, when I proposed it, was rabies, which alone might cut down the foxes (I suspect he would abate his enthusiasm on reflection). He has no time for the special groves where Craig promised twenty-four hour koala service. Such places, he claims, procure the congregation of a breed which, in the wild, is as solitary as the smug female whom we saw by the roadside. Koalas get sick in each other's company. And what was the official answer? Find a cure for the sickness! Wamsley, very clearly, prefers to find a cure for officials. He believes, with the infectious vanity of the dedicated, that using the present federal budget (which, he says, does almost nothing to help and much to aggravate the problem), he could roll back the damage and restore the native environment. On his 35 acres, he offers a sample of what he now proposes to do on a 300,000 acre site on Eyre's Peninsula. The leap excites scepticism, but his method, he swears, is simple and almost infinitely expandable: others may pamper or cosset, he prefers to build fences. The fence keeps out predators – especially the fox – and allows recovery from other European invaders.

Once the fence is in place (about six-feet high and well-skirted, to deter bores), the rest demands only a twenty-hour day. Marshes can be recreated, brush-dwelling marsupials re-introduced; with a firm push, the cycle turns freely again. Wamsley smiles at his new marsh; its deliberate creation, in the suburban hills, convinced his first mother-in-law that he was certifiable. Swamp-rats moved in (an endangered, if unlovely, species) and all kinds of pond-life now abound. He breaks off to ask if you know why Australian swans are black. Because there is so much tannin in the water from the eucalyptus oil that they are better camouflaged by being in mourning. All the while, he is flinging granules to the scurrying marsupials with a sort of urgent intimacy that has no coochie-coochie endearment in it. Hearing of the fire on Kangaroo Island, he denies that these conflagrations are 'natural' or that the seed-scattering banksia has the answer. They are getting worse and worse because the smaller races of kangaroo, which used to eat the brush and so reduced the amount of kindling (and certainly its temperature-raising density), have been exterminated by the fox. Had I noticed that the Flinders Chase park is unfenced? 'No fence, no security, simple as that.'

Wamsley got our vote all right. In my undeniable ignorance,

I would back him against the 'bureaucrats' whom he loathes and who have already put him in jail, for reasons I did not press to discover. Only in South Australia, he claims, could he have done what he has, or do what he means to. Not because SA is more enlightened than his native New South Wales, but because it is more indifferent and has fewer damned laws about how animals can be kept. In NSW he would be obliged by law to pen all the animals which cohabit in his up-and-down, profit-producing, miniature Eden, thus eliminating their symbiotic harmonies. The rough tenderness of the man does not – and is not meant to – conceal a rueful monomania. He loves Australia and scorns most Australians, unless they are bettongs or snakes ('They may be lethal, but they don't attack people – people attack them') or any of the myriad varieties which crawl, scurry, swoop or flit in what is left of what the convicts, and their keepers, called 'The Fatal Shore'. Where the curator of the Adelaide Art Gallery lays stones artfully on parquet, Wamsley would, I suspect, as gladly rip up the floor itself and rediscover the hard reality of unimported rock, and life. Crank and troublemaker? I expect so. Where would the quoll and the potoroo be without him? Good on you, John.

Shades of Michael

What are your first memories of Michael Ayrton?

I first *heard* of MA from Peter Green, at Cambridge in 1952 or '53, when Michael had agreed to do the jacket of *Achilles, His Armour*, as PG rather winsomely entitled his fictional biography of Alcibiades. This was, of course, *before* M's first excursion to Greece. PG was pleased with himself at securing so illustrious a jacketeer. In the early 1950s, when he was still in his thirties, M was already somewhat legendary; he had been famous since the late 1930s (which then seemed divided from us by a wide chasm). He belonged to an intellectual-Bohemian élite (the Chelsea-Fitzrovia axis, which had the BBC and the *New States-man* as its hitching-posts). It remained paramount until the 'Angries', in their disparate and disorganised way, challenged its pieties and supplanted its pundits. Michael's precociousness led him to be left behind by those who were not, in some instances, much older than he. By the late 1950s, the generation which had trusted the Brains Trust (and the proper culture it embodied) was obsolete, like the War Artists who had given many of us our first wide impression of the variety of responses available to public events (Dame Laura Knight will always be an honorary member of The Few, in the light of her paintings of the Battle of Britain).

Michael's attitude to society may have become marginal, as it was increasingly wary, but his alienation (which he felt keenly) was partly due, I suspect, to a feeling of his own that he already

61

knew as many people as he needed; having figured as a prodigy in the world of men like Russell, Huxley, Moore and Augustus John (who once made an absent-minded pass at him, when too drunk to recognise his masculinity), he felt no great urge to rejuvenate his stock of acquaintance with Colin Wilson, Lynn Chadwick, Joe Tilson or Kingsley Amis. Precociousness aged him; early fame put him, prematurely, in a category of has-beens. He retreated into a posture which he had already found congenial, that of the defender of traditional skills, though not of 'academic' styles: thinking he had plenty of time, he declined – unwisely he later thought – to became an ARA. Neither the old nor the new arts establishment ever sought to recruit him again.

His early attack on Picasso, when he was only 23, was continued, in one form or another, throughout his life, culminating in the regrettable *The Midas Consequence*. John Berger wrote his *The Success And Failure of Picasso* at Michael's instigation and because M himself would not undertake it. Ayrton's line of attack, which now seems quite moderate and was often heavy with homage, acknowledged Picasso's genius but saw that Picasso was a pasticheur of other artists and not – as M believed transcendent greatness required – an assimilator of a respected style or styles who then addressed the world armed with their acquired vision, which was compounded seamlessly with his own. What M alleged to be true of Picasso, the *bricoleur* as genius, with his immodest facility (three large paintings a *day*!), has become the mark of the arts in our time, in which parody and cannibalisation, (im)posture and attitudinising (cf. *Time's Arrow*) have supplanted the morality of truthful observation implicit in the primacy of drawing. M's values *became* conservative during the 1960s, not because he changed them but because the tide changed and he chose not to go out, or come in, with it. What had seemed compatible with a certain modernity in the 1940s and 1950s, when 'Englishness' appeared to be a definitive aspect of desirable art, was regarded, by a new generation of critics and artists, as lacking in the shocks to be associated with the new.

Michael was the casualty of a change in fashion which was to disparage intelligence and read any sign of it as a symptom of élitism (unclean! unclean!). Spontaneity and sincerity became the warrants of novelty. Abuse replaced wit and became wisdom. The decision to disdain the place of intelligence in art (or politics) is *the* cultural catastrophe. In Denis Healey's case, for emblematic and important instance, his want of forthrightness, at the time of Michael Foot's accession to the leadership of the Labour Party, suggests that the refusal to admit to being clever, except in the loyal furtherance of stupidity, is a key reason for the dwindling quality of the public philosophy in British society. A certain relationship between intellectuals and 'Socialism' was ruptured by the eviction of condescension from the counsels of the Left. The attempt to raise a new standard dwindled, as the *feu* SDP proves, into a 'TEWT': a technical exercise without troops.

Michael's attitude to art and life was inseparable from the passionate uses of intelligence; he thought that he was rendering his public a service by the ardour of his implications, the intricacy of his allusions. He assumed that a society worth taking such pains for would relish the art which, in the event, it preferred to disparage as 'literary'. He did not question the idea of art as demonstration; teaching was part of doing. This demanding generosity *is* the great tradition (rather than the 'placing' or disparagement of artists) and its loss is, quite literally, demoralising.

How long did you know MA personally?

My first meeting with M was not until the year (1973) when *Fabrications* was published. I was in the *Sunday Times* literary department, cruising for a book to review and Jack Lambert, handing a silvered proof copy to me, said, 'You could try this if you like. Michael Ayrton. No one much likes him.' It was a powerful incentive to find something to say in M's favour. I was startled by the ingenious erudition of the author, although I felt a certain temptation to be as lofty as M himself appeared. Having mused on the curious way in which men with interests in common are somehow impelled to mutual derision, for the greater satisfaction of those with whom they share neither tastes nor culture, I then wrote enthusiastically (albeit in the manner of the work) about the wit, variety and recherché intelligence in *Fabrications*.

Soon afterwards, aware that he had mentioned 'North Essex' in the text, I looked in our local Colchester telephone directory and discovered M's address and number. I wrote asking whether he was ever in our 'mazy' vicinity and invited him to lunch or dine. Soon after *that*, a typewritten letter arrived signed by M, inviting us to lunch at Bradfields. I learned later that all typed letters were written by Elisabeth, in the style of the Master, and that only his handwritten stuff should be taken to come from the horse's fist.

We drove to Bradfields bearing nervous gifts (Perigordine walnuts and a bottle of Châteauneuf du Pape '61). I had no advance advice about M but had a sense that we were about to visit a Famous Artist. I think I remembered some of his wartime stuff and, of course, I recalled Peter Green's awe some twenty years before. The approach to Bradfields was rather impressive, despite the 'Lynn Chadwicks' on which M commented bitterly on that first occasion, referring to the pylons along the valley which loomed over the house with their outstretched arms draped with cables. We drove past the huddled Minotaur and had a sense that this was the house of someone who had, so to say, nailed himself to the landscape and made it his own.

By the time we got out of the car, M's face was, if I am right, round the door, though his body remained inside. He looked as worried as we were, though he hid it less well. What kind of people had he asked, that pained face seemed to wonder, and how endurable could lunch possibly be? We ate roast pheasant, I think, and the cats made themselves at home *very* near the dish, which slightly alarmed us. Our fellow-guests, who arrived after us but were evidently *habitués*, were the Steiners; it was only the second time that I had met them. George spilt red wine on a particularly nice blouse of my wife's and then affected to repair the damage by putting salt on the 'wound'. I was to discover that this was quite a habit of his, metaphorically at least.

My first impression of M was of a man hedged with cautious curiosity; his peek around the corner was emblematic. He and G. spoke with a sort of familiar distance between them, as if they had a private language but not a private understanding. A remembered instance was of M saying that the essential maze was the shortest distance between two points. Such playful conceits are not the stuff of intimacy; they can even suggest a sort of contentiousness. Recently, G. S. said to me, 'Moore was a great artist; Michael was a great MAN.' This was, I am sure, an allusion to his sexual rather than his intellectual scope, although M's range of literacy was very impressive: when he was utterly prone and in great pain, he asked me to bring him some books which he had not read. I chose a selection of what I thought quite arcane volumes from my library (which suddenly seemed very skimpy), but when I showed him what I had brought – including a rare volume of *Jocasta's Crime* by Lord Raglan – he shook his head sadly, like a man who despaired of being shown anything he had not seen before. We were amazed, when he came to our house for the first time, that he recognised *immediately* a very untypical and unsigned Derain drawing, a nude in sanguine pencil. His musical knowledge was hardly less thorough. Shams will always accuse such men of being shams.

As a writer of modern mythology, what do you think of his mythologising; his relocation of the Daedalus myth within himself, and as relevant to our time?

In a sense, all writing in English which is conscious of the history of the language and of metaphor itself is likely to be stained with mythological elements (Iris Murdoch is an instance of a mode quite dissimilar to mine or M's which is, nevertheless, steeped in myth). Being only intermittently in the mythic mode, I am not a strident, or worthy, competitor with M in that domain. His use of the Daedalus myth, in his *writing*, was a wilful and intimate insertion of himself in the Greek world. He came to the academic world as a kind of mature student, exchanging the precocious role for that of the man who makes up for lost time. He relied on Geoffrey Kirk to translate Archilochos for his illustrated responses to that first first-personal poet, whose grouchy swagger was much like M's own. I am not sure that he was not a little *too* deferential to professors of Greek. When he went to Africa, in the last years of his life, he drew with a renewed vigilance: the apes and other fauna from that period are, it seems to me, to be preferred to, for instance, his Archilochan fox.

I suspect that Daedalus' mastery of means and comparative unsureness of touch in human matters may have appealed to M; I have proposed some impertinent glosses in *The Daedalus Dimension*, in the recently published *Of Gods And Men* (Folio Society), which Sarah Raphael has illustrated. *Dédale* by Fran-çoise Frontisi-Ducroux suggests very thoroughly the wealth of material that intrigued M. The charm of myth lies, most evidently, in its timeless relevance: it allows one to escape from one's *specific* circumstances and to inhabit an understanding dignity. Thinking perhaps of Drieu la Rochelle, Malraux spoke of eroticism as a means of escaping from one's epoch; you might look at M as someone who, like many artists, had to escape the times before he could cope with them.

M bet on art being an activity to which the mythical lent authority. This decision (which only a man of intelligence could have wished on himself, in the face of an art-worldwide change in fashion, dating from the late 1950s at least) was to marginalise his fame. His adhesion to traditional skills and interests, which involved a kind of haughty modesty, was dismissed as antiquarian and self-regarding. (But then why should a self-portraitist not regard himself?) The relevance of M's mythologising to 'our time' could be said to be that it insisted on the validity of craft and cunning; it disdained the form of art by publicity of which A. Warhol is the paradigm (let us not, *please*, forget the undiplomatic contempt with which Rothko regarded that pisser on altars).

How deep, as opposed to broad, do you think Ayrton's vast store of knowledge really was?

Is the implication that M was something of a charlatan? I confess I rather hope so. A certain readiness for imposture is essential to intelligence; one can put oneself in the way of the right answer by pretending already to inhabit it. An artist, like a Stanislavskian actor, can prepare. *Imitatio Christi* is the pious paradigm; '*je ne cherche pas*,' etc. is the scandalous parody.

How important do you think political issues were to him, after his extremely political youth?

I remember him saying, rather oddly, that he would prefer to be shot by Communists than by Fascists since he thought that the former really stood for something and that history was on their side, or something of the kind. It occurred to me that that was a reason for wanting to be shot by Fascists, but I did not dwell on the matter, since I have small appetite for being shot by anyone. I suspect that his mother's involvement with the Labour Party, and the period in which he grew up, made it impossible for him to be a Conservative, while his zeal for trenchancy disqualified him as a liberal. He was always sorry that he had not been able to fight in Spain, having presented himself, very young, at the frontier, but this too may have been a gesture of Oedipal piety (rebellion as proof of affiliation). I am not sure that Spain as a place or a culture was very important to him. His homage was to (and against) England rather than Catalonia. He always called Orwell 'Gloomy George' and was unattracted, I think, by the Puritanical masochism which was so much a part of the Orwellian persona. His socialism did not find its spiritual home in the Public Bar; I should have been surprised to see Leonard Bast, or a noble proletarian, at his table.

Have you any conclusive view of Michael Ayrton and his importance?

I miss him more and more. The little 'proof of affection towards Fred' which faces my work table is a constant reminder of him and of our shared passion for the Greek islands and their immortal ghosts (it is indeed an artist's proof of a view of Paros). A visit to his recent show at Austin Desmond and Phipps, in Pied Bull Yard, with its emphasis on Greece, excited all the old rage at the dying of his light (he once told us of a memorable drunken trip down the Thames in the company of Dylan Thomas). It also raised unwanted questions about his true standing. Is it disloyal to ask how fairly, or unfairly, he was treated and whether there was any justice in his *écartement*? Does his putative or proper ranking really matter? He remains a case so intriguing in its aesthetic, social and even deeper implications that it is difficult not to resume the inquest. 'Let not my body be hacked,' Byron said, as he lay dying at Missolonghi, but the case of Byron, like that of Michael, leads even his admirers to probe the old wounds and even to open new ones, in the name of accurate speculation.

M's generosity to students was habitual; it is part of the tradition of apprenticeship which was one of those 'antique courtesies' that Shelley also chose to honour. M once looked with gloomy admiration at Sarah Raphael's early work and said, 'I expect she'll be better than me.' Her retrospective view of Michael is at once loyal and unsentimental: his draughtsmanship had genius, but he failed to look – or to persist in looking – specifically at specific models (mythologising as a method carries the danger of recourse to generalisation which, in visual terms, tends to descriptive cant, the 'literary' gloss: my style cataracts my eye). By reducing *his* models to his models, Sarah Raphael indicated, he missed the essence of their anatomy and became detached from the vitality they could supply. The paradox is that he was accused of being 'autobiographical' but there was something limited in the amount of himself which he injected into his figures, so that they became oddly generalised, but failed – though not always – to become autonomous – forgive the cant! – statements.

M was categorised, at one stage, as an English Romantic, perhaps by himself. But he so tempered instinct with conscientiousness that he was no more a Romantic than Byron (who owed more to the classical Pope than to the 'Lakers'). M's Bohemianism was never reckless, nor was it solitudinous; he said that he was educated in pubs (after leaving school at 15), but he took his bibulous teachers seriously and was always eager to sit for a grand examination. Perhaps one of the laming consequences of his early life was that he was both too close to the critical weekly magazine world and too much in awe of the *monde universitaire*.

His father, Gerald Gould, straddled poetry and journalism; M said that Gould was an excellent judge of novels, except when they were excellent (he thought nothing of *Ulysses*, for instance). M chose to call himself by his mother's name alone, rather than Ayrton-Gould, as his parents styled themselves, because he thought a hyphenated artist was ridiculous (Cavafy might have remarked, ironically, that Gaudier-Breszka was already immortalised, but that is by the way). Gerald Gould's example may have primed a belief, however, that one could be hyphenated in the sense of being both an artist and a ranking critic simultaneously. M's prolific energy (a common aspect of genius) probably promised that doing two things at once was a happy economy, not a divisive stretch. He wanted power as well as status.

Was M ever really a *painter*? He applied pigment (and knew its formal powers) but he did not fully live through it. The outsider may wonder whether there *has* to be a right way of employing paint (affectations of certainty are presumptuous in non-practitioners), but one has a sense that M's paintings are colour*ed*, not colour. His draughtmanship was both his glory and his handicap. I cannot help suspecting that he painted pictures because important artists *must* have work in that masterly class, not because colour conscripted him as imperatively as a pen or a pencil (the little ink studies of Greece to be seen in Pied Bull Yard looked as natural as breathing).

Sarah Raphael does not like the Berlioz canon. Sometimes another artist will 'dislike' something because he or she can imagine doing something similar, sometimes because the work is wholly alien in spirit and conception. I think S.R.'s revulsion from the Berlioz is due to the impurity of Michael's obsession, which was part fantasy, part 'musical', never the response to direct *looking*. M could be sharp-tongued ('Bugger off' he used to say to bores at the Savile Club, which was not the road to popularity), but he was no iconoclast: he craved idols, you might say, with Berlioz literally *en tête* (that brow, that jaw, that nose!). The disposition to venerate could perhaps be attributed to a frustrated need for a *responsible* father, by which I mean one with serious responses; the casualness of his own gave rise to amusing stories, but one does not look to a father merely to furnish anecdotes. As a father himself, M was indulgent and attentive to his step-daughters, but disdained to make contact with an illegitimate son when the opportunity arose, in France, many years after his birth. 'Splitting', one could argue, was an habitual tactic, though I distrust these categorising formulae.

It is part of M's notion of himself as Daedalus that he became a member of a divine and modest (because perfectionist) fraternity, a fundamental, hence irreplaceable, concept. Intrude a self-referential 'I' into the term instead of the logician's 'p' and you have conceit, which turns the myth from gold to silver. Daedalus himself never thought of himself as Daedalus. Did the reverent insolence of M's impersonation betoken a kind of independent dependence, a need for reinforcing imposture from which Daedalus himself – never working in a silver age! – was wholly insulated? Michael was less of a scoundrel in art than his master; he kept his wickedness for the bedroom, where Daedalus had no renowned championship. Yet the erotic in M's art was always a little precious. Even when he had the licence, in his Verlaine illustrations, of the specialised 'art book' trade (in the days before fucking became a public sport), M depended on a certain respectability, in his audience, in order to spring his careful shocks. His appetite for myth – the authenticating precedent which he could then gloss – suggests a respect for the given, a need for the reassurance given by earlier masters (the adulterer's fetish); he wanted, one could say, very Englishly, both to go out of bounds and to be tied to a good old school. His pedantries accompanied an audacity which was also a tribute to the beauty of the rules which modernism defined itself by challenging, that very modernism in which he also wanted to have a stake. His unsociable 'Social-ism' is of a piece with this straddling aesthetico-ethical strain.

M was no sort of coward, nor was he a toady. He went to Spain at the age of 15, in defiance of his Socialist mother's wishes, and in ignorance of her reach, in order to enrol in the army of the Republic. Mrs Ayrton-Gould MP, was able to pull strings to have him excluded from the Spanish arena; he went to Vienna and then on to Paris, where he established his virility in a peaceful mode, before returning to England in time for the war in which he never fought. Although called up (asked his religion, he wrote 'Gnostic', which his flight-sergeant corrected to 'C. of E.', a correction that was not corrected), he was soon invalided out.

Despite his veneration for the Renaissance masters, as far back as Barna da Siena (a typically arcane totem), M never displayed any work, to my unthorough knowledge, in which Christian allusions figured importantly. The Greek world was a providential cover for his iconic urges (as it had been for the Renaissance painters of an unorthodox bent, for whom the ancient canon's place in Christian apologetics was a happy – often literary – excuse for pretty Paganism). M outflanked Christian art, without having to confront or overtly to dissent from it (it could be said that he followed, or equalled, Picasso in this untypical reticence). I am, of course, in no way *accusing* M of flinching from the treatment of Christian motifs to be seen, for example, in Graham Sutherland's you-asked-for-it crucifixion in Coventry Cathedral, though one can guess at a certain *pudeur* which is absent, most obviously, in Dali's un-nailed St John of the Cross version. Such commissioned muta-bility was, happily, alien to M.

Was there, nevertheless, a flaw in M's posture to art, in his constitutional attitude to it?

Why is one tempted to lend straw to those who would make bricks to throw at a friend? Should I not admit the suspicion that there was, in M's whole scheme, some persistent reluctance to face *something*, a deviation which disposed him to decentralise his personality? I do not in the least imagine that we can find models of true alignment in human beings nor that perfectly adjusted characters, if they could be spotted, would necessarily produce good art, but it is not *pointless* to notice where warps and detours occur nor uninteresting to speculate on their 'geological' source. Is it disrespectful or disloyal to wonder whether the largely unacknowledged stratum in M's character is his dubious Jewishness? Here was a marginality (in its time) which was without the sweet dangers of eroticism or the convivial exhilarations of alcohol. The loneliness of the artist was more easily assuaged (and more delectably glamorous) than that of the Jew. M did not *deny* his Jewish connections: he boasted that Israel Zangwill was his great-uncle, by marriage, but he had no *use* for being a Jew. Why should he have? It is not a matter of morals, still less of faith; it is more to do with who one thinks one is, and such thought led M to Daedalus and the enveloping comfort of the Greek obsession. There is no need to believe that M was *guilty* about his indifference to the (traditionally anti-iconic) tradition of Judaism, but the fervour of his political views – which were generalised by his Left-wing sympathies – was perhaps keener for the assumed anti-anti-Semitism of the Old Left. I am arguing for no correct artistic or social attitude to one's own or anyone else's Jewishness. But the 'disappearing Jew' – of which Houdini's escapism supplies a marvellously showy 'period' instance – was, as Heine's baptism notoriously announced, a standard figure in the world of European art: the outsider traded his obsolete specificity for a noble and 'higher' model. Why not? The attempt, unfortunately or no, precipitates all the demons of our time. R. J. Kitaj's jejune candours, in *The Diaspora Jew*, show how a sophisticated artist can be given an uneasy conscience by 'irrelevances'. Michael's character was established before the *Shoah*; thus he had better reason to feel that to be identified as a Jew was simply to take on the 'fossil' identity which Arnold Toynbee denounced.

M seemed almost to invite the rejections which hurt him so much. As a critic, he no doubt imagined (don't they all?) that he was speaking for standards, not for himself, but victims seldom accept strictures in that spirit; Michael's bided their time, and it soon came. Was he perhaps drawn to criticism *because* it alerted him to flaws which he feared were his own? Did he not seek, in his almost excessively *worked* essays, to fortify himself against temptations which were all too tempting? If so, the trap and the trench were one. Certainly – like the Jew who can always recognise a Jew! – he was almost morbidly conscious of what he could be accused of being: the facile, but parasitic, pasticheur and parodist whose sublimely reprehensible instance, in M's own book, was Picasso. Guilt and election are sought by the same association. In this gesture of quasi-camp ostentation, M took on the lineaments of the brazen pre-Wolfenden homosexuals who dared to flaunt what they would have been wise to conceal: his attack on Picasso demanded that he be classed with the genius he damned with unfaint praise. This was not to be forgiven, though I cannot find it unforgivable. A not always unspoken 'How dare he?' pursues Michael even now; his critics can be too malicious in their efforts to prove that they are cleverer than he is, which is the danger clever artists run. Some men can be hit with impunity only after the bell. They are dug up to be knocked down again.

How 'English' was Michael Ayrton's art?

His insularity was of a piece with his times, but it seems insignificant now, in the period of mass tourism, in which art itself has joined (when I was in Valencia in December, the Velasquez self-portrait and the Goyas were away on their holidays). It was while compiling a now dustily forgotten compendium of 'English drawings' that he discovered his unelected affinity with Wyndham Lewis. M's encounter with 'The Enemy' might have been bruising, but he showed himself surprisingly motherly-fatherly-brotherly in accommodating himself to Lewis, who was going blind. Lewis had affected to be an early admirer of Hitler, but he and the admirer of 'Socialism', of which Stalin's Russia was, at least at one stage, taken to be a bright example by New Statesmanites (Michael did a typical portrait of the elastic editor, Kingsley Martin), found that when it came to draughtsmanship they were almost indistinguishable in taste and accomplishment. (Was either man a colorist of the same merit?) Lewis's and Michael's confidence sprang, one can guess, from the incontrovertible, they-can't-take-that-away-from-me brilliance of *their* line (and never mind the Party). M became, for a while, Wyndham Lewis's 'secretary'. The assumption of a lowly office was also an assertion of parity.

Could it be argued that there was a prospect of inheritance, even of succession, in succouring the doomed dinosaur?

Lewis had deliberately chosen to be The Enemy, but M chose only to be the enemy's stretcher-bearer. The red cross he wore in his approach to the flagging Titan was both brave and neutral. Did M envy Lewis his salient solitude, the result less of being ignored than of having solicited pariahdom? Somewhere along the line, M was dedicated to the seduction of an audience which Lewis preferred to intimidate. Not for nothing, perhaps, was WL said to have the face of a failed rapist, since what we admire, however furtively, in the pervert, whether the killer or the sadist, is his willingness to emblazon his own loneliness, a rejection of sympathy which gives him the autonomy of heroism and earns, for instance, Hannibal Lector the strange adulation of herbivorous audiences who can bless him with a sort of 'artistic' stylishness, with flesh as his medium. You could push a point and say that M was wary where Lewis (the gun!) was war-ry.

How do you think Michael Ayrton wanted to be seen?

There is no scandal in having an opinion of oneself which one would like to have shared. M was not a snob, but he was accustomed to the company of the famous. His habit of seeking clever company implies an emulous modesty: what artist does not want to be worthy of the highest tables (Daedalus was a treacherously eager guest of Minos)? M's prodigious misfortune was to be picked out as a potential master before he had ceased to be *imberbe*; the beard he later grew was as if it were false: it first masked his youth and then it denied his age, but it never *fitted*. (Did it add an involuntary foreignness to his face, a Mediterranean fringe?) One understands him best by attempting to re-imagine that England to whose art he wanted to add (Stephen Potter, the BBC man, made 'Mediterranean' a term of disparagement in his *Oneupmanship*). Rebel and curator, there was caution even in Michael's most incautious work. His nudes may have been largely of his anatomy (for a lover of women, he seems not greatly to have loved the female form), but they were – as John Berger remarked of Renoir's women – somehow always *clothed*, in M's case in a conventional suit of flesh pegged on expected bones. (His essay on Michelangelo's 'imprisoned' figures offers clues as to how he may have regarded his own recurrent practice, in which *finish* gave the impression of conclusive confidence.)

The sculpture looks weakest when it is least 'artificial': in Pied Bull Yard, the couple lying – post-coitally perhaps – on a bronze saucer are triste only in their jellified solidity, their want of tensile cohesion (no wonder art critics, poor tongueless souls, have recourse to heavy jargon!). The fact that the pair I am thinking of carry no mythical tag is a sign of what risks M took when he sent his bronze children nameless into the world. It is tempting to puzzle over the failures of certain artists, although I would not willingly give ammunition to Michael's strangely numerous and unremitting enemies; in his case, 'failure' has nothing to do with incompetence but much more with a kind of misreading which only the highest literacy could manage. 'Old Henry', as M called Moore, was incapable of that kind of considered error; he was pretentious only in the undamaging appropriation, almost as an afterthought, it seems, of cultural tags: it hardly matters that his warriors are not very Greek, because the bronze itself – as distinct from the catalogued title – carries almost no allusive affectations, whereas Michael's *work* insisted on parading its provenance: falsified by what it relied on for authenticity, it was at least sometimes lamed by its own crutches.

M's *love* of métier, his sedulous joy at being Daedalean, robs him of the insouciance of Daedalus himself. Haunted and informed by the Greek thing, he could not unfailingly make the mythic transcend the peculiar. Was he too manifestly hungry for a tradition into which he could hope to insert himself without trace? Despite and because of his sense of being an outsider, if not the 'free-thinking Jew' whom Mr Eliot would have excluded from his Christian polity, perhaps he carried his icons too high. Moore made heroic emblems which people might assimilate to the Greeks but which, in truth, justified themselves independently of the nominal cloak he threw over them. M was far more pious and yet only occasionally achieved that unquestionable image which Daedalus could have been deceived into taking for his own in the same way as real bees were lured to Michael's artful golden honeycomb, fashioned in the *cire perdue* tradition of the Master himself. (Lost wax cost Daedalus his son, as the Ayrton Icarus on our terrace reminds us.)

Are you happy with what you have said about Michael Ayrton?

He was a draughtsman of genius; he was a painter of talent; Moore said that he would be regarded as a minor master of sculpture. I loved the man and he was not, I fear, an undeniably central figure in modern English art. I am not sure that it matters which precise niche we put him in, or whether such precision is possible. His intensity of purpose is itself an exemplary anachronism: alien to the media-led art-world of today, he continues to celebrate a hermetic way of life it is increasingly difficult, and all the more valuable, for an artist to sustain.

Tunc and Nunc

'Caesar attacks the Belgians' was the first sentence my Latin class was called upon to translate. *Caesar oppugnat Belgas* was the correct answer, but no one told us why he did so or, more significantly, that the Belgae were a Celtic tribe with plenty of cousins in Britain. Caesar's 55 BC reconnaissance in force, which put down a marker for the subsequent Roman interest in ruling Britannia, was part of the divine Julius's campaign to crush the Gauls and conscript them, *nolentes volentes*, to civilisation. One could not ask for a more meticulous or scholarly assessment of what Britain meant to the Romans, or Rome to Britons, than Peter Salway's monumental study, *The Romans* (in which I found only one venial misprint).

Although the Roman invaders had some problems with the choppiness of the Channel, it seems to have baulked them less than it did Napoleon or Hitler, probably because the local tribes had no fleet with which to challenge them. In ancient times, Professor Salway argues, the Channel was seen more as a river than a barrier. British trade with the continent pre-dated the Roman invasion; iron, lead and gold had already been found in desirable quantities. There were Belgians to attack on both banks.

When, in AD 43 Claudius incorporated Britain decisively in the empire, its conquest was both a propaganda *coup* – intended to give the pedantic emperor military laurels – and a profitable acquisition. In the following four centuries, Britannia sometimes proved a fateful element in the political equations of the empire: Constantine the Great was not the only emperor whose power

base was garnished with legions stationed in Colchester, Ciren-
cester or York. As all East Anglians know, Colchester claims to
be Britain's 'first recorded town'. It might have remained the
capital city, just as it is still a garrison town, had it not been for
the revolt led by Boudicca (as scholars now prefer to call the legendary Boedicea) in AD 60, a century after Julius first tested the
British waters. When the enraged queen had done her worst, the
administrative capital decamped to a less stroppy neighbourhood.

London soon became the centre of the network of roads
which reached westwards to Cornwall (where the tin came
from) and north towards Caledonia, where first Hadrian's and
then the Antonine Wall (shorter, but further north) were built
to impress and bracket off the untamed tribes who were later
called Picts and Scots. Their troublesomeness may have been
mitigated as much by trade (and unofficial inter-marriage) with
the garrisons on and around the Walls as by the Romans' deeply
entrenched show of here-to-stay determination.

Even Boudicca's short-lived creation of a National Liberation
Front was inspired less by patriotic indignation than by the
cack-handedness of Decianus Catus, the provincial procurator,
and his officers. Boudicca's unrebellious husband, King Prasu-
tagus, had left his East Anglian kingdom to the Roman emperor
as co-heir with his two daughters, but Catus' men proceeded to
appropriate the kingdom, enslave the Iceni, steal their goods
and rape (among others, no doubt) the royal daughters. The
widowed queen herself was flogged, but not into submission.
She recruited neighbouring tribes and went, literally, to town:
Colchester was probably delivered to her without difficulty by a
'fifth column' which outnumbered, and soon helped to murder,
its Roman inhabitants.

The sizeable temple of the Imperial Cult was a prime target,
not least because the locally recruited priests were being ruined
by the conspicuous fortunes it was their enforced privilege to
lavish on it. One of the prime purposes of Roman religion was
to unify the empire in respect, but piety and extortion were
often close. The later attraction of Christianity may have been
partly prudential: in Britain, it was among the local upper
classes that it eventually spread most quickly. Almost undoubtedly, it made fewer practical, if greater spiritual claims, on
them. 'Privatisation' of the funds held in Pagan temples also
enabled certain late emperors to reflate their economies.

As for Boudicca, she scythed and burned her way to spectacular, but very temporary, success. While her chariots were cutting a swathe towards London, some seventy thousand Romans and collaborators were hanged, burned or crucified, so Tacitus promises, in an orgy of impractical murder (taking no prisoners meant having no bargaining position if things turned sour, and no slaves for sale if they did not). The Brits were on the rampage, in numbers, rather than involved in any disciplined reconquest, although their by-passing of Roman garrisons led them to invent a sort of *blitzkrieg* which wrong-footed the colonists and spread panic as far south as Verulamium (St Alban's), which was thoroughly sacked.

The Roman governor, Suetonius Paullinus, an experienced general, gradually took control of the situation. The final battle, 'perhaps near Mancetter or Towcester on Watling Street', was watched, like some gladiatorial display, by the British supporters (mostly women and children) in the wagons which followed the motley, multitudinous army. This time Roman skill trumped British grit; the show turned into a massacre when the narrowness of the site and dense woods deprived the queen's chariots of their previously alarming mobility. Eighty thousand Britons – spectators and warriors alike – died or were slaughtered later; Boudicca escaped, but either killed herself soon afterwards (as Tacitus tells it) or fell sick and died (as Dio would have it). Either way, serious British resistance was at an end and did not recur for over three hundred years. As for Colchester, it remained a somewhat haunted corner of a foreign field, so far as the Romans were concerned, although its oysters were soon renowned. They were transported in all directions, either at great speed or in water-tanks.

The pacification of the province was both thorough and, so far as the local 'gentry' were concerned, increasingly agreeable. Provided they had things all their way, the Romans were indulgent imperialists. Their habit of accommodating local toffs, provided they consented to be Romanised, was to be followed by the British themselves when they became the somewhat briefer masters of the world. The degree of restlessness among the natives has probably been exaggerated. Our top-heavy idea of imperial Rome tends to be lurid with civil wars, as one candidate after another donned the purple or was rudely stripped of it, but Salway's undramatic thoroughness produces detailed evidence that the lesser lights of the Roman world often burned steadily and with remarkable efficiency.

Despite all the in-fighting at the top, it remained an enforcea-
ble law that civilians should not carry weapons: the inference is
that, in both town and country, security could be assured by the
often sparse garrisons. As for the chain of command, imperial
mail sometimes covered two hundred miles in twenty-four
hours. The system of *mansiones*, post-houses, meant that the
emperor's friends could travel widely and without much risk.
Even common soldiers were moved with some panache from
east to west: we read of Syrians stationed in Britain.

For the emperor, the profits of stability had to be balanced
against the danger of creating fiefs from which, as often
happened, an imperial pretender, having ingratiated himself
with his men, by success or sweeteners (preferably both), could
take the field against the emperor who had promoted him.
Britain could brew both beer (its price was fixed, by Diocletian,
at twice that of Egyptian) and trouble. Indeed, the final Roman
evacuation of the island was probably due less to pressure from
the usual suspects, the Picts and Scots, than from that eye for
the main chance – the imperial purple – which is to be observed
in even the last of the provincial colonels.

To judge from the archaeological evidence, Britannia without
the Romans was, for some time, almost indistinguishable from
the placid island which had accommodated them for almost
half a millennium. Christianity was slower to prevail than our
pious school-books promised and, so far from being a 'slave
religion', it seems to have filtered downwards. The Church not
only replaced the imperial authority but, emanating from Rome,
soon mimicked its diocesan style, if rarely its tolerance.

Constantine the Great's 'conversion', in the early fourth century, had been as much a Machiavellian as a metaphysical move.
His triumph at the Milvian Bridge, in which élite legions from
Britain played a crucial part, has long been represented as the
vindication of the True Faith, but Salway reminds us that Max-
entius, his defeated rival, had also advertised his willingness to
tolerate, and perhaps even embrace, Christianity. A universal
religion – the irreverent might say *any* universal religion – offered
the best hope of unifying the increasingly fractured empire which
was to have a second coming, of a kind, in Christendom, and
perhaps a third, in the invasive EEC's Treaty of Rome. The
English language and English topography, law and customs (not
least the cult of the country house) still owe a good deal to
invaders who, in so many respects, never left these shores.

The Reclining Buddha

Everyone warns you against Bangkok: it may have been a wonderful place a decade or three ago, but today it is one enormous traffic jam. Step out of your taxi or *tuk-tuk* (a sort of motorised rickshaw) and the pavements are said to be perilous with prehensile salesmen or rapacious pickpockets. The nights – watch out! – are unsavoury with German and Japanese executives, whose work-rate has been rewarded by packaged opportunities for a sexual blow-out. There they are leering through two-way mirrors in the mass cat-houses of Patpong before giving the number of the pubescent girls of their choice. You will probably find Benidorm more subtle.

Well, Bangkok certainly is a huge bazaar where every hour is rush-hour. Genuinely fake designer T-shirts go for little more than a couple of pounds; Chinese tailors will reproduce your favourite suit overnight, in wool or silk, for a price as low as your bargaining skills can make it. Even as you haggle, old buildings are being ripped down and ostentatious tower blocks, in the pile 'em-high international style, surge into the polluted air. A building worker gets 110 baht (not quite three pounds) for a dawn to dusk shift, which accounts for a skyline skeletal with tower cranes and a ground-plan pitted with incipient bargain basements. However, perhaps because there are so many whores, perhaps because Thai wives, so a long-resident doctor friend assured me, make a happy habit of keeping their husbands sexually sated, a woman can walk safely, anywhere, any time: she *may* be robbed, but she will not be sexually assaulted, which is more than one can say in Wimbledon.

The residue of Bangkok's antique charm is to be found along the curved axis of the Chao Phraya river, a broad, turbid and uncluttered highway, the colour of milk chocolate, on which the peep-peeping conductors of the water-buses regulate a whistle-stopped traffic that comes and goes with relentless urgency. Those in too much of a hurry to wait at the undulating quay for cheap public transport can hire a long boat. Its outboard motor, at the end of an extended and manipulable steel arm, makes its pilot into a *Grand Prix* gondolier. The accelerating whine of the engine and the pony-tail of water spewed over the wake make sure that no one travels inconspicuously.

The unspoiled precincts of Bangkok lie only a few water-bus stops from the excellent Oriental Hotel, which still has some of the (now very expensive) allure which made it one of Somerset Maugham's favourite stopping places on his way to tap Malayan rubber-planters for tales of colonial life in the great days of empire, tiffin and mosquito-netted adultery. The Grand Palace, sequestered behind blanched walls, contains Wat Phra Kaeo, where the famous 'Emerald' Buddha (actually made out of jade) casts his squat, green spell from the top of an altar dazzling with votive gold. No more than two feet high, the jade Buddha has a peripatetic history: it was brought to Bangkok only in 1779, when Rama I founded the city after the destruction of the old capital, Ayutthaya, by the Burmese who were incensed, legend asserts, by the refusal of the then King of Siam to give them one of his seven white elephants.

The Emerald Buddha is becomingly modest, but I did not feel the force of its salutary charisma. The Reclining Buddha in the adjacent Wat Po ('Wat' signifies temple complex) is quite another matter. If you come on it without foreknowledge, it is as amazing as Pheidias' statue of Olympian Zeus must have been to those who went to see the Olympic games in ancient Greece and were faced, in the luminous gloom of the temple, with the seated chryselephantine figure of the father of Gods and men.

Buddha is more man than God. Not the smallest of the charms of his religion is the modesty of its pretensions. No claim is made of privileged access to divine favour; the saffron-robed monks give sensible, somewhat fatalist, advice: while they recommend virtue – especially when it takes the form of generosity to religious foundations – they do not deplore, even if they abstain from, most of the pleasures of the flesh.

The Reclining Buddha of Wat Po is enclosed in a chapel which is only slightly larger, and longer, than the glittering forty-five metre figure it contains. Since the Buddha is recumbent, you have the disconcerting impression that it is bigger than what houses it. Like the seated statue of Zeus, if it were to rise to its feet, it would burst through the roof and shatter the edifice surrounding it. However, the posture of the Buddha, and the position of its feet, one horizontally posed above the other, signify that the figure is dying. That, in a sense, is the good news: the great spirit is about to enter Nirvana, a destination reserved for those who, having attained the highest human condition, are not obliged to be recycled for another testing life on earth.

So massive is the loll of the Buddha's unsuffering body, so broad the shoulders above which the serene head, with its gold-pimpled head-dress and spike of a crown, is propped on an acute-angled elbow, that it impresses but does not intimidate: Buddhist doctrine threatens you with no hell worse than a dog's life here below. The core of the reclining Buddha is of brick, covered with plaster, but his gilded skin has a lissom gleam such as the now vanished Olympian Zeus must have had when anointed with oil. Only the soles of Buddha's feet are not gilt, but black: the whorls on each of the ten aligned toes are inlaid with mother-of-pearl lozenges, the size of dominoes. They display the one hundred and eight *lakshanas* which, Paul Gray and Lucy Ridout's guidebook told us, are 'the auspicious signs which distinguish the true Buddha'. How nice that modern scientific myth also claims that, in finger-prints, concentric whorls are symptoms of rare intelligence!

After you have looked up at Buddha's unsoiled soles, you buy a few bahts' worth of tiny discs, each worth twenty-five satang, and contribute to the pious chink and chime as you put one in each of the one hundred and eight metal bowls along the wall. You leave the temple both exhilarated and frustrated. Because of the narrowness of the building, it is impossible ever to back away and see the whole of the figure in one wide view. The nearer you get, the more partial your vision, and the greater the sense of the Buddha's elusive mass. On the other hand, the lack of accusation in the image, in contrast to that of any crucified Christ, blesses you with a certain lightheartedness. This Buddha may dwarf but he does not belittle the visitor. Nor is the sacred unsmiling or wholly unworldly: the lady who changes your money into alms has a kettle hanging just below the sacred figure and sees no scandal in making herself a cup of tea.

The altars outside the chapel are tasty with practical picnics; the food is left as a tribute for the monks who have no source of nourishment but the gifts of their friends and families (nearly all male Thais become monks for at least a brief term during their lives). Monks eat only twice a day, at 7 a.m. and then again before noon, but they eat well, as do most people, most of the time. A Thai friend told us that only about two thousand people do serious work in Bangkok: the others are all involved in selling, preparing or eating food. You can certainly eat copiously, cheaply and – given reasonable hygienic prudence (and dishes undepthcharged with chilis) – with no savage gastric consequences, even in the most basic street stall.

The aura of Wat Po's Reclining Buddha may be unique, but it is mirrored, if not matched, by any number of reclining figures elsewhere. The most memorable one we found in the open air outside the ruins of Ayutthaya (the site can be reached after a few hours' chug up the river from Bangkok). The open air Buddha – not quite as long as that in Wat Po – was swagged in a saffron robe during restoration work. His lips are curved in something very close to what Western art historians call 'the Anatolian smile', which can be seen on sixth century *kouroi*; Buddha resembles an unriotous version of the androgynous Greek god, Dionysos, who grooved into Europe from the East at about the time of Buddha's birth. Pillowed on a bolster of lotus flowers, the dying Buddha regards the world he is leaving with aloof, but not unamused, indulgence. While he advertises the narcotic bliss of Nirvana, he does not enjoin anyone to make penitential haste to join him there. There are many less tolerant, and less plausible, examples to follow than that of such an unassertive paragon.

Byron's Freedom and Ours

> Eternal Spirit of the chainless Mind!
> Brightest in dungeons, Liberty! thou art
> For there thy habitation is the heart –
> The heart which Love of thee alone can bind;
> And when thy sons to fetters are consign'd –
> To fetters and the damp vault's dayless gloom,
> Their country conquers with their martyrdom,
> And Freedom's fame finds wings on every wind.
>
> Byron, Sonnet on Chillon

You will recognise the extract from Byron's famous and – as the poet himself admitted – glib response to a touristic visit to the castle of Chillon. The sonnet celebrates Bonnivard, the Swiss hero whose long imprisonment and final vindication gave martyrdom a happy ending. For Byron, Bonnivard was an out-of-the-guidebook symbol of what one man could achieve in opposition to religious intolerance, the impersonation of Liberty. He is also held up as an advertisement for 'freedom's fame'. What I want to broach today is what freedom means to us, how it is to be fostered and what its prospects are in a future Europe.

What is freedom? And is it always the same thing as liberty? Bonnivard's fellow-citizens, the Swiss, are obliged to follow the French in being unable to make any verbal distinction between the two: *liberté* must cover both terms. The difficulty which Frenchmen have always had in finding common ground with

84

each other may not be *caused*, but it is certainly *symbolised*, by the linguistic poverty which requires them to use a single term to designate individual, metaphysical and political freedom. Of course, even for us the meanings of liberty and of freedom converge. However, we can perhaps agree that liberty is a somewhat more political than personal concept, whereas freedom belongs more commonly to the individual. In English, since we have both terms, we can more readily make the distinction between public and private freedom than can many continentals.

Is it entirely by chance that French intellectuals – often aping the Germans – seek philosophical systems to justify or from which to deduce the possibility of liberty? What Jean-Paul Sartre called 'contingency' disturbed and dismayed him: he needed to prove that he was free before freedom could become real to him. In its pursuit, he began a tetralogy of novels called *Les Chemins de la Liberté*, but all his roads led to an inconclusive destination. His craving for a convincingly commanding philosophy of liberty led him to travel hopefully with the Communists and to undertake the search for truth while toting the baggage of fraudulence.

The British, by eminent contrast with the continentals, have felt no pressing need for metaphysical or world-political warrants. However misguided John Locke may have been with his notion of the new-born mind as a *tabula rasa*, his deeply influential ideas were based on what he took to be an empirical assessment of human possibilities. Although, as students sometimes discover to their surprise, he referred to God with considerable frequency in his disparagement of preconceptions, Locke proved to be the sponsor of a secular democratic philosophy, without any over-arching metaphysical scheme.

European pundits, on the other hand, even when they reacted against the moral *imperium* of the Catholic Church, often proposed a substitute orthodoxy for that of Rome. The Common Market itself, despite its unassuming secular framework, was the practical work of Adenauer, de Gasperi and de Gaulle, for whom Catholicism was a common underlying allegiance. Who can say that there was no symbolic significance in the treaty being signed in Rome?

European Socialism also remains almost as much a religion as a political movement; the French Left still describes itself as a family, with all the kissing cousinage and Oedipal affiliations which that institution, so hated by André Gide, could be expected to offer. The many scandals of François Mitterrand's reign have been excused, and amnestied, not least because the sly enrichment of the family's fortune could not be regarded as wholly unforgivable. To Left and Right then, Europe has a civilisation in which special pleading and dispassionate witness – Sartre as against Raymond Aron – are in more or less compatible symbiosis: partisan or patriotic loyalty excuses falsehood; science and honour demand truth. Montesquieu said that one could not refuse to die for one's country, but that nothing obliged one to tell lies for it. This view, we may be sure, was not expressed in the twentieth century.

If diversity and division had not been the often ruinous rule, why would Europeans hanker so fervently after unity? When democracy began, in ancient Athens, it was less the expression of an abstract ideal than a practical means of changing the leadership without bloodshed. Internal divisions were healed, or finessed, by the wilful creation of a society which then became free to bleed others, not itself. The United Kingdom learned something of the same trick, in 1688, when the blood-less overthrow of the Stuarts cleared the decks for imperial ambitions. Both France and England may have executed a king, but the French continued to slaughter each other and never embraced the *ménagements* of democracy. The events of 1940–44, in which reactionary Vichy was finally suppressed by the forces of Freedom, can be read as the continuation of civil war by other means. The ritual obligation for French presidents to say '*Vive la République*' in the same breath as saying '*Vive La France*' suggests how the former – partisan – phrase needs to be validated by association with the wholeheartedness of the latter. There are, of course, those who will now say that the unity of the United Kingdom is also a matter of will rather than of manifest fact, but for the best part of three centuries, expediency inclined the British to a prudently unphilosophical pragmatism.

Nostalgia for a single metaphysical currency has had much less charm in Anglo-Saxon countries than within the ancient constituency of Catholicism. During the centuries of British ascendancy, tolerance was the moral correlative of Free Trade. The British lack of religious dogmatism, allied with their famous sense of humour, was an aspect of their sporting refusal to take anything but their own primacy very seriously. Their undog-

matic Christianity has been a ceremonial and sentimental adhe-
sive, rarely a normative code; the piety of Anglicans has had
more in common with the Athenian creators of democracy than
with the interpreters, inheritors and inculcators of Holy Writ.
Anglicanism's cheerful hymns and eloquent texts have created
common rather than sanctimonious ground. In general, only
foreigners, like T. S. Eliot and Hilaire Belloc, have wanted to
create an ardently exclusive Christian society; the natives have,
on the whole, preferred pomp to piety and snobs to moralists.
Embarrassed by what Byron called 'enthusy-musy' (the unsmiling excess of religious passion), the English public and private
vocabulary, compounded of irony and foul-mouthedness, has
come to embrace social and regional variety. In its unpatterned
but colourful prolixity, English became rich, but not logical; its
literature, whatever Leavisite puritans might wish to ordain,
belongs more to a free associational playground than to a school
of morals. In a society without a written constitution, more or
less comfortably at home with its contradictions, the British
have found their common ground above all in a common
language. Unequally articulated, often as violent in its expletives
as it can be insufferable in its pomposities, the language conveys
the unevenness of the social landscape, yet even its least amiable
clauses, its irregular grammar and reckless spelling, its rank
obscenities and its airless sublimities stand for a ramshackle
freedom which has rarely been either heartlessly partisan or
ideologically savage. The British have attached more importance
to being free than to doctrines of Liberty.

If it is worth preserving, it is worth asking what we do, and
what we should, mean by common ground. Need it entail more
than the possession of a common, preferably large, vocabulary?
Can it involve anything less? The speaking of other languages,
more recherché, cruder or more refined, or of street argots and
clannish codes, is not ruled out, still less disparaged, by attaching fundamental significance to a common language. But without it, how can there be any humane exchange of ideas?
Civilisation, I have to suggest, is to do with what we say and
what we read, not to large measures of agreement between
politicians. When people can no longer disagree intelligibly, a
society disintegrates; where they need interpreters, they cannot
either unite or emerge from conflict into unbelittling
compromise.

Free speech is not an accorded privilege, still less a polite fiction; it is the defining condition of a free society. The supposed weaknesses of democracy, its pattering divisions, are precisely what render it articulate, and hence capable, as Wittgenstein said, of saying the new thing in the old language. I remember being in an unusually silent Athens during the rule of the Colonels and telling a Greek friend how England was loud with the diatribes of opposing parties. 'It sounds wonderful,' he said.

In a society of free men, argument replaces *fiat*; the genius of ancient Athens lay in creating a society in which only the will of the majority could translate dissent into decision. It is true that women were not enfranchised, that part of the economic muscle was provided by slaves and that Athens itself was a domineering advocate of its own ideas. Yet, with all their faults, the Athenians – like the British – created a society, whose literature reflected both its boldness and its vanity, in which freedom was both the end and the means. It is a pretty coincidence, at least for admirers of Friedrich von Hayek and Milton Friedman, that when the Athenian populace came to have a meeting place, they used the agora, which means 'market', for their gatherings. However, the auditorium of the theatre of Dionysos, a second civic space where entertaining (and alarming) debate – ritualised in the formality of tragic dialogue – took place under critical surveillance by the (male) citizens, was a no less vital element in the topography and the evolution of freedom. Literature is not a luxury; it is the education of the people. When a society disdains high art, and sponsors vulgarity, it is not honouring the wishes of the people but deliberately depriving them of the ability to wish for anything better than what they have or are given. Only literature can challenge the sanctity of the cliché, which can now be found in all departments of politics and bureaucracy. The common ground does not have to be level; it need only be accessible. It is an area where loutish or lordly ambushes do not threaten and where the free, perhaps loud, play of opinions and ideas can take place without intimidation. It is, above all, no one's property.

What could ever guarantee the civility on which our common tenancy and our common freedom are posited? The claim that it is natural to be a democrat and respect the views of others is an ardent fiction, more noble than Plato's so-called 'noble lie', but no less synthetic. The possession of a common vocabulary does not imply that we should all say the same, politically correct things (arguably, it implies the opposite), still less that what we say should be without nuance or provocation. Community implies that we may argue about meanings, but that no one can claim privileged knowledge of what a word means, or 'should' mean, in such a way that others are forced to use it in a tendentious sense: a common language must be the vessel of clarity, but – unlike 'basic English', for instance – it must not be hostile to nuance. It announces itself not only by its general intelligibility but also by its capacity to express and then digest disagreement in such a way that its grammar, in the widest sense, becomes an impersonal corrective, capable of jibbing at nonsense, like a cough from a tactful judge, and innately disposed to favour coherent answers to social and moral questions. Through a civilised language, even the dead retain the vote and add their wisdom to our arguments.

It is in this sense that great writers and wise citizens can hope for immortality in the literature and speech of an unabased society. I was accused, not long ago, by a posturing essayist, of affecting to have read books I had not read. I hope that the charge was not true in the mischievous sense in which it was brought, but if it can hardly fail to be true, to some degree, of anyone who has ever underprepared an exam or quoted an author, it is true also in the more amiable sense that our intelligence, our wit and even our prejudices are supplied above all by those whose language we use and whose books we feel that we know, even when we have not actually read them. If we cheapen the language, we limit our children's freedom by limiting the possibility of its expression. Bad or dishonest writing is a kind of social poison, but so is bad or dishonest *talking*.

Vladimir Nabokov was unique in forecasting the collapse of the Soviet Union on linguistic grounds alone: he claimed, improbably but rightly, that the great Russian language itself would eventually evict those who crushed its subtleties. How typical that he, as an entomologist, should nominate as the fundamental rule of nature 'the survival of the frailest'! What could be less muscular than mere words? Yet the language of Pushkin could not tolerate its usurpation by sloganeers. Oppression may kill, but nothing cannot oblige us to take it seriously. Only a dandy and self-conscious artist such as Nabokov could have dared to concede no distinction between aesthetic and ethical revulsion: he regarded the cruelty and the prose style of the Soviets with the same disgust. A regime whose vocabulary debarred grace and gave barbarism its foul mouth could not, in his view, fail to dwindle into ridiculous chaos.

All totalitarianism falls into self-defeating contradiction the moment it tries to deny that freedom of choice which the existence of negation – the ability to say 'no' – itself guarantees. This freedom is not a fortunate grace; it derives from the bald fact that whatever can be asserted can also be denied. This 'irresponsibility' in language is loudly shivered at by George Steiner, in *Language and Silence* and elsewhere, but he confuses the fancied stimulus of censorship with the dividends of reticence: it is precisely because language has, as he might say, no morals (which grammar somewhat denies) that it can *always* respond.

As Antigone's defiance of Creon reminds us, the right to say 'no' is ineradicably, perhaps duplicitously, embedded in any viable language; it may be repressed, it may even be punished by death, as in Antigone's and in Mandelstam's case, but no enduring language, and hence no society, is conceivable without the possibility of denial and of its political correlative, opposition (Byron claimed to have been born for it). This may provide frail comfort under tyrannies whose first act is to assert their monopoly of the negative, but the permanent loss of the right to say 'no' is a logico-empirical impossibility. Freedom of speech is – as Lévi-Strauss might say – *embedded* in the notion of language itself; almost as soon as human beings can say anything, they begin to say 'yes' or 'no'. In view of this, no deep psychological or philosophical analysis of mind is required to establish the existence of free will. Whether or not we are programmed by the double helix (Shakespeare's mortal coil), the ineradicable ambivalence of language promises that man can always demand freedom, even if the consequence is that – like Antigone – he or she literally negates himself. Whether we like it or not, the contrariness of speech will invariably rupture every monolithic programme and interdict every interdiction. Duplicity (which sex and the reproductive process mirror and perhaps sponsor) exerts the same slow, green pressure as a blade of grass when it threads the weak spots in a slab of Portland stone and finally finds its piercing way to the light.

Who can say, or needs to discover, to what degree Nabokov's *méchanceté* ('wickedness' does not quite convey the French word's combination of sly perversity and contrary egotism) was motivated by snobbish disdain for the vulgarity of the Soviet rulers and for the mundane conformity in which they sought to mould human activity? The libertine and the apostle of liberty have close, if unreliable, affinities. Byron, to whom Nabokov's *Ada* pays skittishly outrageous tribute, is the great European example of the insider–outsider, a Janus whose ambivalence in sexual and social matters rendered him both scandal and totem (in this regard, lame Byron limped after lame Oedipus, his senior in mythology). If his lordship was taken a little too seriously on the Continent, where the translators usually missed his teasing ironies, and too lightly in England, where it was convenient to read his political radicalism for a way of disguising his moral turpitude, Byron remains the advocate of a kind of liberty which glories in commonness and common sense, though George Gordon himself would not, I suspect, ever choose to renounce his peerage.

Unsurprisingly, Byron was anathema to the Victorians. The presumptuous destruction of his journals, by his own publisher, John Murray, and his intimate friends Hobhouse and Tom Moore, was an act of iniquitous devotion by men who sought to protect the poet's reputation in the eyes of posterity by a prophylactic *auto-da-fé*. Byron has, none the less, become a by-word for outrageousness. He expressed his craving for liberty by wanting to have, and do, things both ways. Kingsley Amis's latest novel is called *You Can't Do Both* (I yield to no one as a prompt reader of his titles), but Byron refutes him and remains, for selective persons, the rampant example of the capital I-dealism to which 'permissiveness' can lead, assuming that you have the talent, the profile and the money.

The term 'permissiveness' belongs, of course, squarely to the rhetoric of repression: it suggests that free behaviour is the result only of whatever licences are accorded by central authority. In the rhetoric of liberty, on the other hand, freedom derives not from a *relaxation* of rules but from the conscious capacity to set, and then to honour, them. Free people, the libertarian argues, do not speak or act freely as the result of a ukase; the smiles of those who make a *show* of being free, or happy, as peasants did in Soviet propaganda films, demonstrate precisely what it is not to be either free or happy. Nabokov regarded the 'art' which framed and procured these false images as the very instance of aesthetic treason. In our own comfortably untragic, merely sad and comic world, we are less often bullied into acquiescence with the prevailing 'ideology' than tickled into it by the media to whom circulation and viewing figures are the measure of what is worthwhile. In the perverted Benthamite reckonings of the networks, the applause of the mass audience is equated with what is good for it. When freedom of choice becomes a matter of economics, to dissent from the majority taste can be conveniently stigmatised as undemocratic; 'élitism' is now a denunciatory term applied to all suspected of not clapping with due enthusiasm to the majority's beat. Freedom *from* choice is the luxury offered by all extremists.

It is no part of democratic loyalty to endorse, or share, the tastes or opinions of the majority. The rule of the majority is a democratic way of selecting a line of action, not of determining its virtues. Even if 99.9 per cent of the population agreed that something should be done, it would do nothing to prove that it was *right* to do it; ethical and aesthetic issues cannot be resolved by a show of hands. Furthermore, whatever it may say in stone on every *Mairie* in France, equality is not a function of liberty nor liberty its synonym. It is impossible, as Jonathan Sumption and Keith Joseph once argued, on Hayekian principles, for a society to enjoy liberty and yet ordain equality. This does not entail that it is wrong, still less that it is unfeasible, to legislate piece-meal against unjust inequalities, especially in the field of opportunity (though here the tendency of the talented to prevail cannot be read, without disastrous results, as a symptom of injustice). Equality before the law has nothing to do with status and everything to do with procedural honesty. When Margaret Drabble argues, apparently sincerely, for everyone to have the same salary, she reveals the limitations of sincerity: such equality would bring human intercourse to a halt.

The apparently self-evident justice of one-man/one-vote does nothing to establish the equal value of everyone's opinion. It is only because it is impossible to evaluate the proper weight to be given to the wise man's view as against the fool's, or the charlatan's, that a free society *postulates* an equality which nothing suggests to be a fact of nature. No fiction is more polite than the allegation that your idea is as good as mine, or his, or hers. The intelligent and the knowledgeable may, in practice, have only one vote but, luckily for society, they have other means of making their influence count. It was not for nothing that the Greeks postulated a God *peitho*, who was the patron of persuasion.

To give equal weight to every citizen's vote does not in any way confer the force of *truth* on, for instance, the referendum (it is nearly always those with peremptory temperaments, like Mrs Thatcher, who – if only when baulked – find sudden virtue in the corporate yell). If what the majority voted for thereby became true or even, supposedly, right (rather than current policy or law), the rule of majorities would be as prejudicial to freedom as it would be dangerous to art, science and honour. There is neither paradox nor puzzle here, though confusions can be engendered by a false account of what democracy means or by demagogic appeals to 'the people' and its *Volkisch* infallibility. 'The people' do not come into their liberated own if their orchestrated yes or no is declared to be the last word; they are more often led into bondage in the trappings of freedom. The referendum has signed away more liberties than it ever procured; its use in Switzerland appears benign, but even there it is a device, however pragmatic, which gives a spurious unity to a trinity of disparate communities. In general, we may depend upon it that those who clamour for freedom from the inadequacies of politicians by advocating constant reference to 'all the people' are the barkers of the autocrat. Given influence or office, they soon become the willing sycophants of the powerful: Montaigne's friend, Étienne de la Boétie drew their stinging portraits, with precocious accuracy, more than four and a half centuries ago, in his *Discours de la servitude volontaire*.

The origins of liberty and of the burden of freedom are both historical and mythical. The fundamental myth which haunts the Western imagination is that of Eden. Before the Fall, Adam and Eve were allegedly at one with God and in a state of innocence; they neither did evil nor were they acquainted with even the possibility of doing it. They could supposedly 'speak' to animals and knew the true names of everything in nature. Wittgenstein may have maintained that if lions could talk, we could not understand them, but he came after the Fall.

Were Adam and Eve free when in their paradisaical state? They were free *of* freedom, one might say. As God's creatures, they were not His slaves, but their happiness was conditional on honouring His ordinance that they should *not* do something: the Tree of Knowledge was expressly forbidden them, just as the locked room in the castle was out of bounds to Bluebeard's bride. In each case, the avoidance of undue curiosity entailed both happiness and – dare one say? – immaturity. At the root of our notion of freedom there lies an uneasy relationship with knowledge; God might be accused of having given an unfairly alluring flavour to the fruit he advised against tasting. By decreeing what should not be done, He instigated that long fascination with the forbidden which Nabokov underlined, with delicate crudeness, when he pointed out that incest and nicest were anagrams of each other.

Eve's seduction by the snake gave her an appetite for the forbidden which was synonymous with 'knowledge'. Some feminists see a distorted version of the mother goddess, Cybele, in the wicked snake. On their view, the male-oriented myth of Genesis was designed to disparage female power; it is not implausible to see the serpentine solicitation of Eve as a gesture of liberation from male dominance. On this account, Eve was being recruited to the female side in order to *recover* lost powers; the knowledge which was forbidden her was, one might say, *already* hers, although she did not know it. Her 'innocence' was a form of repression from which the snake sought to deliver her.

According to the more conventional reading, it was not Eve's desire to retrieve intellectual insights which disposed her to bite the apple. Milton's 'first disobedience' denoted an end to the unthinking bliss which Eden continues to symbolise. Whatever the charms of feminist revision, it is difficult now not to see Eve's *acte gratuit* as the source of her (and our) inexorable 'freedom', of which exile from blissful innocence is an inevitable ingredient.

If one pursued the counter-reading of the Eden myth, it could be said falsely to portray the woman as the *cause* of our unhappy state in which, in fact, she has been unjustly enslaved by the male. More commonly, though less wittily, Eve's deviance, or defiance, has been seen as an original sin from whose yoke humanity can never be free until it is redeemed by a Second Coming. Only then will those who merit salvation, or by Grace are granted it, return to a condition of timeless Edenic innocence in which, I daresay, they can all enjoy Ms Drabble's minimum/maximum wage, since time will have a stop.

Presumably the Millennium will put an end not only to wage differentials but also to the pursuit of knowledge, which the Fall began. Man's appetite for knowledge is a function of his ejection from that seamless continuity with Reality which his unfallen state accorded him. It is tempting to ask whether the freedom which enabled Eve to 'sin' was superfluous to the needs of the first couple. Had God not granted them the possibility of diverging from His commands, what defect would it have entailed in their blissful state, other than denying them the chance to ruin it? It is pious to claim that generosity impelled God to give man the freedom to choose to be obedient, without which good behaviour would have lacked merit. A less genial view might be that the giving of free will to Adam and Eve was an act of divine *méchanceté*, of Nabakovian ingenuity, on the part of a deity who, given His omniscience, must have known (since He knew everything) that Eve would never resist the blandishments of the serpent.

The theological cruxes which have for so long filled the Garden of Eden with their brambled skeins cannot, of course, be straightened out by playful recension; their wrangling complexity denotes the problem which man has had in deciding both what he is and what he wants to be. The notion of the natural law, enacted by St Thomas and implicit – in secular form – in the idea of Universal Human Rights, is sustained by the hope, the dream or the fantasy of a recovered Eden. By conscious virtue or responsible planning, it is hoped that humanity can recoup its innocence without losing its knowledge. The return to such a state of natural balance and righteous respect depends on the belief that a condition of more or less Edenic stability will necessarily follow from the elimination of abuses. The assumption is that worldwide harmony can be restored. Universal Rights, on this reckoning, have a sort of *republican* divinity: they constitute the unfortunately lapsed blueprint of what was, or could be, the fundamental code for human freedom.

Unfortunately, perhaps, it does not demand the cynicism of Talleyrand to see that the unity of Europe and the notion of its socially contracted harmony amount to a sentimental fiction. The fundamental diversity of human beings is as certain as their superficial fraternity. The good and the bad news are delivered, as so often, in the same package. It is practically inconceivable that Europe can arrive at standardised habits in public or private affairs or that, if it did, it would still be capable of civilised progress. The recognition of our fragile prospects for survival in diversity may be salutary, but to cater only for survival cannot make life worth living nor provide a liberating prospectus. Resignation and modesty may, at times, be seemly but the lure of the unknown, to which we all accede in the exercise of freedom, must always trump them. The myth of Prometheus and his rejection of submission even to the will of Zeus promises that the heretic has his long pertinence to the grammar of European motives. We cannot agree to be obedient to any authority, whether forceful or benign, without betraying what, in a deep sense, Wittgenstein called our language.

The horrid example of the Romantics, with their penchant for the innate wisdom of the *Volk*, threatens to foul any discussion of the naturalness of defining a people by its language, but it is, I think, possible to find a way of both ennobling and extending the limits of community without embracing the nonsense of the *Volk*'s right to 'self-determination'. In fact, the myth which Aeschylus revised, renovated and, to a degree, invented in *The Oresteia* lies deeply embedded in the European language, that nexus of metaphors and forms which, transcending national languages, supplies our fractured community with its abiding hopes and fears. It is this conjunction of what we dread with what we must learn to treasure which Aeschylus so unforgettably contrived in the resolution of the conflict between the old chthonic forces, the so-called Furies, and the new divinities on Mount Olympus. The genius of Aeschylus lay in seeing that unless the darkness can be recruited to harmony with the light, unless what we fear becomes incorporated and useful in what we hope, there is no chance of achieving what Wittgenstein meant when he spoke of saying 'the new thing in the old language'. The single currency of a mint language could create only a false Eden, in which some snake will always be found to cozen some man or some woman into reverting to the bloody ways which bland formulae have sought to occlude.

What political system has ever been more insolent with supposition or more freely *fabricated* than Athenian democracy? Its procedures were in no way a *natural* development; it derived, in the first instance, from sly contrivance by Kleisthenes, who used the tradition of tribal voting in order to break the power of the old aristocrats and, by the wilful creation of an intelligently confusing arrangement of new tribes and procedures, gave Athens a new cohesion. He resolved contradictions which might have led to civil rupture and used their energy to compound Athenian strength.

Aeschylus celebrates the synthetic unity of the old and the new Gods, and of the citizens who look to them for guidance. In his myth too, feminists can find sources of indignation. The evil which blighted Greece derived, men claimed, from Helen the destroyer and her twin sister, born of the same egg, Klytemnestra, who killed the returning Agamemnon and began the trail of blood which ended on the Areopagus in Orestes' amnesty. However, even in the course of liberating Athens from the automatic pollution which the old laws decreed, Aeschylus recognises, though finally he does not honour, Klytemnestra's rage at the sacrifice of Iphigeneia. We cannot ever arrive at a new and clean beginning, immaculately free of the dark gods whom Aeschylus and Athens were wise enough to incorporate (and tactfully re-name) rather than to repress. The imprisoned liberty which Byron saluted in his sonnet on Chillon may well have uglier cell-mates who, crushed by bland edicts, can also find dangerous wings unless their force is recruited to the common knowledge and freely acknowledged, even savoured, by those who find it alien. The process of ennobling the savage and of reconciling the incompatible is not a matter of extending rights or of posed hand-shakes; it requires the kind of imaginative harnessing of old hatreds into energetic common purposes and in the excavation of common ground of which Aeschylus furnished abiding paradigms both in *The Oresteia* and in his Prometheus. In each case, compromise is revealed as an agonising and dangerous choice, not a bland business of bureaucratic communiques; freedom from the old demons requires their conscious co-optation in fresh enterprise and, as Spinoza first said, and the Communist party mischievously parroted, the recognition of a certain kind of necessity. If freedom is indivisible, it is also the fruit of division; duplicity – yes *and* no – is both our nature and our fate. Why else do we so often see the masks of comedy and tragedy hanging, two-facedly, from the same nail?

Look Here Upon
this Picture

Why Venice? In April 1816, Byron left England, for what turned out to be the last time. He had taken the Dover road in his specially commissioned, Napoleonic travelling coach complete with library. The grandiose conveyance would have cost him five hundred pounds, had he had the means to pay Mr Baxter's bill. He left behind many other unpaid accounts – the bailiffs were already emptying his rented house at 13, Piccadilly Terrace – as well as a vengeful wife with Christian principles. London's 'rogues' gallery' (as Byron once called the *beau monde*) was garrulous with allegations of his heterodoxy and/or homosexuality. Those who acquitted him of being a revolutionary were hot to credit him with incestuous relations with his half-sister, Augusta Leigh. Unlike Oscar Wilde, Byron looked forward to a world elsewhere. He did not dawdle about waiting for martyrdom: *Don Juan* would serve as his *De Profundis*. Venice, humiliatingly 'liberated' by Byron's 'little pagod' Napoleon, now in St Helena, was more attractive than a victorious London in thrall to Wellington ('they worship any bloody booby who breaks heads').

Childe Harold's grand tour had left Byron with youthful memories of unclouded skies, and of the pleasures to be found under them. Although there was an allusion to Venice in the poem which authorised him to wake up famous, Byron had not, on that first excursion, gone to Italy. However, he had long fancied the intersection of East and West where St Mark's parade of riches still mocked their looted source and Venice's

quondam master, Byzantium. If Constantinople's prancing
horses now dignified an impotent Serenissima, no longer mis-
tress of the Adriatic, or – since Buonaparte's conquests – even
of herself, Venice was at least somewhere a man could swim
and not walk (Byron did not limp in the water), and where
transgression had no bad name. The Rialto might no longer
supply a brave offshore refuge for the wretched peasants, in
flight from Lombards or Goths, who had founded the city
'throned on its seventy isles', but it still offered soft asylum to a
poet who, having wrecked his English life, was well-heeled
enough (in one sense at least) to emigrate to the appetising husk
of a decadent supremacy. Did not London have the same allure
for American 'fugitives' in the 1960s?

Not yet thirty, Byron was already England's most famous
poet, for whom 'the tight little island' had begun to pinch. Was
he the victim of a political conspiracy? Did the Tories run him
out of the country? He was more probably paying for the
consequences of domestic wilfulness. He was, if only temporarily, unable to pay for anything else very much. No small part
of the lure of abroad was that it was cheaper than London:
towards the end of his self-indulgent three years or so in Venice
(by which time he had sold the Byrons' ancestral home, Newstead Manor, and was again in the chips), his lordship calculated
that he had spent less than five thousand pounds. He had had
to be very extravagant to do so. His whores, of both sexes, cost
him more than the rent of the *palazzo* Mocenigo or the salaries
of his fourteen servants (there was also, of course, his menagerie
to feed: like Alan Clark, a prosaic modern Byron, he was often
more tenderly disposed to animals than to people).

At first, Byron's only forwarding address was '*Poste restante,
à Geneve*' (he gave it to Claire Claremont, never expecting her
to forward her intrusive self, as she soon did). However, he was
already toying with Venice, 'the greenest island of his imagination', as a final refuge. If, at the end of 1820, when writing
from Ravenna to his estranged wife, Annabella, he claimed that
he had meant to go to Turkey ('and am not sure that I shall not
finish with it'), he had by then surfeited on the pleasures of the
Serenissima. His disreputable adventures had culminated (as his
presence at Ravenna proved, though he did not advertise the
fact to Annabella) in his sentimental 'last attachment' to the
Countess Teresa Guiccioli.

He would go no more a-roving, except to Missolonghi and

his tragi-comic death in the cause of Greek independence. His wry last words were '*E finita la commedia*'. He was an actor who found his happiest parts in the Venice of Goldoni. In the tradition of the *commedia dell'arte*, given that he was a lord, he devised a plot, and an ending, worthily frilled with heroic irony. One of the first things which had impressed Byron in Italy was the famous *improvisatore* Sgricci, whom he saw, and heard, at La Scala, in Milan in October of 1816, soon after his arrival from Geneva.

When, in reply to querulous comments from London, he later told his friendly critics that Don Juan had no 'plan', it indicated how far he had been recruited into the unEnglish uses of spontaneity (Jerome McGann has detected a 'Wittgensteinian' modernity in the poem's sprawling proliferation of instances and its lack of conclusive argument). If Byron understood Italian – learnt, from his young lover Nicholas Giraud, on his first trip to Greece, in return for teaching the boy to swim – his audience, and target, remained English ('. . . I did not write to the Italians,' he wrote to Samuel Rogers in March 1818, 'nor *for* the Italians, nor *of* the Italians'). Nevertheless, the improvisatory skittishness of his Venetian work paid tribute to local buffoonery. Nervous of a theatrical audience's pitiless verdict (isolated in Venice, he was alarmed, and enraged, to hear of an unauthorised production of *Marino Faliero* at Drury Lane), Byron relished opportunities for ventriloquial imposture. He was in his mutable element when he donned the impudent masks which effaced quotidian identity and made all the Venetian world a stage in the *Carnevale*, that sensual farewell-to-flesh before Lenten abstinence.

Byron and John Cam Hobhouse, his habitual straight man, finally embarked for Venice at Mestre, in pouring rain, on 10 November 1816, and huddled under shelter until 'a boatman cried out to us – "The Rialto" – shortly afterwards we landed under the *Hotel of Great Britain* . . . and were shown up a magnificent flight of stairs into rooms whose gilding & painted silks showed they belonged to better people in better times . . .' The same was true of Venice. According to local myth, the Contessa Benzoni – who still had her salon and a long-time admirer, the Cavalier Giuseppe Rangone, besotted enough to describe the almost seventy-year-old, sausage-shaped countess to Byron one morning as '*Rugiadosa*' ('dewy') – had danced around the liberty tree in her beautiful youth with the young

Ugo Foscolo, 'dressed in an Athenian petticoat open along the flanks, with a vest which left her breast free'.

Venice's putative freedom lasted less long than the Contessa's youth: its population had dwindled and so had its prosperity. However, its crumbling beauty had the dilapidated charm which Newstead Abbey had also possessed when, by a fluke of inheritance (he was not in the direct line of baronial succession), Byron had come into it at the age of eleven. In Venice, he looked for a home from home, obligingly garnished with a past more glamorous and mementos less painful than Newstead.

On 11 November, the morning after their arrival, Byron and Hobhouse went to the *Palazzo Dogale* and saw the portraits of the Doges, the last of whom, Ludovico Manin, had surrendered his ducal hat less than twenty years before. Hobhouse observed that Byron was 'most impressed' with the black veiled space allotted to Marino Faliero, 'who was beheaded on the stairs in the yard for conspiracy against the state in 1355'. His response to Faliero's want of flattering depiction would be to supply one, in the form of a 'tragedy' which was both Shakespearian in diction and artful in its avoidance of an Othellan echo, even if Faliero too had rendered Venice some service.

Despite the offence he is shown to take at Michele Steno's notorious *graffito* (which was not, in historical fact, about the actual Doge's idealised wife Angiolina), Byron's Marino Faliero is depicted as more irascible than jealous, more self-destructive than mischievously lured into treason (Byron took the part of Iago, very well, they say, in amateur dramatics in Rome). In the preface to his play, Byron cites a passage from Langier which suggests the elective affinity he felt with the disgraced Doge: '*Tale fu il fine ignominioso di un'uomo, che la sua nascita, la sua età, il suo carattere dovevano tener lontano dalle passioni produttrici di grandi delitti.*'

The dread, and thrill, of a great fall haunted and excited Byron. Marino Faliero was an old man cursed by a violent temper (there was a historical incident in Faliero's youth when he struck a Treviso priest who was dilatory in serving the Host), but his *hubris* – never forget Byron's classical education, as he did not – became fatal only when he took ruinous offence at a small provocation. Faliero's emotional and social instability were easily assumed by a writer who, better than his critics (and many historians), had an observant sense of the disproportionate nature of human causes and their effects: '. . . a basin of

water spilt on Mrs Masham's gown deprived the Duke of
Marlborough of his command, and led to the inglorious peace
of Utrecht ... Louis XIV was plunged into the most desolating
wars, because his minister was nettled at his finding fault with a
window, and wished to give him another occupation ... etc.'

The works of what passes for Byron's maturity owe much of
their imagery, form and recklessness to Venetian experience. In
the *palazzo* Mocenigo, on the Grand Canal, and in the Palladian
Villa Foscarini at La Mira, the Childe ripened and – in some
eyes, degenerated – into Don Juan. If he could scarcely have
made bolder or more prolific use of his unserene life in Venice,
it remains a shame that Byron did not prefer, for summer
purposes, to rent the Villa Foscari, known as La Malcontenta,
at Gambarare di Mira. It may be a lugubrious pile (with gigantic
murals by Battista Franco that recall Giulio Romano's in the
Palazzo Te, at Mantova) but it could have supplied a tasty
donneé concerning *le donne*. Imagine, for instance, if Byron had
surmised that the flagrantly ardent lady for whom it was named
(though it was built long after her sullen exile from Venice),
was only *pretending* to be wretched on the Brenta, in order to
be free to pursue more local pleasures, perhaps with such a girl
as Margarita Cogni, *La Fornarina*, whose figure 'to breed
gladiators from' Byron admired while cruising, on horseback,
along the banks of the river. (There were said to be eight horses
in Venice: four on the façade of St Mark's and four in Byron's
stables, either at La Mira or on the Lido, where he exercised
them, and they him, in the winter.)

Venetian themes and styles are most clearly expressed, of
course, in *Beppo*, and in his plays, *Marino Faliero* and *The Two
Foscari*, but the *ottava rima* of Don Juan has a cursive flippancy
which reeks, sweetly and persistently, of Venice. The unprint-
able satirist Pietro Buratti probably primed the insolence whose
levity would lead the poet to say that his intention in Don Juan
was nothing more than to 'giggle and make giggle'. If Buratti's
insolent verses meant that 'every six months or so, by the
governor's orders, he pays a visit to one of the prisons of
Venice', Byron's status as an English peer, no less than the alien
inscrutability of his verses, secured immunity from Austrian
censoriousness; he was more familiar with palaces than prisons,
even if – like Piranesi, whose work he must have seen, though
he does not remark it – he suffered, painlessly, from a fascination with dungeons (Chillon, for instance) and with torture

chambers. Like Jacopo Foscari, he had been 'racked', if thera-
peutically, by the quacks who tried to wrench his lame leg into
conformity.

Byron was born to entertain opposites rather than 'for
opposition', as the cant insists; his ambiguity – as saint and
sinner, bully and victim, poet and hack, etc. – was, perhaps, a
function of his dexterous lameness. His privileged curse rendered him sensitive to the twists of fate: he could sympathise
easily, even emulously, with the tight-rope lives of men like
Marino Faliero or Francesco Carmagnola, both of whom rose
high before losing their heads to the Venetian oligarchs.

It is surprising that Carmagnola, the great *condottiere*, did
not figure among Byron's *dramatis personae*: in 1432, deceived
into returning to his employers' territory, he had been greeted
like a prince and, at the last moment, conducted across the
Bridge of Sighs to the lead-roofed cells. He was to cross it again
only on the way to his execution under the eyes of Doge Foscari
whose own fate was to prove hardly less ignominious and
certainly more painful. The reason that Carmagnola did not
catch Byron's eye for dramatic peripeteia may have been that
the *condottiere* did not figure among any of the portraits on
local display; he did not even announce himself, as Marino
Faliero did, by the black-marked *absence* of a portrait. Byron
may not have been a great appreciator of art, but he was to the
highest degree suggestible. Real and imagined worlds found a
permeable frontier, and a *bureau de change*, in his mutable
mind. His penchant for puns is part of the commerce he
entertained between the straight account of a thing and its
possible subversions; Picasso often played the same sort of
games with imagery.

Byron had that sympathetic egotism which expresses its
genius more by imagining itself in the place of others than by
an aloof account of their distinct qualities. He 'painted' not by
standing back from his subject but by insinuating himself in it.
He was not so much all things to all men as all men to himself;
an English lord, born in Scotland, who acted as if parodying an
English lord (hence his articulate want of reticence); he became
what he was by impersonating himself. Imitation was both a
provocative defence – above all against anyone who might
remark his lameness – and an aggressive form of deference;
hence perhaps his (intermittent) sympathy for Jews and the
defiant solitude in which he appropriated Shylock to say 'I

will neither love ye nor fear ye ... I will neither eat with ye, drink with ye, nor pray with ye.' He was the type of marked man who felt at home in an exile where the only thing different about him, so far as the natives were concerned, was *everything*.

Nevertheless, few contributions to literature have been more *sociable* than Byron's. Even his solitude was peopled by loquacious ghosts and menacing *commendatori* (and, of course, *commendatrici*). His merit as a poet can hardly be divorced from his ingenuity as an actor. In the manner of the dandy he longed (too plumply) to be, he liked nothing better than to be buttoned – oh, like a flashy foil too! – into a new personality. A master of the mimetic, he drew his inspiration – for instance, in *Beppo* – more often from an accidental *donnée* than from literary sources. In this, he resembled his deferential acquaintance Henri Beyle, who so successfully became Stendhal that his real name sounds like a pseudonym and whose *Le Rouge et Le Noir* derived from a *fait divers* seen in a newspaper. Byron and Stendhal met in Milan in 1816 and had some lively conversation, though the Frenchman was muffled by shyness at confronting so famous a personality.

The poet was, in particular, *impressionable*. 'I hate things *all fiction*,' he told Murray in a letter in the spring of 1817, 'and therefore the *Merchant* and *Othello* have no great associations to me.' This confession did not prevent G. Wilson Knight from finding a plethora of involuntary (?) allusions to both plays – and to *Timon of Athens* – in Byron's Venetian life and letters. Why not? Byron was both spontaneous *and* a striker of attitudes. When he posed for Thorwaldsen, in Rome, the sculptor said, 'You need not assume that look'; to which his subject retorted, 'That is my expression.' He took such pleasure in fresh sensations that he could try on a character, or a way of life, like a hat which could later be thrown aside. Consistency was the drabbest of proprieties, although *accuracy* – which he found wanting in his ninety-two volume edition of Voltaire – remained a 'scholarly' virtue he respected; it was seconded, in his own not *always* accurate case, by a prodigious, gliding memory. Although no unquestioning recruit to the Romantics, Byron shared their cult of energy (he took sexual performance to be its proper measure) and depended on the immediacy of his responses for proof of his genius. 'Mill away right and left'

– his pugilist tutor Jackson's motto – became a lifelong watchword.

In many ways, mimetic skill like Byron's is also likely to be conventional; it relies, for its competent impertinence, on familiarity with the rules it breaks, or challenges. The iconoclastic Shelley spoke of 'the antique courtesies' which he would always respect; Byron was in similar case: whatever his affectations of devilish outsiderdom, he also wanted to belong to the world in which Douglas Kinnaird, his London confidant and honorary treasurer during his Venetian residence, was so grandly at home. Hence Byron's response to the arts of painting and sculpture had more in common with that of the average Regency *dilettante* than with, say, the informed astringency of Baudelaire half a century later. His lordship would not have taken it as a compliment to be called an intellectual, although he knew that the word, when he applied it to his mathematician wife, rhymed prettily with 'hen-pecked you all'.

Byron's work was sufficiently picturesque ('The Assyrian came down like the wolf on the fold,' we all remember, 'And his cohorts were *gleaming in purple and gold*') for him to have a naïve appetite both for a good likeness and for dramatic effect. If pretentiousness was part of his literary repertoire, painting and sculpture – unlike the literary classics and Shakespeare, whose reputation shadowed him, and whom he swerved to elude – lay beyond his scholarly terms of reference: he approached them, as he did Venice, with unguarded curiosity and admitted want of expertise. Yet he had his quick opinions about art. He wrote to his publisher, John Murray, 'The Flemish school, such as I saw it in Flanders, I utterly detested, despised and abhorred,' while to John Cam Hobhouse, he remarked 'As for Rubens . . . he seems to me . . . the most glaring – flaring – staring harlotry impostor that ever passed a trick upon the senses of mankind . . . I never saw such an assemblage of florid nightmares as his canvas contains; his portraits seemed clothed in pulpit cushions.' The rhyming sequence of his denunciation suggests that wordy playfulness easily took over from rigorous appreciation when it came to something as marginally interesting as old(ish) masters.

Beppo was his prototypical tribute to Venice. In its frisky *ottava rima* he found an ideal way to 'paint' the local scene and to find the crossing point between the vivid appearance of the place and its representation in art:

'They've pretty faces yet, these same Venetians
   Black eyes, arch'd brows, and sweet expressions still;
Such as of old were copied from the Grecians
   In ancient arts by moderns mimick'd ill;
And like so many Venuses of Titian's
   (The best's at Florence – see it, if ye will),
They look when leaning over the balcony,
   Or stepp'd from out a picture by Giorgione,

'Whose tints are truth and beauty at their best;
   And when you to Manfrini's palace go,
That picture (howsoever fine the rest)
   Is loveliest to my mind of all the show;
It may perhaps be also to *your* zest,
   And that's the cause I rhyme upon it so:
'Tis but a portrait of his son, and wife,
   And self, but *such* a woman! love in life!'

The facility with which Byron travels between life and its double, in art, cannot conceal his preference for the former, which supplies the latter's certificate (in this he shares something, if never his wit, with the art critic Paul Johnson). Byron's disgust with Rubens, we may guess, was somewhat *practical*: it owed something to his distaste for women once they had grown 'flummety'. Whatever his pederastic diversions, the beauty of women, if not their characters, determined what he admired most keenly: 'Italian beauty! didst thou not inspire Raphael, who died in thy embrace . . .?' When he saw the *Helen* of Canova, in the house of the Countess d'Albrizzi, whose *conversazioni* he attended, he told Murray that it was 'without exception to my mind the most perfectly beautiful of human conceptions – and far beyond my ideas of human execution'. Given that he was playing the connoisseur with his publisher (and condescending to a show of equality), his appended verses confirmed his tendency to evasive flippancy when called upon to respond to art:

'What nature *could* – but *would not* do –
   And Beauty and Canova *can*!
Beyond imagination's power –
   Beyond the Bard's defeated art,

With immortality her dower –
Behold the *Helen* of the *heart*!'

As if to get off his aesthetic high horse as soon as may be, he adds: 'Talking of the "heart" reminds me that I have fallen in love – which except falling into the Canal (and that would be useless as I swim) is the best (or worst) thing I could do . . .' He remounted on another occasion, to tell Murray, in a letter of 14 April 1817, of (another?) visit to the Manfrini palace where he saw Titian's portrait of *Ariosto*, 'surpassing all my anticipation of the power of painting – it is the poetry of portrait – & the portrait of poetry . . .' After this vacuously chiasmic play, he sounds more throat-clearingly earnest when he goes on,

What struck me most in the general collection was the extreme resemblance of the style of the female faces in the mass of pictures – so many centuries or generations old – to those you see & meet every day amongst existing Italians. – The Queen of Cyprus & Giorgione's wife – particularly the latter – are Venetians as it were of yesterday . . . You must recollect however – that I know nothing of painting – & that I detest it – unless it reminds me of something I have seen or think it possible to see – for which [reason] I spit upon and abhor all the saints & subjects of one half the impostures I see in the churches & palaces – & when in Flanders, I never was so disgusted in my life as with Rubens & his eternal wives & infernal glare of colours – as they appeared to me – & in Spain I did not think much of Murillo & Velasquez. – Depend upon it of all the arts it is the most artificial and unnatural – and that by which the nonsense of mankind is most imposed upon. – I never yet saw the picture – or the statue – which came within a league of my conception or expectation – but I have seen many mountains & Seas – & Rivers and views – & two or three women – who went as far beyond it – besides some horses; and a Lion (at Veli Pasha's) in the Morea and a tiger at supper in Exeter 'change.

There are other examples of Byron's skittishness when confronted with masterpieces: 'I beg to conclude,' he wrote to Murray, in May 1817, 'by wishing Mr Southey damned – not as a poet – but as a politician. There is a place in Michael Angelo's last judgment in the Sistine Chapel which would just suit him ...' And a few days later, he wrote, 'The Apollo Belvedere is the image of Lady Adelaide Forbes – I think I never saw such a likeness.' It is not surprising that Byron inscribed his name on the temple at Sounium, among other places: he found it difficult not to insert himself, or his opinions, wherever he happened to be. The number of hotels named after him returns the compliment.

Byron's time in Venice was divided between industry and venery. He showed little interest in art and rather less in music (of which there was still a great deal), although he did say that the sound of the organ disposed him to favour the Catholicism in which he had his and Claire Clairmont's natural daughter, Allegra, raised for the few sorry years that she lived. Opinion-ated eclecticism was always his style, but the best museum in Venice was Venice itself. The visual arts were always trumped, in his eyes, by natural landscape and female beauty. Perhaps we shall never again understand to what degree painting, especially portraiture, could be a mere trade to a milord like Byron. The mechanical reproduction of works of art, so far from derogating from their worth and mystique, has given 'originals' an aura of remote uniqueness. Photography has dignified the portrait, not – as was generally feared – destroyed it. Byron's own work with its next-slide-please succession of scenic enchantments, presages both the travel literature, and journalism, of today and the sort of self-mocking, self-advancing 'postcards from abroad' from which Clive James makes a fatter living than ever Byron did from his garrulous jaunts.

Selected Bibliography

Byron, *The Poetical Works* (Oxford)
Leslie A. Marchand (ed.), *Byron's Letters and Journals; Byron, a biography*
G. Wilson Knight, *Byron and Shakespeare*
Donata Battilotti, *Le Ville di Palladio*
Donald M. Nicol, *Byzantium and Venice*
John-Julius Norwich, *Venice The Greatness and the Fall*
Jerome McGann, *Byron In Context*
Frederic Raphael, *Byron*

Nostalgia

If the average voter were to be returned to the Garden of Eden, he would immediately complain about the fall in his living standards. To most people, such a move would smack more of forcible repatriation than of the recovery of primal bliss. Yet the fantasy of a past more beautiful, more simple and more blessed than the present is inseparable from the human condition. Nostalgia – the pain which arises from separation from home – is so keen and so universal that Edenic fantasies, and longings, lead mankind to believe in and long for those careless yesterdays when all our troubles seemed so far away. Exclusion and hope are twins.

The body's clock carries us irresistibly, it seems, in one direction, but our minds turn us, as Scott Fitzgerald put it in *The Great Gatsby*, into 'boats against the current'. We are forever aching to be carried back to first loves, childhood Arcadias, uterine security. Freud talked of 'Oceanic feelings', the illusion of guilt-free drift in a timeless world where egotism is abated and we moon in tune with the music of the spheres. Freud fancied that such feelings echoed the sentiments of the unborn child, happily coddled in a sea of amniotic fluid. The novelist Thomas Wolfe (*not* the author of *Bonfire of the Vanities*) once wrote a book of which the callous title alone remains forbiddingly durable: *You Can't Go Home Again*. It is the ultimate denial of hope. The age-old exiles' toast, 'Next year in Jerusalem', was the wishful denial of such a denial.

The American dream is of a future which enshrines a past

which was, in most cases, neither happier nor much more secure than the present but in which Andy Hardy plays forever with Tom Sawyer and the girl next door stays as sweet as she was. There is nothing new in such nostalgia: the Romans made constant sentimental appeal to the *mos maiorum*: what wiser, better men did (often *very* unsentimentally) in the old days. What would more happily suit today's England, in its nostalgic malaise, than the discovery of a thousand new Jane Austen novels, each of which could be translated into hours and hours of television to serve in the office of a wall against the intrusion of unpalatable modernity? Who cares that Jane's heroines, in their author's day, would have lost their (few) rights, even over their own persons, as soon as they found their Mr Darcy, that everyone's expectation of life was brief and that, in a world without anaesthetics, let alone antibiotics, the smallest operation was agonising, the least infection lethal?

What are books for but to bind the elusive past into proximity? European literature begins with the Greeks and the Jews. In both, the fall from grace is a recurrent theme; the lure of its recovery arms prophets with their reproachful fervour and poets with their bitter bite. The Hebrew Bible would have us believe that there is a cure, in Abraham's bosom, for Adam and Eve's expulsion from timeless simplicity. The eighth-century BC Greek poet Hesiod, whose *Works and Days* was the first gardening book, lamented the labour which the surly earth now required. In the Golden Age, it had supplied punctual crops without any need to turn the soil.

Dante's *Inferno* revised the pagan underworld for Christian sinners and infidels. Amid its torments, the damned were cruelly privileged to retain memories of earlier happiness. Yet among all the debilities of age, we fear amnesia more than physical decrepitude: nostalgia is better than blankness. Memories garnish the pension fund of the spirit. General de Gaulle called senility 'a ship-wreck', but had the consolation of being able to pen his memoirs and reprise his first love, *La France*, until sudden death felled him.

Nostalgia has a prime place in the fundamental fictions of Western literature. *The Odyssey* is a protracted lament, on the part of its cunning hero, over the years of his separation from his modest kingdom, Ithaca, and from Penelope, the faithful wife to whom he is, as males tend to think understandable, faithful only in his fashion. Odysseus' nostalgia is both genuine and convenient. His longing for home and for his true wife allows him to slip away, 'home free' as they say, from the erotic bondage of the nymph Calypso. Nostalgia gives warrant to his ruses and lends muscle to his resolve.

The early twentieth-century Alexandrian poet, Constantine Cavafy, warns those who emulate Odysseus against plotting too straight a course for home:

> As you set out for Ithaka
> hope your road is a long one,
> full of adventure, full of discovery,
> Laistrygonians, Cyclops,
> angry Poseidon – don't be afraid of them . . .
>
> Hope your road is a long one.
> May there be summer mornings when,
> with what pleasure, what joy,
> you enter harbours you're seeing for the first time. . . .
>
> Keep Ithaka always in your mind.
> Arriving there is what you're destined for.
> But don't hurry the journey at all.
> Better if it lasts for years,
> so you're old by the time you reach the island,
> wealthy with all you've gained on the way,
> not expecting Ithaka to make you rich . . .
>
> Wise as you will have become, so full of experience,
> you'll have understood by then what these Ithakas mean.

The sweetness of nostalgia is sharpened by its pain. The imagination affects to predict the future, but it works more fervently and ingeniously in retrospect. The myth of 'the eternal return' promises that life is cyclic and that, somehow, what is lost can be retrieved: 'God and sinner reconciled'. It is a promise which, against banal plausibilities, we cannot but hope will be kept. In *The Go-Between*, L. P. Hartley famously called the past 'another country', where they do things differently. It is one to which we dream of obtaining a visa and in which, landed once more, we like to think that we will not misuse our opportunities. Francis Coppola's *Peggy Sue Got Married* is a filmic myth of such a return, and its delusive salvation. Nostalgia promises that, given another chance, first love will last and that the time we squandered will be duly spent. Yet man is straddled between pleasure and work, frivolity and earnestness. If I were to be returned to the Cambridge of the early 1950s, would I take the opportunity to be a totally diligent scholar, hunched over *Advanced Greek Prose Composition* and filling my reading list with evidence of midnight-oil well burnt? Or should I – second time around – abandon *quondam* suburban timidities and advance myself shamelessly in the ambitious vanities of the literary and theatrical world? In all probability, I should once again fall between two stools.

Novelists have always traded in nostalgia. Perhaps one becomes a writer in order to find fuel, and excuse, to remount the stream of time, to refashion failure into success and folly into royalties. Proust's *A la Recherche du Temps Perdu* is a wilful *retour aux sources*, a protracted and sophisticated revival of lost days, lost love, lost innocence. In its last volume, the narrator persuades himself (and us?) that transcience and grey hair can be defeated by art. The writer often does his best to recast his memories so that, as Vladimir Nabokov imagined, he *can* go home again, even when the mansion has been despoiled, society dismembered, Eden defoliated and innocent love Lolita-fied.

Nabokov used art to avoid inevitability. With what seemed to progressive minds to be solipsistic absurdity, he denied the future to the Soviet Union on the stylistic grounds that the Communists had so crucified the great Russian language that it was bound, he insisted, to rise up and bounce them. What élitist arrogance! And what fanciful accuracy! During all his adult life, Nabobov yearned for the lost pre-Revolutionary world, in which his father had been a shining instance of enlightened aristocracy: the millionaire Nabokov senior was a liberal for whom his son felt so unwavering a love that he held its evidence enough to refute Freud. Nabokov's nostalgia was not for the pampered luxuries of his childhood but for that slower clock, before the fall, which allowed every second to be steeped in sensations, and every sensation as intricately coloured as a butterfly's wings. Nabokov glossed Darwin and spoke, as an entomologist, of the sweetest of nature's laws: 'the survival of the frailest'. While the tyrannosauri had blundered heavily towards their overweight extinction, the skittish butterfly – at once ephemera and eternal – survived their clumsy tyranny with the resilience of powerlessness: beauty beats the beast. Such is the bet, not always won, which every true artist has to make.

Nostalgia recalls a world indifferent to cost-effectiveness; the past is stocked with invaluable moments which money can neither supply nor supplant. I am fortunate in being victim to many nostalgias. My first remembered home was in the America of the Depression. I recall queues of cloth-capped, shuffling and hungry men as we drove, in a Ford with a 'rumble-seat' in the boot, where my grandmother sat in exposed dignity, from Chicago to New York. How luxurious modest security was in the days when a dime was a dime!

I was a small American boy until I was seven years old. It was not the Jesuits who determined my early consciousness, but Joe Louis and Babe Ruth, Macy's and Saks Fifth Avenue, Guy Lombardo and the Good-Humour Man, Dorothy Parker and Robert Benchley, Bing Crosby and Eddie Kantor and Jack Benny and Uncle Don (the children's radio favourite who thought the microphone was already switched off when he said, 'Goodnight, you little bastards', and was never aired again).

I sometimes feel as if I left a phantom self to grow up in New York, to go to Columbia or Harvard (maybe). My career in Hollywood, such as it has been, is perhaps a furtive *retour aux sources*. When I write a novel about Americans, as I am at present, I have fantasies of a return to a world in which I do not remember ever crying. My memories of tears begin when I came to my father's birthplace, England, and learnt home-sickness at a good school.

England's present nostalgia for the days of imperial dominance may well be typical of what Lewis Namier called 'Vanished Supremacies'. The Euro-sceptic resentment of 'Brussels' is the 'reasoned' xenophobia which dares not snarl its name. Having severed umbilical affinities with the Commonwealth, the British – like Thomas Wolfe's hero – are unable to go home, or away, again with the old confidence. An island of steadily increasing prosperity feels diminished by the loss of the oceanic feeling which was induced, even among the lower classes, by Britannia's ruling the waves. They, and their one time betters, are hobbled by nostalgia for a Paradise Lost which, should they manage to get back to it, they would discover to be Edenic only for a very few. Yet little Englanders are persuaded that bitching and binding can retrieve what diminished power cannot. They are encouraged to imagine that they can redeem the past not by art, or purposeful effort, but by getting lucky in the 'great' national lottery (or by lobbying for hand-outs). They will then have tickets to emigrate to the past, or a country, such as Jimmy Goldsmith's Mexico, where tracts of the primal garden are still for sale to those who can afford to fence and police them. The angel who bars the way back into paradise is there transformed into a private security guard who checks the computer to see if Adam and Eve are rich enough to qualify for entry.

The Poems of C. P. Cavafy

A few years ago, we were in the tiny, tragic Greek island of Kastelorizo, which was once the most prosperous, as well as the most remote (from Athens), of the Dodecanese. Owing to a wartime drama whose details have been shrouded in possibly deliberate mystery, Kastelorizo is now almost entirely depopulated (it was the location for the film *Mediterraneo*). Its inhabitants and their descendants form a diaspora with a large colony in Australia, from which some 'Kazzies' have returned to reclaim their ruined family houses. Hence you sometimes hear a strange accent, Hellenic-Strine in the few bars and *tavernas*. In one of them, I also heard a woman of a certain age speaking the rather florid French which marked her as a Levantine. I asked her if she was, by any chance, from Alexandria, the city Larry Durrell so notoriously called 'the winepress of love'.

'Oui, Monsieur!'

And had she by any chance known Cavafy the poet? 'Mais bien sûr! Je l'ai souvent taquiné dans la rue.' She had often teased him in the street. I did not press her to tell us what taunts she had shouted after the man who, in E.M. Forster's phrase, stood 'absolutely motionless at a slight angle to the universe'. Did she say he was queer or poor or just that he was a poet? All were true.

By coincidence, the French use the expression *taquiner la Muse* where we might say that someone 'dabbles in poetry'. A meticulous civil servant by reluctant profession, Constantine Cavafy was an amateur in the sweetest sense; he was a lover whose love was reserved for boys (and their memory) and for the Muse. No poet could have been less professional – I do not think he ever *sold* a poem – or more dedicated. His work – like Wittgenstein's – was 'published', in manuscript, only to a favoured few. Keeping his constantly revised verses in a folder, he neither courted fame nor, in his lifetime, procured it.

Cavafy, who was born in 1863 and died in 1933, belonged to an ancient city and to a cosmopolitan society which no longer exists. Wilfully founded by Alexander the Great and boldly seized, on Alexander's death, by one of his generals (whose family, the Ptolemies, ruled it until the Romans filched it from them), polyglot, multi-racial Alexandria was no less wilfully dismembered, in 1956, by President Nasser, in the name of pan-Arabism. Its present derelict condition and negligible status honour an 'idea' which was, as one of Durrell's characters would say, *de la grande bogue* (the Egyptians do not, in private, think of themselves as Arabs).

In their arrogant insecurity, the Alexandrians created a culture and a legend, an impacted palimpsest of languages and memories, of passions and conceits from which Cavafy's provincial genius fashioned something universal. How odd that one can come to love poets as I love Cavafy, whose defining homosexuality was never 'gay' and for which I feel no affinity! Since it has become fashionable for literary persons to boast of the masterpieces they have never read, I may be forgiven for confessing that modern Greek poetry, from Seferis, through Ritsos (wrongly ignored by Western readers) to Elytis and Panselinos, means much more to me than, say, Wordsworth or Shelley or Pound or Eliot or Larkin (with whose apparently pinched scope Cavafy has something in common).

If it were not for the noble and doubtless uncommercial *en regard* editions once published by Jonathan Cape (of Seferis) and Hogarth (of Cavafy), I might not have read them in the original with such affectations of ease, but with the Greek on one page and Keeley and Sherrard's miraculous perspicuity on the other, there is no escape from doing the thing properly. Why else should one have suffered all those dusty years of ancient Greek? The scholarship of Cavafy's verse seems to offer a way back to the roots of the discriminating, yet convergent, Mediterranean culture which modern parochialisms have shattered. If only it were true, as Herakleitus claimed, that the road up and the road down were the same road!

George Seferis, the native of Smyrna who became a Greek ambassador after his family was evicted from Asia Minor, lived long enough to win a Nobel Prize – oh these damned prizes! – which it is unlikely Cavafy, his master, would ever have been awarded, even if he had survived beyond his seventy years. Seferis' work is showy with modish influences and fruity with fine phrases; although magnificent, it smacks of posturing. Cavafy's poems are sly, but not slight, dry but not desiccated; with pride and resignation at their heart, they are influenced by the Greek tradition, not by André Breton or Eliot, though their author lived, as a child, in England (his *King Claudius* is a heterodox gloss on Hamlet).

Cavafy spoke, with bitter prescience – in 1904! – of the barbarians who were said to be coming and whose failure to materialise disappointed the citizens whom they had come to despoil: 'Because night has fallen and the barbarians haven't come/ And some of our men just in from the border say/ there are no barbarians any longer/. Now what is going to happen to us without barbarians?/ Those people were a kind of solution.'

The citizens had only to wait a few decades longer: the barbarians are in all our cities now. Who else have wrecked the Classical departments of our great universities or destroyed the library in Sarajevo just as they once destroyed the one in Alexandria? Cavafy's exquisitely *angst*-ridden poems, which – for the happy few – are also stories, and phylacteries, honour the view of that other Alexandrian, Callimachus, his contemporary though he died more than two millennia before him: 'Big books, big junk.'

As for our fellow-citizens, the barbarians, should we seek another city to replace the one they have ruined? Cavafy had the rueful answer: '*Kainourious topous then tha'vrees*'. 'You will not find a new country . . . Now that you have wasted your life here, in this small corner,/ you've destroyed it everywhere in the world.' Yet the same poet said that we should honour the men who held the pass at Thermopylae, though they foresaw, some of them, that Ephialtes, the traitor, would render their bravery futile and 'the Medes would break through after all'. Honour Cavafy, too, who won no prizes, the best of poets.

Night and Day with
Mr Cheever

Journals/diaries/notebooks, what is the difference? There is something pretentious, to English ears at least, about 'journals': what are they but the diaries of those who think well of themselves? If not intended for publication, they resemble the Christmas cards which King John addressed to himself because nobody loved him; if composed for posterity, how shall their narcissism be excused? Although journals can be secretive and confessional, containing unmitigated truths about self and friends which tact, libel laws and common decency render unpublishable during a man's lifetime, they often supply a posthumous lode on which what Henry James called 'publishing scoundrels' cannot wait to get their helpful hands. However breast-beating or fly-opening, they are also not uncommonly a shrewd form of delayed self-advertisement: when a writer's novels lose their charm, soul-searching goes marching on. Mrs Woolf is a lot more interesting than Mrs Dalloway.

Was John Cheever a writer of sufficient importance for us to want to examine the parings of his soul and the evidence of his body with forensic thoroughness? This selection from John Cheever's *Journals*, amounting to almost 400 pages, has been made by Robert Gottlieb, his regular publisher and sometime editor of *The New Yorker*, where the bulk of Cheever's output appeared, from the 1930s onwards. His afterword tells us that he has chosen only about five per cent of the millions of words available to his scissors. Frankly, after protracted exposure to Cheever's bibulous lamentations, mostly about his 'lewd' desires

(and their frustration), one can be grateful for Gottlieb's exci-
sions, but still wonder on what logic – apart from prurience –
the selection has been made. If the rest of the journals are the
same, only more so, that is one thing, but if there are more
literary observations (the few on show are modest, but very
shrewd), more outlines for stories, something about Cheever's
wartime service, then Gottlieb has done us a vulgar disservice
by harping on booze and fucks. Some account of the grounds
for inclusion should have been given in order to know whether
we should press for further extracts or be grateful to have been
spared voluminous torrents of self-pity.

American writers seem to depend heavily on editors in the
Max Perkins tradition, like Gottlieb. Perhaps their penchant for
clutching at such straws has something to do with how much
they drink. Cheever was the kind of alcoholic who, in the depths
of his addiction, started the day with a liquid breakfast. The
wonder is that he was capable not only of writing coherent
sentences but also of raising and keeping (and often deceiving)
a family. His *cacoethes scribendi* must have been as compulsive
as his appetite for the sauce. If his novels seem mannered and,
even in the case of the notorious, best-selling *Falconer*, calculat-
edly sensational, his best short stories – 'Torch Song' is my
favourite – are as good as anyone's. They suffer from a certain
prolixity, reflecting *The New Yorker*'s regular diffuseness, but
they are superb variations on the theme of the anguish of the
man on the commuter train. J. P. Marquand and John O'Hara
travelled the same lines, though Marquand was more satirical
(and more squeamish) and O'Hara also dealt with a world
beyond Cheever's obsessive scope. Both highly professional
writers are honoured with emulous applause here, as is John
Updike, the king of New England, whose death was mischievously reported to Cheever, thus prompting a premature obituary
of generous accuracy. Cheever was a sex'n'Christianity man,
like Updike, and is not only deeply moved (intermittently) by
candles and ceremonial, but also uses religion as a spiritual
swizzle-stick to put fizz into his accusations against his wife,
who is said to lack the charity unfailingly to appreciate the piss-
artist she had married.

The heart of the matter, as Susie Cheever's memoir of her
father has already revealed, is that John Cheever, husband,
father and Pulitzer prizewinner, was a randy sonofabitch who
not only fancied young girls with big breasts and slim waists

but also, and more shockingly, had a number of homosexual affairs, although he refused to consider himself a total fruit-cake by quite a long chalk. What happened to Nigel Nicolson, when he discovered that Harold and Vita were no ordinary couple (the idea!), happened to the Cheevers in spades. Daddy did not just write about people who went to hell on the same train every night, he was one of the damned himself.

We are always being promised by militant tolerationists that man is naturally bisexual, but is he necessarily naturally a commuter with a house and a mortgage and a wife who (he imagines) doesn't know and kids who mustn't? Whatever else he may be, man – the un-naked ape – is also naturally unnatural, a fabricator of morals and things, such as books and relationships, which require dedication and decision and which give a sense to his life that cannot be trumped (though they are constantly menaced) by sexual pre-emptions. Cheever's saving grace is that, for all his remorseful self-indulgence, he wants to love his wife and his children and all the joys of the American way; he does not dismiss the bourgeois life as hypocrisy, he just wants regular doses of the other. Man is a forked creature and none was more forked than poor dear Johnny.

Gottlieb has, I have no doubt, been as tactful as he knows how. Having had their help in hanging the family's dirty linen on the line, he thanks the Cheever children for their forbearance and they, I daresay, thanked him for his cheque (the *New Yorker* did its long-serving author long-winded honour) and his solemn services, although they did not include any footnotes which would enable an English audience, in particular, to know who Saul B. and other shoulder-rubbing, initials-only celebrities really were. We have to assume that the juicy bits were what remained, along with a lot of stuff about the weather of which, as Updike has often proved, there is no shortage on the East Coast. Cheever even accuses the air of being 'omniscient', in which case it knows more than I do, including what the hell that is supposed to mean.

Cheever's wife, Mary, gets most of the stick (and, to be blunt, quite a lot of the radish too): he 'mounts' her often enough to make one feel he missed a career in the cavalry. *Odi et amo* gets stretched way beyond Catullus' original couplet here; John and Mary can neither get along nor separate, although divorce is irregularly proposed and accepted. Mrs Cheever is accused of being cruel, unloving, vicious, indifferent and unappreciative, but I suspect that it needed a lot of that good old forbearance to stay as sweet as she was. Love sometimes supplants hates, even in this furtive record, but Cheever – though no sort of a Bohemian and suffering from all the hang-ups about queerness available to a man born just before World War One – rarely ceased to rail about the bondage to which marriage consigned him. One cannot readily conceive of the angel who would have been able to give him what he wanted.

There are shrewd passages here and there are self-lacerating ones with which it would require rare gifts of hard-heartedness not to sympathise, but Cheever's maunderings finally get you down. Of course, drink ran in the family (his brother died of it) and a man cannot be blamed for his genetic programme; it's just that – as I was telling my journal a moment ago – I have no appetite to sit through it with him.

Anti-Semitism Can Be Fun

If Mr Major had been less scrupulous (or, as Alan Clark might say, more efficient), he would never have announced a moral crisis without proposing a scapegoat whose extirpation would reverse the blight. By failing to supply an identifiable cause, the Prime Minister offered his opponents the chance to point accusing fingers at him. Those who start Crusades must take care first to nominate their Saracens. Mrs Thatcher's providential 'enemy within' was the Unions, to whose malign influence the Winter of Discontent and all subsequent misfortunes could be attributed. What comfort is a nanny without a bogey-man?

Until 1945, it had often been 'the Jews' who, in the eyes and on the lips of articulate theorists and ranking intellectuals, had engineered or schemingly profited from the decline of major European powers whose mighty muscles were mysteriously useless against 'a little white-faced Jew in a bathchair with an eye just like a rattlesnake' (hats off to John Buchan, Lord Tweedsmuir). It is of course, to the moral credit of Mr Major that he refrains from recourse to a routine of unreason which served Christendom so well for so long, but it can also be argued (or at least hoped) that anti-Semitism, though still the 'suburban prejudice' which Ezra Pound pretended – very

Review of Bryan Cheyette, *Constructions of 'the Jew' in English Literature and Society: racial representations 1875–1945*, in the *Spectator*, 1993.

belatedly – to regret, no longer serves as a convincing remedy for 'decline'. A Jew may still be vilified (and sometimes, like Robert Maxwell, be vile) but 'the Jews', as a sort of abstract entity, are no longer a plausible target for paranoid delusions except on the part of even greater crackpots than Hilaire Belloc.

This unreliable redemption owes less to the recognition of Jewish virtues (or the existence of Israel) than to the fact that no plausibly fiendish conspirators, however well-oiled their bathchairs, could have schemed to procure for themselves the fate of the Jews in the present century (I write this on the fiftieth anniversary of the deportation of the Jewish population of Bordeaux, a crime whose unpunished authors, so Lord Mayhew and his friends would doubtless argue, are now the victims of unforgivingly vindictive persecution by memory).

If more or less virulent 'social' anti-Semitism is not unknown today, the full-blown Socialism of Fools – as a political theory of the kind variously endorsed by H.G.Wells, Bernard Shaw, the Chester-Belloc fraternity, D.H. Lawrence and Wyndham Lewis, not to mention the sainted Virginia Woolf and her acolytes – is no longer respectable. Cheapness and nastiness splutter on in Philip Larkin and Richard Ingrams and their epigoni and they find a mutation in the anti-Israelism of pin-striped poseurs like Gore Vidal, but as a lightning conductor, anti-Semitism has lost its salutary powers and hence its pied-piping charm.

Ignoring instructive, non-canonical instances such as Maugham's *The Alien Corn*, Bryan Cheyette has trotted out the usual moribund texts for his analysis of the pathology of 'the Jew' as depicted in English literature from 1875 until 1945, when the threadbare mechanism – and murderous consequences – of scapegoatery became disenchantingly clear even to the cleverest minds. However, one of the putatively finest of them, T. S. Eliot, saw no prompt need to revise his philosophy or apologise for a spite which, we are promised by close-to-the-throne memoirists, he never displayed towards 'individual Jews' (a testimony more to his cowardice than to his morals). His reputation remains largely untarnished; 'money in furs' is one thing, but when did money from *Cats* do anybody any harm?

Despite the moment of Belsen, when unmitigated reality shredded the Modernists' mediating fabric of literary perversity, the Eng. Lit. establishment has managed pretty well to patch the reputations of the idols to whom their critical ascendancy is committed. Only an occasional twitch of published dismay at the 'authoritarian' philosophies of certain enshrined authors suggests that a few academics have seen that something just may be wrong with traditional reverences. Such fawning quibbles can – if suitably processed and rigged, like Dr Cheyette's, with an *apparatus criticus* – be retailed to the university libraries where Pound and Eliot and other putative 'thinkers' continue to be importantly curricular.

Is it their fault, it is sometimes asked, if 'our' best writers have repeatedly been interpreted as having authorised genocide? (Briefly: if justly, yes.) It does not, in truth, require much coercive interpretation to see that T. S. Eliot could play the modern-dress version of Henry II in *Murder in the Cathedral* to a fare-thee-well and that 'Will no one rid me, etc?' was a speech that came easily to him. As for G. B. S., his amusing playfulness endorsed the right of a state to practise 'civilised' eugenics, by which, perhaps, he meant gas not the axe. H. G. Wells, the apostle of science, shared Chesterton's grave view of the Marconi affair (fatso regarded it as 'a turning point in world history', which shows what insularity does to taxonomies of significance). We are informed, on page 123 of this Cambridge University Press book, that H.G. considered that the 'fundamental idea of socialism was the "scientific" replacement of "order by disorder"', when presumably the precise opposite was his view. We are also told, within a few pages, first that Herbert Samuel and then that Rufus Isaacs – both of whom are said to have been 'protaganists [*sic*]' in the Marconi scandal – was portrayed as 'Lewis' in *The New Machiavelli*. Nor, it seems, does the CUP run to a proof-reader who knows how to spell foreignness.

However, the greatest weakness here is a failure to broach the unspeakable possibility that, in the tradition of *The Merchant* and *The Jew of Malta*, the anti-Semitism of English authors is as gloatingly frivolous as it is habitually malevolent. The invention of villains is an artistic trope like any other, and a rather more enjoyable one than supplying the virtuous. What academics cannot easily imagine is that anti-Semitism was, and sometimes is, *fun*. If one is capable – and plenty of really, really classy literary people clearly are – of suspending all humane impulse or sense of shame, the Holocaust itself can – as Martin Amis, in *Time's Arrow*, was the tremendously brave first to see – be reclothed in the lineaments of comedy. What irony could better testify to the vanity of human schemes than the fact that six million people could be done to death by a Great Civilisation for no good reason whatsoever? We shall never come within range of understanding the bizarre ideas of Very Great Writers Indeed until someone begins to see that malice and unfairness, exaggeration and fabrication lie at the heart of the literary enterprise (or do we still seriously want to argue that, for instance, Evelyn Waugh was a *moralist*?). What the authors under scrutiny have in common is not some geo-political insight but the habit of crowd-pleasing authorship.

The scrupulous consistencies which professorial persons have supplied (for instance Christopher Ricks in *T. S. Eliot and Prejudice*), in order to truss the rupture – and protect their investment – in the key reputations of European culture, since 1945, deserve a more caustic examination than tenured caution is liable to give it. The latest lit. crit. cant is inadequate to deal with an issue which cries out for closer political and psychological correlations. Since he refrains from any sign of humour or irony, Cheyette also neglects to observe the comedy of a metic like Eliot or Pound, a Papist like Chesterton or the half-frog Belloc (or the scarcely mentioned Graham Greene), a bespectacled toady like Kipling, a *petit bourgeois* Civil Servant like Trollope, or a self-proclaimed 'Enemy' like Wyndham Lewis auditioning for the role of Dictator of Omnium in order to arrest the undermining of a power structure in which their own place was marginal. How sweet to lay off their own various foreignnesses on the Eternal Foreigner!

The usual insularity prevents Cheyette from employing – or even acknowledging – René Girard's highly suggestive accounts of the scapegoat mechanism (and its limits); much more profoundly than Karl Miller, Girard has examined the mirroring uses of duplicity in order to make coherent sense of the recurrence, left and right, of the conspiracy theory. Nevertheless, there are instructive things to be found in a study which is too frequently a jargon-shod trudge – how can anyone use 'to foreground' as a verb? – through the old, old stories. To read this book alongside Geoffrey H. Hartmann's unnerving symposium, *Holocaust Remembrance* (published by Blackwell), is to be reminded that even the stalest dust can still be noxious.

Cohn-Sherbok's Solution

The world is full of hatreds; no injunction is more admirable or less honoured than the one about loving thy neighbour as thyself, although it certainly makes people careful about whom they live next to. The separation of races, tribes and religions from each other is sometimes the consequence of arrogance, sometimes of fear; it can be a choice or an imposition, privilege or punishment. In the case of the Jews, contempt and envy, fear and respect, disgust and fascination have worked in tandem, doubling and redoubling their particularity.

How odd of God to choose the Jews! The old jingle still rings a bell. That God's own Son should also be a Jew has been an embarrassment from which theologians, philosophers and crackpots (not always to be distinguished from each other) have frequently sought to escape, most obviously by postulating a spurious distinction between Aryans and Semites. This 'theory' had a providential place in the self-advancement of nineteenth-century Germany, whose nationalists belatedly claimed a fundamental role in European culture. The glory which was Ancient Greece began – so po-faced Teutons claimed – with migrant folk who started from, or very near, Schleswig-Holstein. Jesus himself, it was maintained, came of similar stock; the fact that he was raised among Jews, in whose religious traditions he

Review of Dan Cohn-Sherbok, *The Crucified Jew*, in the *Sunday Times*, 1992.

discovered most of his ideas and all his terms of reference, was his blue-eyed misfortune and served only to give that damnable race a chance to procure His death and so condemn themselves to eternal vagrancy and universal execration.

It is wise to keep a straight face when recounting the myth which, in the lifetime of anyone over fifty, justified the murder of six million people, of whom two million were children. The absurdity of the arguments, the falseness of the charges (especially of ritual murder), the grotesqueness of the 'morality', which made The Jew into the Devil's legate and Judaism the principle of Evil would be laughed out of any rational court, but how often is man the reasonable creature he sometimes likes to think himself? As Pascal reminded us, the heart has its reasons that Reason cannot know, and at the heart of European ideology lies Christianity. To sustain the beauty of its architecture, the nobility of its literature and music, the self-confidence of its mission (in which civilisation and conquest were head and tail of the same coin), Christendom depended on the blessings of a God appropriated from a Levantine tribe with pretensions to divine favour.

If the Jews themselves regarded their selection less as a warrant for empire than as a burden of service to a Father who was always demanding and often punitive, Christianity made them into deicides, who had rejected and murdered God's son and had no abiding place in the divine scheme, except to serve as Awful Warnings (the excuse which Pascal gave for their continued presence on earth and the only one for not exterminating them). In his brisk, somewhat artless manner – in which 'mitigate against' is not the only unhappy phrase – Dan Cohn-Sherbok has told an old, old story; it reminds one of Lewis Namier's notorious observation that the Jews do not have a history but only a martyrology.

Although Rabbi Cohn-Sherbok is more interested in reconciliation than polemics, he cannot render a true account of the relations between Christianity and Judaism without a long indictment of Christian practice, in which theft and murder have figured with exponential thoroughness. The greater the crime, the greater the justification required for it: in order to deserve spoliation and extinction, the Jews have had to be accused of whatever deeds might render them the proper recipients of their fate. Deicide, a plan to take over the whole world (precisely the benign purpose of the Catholic Church which underwrote anti-Semitism), hatred and exploitation of all Gentiles were – and are – attributed to a small, fiendish rabble of supposedly single-minded confederates who were also regarded as too feeble in muscle, argument and culture to belong to civilisation and yet against whom an endless battle had to be fought and, without ruthless tactics, was likely to be lost.

Rabbi Cohn-Sherbok's announced theme is *Christian* anti-Semitism and his method is descriptive, not schematic: he provides incontrovertible evidence, but no general theory. A sequence of more or less well-known instances, culminating in the Holocaust, makes it clear that Christian charity is less reliable than Christian malice: Pope Pius XII justified his failure to condemn the extermination of the Jews by saying 'millions of Catholics serve in the German armies. Shall I bring them into conflicts of conscience?'

Today, Cohn-Sherbok finds optimistic consolation in the convergence of Christian and Jewish attitudes to the God whom they affect to worship in common. Here is part of the 'Christo-logical understanding of the Holocaust' formulated by the Swiss theologian Clemens Thoma:

> ... Auschwitz is the most eminent modern sign of the inmost relationship and oneness of the Jewish martyrs ... with the crucified Christ, although the Jews affected here could not have been aware of this. The Holocaust is thus, for the believing Christian, an important sign of the unbreakable unity, founded upon Christ crucified, of Judaism and Christianity in spite of all breaks, separate ways and misunderstandings.

I have some problems with this passage. One of them is that it is almost entirely void of intelligible, let alone verifiable, meaning. 'The Jews affected here' is a memorable meiosis indeed, when it denotes millions who were choked, starved or tortured to death in the name of German culture. Cohn-Sherbok's desire to see all religions ascending the same mountain from different sides (another Panglossian image from modern theology) is both honourable in its general piety and an impediment to intellectual, historical and philosophical clear-thinking. He has no argued purpose and no trenchant vision of the cause or conceivable 'cure' of anti-Semitism; for him, it is sometimes an aspect of theocratic or political opportunism, sometimes a personal sentiment, sometimes the fault of certain

Jewish habits (however understandably contracted), sometimes of failures of communication.

Is he wrong? He is right *and* wrong: he is right that many 'beliefs' – almost always the enemies of knowledge, rarely its pale precursors – combine to make the Jew an emblematic scapegoat, but he is wrong in failing to confront the unpalatable truth that anti-Semitism is literally fundamental to Christianity and to the good conscience of those who speak in its name: the metaphysical 'positive', which is Christianity, *requires* a negative which is Judaism, just as The Aryan superman needed a Semitic under-man. T. S. Eliot's 'the jew is underneath the lot' is *not* a casual, off-day phrase but typical of a serious strand in the noblest, as well as the trashiest, European literature.

The resentments and suspicions of individuals would never coalesce into murderousness without an enabling logic which licensed (and promoted) the absurd idea that negativing the negative – killing the Jews – could create a wholly (and Holy) positive world. The fatuousness of the argument has not impeded its frequent and distinguished advancement; it is part of the value-system of western society. This is not an accusation, just a simple truth. And what can be done about it? Almost certainly very little, but it can and should be faced, as René Girard – uncited, like Norman Cohn, in the ragbag bibliography – has attempted in *Violence and The Sacred*, his essentially Protestant treatment of the scapegoat theme.

A post-ideological study of the uses of anti-Semitism in politics, religion and nationalism awaits its author, who will need to be much more outspoken and probably more embarrassing than any well-intentioned minister. Meanwhile, the obfuscation of human savagery by a fog of theological blather will do nothing to replace the categorical simplicity of the commandment 'Thou shalt not kill'. The one about 'bearing false witness' might be worth another glance too, but one mustn't make waves, must one?

Dreyfus Revisited

Miscarriages of justice are sometimes paraded as the glory of civilised states. The admission of error, however reluctant, is said to be evidence of the good faith of those who run the system. No error was more notorious, or less willingly admitted, than the one which led to the conviction of Alfred Dreyfus and none had more prolonged repercussions on the politics, morals and even the history of a great power. France had, perhaps, been divided in two ever since the Revolution, but the cleavage between Dreyfusards and supporters of the Army and the Church grew so deep that it could be said not to have healed even now, almost a century later.

The facts are scarcely in dispute. Alfred Dreyfus, an Alsatian Jew whose family had grown very rich in the textile trade, chose the French army as a career, apparently out of patriotic enthusiasm after the amputation of Alsace as a result of the Franco-Prussian war. He was a diligent student at the Polytechnic (France's most demanding *Grande Ecole*) and had all the qualities – including excellent horsemanship – appropriate to a successful career, except that he lacked the robust clubbability of his Gentile contemporaries. Dreyfus' reluctance to mix with others, his tendency to keep himself to himself and to rely on dry excellence to commend him to his superiors, may have been

---

Review of Michael Burns, *Dreyfus: A Family Affair 1789–1945*, in the *Sunday Times*, 1992.

due to a certain maturity they lacked; it may, as was often implied, have derived from his being a Jew. It did not make him popular, although those who might have been happy to see him disqualified from the higher ranks were unable to find official reasons to exclude him.

The discovery, in 1894, that there was a traitor in – or with access to – the General Staff – converted those who had vaguely disliked Captain Dreyfus into his credulous, implacable enemies. Defeat in the Franco-Prussian war still excited the desire for revenge and the fear of further humiliation. It was tempting to believe that only treachery could tip the balance next time. The enemy within might be devilish difficult to detect (hence his discovery became a sort of military triumph), but he was a scapegoat who could be punished, and so redeem the Army's prestige, without the risk of any serious battle. Despite the venal and corrupt character of Esterhazy, the actual villain, Dreyfus – who certainly did not need the money – was the 'natural' suspect.

Although he protested his innocence from the very first, he did so in the rigidly self-controlled manner which had always failed to charm and now signally failed to convince his fellow-officers. Dreyfus was a Jew who wanted nothing more than to be as unemotional, honourable and correct as he believed all true Frenchmen to be; perhaps his tragi-comedy was that he was indeed all of these things, but that Frenchmen – at least those who judged, pilloried and degraded him – were not.

From the very first, the evidence was literally flimsy: it consisted of a *bordereau*, a scrap of paper supposedly retrieved by a patriotic charwoman from a waste-basket in the German embassy, on which notes containing secret information had been written in a hand which the usual experts swore belonged to Dreyfus. The obvious discrepancies were proof of the man's swinish cunning in disguising his writing. He was court-martialled, sentenced to life imprisonment, publicly stripped of his commission, his sword broken across an NCO's knee, and – like all France's bad rubbish – transported to Devil's Island. He was pursued by cries of 'Death to the Jew!', against which he raised his thin voice to insist that he was an innocent man.

He had been defended by Edgar Demange, 'a fervent Catholic and a profound admirer of the Army', who took the case only after being utterly convinced that the evidence against the Jew was derisory. Forzinetti, the governor of the jail where Dreyfus was held, was equally certain of his prisoner's innocence. Yet the force of anti-Semitic frenzy, fostered by Edouard Drumont's newspaper, *La Libre Parole*, rendered all protest 'unpatriotic'. It took five years of brave and determined argument and protest to bring Dreyfus back – after hellish and sadistic treatment – for a re-trial at which he was again convicted, at which point he applied for, and received, the clemency of President Loubet.

His most intransigent supporters now felt 'betrayed': they would have preferred to have his sufferings prolonged in order to derive the maximum political and 'moral' advantage from the now manifest bad faith of their reactionary enemies. Dreyfus was reinstated in the army, given the Légion d'honneur and finally, during the Great War, was promoted Lieutenant-Colonel and put in command of an ammunition column.

The end? By no means: the division of France into Dreyfus-ards and anti-Dreyfusards did not die with him (and he lived on until 1935). The Affair had been – and remained – a fight for the high political and moral ground, however muddy the approaches. The man himself was scorned by his enemies and not always saluted by his friends. Historians have preferred to look at the implications, the significance, the paradoxes and the ironies of the case rather than to concentrate on the 'banality' of Dreyfus' personal ordeal. It may be that he was innocent, but he was also (we are promised) a bore. Even his lamentations were prosaic; rather witlessly, he proclaimed his love for France, his belief in the honour of the Army, his concern for his family. What intellectual or political Ultra could warm to such a priggish paragon?

There have been hundreds, perhaps thousands of books about the case and almost all of them sigh over the lack-lustre protagonist and – according to their political bent – prefer to look elsewhere for the heart of the matter. Sub-titling his study 'A Family Affair', Michael Burns concentrates, rewardingly, on the supposed banalities – in particular, the savage strain imposed on Dreyfus' wife and children. Lucie was by no means the vapid little woman derided by those who have not read, or cannot appreciate, the tenderness of her letters or noticed the resourcefulness of her fidelity. Honour is given above all, and rightly, to the prodigious stamina and unwavering courage of Alfred's brother, Mathieu, who was strong without being strident and determined without being pig-headed.

In an easy style, without polemics or sarcasm, Burns dismantles quite a few myths (not least of the 'understandable' animus of Dreyfus' accusers), without being diverted from the long and moving thrust of his narrative, which takes us on from the rehabilitation into the family's brave and tragic contribution both during the Great War and in the Resistance, in which its men and women again played a heroic part.

During the latter period, Charles Maurras – the prime intellectual enemy of Dreyfus – deliberately published the names and addresses of Jews whose arrest he demanded and whose murder he thus contrived. When Maurras – for whose 'royalism' T. S. Eliot OM never withdrew his admiration – was convicted, after the Liberation, of commerce with the enemy and sentenced (with ample justice) to life imprisonment and 'national degradation', he cried out 'C'est la revanche de Dreyfus!'

It is tempting to see The Affair as a rehearsal for genocide, but it was also evidence that a free society – albeit capable of fraud, vindictiveness and malignant myopia – could purge its faults. The reactionary losers in the case drew the conclusion that only a rigged society – and not merely a rigged court – could deliver verdicts in sweet accord with their prejudices. Vichy and its racism were the consequence; we must be allowed to hope that the Front National, and Jean-Marie Le Pen, its *chef*, are not going to be the rough beasts who shamble towards Paris for their rebirth.

A Strange Englishman

Every time I climb the stairs of the London Library and see the framed faces of T. S. Eliot and Harold Nicolson looking down at me, with the required air of quizzical serenity which dated photography required of eminent contemporaries, I make an unsubtle gesture in their presidential direction (assuming no other member is there to witness my puerility). Harold Nicolson's 'Marginal Comment', in the *Spectator*, was my favourite weekly reading in Charterhouse library, but he was also the man whose unputdownable diaries confess that he could never bring himself to dive into a steamship's swimming-pool after a possible Jew had been in it (I shall refrain from facile speculation about why Nicolson bothered with suspicions about what people might be hiding about themselves). As for Eliot, his distaste for 'free-thinking Jews' is not a secret, although it is regarded by fastidious persons as witless or vindictive to attach any sullen significance to it.

There have certainly been innumerable villains more villainous, if no less priggish, than the late Thomas Stearns Eliot OM. When it comes to having a go at poor Tom, I have, in truth, arrived rather late at the pillory where his image has long been a venerable target for literary brickbats; if fame endures, laurels have a regular way of turning into rotten tomatoes, as Churchill's brave detractors prove. Eliot was one of the first to disparage himself, when he spoke of how 'beastly' he was in his 'suit of clerical cut', but his attempts at prophylaxis did not quite do the immunising trick; poets are prone to regard him rather as painters do Picasso, a man who pre-empted the field and continues to cast a suffocating shadow, even if the bottoms of its trousers are rolled.

Being of prosaic temper, I have no sustained aesthetic quarrel with Uncle Tom. I am more disgusted with my own attitude to him (and of the docility with which I acquired it) than with his work. Indeed, when re-reading his verse, I was surprised to find how amusing much of it still was, or perhaps had become. There is something both charming and disconcerting in the discovery that so strange a God had more of a sense of humour than adolescent piety ever cared to notice.

I came to England from America in 1938 and from that time on, my youth became a perpetual examination, not to say endurance test, although I endured nothing much more terrible than Greek irregular verbs and the company of the sons of the English bourgeoisie. Unlike Mr Eliot, who came from St Louis by way of more respectable Boston, I was a Chicago-born New Yorker, but I too was rather promptly overwhelmed by England (my father's birthplace) and quick, to the point of servility, to adopt whatever local colour would homogenise me, as far as possible, with my new-found land and conceal my lamentable origins. Like Eliot, I had returned to where I had never been and did my best to seem a native.

How damaging a confession is it to say that I have not read Eliot regularly since my twenties? When Nabokov maintained that H. G. Wells was a better novelist than Conrad, some scandalised academic demanded when he had last read any Wells, to which the old Russian tease replied that he had found him excellent at the age of fifteen and saw no reason to disillusion himself by re-reading *Kipps* or *The War of the Worlds*. Eliot had, of course, already been challenged and even – in certain circles – debunked by the time I went to Cambridge in the early 1950s, but to an eager ape of High Culture he remained an emblematic, even normative figure (we donned the vocabulary of pretentiousness even more promptly than our skimpy, obligatory gowns). Eliot was always *Mr* Eliot, of course; an unmitred, secular bishop who appeared to preside over English with infallibility. He was the medicine Dr Leavis gave his patients; though I was never on his panel, I tried to follow his prescriptions. Since Cambridge already had all the precociously desiccated editors it needed, it was prudent to stick to philosophy, in which department Mr Eliot was said to have failed, having been first instructed and then cuckolded by Bertrand Russell.

It is easier to confess one's (few) ancient indiscretions than one's (many) naïvetés, but there it is: England, in that wedge of time between Triumph and Suez, was a place of persuasive propriety in which hierarchies held an apparently unquestionably totemic place. Mr Eliot's *quondam* Americanism and his announced conversion to England (echoing that of Henry James a generation or two earlier) seemed to warrant, if not require, the adoption of a senescent style, an allusive guardedness. Of course, there were those who followed Dr Leavis's *other* favourite formula and opted for undiluted D. H. Lawrence. However, even for literati who chose that red-blooded diet, Eliot served as a sort of Friday fish, boneless and blanched, but essential to a balanced intake.

When I read a bundle of Eliot's 1950s' essays again the other day, the taste of dust was overwhelming enough to explain why *Lucky Jim* seemed such a liberation. Eliot's audiences were always respectable and he addressed them in a comma-littered, convoluted style appropriate to a Peter Sellers' imitation of a Bombay BA (failed). He combined wilfully unprogressive sentiments with his own brand of winsomeness: 'my main motive has been to unsettle your minds, rather than to impose a theory; and when I have gone on defining, I have not been thinking of convincing, though you may have been thinking of your next cocktail party.' Such was the conclusion of a lecture about education, about which, in characteristic fashion, he both affected to be no sort of an expert and to be wiser than most.

The more you read his prose, the more you have the impression of an impressionist, a man who became more and more competent at imitating what others took him to be. The cultural breadth which he advertised, as an Anglo-American, enabled him to conceal the degree of his fawning condescensions with regard to an England where he was always more of an *arriviste* than he wanted to be reminded. While affecting refined sensibilities and an exemplary moral earnestness, he was in reality a man of flexible rigour and duplicitous integrity. As with Graham Greene (another fallen idol), one became only belatedly conscious of how eclectic were the issues with which English morality was concerned; the sins which their Gods were asked to be big enough to forgive were usually domestic and often thought up in order to give Him something a little teasing to think about.

By his scrupulous reticence, Eliot encouraged the English to believe that personal hygiene, in the moral sphere, should be their main concern. If he spoke loftily of the Destiny of Man, he was sedulously indifferent to what men had actually done in the years when he was frowning over manuscripts at Faber's. It may be that there was little that old Tom could have done to change the course of twentieth-century history; I do not wish to cudgel him for not interposing his person between the SS and their victims, but he could, in the safety of his mandarin impersonation, have lifted his pen. Neither during nor after the war did he allude to the Holocaust in any but the most cursory manner; like Graham Greene, he maintained the fabric of insular complacency while affecting to be a citizen of the world. Had he confined himself to the elegant mortifications of his poetic compositions, it might be unfair to chide him, but he showed a steady mock-reluctant zeal for addressing solemn audiences on Serious Matters. Inadvertently, he could some-times reveal the degree of callousness of which perhaps only a sensitive soul is capable, for instance when he regretted what had happened, after the war, to Charles Maurras, of whose *Action Française* he had been a youthful admirer. Maurras was, it is true, condemned to 'national disgrace', but if it is unbecom-ing to applaud the punishment of an old man, it is worth saying (as Eliot never did) that one of Maurras' habits during the war was to publish the names and addresses of Jews whom he incited the occupying authorities to take care of in their own way. Eliot's cowardice, of which his aptitude for the recherché is the objective correlative, was part of an intellectual tendency – never, of course, a conspiracy – to find very quiet excuses for the inexcusable, especially when committed by sociably or artistically elevated persons (Eliot was prompter to sympathise with Pound than with anyone spawned in an estaminet).

Eliot and Graham Greene, in their very different ways, were determined to save Christendom from aspersions on its honour, even if it meant ignoring the truth. Their bad faith has a cardinal place in the superficiality of the post-war reaction to Nazism. As late as 1970, a cosmopolitan lecturer of rare quality blighted his academic prospects in Britain by a discreetly forthright jibe at Eliot's failure ever to regret, let alone retract, his 'the rats are underneath the piles/ the jew is underneath the lot' remarks. There was, of course, no shortage of tenured professors, with good prospects from the Eliot business, to deplore George Steiner's sense of timing in attacking T.S.E. in a lecture which bore his name. Some people will never learn how to behave, will they?

That Eliot was a hollow man with no abiding convictions – except the need for respectability – hardly puts him high in the class of villainy, but it was precisely that he was also such a hero, in one sense, certainly such a master of the poetic straight face, that makes his memory cling until one feels like a sort of inverted Heracles wrestling with Proteus: one longs to have the old man revert to the lion one always imagined him to be. At least one would then have been in awe of a genuine king of the jungle, rather than of the domesticated, doctored Tom his biographers reveal him to have been.

Inventions of the March Hare

Just over forty years ago, T. S. Eliot wrote, in an occasional poem: 'There are several attitudes towards Christmas'. Today, there are several attitudes towards Mr Eliot (as my generation was induced, not least by Leavisites, to call him). That we are no longer dragooned into pious deference does not entail that Eliot should be downgraded from mastery, still less that he be evicted from respect in the way in which Milton was, supposedly, by Leavis (with Eliot's nuanced if temporary acquiescence, although – and because? – Milton was, as this edition proves, his potent and frequent inspiration).

It is not, however, impertinent to attempt, as Leavis used to say, to 'place' a now less mysterious Eliot towards the end of a century during which he has been, so to say, the head of the poetic corner. Christopher Ricks' meticulous edition of *The March Hare* which contains – mostly petty, if appetising – variants of early poems, as well as some purportedly scandalous hot-cakes *juvenilia*, seems to come as a timely, not to say timed, response to the renewed so-called 'spat' concerning Eliot's anti-Semitism. The naughty, negligible verses turn out to be of a more or less traditional, rugger-bugger crudeness, and would not be chosen for changing room song-sheets unless their author's name lent them popularity.

Review of T.S. Eliot, *Inventions of the March Hare* in the *Times Educational Supplement*, 1996.

The issue of Eliot's attitude towards Jews (or jews) was revived recently by Anthony Julius, after George Steiner first raised it, with *parvenu* courage, in *In Bluebeard's Castle*. Julius' *T. S. Eliot, Anti-Semitism and Literary Form* was a courteous (and, I insist, an unrepetitive) appreciation of Eliot's unnerving ability to breach aesthetic norms by proving that he could base good poems on evil ideas. Julius' scholarly caution did not exempt him from sighing, wincing responses '*de-ci, de-là*', as Eliot put it in 'Mélange Adultère de Tout'. There are, it emerged (after a certain disconcerted delay), powerful 'reasons', or at least motives, for continuing to repulse attempts to dethrone Mr Eliot from the position of sagacious 'sainthood' in which Noel Annan and other masters of the subtler arts remain willing to niche him.

Their cant could hardly be more kneelingly expressed than in Lord Annan's *Our Age*:

> ... as the years passed his poetry reached new heights until it culminated in *Four Quartets*.
>
> The generation that succeeded ours did not have the experience of growing up at a time when a great poet was publishing, who changed the style of poetry as Wordsworth had, and when each new publication did not diminish but added to his reputation. As each *Quartet* appeared during the war in its paper cover you were humbled. Eliot's modesty and gentleness reminded you of other worlds of sin, repentance and death whether or not you were a Christian ... Eliot taught me that opinions, prejudices, beliefs are an inescapable part of a vision of life, but to be moved and touched by that vision does not mean that you have to sign a contract with the poet and implement all its clauses.'
>
> [The punctuation, or its absence, is Lord Annan's.]

What emerges from this honeyed paragraph is a po-faced version of the estimate of Eliot's achievement and character which has become clingingly canonic. Within it are concealed complacencies and happy-few reticences of a kind typical of those who prefer to have their cultural cakes and eat them too. The image of Eliot climbing, climbing until he is so far above the common herd that we can only be 'humbled' has been keenly burnished by his acolytes. Their immaculate *homo Faber* (untainted by the unfortunate excesses of his *miglior fabbro*, Ezra Pound) still approximates to the role of demiurge, or demi-

God. To challenge him is to challenge their world-view; their eminence sits on a giant's shoulders and they wobble nervously at any suggestion that he might have clay feet.

Does re-reading Eliot justify the conclusion that *Four Quartets* is as great as the wartime Annan thought? My impression is that Eliot peaked early, and brilliantly. By the end of the 1920s, he showed signs of yielding to that self-parodic temptation which afflicts those to whom success – in the mundane, famous sense to which the greatest writers are rarely as indifferent as they pretend – comes with dignifying publicity. Much is said, by those who advance it as a way of hushing criticism, about Eliot's personal unhappiness during his first marriage, less about his uses of eminence. If Eliot himself, at much-quoted times, alleged that *The Waste Land* was 'a personal and wholly insignificant grouse against life', his sly masterpiece was also a claim to fame; and it was almost instantly honoured.

The lampooning rage with which he can be seen, in *The March Hare*, to have responded to Jack Squire's curtailment of his reviewing for the *Spectator* suggests a zeal for influence in the literary/social world which his own editorship of *The Criterion* somewhat satisfied. It is not my purpose here to re-heat coals over which to drag a dead poet, but it must be said that it is *very* convenient, on the part of his *purs et durs*, to use 'The Intentional Fallacy' (an 'axiom' of criticism which was vigorously and cogently questioned by William Empson) to render Eliot's political *obiter dicta* – whether callow or callous – irrelevant to his reputation. What should we make of apparently purposeful verses such as these from *Choruses from the Rock*: '. . . A Church for all/And a job for each/Each man to his work.'? If you cannot smell a whiff of corporatism and enforced belief in that, you have a poor nose for the scents of the twentieth century.

That a man without any clear practical project should pose as a political 'thinker' and dignify, if not endorse, anti-democratic (i.e. fascistic) ideas cannot escape scrupulous criticism, even in a 'saint'. Eliot himself wrote, in 1927, 'we cannot be *primarily* interested in any writer's nerves . . . or in anyone's heredity *except for the purpose of knowing to what extent that writer's individuality distorts or detracts from the objective truth which he perceives*'. Eliot emphasised the 'primarily'; the longer emphasis is mine, but much the same point is upheld by both: the work may be hermetically considered only as the work, but the individual character and history of the writer, and the way in which they hobble his stride or impair the generosity (let us say) of his vision, are bound to excite our interest and, at times, our reproach. To deny their relevance is to 'save the phenomena' at the price of wearing blinkers. (Something of this attitude is to be found in the privileging of the *'longue durée'* by French historians, Fernand Braudel *en tête*, for whom close attention to specific details reveal flaws in their beloved France too recent and too rancid for comfort.)

What is remarkable about Eliot's response to the war (in which, morally – even 'religiously' – speaking, it can be argued that the Holocaust was the supreme 'event') is, as Steiner hinted, that it appears hardly to have occurred. What then did the war mean to Eliot? What kind of Christianity did *Four Quartets* assert or embellish? Eliot did not only more or less ignore what happened to Europe's Jews (as did the Foreign Office, which contributed to it by attitudes not very different, in their fastidious inhumanity, from the poet's); in the murky light of his editorial lucubrations and sponsorships during the *entre deux guerres*, he could be said to have remained in elderly, wilfully ignorant retreat during the whole of the war, and after. He is the Albert Speer of Parnassus, too fastidious to have an accurate conscience.

As a young man, his only acknowledgement of the Great War was, it appears, his decision not to risk submarine attack by returning to defend his Harvard thesis, on F. H. Bradley, in 1916. His only published contribution to 'the war effort' between 1939 and 1945 consisted of the jejune lines entitled 'To The Indians who Died in Africa' (1943). Written for *Queen Mary's Book for India*, the poem, such as it is, looks to have been prompted more by royalist deference than by respect for anyone whose 'destination is his own village'.

In his Clark Lectures, Robert Graves did not spare Eliot, and other militant stay-at-homes under the rubric 'These Be Thy Gods, O Israel', for their lack of active service in the Great War, but Graves' scorn was dismissed as eccentric. Proximity to the front is, perhaps, a dubious form of aesthetic measure, but to write lines such as 'There will be time to murder and create . . .' without any experience of blood (except on bed-sheets) is hardly pretty. Eliot's sustained respect for Isaac Rosenberg, who was killed on the Western front, may be evidence less of his putative (personal) philo-Semitism than of a certain sense of the uneasiness of those who, as Dr Johnson put it, had not 'been for a soldier'.

Even in civilian society, Eliot was a very specialised sort of observer. He did not seem to relate to people, but to types (poems are often more like the *plots* or maquettes for novels than they are like details from them). Eliot's generalising style was acutely analysed, by Empson, as akin to that of Henry James: 'sweetly funny in its way, but a patent attempt to cheat'. The snob and the *arriviste* tend to be at one in their alert assimilation of the social odds, the ins and the outs: in their wilful accuracy they can become almost involuntary satirists of what they crave to please. They 'cheat' by making knowingness a form of knowledge; they hint at what they themselves have only guessed (Max Beerbohm's cartoon of James showed him sniffing shoes in a nocturnal hotel corridor in order to deduce the activities of those behind closed doors). For whatever reasons, Eliot was better at catching atmosphere than at closing with specific character or incident. This is less an accusation than what, in his French mask, Eliot might have called a *constation*. He remarked, however, in 'Sweeney Erect', 'The lengthened shadow of a man/ Is history, said Emerson/ Who had not seen the silhouette/ Of Sweeney straddled in the sun'. It is not Eliot's *fault* that his shadow is now less majestic in the light of history which entirely eluded his imaginative grasp or his conscientious response. Yet it is a *fact* that he established – silhouetted – himself as the commentator on the century, as well as its leading English language poet. Our assessment of him cannot, and should not, ignore occasions when he was 'At times, indeed, almost ridiculous – /Almost, at times, the Fool', as he said in 'The Love Song of J. Alfred Prufrock' (1917).

One does not legitimately criticise a writer for not achieving what was beyond, or marginal to, his chosen scope. But it does not follow that the observation of his limits, and limitations, is irrelevant to assessing his achievement (or even to underlining it). Also in *Prufrock*, Eliot – while claiming to be 'no prophet' – had the foresight to remark 'I have seen the moment of my greatness flicker' and in 'Conversation Galante' the question is posed 'And "Are we then so serious?"'. The determination to regard Eliot *seriously* is, I suspect, part of what has led us to misunderstand and perhaps even to underestimate him (his capacity for 'camp' comes out as soon as you read his verses aloud: the 'Fragment of a prologue', written forty years before Harold Pinter, is a superb proleptic criticism by example).

Christopher Ricks' exemplary, not to say precious, editing of *The March Hare* is part of a sustained solemnifying process. The printing of the supposedly naughty, in fact egregiously puerile, Bolo verses is typical of an age in which it is supposedly endearing to learn of the 'human' side of the princes, real or literary, who govern us. It would be better to 'teach' Eliot as a controversial polymath (we can afford to drop his comma between the two), vivid with contradictions and riven by vices as well as virtues, than to 'preserve the phenomena' by the kind of perverse ingenuity which renders the poet inhuman and the critic disingenuous.

'The British race assured of a mission/ Performed it, but left much at home unsure/ Of all that was in the past, you eat the fruit, either rotten or ripe.' Trust the poem, not the poet.

In the Case of
Julius v. Mr Eliot

Still in his thirties, Anthony Julius has an uneven fame: he is both the high-flying lawyer representing the Princess of Wales, in her impending divorce from Prince Charles, and the author of *T. S. Eliot, Anti-Semitism and Literary Form*, a serious study which has been greeted, in literary circles, with conspicuous reticence. Although published by the Cambridge University Press, it has not been reviewed in the *Times Literary Supplement* or in most of the major newspapers. Since Dr Julius – his book is a revised, successful PhD thesis – took two years out from his legal career in order to train for and acquire the intellectual muscle, and warrant, to get into the ring with Mr Eliot, he might be excused for expecting at least a chorus of welcome obloquy after a Rocky-like training period which qualified him to challenge one of the champions of High Culture.

By contrast, as Princess Diana's legal counsel, Julius has become a gossip column celebrity, the minutiae of whose office politics merit newsprinted attention: we have been treated to headlined promises that his usual secretary at Mishcon, De Reya was miffed when he imported a different (tighter-lipped) typist to deal with palatial business. It has also been exclusively disclosed that some of his colleagues detected symptoms of hubristic vanity in his bearing: like Eliot's Princess Volupine, Diana both lends kudos to her escorts and excites envy in those whose arm, or advice, she disdains to take.

Perhaps the muted reception of Julius' book on Eliot proves only that enough is more than enough. After the play and film of *Tom and Viv*, with all their re-heated simplifications, have we not had a surfeit of cattishness at the expense of the young(ish) Tom's flat-footed fogeydom? It may be true that he could neither satisfy his first wife – his long-lived second, Valerie makes do with Keeper of the Flame self-satisfaction – nor be convincingly kosherised, but need we go on *and on* about his ill-considered *jeux d'esprit* (the obvious pun supplies their subject)? Has Mr E. not achieved the usual English transition from *vieillard terrible* to cuddly cult-figure? His old publishing house, Faber and Faber, grows gorgeously rich not so much on his poetic reprints, however canonic, as on the royalties from *Cats*. It is somewhat sweet that the author who referred so scathingly to 'money in furs', should have been purringly immortalised by tuneful pussies. Does what is left of God sometimes take the form of a Cheshire cat, of whom there is nothing to be seen but an ironic smile?

If there have been murmurs of dismay at Julius' re-opening of the dated charges of anti-Semitism against Old Tom, critics have preferred to be sighingly sympathetic to the emotional – albeit anachronistic – reaction of a young, post-Holocaust Jew to the poet who declared, in the 1920 poem 'Burbank with a Baedeker: Bleistein with a Cigar', that 'the rats are underneath the piles/the jew is underneath the lot.' However, did not Theophile Gauthier once say *Tout passe?* (No, Théophile Gautier did.) Be that as it may, is it not time everything did?

For as long as anyone can remember, the standard response to Jews – and others, if any – who sought to evict Eliot from the sainted niche in which his merits, no less than his anglophile pose installed him has been to deplore his persecutors' unsubtle organs of appreciation. Sensitive critics like Christopher Ricks (assuming there *is* anyone like Christopher Ricks) have displayed, in detailed detail, with what straight-faced skittishness Eliot played the controversial polymath. By donning grotesque masks of unreason, of despair and of mythological *personae*, was he not simply 'doing the police', as he used to say, in a variety of cunningly subversive voices?

This by now routine defence insists that, like any other dramatist or dramatiser, Eliot cannot *legitimately* be identified with those whom he impersonates or whose platitudes he gilds, or makes glitter, with such scintillating derision. Julius treats these suave disclaimers with merciless courtesy; he does British justice to Eliot's professorial apologists, by listening respectfully to them and believing no more than every other word they say. In this unusual fashion, he proves himself at times a greater. and always more honest, admirer of Eliot than those who habitually plaster him with saintliness: the unintimidated Julius may attack the poet's anti-Semitism, but its nuanced malice and his own intelligence do not prevent him from saluting its generative place in Old Possum's feline arsenal.

Julius' book is mould-breaking without being merely debunking. Its diffident impact is only underlined by the affectations of *déjà vu* with which academics on both sides of the Atlantic have chosen, pretty well, to ignore it. What is extremely rare, if not unique, is Julius' assertion that Eliot's dismissive disdain was not a dramatic device or even an ill-advised lapse on the great man's part, but an integral and seminal aspect of his imagination. Eliot, Julius argues, saw the Jews as a blot, not a menace; their physical stuntedness was the objective correlative of their spiritual atrophy. They were a practical joke he liked to crack, like a bad egg. They were not a threat but an embarrassment.

Julius rejects the fudgy dogma (so often propounded by John Carey, Christopher Ricks and all that *galère*) that, since great poetry cannot be anti-Semitic and since Eliot certainly is a great poet, he cannot, logically, be hostile to Jews. Julius comes to the disconcerting conclusion that poems such as 'Sweeney among the Nightingales' are both great literature *and* anti-Semitic. Despite what Wittgenstein (or Jean-Paul Sartre) said to the contrary, aesthetics and ethics have no necessary equivalence or symmetry; there can, after all, be 'good' right-wing literature. (Come to think of it, what would literature be without its prejudices, of which grammar is the abstract guardian? Mere accountancy!) With footnoted defiance, Julius breaches *and* honours the fastidious conventions of academic custom. His only naïveté is in supposing, if he does, that such candid duplicity can secure him the admiration more properly reserved, in critical circles, for hypocrisy.

It has always been held to be a sign of naïvéte – an intellectual sin far graver than malice or vindictiveness – to attribute propositional content to poetry. Prose may incidentally embrace metaphors, but poetry *is* metaphor and hence *sui generis* true or false assertions about the world can never properly be extracted from it. Julius cries 'humbug' to this recension of the old claim to 'benefit of clergy', and rightly. Yet like Eliot, he is at once subversive and respectful of tradition; *en bon Anglais*, he is prudent enough to shout without raising his voice. His attack on literary evaluation is intended to be a contribution to it. Parody is the sincerest, and most painstaking, form of criticism.

I once said of Arthur Schlesinger Jr., in reviewing a heavy volume of essays in which he took as much space in discussing the (negligible) role of the vice-president of the United States as Thucydides did to describe the defeat of the Athenian armada in the Great Harbour of Syracuse, during the Peloponnesian War, that there were 'few dark corners on which he fails to shed fresh dust'. If there is a trace of urgent dustiness in Julius, he differs from the smug junior Schlesinger (can anyone still take the toadying biographer of Robert Kennedy seriously?) in being genuinely enlightening. He is particularly forceful in exposing the supercilious stratagems with which Eng. Lit. pundits have sought, systematically, to obscure or excuse the vulgar animus of protected specimens in the modern canon.

Although Ezra Pound's anti-Semitism is so manifest (and programmatically murderous) that only the most refined minds are scrupulous enough to deny its centrality in his work, one of Julius' problems is that for a Jew to harp on malice towards Jews can still be taken as evidence of undue sensitivity. Discreet Shylockian sufferance is much to be preferred to being a cry-baby. I was once on a panel at Stratford, faced by rows of culture-tripping Japanese, after a production of *The Merchant of Venice* in which Shylock, played by Ian McDiarmuid, wore a yellow hat, spoke with a stereotypical Jewy lisp and played for self-inflicted laughs. In the discussion, McDiarmuid denied angrily that he would ever have anything to do with anything that endorsed anti-Semitism. To which, in my crowd-displeasing way, I asked whether this did not amount to resignation from Western European culture.

It is, I daresay, in response to such loutish cosmopolitan sarcasm that Professor Denis Donoghue impatiently advises Jews to have a sense of humour as willing to let bygones be bygones as that of the Irish. None of *them*, we may deduce, ever complain about such antique grievances as the behaviour of Oliver Cromwell. And what Irishman would today remind the English of how little they did to alleviate the potato famine or draw attention to the cynicism with which London divided and still rules part of the Ireland it colonised? Holocaust denial, Donoghue might argue, is the possibly deplorable backlash which the Jews have brought on themselves by an undue number of visits to the wailing wall. In fact, Jews such as Delmore Schwartz, who scarcely hid their origins, are shown to have been contortedly 'forgiving' when it came to their idols. Lionel Trilling paid almost as alienating a price as Heinrich Heine in offering deferential dues to the Christian establishment.

Before the war, Sir Lewis Namier declined to write a history of his own people on the grounds that the Jews did not properly have a history, only a martyrology. According to Julius' reading, Eliot's 'A Song for Simeon' (1928) testifies to even the most honourable Jew's marginal role by the way in which Simeon greets the arrival of Jesus in the guise of a resigned, soon to be dispossessed, witness (witness is, of course, the root meaning of martyr). St Paul's 'New Covenant' relegated the Chosen People to the exemplary position of rejected wanderers (Blaise Pascal took the same view of them in the seventeenth century); they have been forced to pay the long price of their incredulity ever since.

The caesura between BC and AD was fatal for Jewish fortunes. At their peak, in the early Roman empire, Jews constituted ten percent of the population of the known world; their diabolisation by the Fathers of the Church (St John Chrysostom, the golden-mouthed, led the way) reveals the fabricated cohesion of the so-called 'Judaeo–Christian tradition'. In fact, the rupture between Jews and Christians was as dire for the former as it was promotional to the latter. The historically valid Judaeo/Christian tradition is of one-sided malevolence; to justify their malice, Christians discovered regular 'evidence' of what the usual suspects were up to. Ritual murder, poisoned wells and lamentable standards of personal hygiene were the outward and visible signs of an inward and spiritual gracelessness. Muslims, on the other hand, were ridiculed for excessive washing; good Christians, inspired perhaps by St Francis's charitable attitude to infestation, did not have to indulge in bathing more than once a year.

In his many studies of the relation between violence and religion, René Girard has pointed out that 'the scapegoat mechanism', which stigmatises the outcast – and preferably weak – Other, is a standard recipe when a society feels in danger of fracture or disintegration; victimisers have to see themselves as victims. One of the curious, and unforeseen, consequences of expelling or killing scapegoats is that they later become objects of superstitious veneration. Supernatural and magic powers are attributed to the bloody nuisance whose maltreatment has enabled society to recover its poise. Jesus remarked that the stone which the builder rejected became the head of the corner; Dionysos made the same point. The Jew becomes an unexpected instance of the same process; time and again, he is dismissed from Christian society, only subsequently to be credited (though not by Mr Eliot) with the mythical, tentacular omnipotence which sponsors rekindling the fuse of violence. Not wholly by chance was Mircea Eliade both the scholarly apostle of the theory of eternal return *and* a committed Fascist.

David Pryce-Jones once told me that on the eve of his execution Julius Streicher, the Nazi 'Jew-baiter', informed his jailers that he now realised that he had been completely wrong about the Jews. On being told that it was a little late for repentance, Streicher explained that he had not exaggerated the worldly power of the Jews, but rather underestimated it: since they were clearly invincible, he now wanted to be on their side. If they had survived the Holocaust, they were a club worth joining.

In more refined calculations, however, the sorry survival of the Jews is coincidental with, and a validation of, the history of Christianity. Hence the false naïveté of the post-war Eliot's 'refutation' of charges of anti-Semitism by asserting that, since he was a Christian, he could not possibly be anti-Semitic. Even if it was technically a 'sin' to hate Jews (or anyone else), such sinfulness was scarcely a practical impossibility; sins have. after all, been known to be committed. Be that as it may, Eliot became quite tetchy, after 1945; when 'libelled' by uncouth contributors to the *Times Literary Supplement*, he demanded 'evidence' or retraction, quite as if he had never printed the propositional, prosaic remarks in *After Strange Gods* calling for a very limited number of 'free-thinking Jews' in any putative Christian society. His ideal state would require the exclusion of Jews who tried to pass for common citizens (Maurras too was particularly venomous about those who changed their names). Father Coughlin and Ole Ez and the Great Tom were brothers under the skin. The Rev. Farrakhan is but the latest witless recruit to their fraternity.

In his 1970 T. S. Eliot Memorial Lecture, George Steiner mimicked the *arriviste*'s cautious nerve when he adverted to Eliot's mutedly regretful references to the recent Holocaust, in *Some Notes towards the Re-definition of Culture* (still awaiting

Andrew Lloyd-Webber's musical version). Steiner has claimed that his polemic wariness contributed to the frustration he encountered when seeking preferment in Oxford or Cambridge. In the printed lectures, entitled *In Bluebeard's Castle*, probably his best and certainly his most cogently argued work, he trod delicately, yet broke academic step by dealing openly with Eliot's reluctant retreat from the quasi-Fascist ideology with which he had certainly flirted in the *entre deux guerres*. At that time, old Tom all but got into bed, in a spiritual sense, with Charles Maurras, whose Action française movement was avowedly based on anti-Semitism. In 1940, Maurras notoriously remarked that France's defeat was 'providential'. What we shall never know, luckily for us and, I suspect, for his reputation, is what posture Eliot would have struck in a London as providentially subject to the Nazis as occupied France.

I have suggested elsewhere that there is something no less providential, in an amiable but not wholly dissimilar sense, in the creation of the European Community. The vanished Jews of Europe provide an unspoken but fundamental reason for the kind of 'fresh beginning' which will consign them to honourable oblivion. By 'fundamental' I mean that the blood of Europe's Jews has provided the basic cement which links their active and passive persecutors in a pact of righteous silence. Why else was the recent suggestion by President Clinton that dispossessed European Jews should be allowed to sue, independently or as members of a 'community', for the return of their stolen property greeted as another example of clod-hopping Yankee crassness? Chancellor Adenauer's prophylactic payment of 'compensation' to the nascent state of Israel was both a confession of guilt and a well-timed act of early redemption (buying back) of Germany's good name: *mea culpa* and *raison d'état* went economically together.

How much does it all matter now? How much does *anything* matter now, unless we have available footage to illustrate it? The place of the Jews, even in the demonology of their enemies, has changed beyond foreseeable regression since the Holocaust and the establishment of the state of Israel. There are those, of whom George Steiner is the most rampantly outspoken, who wonder whether Hitler was not, in some sense, the unacknowledged sponsor, even the necessary cause, of the Jewish state and whether the Jews are not fated to disappear, as 'the people of the book', as much because of Zionism as because of the

Holocaust. Having acquired a land, Steiner laments, they are no longer rooted in the text, in the intellect, in what D. H. Lawrence called 'disinterested speculation'. Anti-Semitism certainly did not die with Hitler, but his murderous example rendered it obscene as a philosophy or, except to crackpots and headline-hoggers, as an explanation of 'the way we live now' (to cite the title of Trollope's novelistic contribution to the canon). Winston Churchill once told one of Hitler's leg-men to advise his master that anti-Semitism was a 'good starter but a bad stayer', and so it seems, bloodily, to have proved.

In the light of twentieth-century experience, it should be strange that, of all our strange gods, the anti-Semitic figures in the literary pantheon have retained their centrality. Myths of Jewish cunning and clannish manipulation could hardly survive the Holocaust any better than the benign God Whom, supposedly, Jew and Christian had in common. Not the least intriguing of recent discoveries – published in France – is that of a suppressed Papal Encyclical, commissioned by Pius XI in 1938, in which a Jesuit and a Dominican, among others, argued for an unequivocal condemnation of anti-Semitism and racism. Pius XI died before he could sign the *imprimatur* and Eugenio Pacelli, Pius Xll, had it shelved. This palpable cowardice has not been held against him by those who maintain that he 'saved' many thousands of Jews by his tacit tact. Eliot's obsequious post-war decorum was of a piece with Pacelli's concern more with Christian continuity than with Christian witness.

What mattered in 1945 was the preservation of appearances; a complete rejection of what had led up to the *Shoah* would have been tantamount to a repudiation of the whole language of Western thought. It was literally unthinkable. The preservation of Eliot, as the head of the corner, was the academy's compact with prudent oblivion. Am I saying that he was not a great poet? Must I? I prefer to remember what a French academician wrote not long ago: as a young *lycéen*, he was an impotent witness of the arrest of the Jewish members of his class. He became an influential critic and made a considerable career in literature, but he was, he confessed, never able to think that writing was quite as supremely important as cultural pundits would have us believe. Somerset Maugham remarked long ago, when someone accused a (fictional) character of being a lousy poet because he behaved despicably, that he was, on the contrary, a great poet; he was a lousy *man*. Mr

Eliot, intimidating impostor, prosing *poseur* and genius, was of the same *galère*.

The comedy of his intrusive centrality is that the man from St Louis was himself, in Maurras' terms, a *métèque*, a camouflaged foreigner in an England where anti-Semitism was, and perhaps is often a casual social prejudice but never a plausible political programme. The refusal to be scandalised by Anthony Julius' book is, I daresay, not itself a scandal. The Jews have had a happy history in Britain, despite flurries of malice and, sometimes, of murder. Benjamin Disraeli is the only Victorian figure who is still instantly recognised by his nickname, Dizzy, and the most famous English Jews, despite the malpractice of those like Robert Maxwell, are remembered for their benefactions and their genius rather than for their misdeeds. English tolerance may be almost indistinguishable from indifference, but is London wholly misguided in being more interested in Anthony Julius as Princess Di's worthy liegeman than in Dr Julius, the shedder of indignant dust?

Finkielkraut's
Imaginary Jew

Not long ago, I remarked in a review on the difficulty which Jewish historians have had in finding a style appropriate to dealing with the Holocaust. For fear of being accused of 'emotionalism', they usually adopt a measured and clerk-of-the-courtly tone: Martin Gilbert's wilful pedestrianism is the limit instance. It is impossible to imagine what a *due* response might be, in what vocabulary it could be couched or, if it matters, what purpose it would serve. As it is, even the most combative Jewish historians are inclined to present the Holocaust in terms which imply no unbridgeable distinction between them and their Gentile colleagues. So far from ranting and raving, the literature of the Holocaust is almost unnervingly sane; Primo Levi's attempt to be 'scientific' is the noblest instance of keeping one's voice down the better to make it carry. My article provoked only two, anonymous, responses: one was the usual margin-to-margin montage of cuttings from miscellaneous sources, reminding me that 'the Jews' had armed Bismarck, massacred the Amalekites, been Rothschilds and had only themselves to blame; the other, more economical, enclosed my article with the word YAWN written across it in black marker.

The fear of being boring is both the enemy of justice and a proper specific against repetition or, as they say, banging on. In

---

A review of Alain Finkielkraut, *The Imaginary Jew* (trs. Kevin O'Neill & David Suchoff), in the *Times Literary Supplement*, 1994.

fact, the mutedness of English and Jewish and English Jewish consideration of the Holocaust was deafening for at least a decade after the war, until Lord Russell of Liverpool, for motives which may not have been wholly noble, wrote *The Scourge of the Swastika*. Raul Hilberg's *The Destruction of the European Jews* and Hannah Arendt's *Eichmann In Jerusalem* broke the concordat of reticence, but combined to give the impression that the six million had gone bleatingly to their deaths. Only Elie Wiesel remarked, rightly, that the sheepishness of the victims was nothing to that of their killers, who acquiesced in murder with scarcely a mutter of dissent or revulsion. One of the sustaining myths of exculpation was that many of the mechanicals were concripts who had to kill or be killed, although no case has ever been cited of a German or any other national being punished, let alone shot, for refusing to take part (cf. Christopher R. Browning's *Ordinary Men*). When it comes to the attitude of the Allies and of the Catholic Church, one has only to ironise on their inertia to be reminded how busy everybody was and that Pope Pius XII was a saint. As for the British Foreign Office, when faced with the possibility of their escape, Anthony Eden asked, in the tone of a pedlar spreading his hands, what he was supposed to do with a million Jews. Frank Roberts very much saw his point and later rose to the highest diplomatic positions.

Those who survived the war did so with a variety of emotions and prospects. English Jews were, of course, the luckiest, though rarely the loudest. Of the thirty thousand or so Polish Jews still alive (one per cent of the pre-war Jewish population of that most Christian country), many met pogroms when they attempted to resume their lives and recover their property (the motive of theft is often ignored in the search for 'deep' reasons for the *Shoah*, although Claude Lanzmann's film displays its prevalence). In France, returning or surviving French Jews – about two-thirds of the community – were wary of making waves; those of alien birth were even more self-effacing. As Alain Finkielkraut reminds us, when Jean-Paul Sartre published his portrait of the anti-Semite, his outspokenness excited almost embarrassing gratitude, even though he showed little knowledge of Judaism and was as much concerned to disparage the Right as to make common cause with the Jews, whom he called upon – with patronising camaraderie – to 'assume' their identity, rather than flinch from it. Nevertheless, his pamphlet was of capital importance at a time when the establishment of the state of Israel was still being baulked by Britain and when the Jewish will to survive might well have fallen beyond recovery. Sartre's pro-Semitic (and later guardedly pro-Israel) attitude was to last into the 1970s by which time the Palestinians had become the *chouchous* of the Left.

In 1967, the French government also changed its posture. The usefulness of Israel, as an ally against the Arabs, had evaporated after the Evian agreements to end the Algerian war. General de Gaulle's declaration, that the Jews were 'un peuple d'élite, sûr de lui-même, et dominateur', provoked Raymond Aron, the very instance of an assimilated, unreligious citizen of the Republic, to reaffirm his Jewishness and round on the man to whom he had rallied in 1940. Aron was unequivocal but not intemperate: belonging to a family whose members had long been *heureux comme Dieu en France*, he saw no contradiction in being a Jew and a Frenchman (Alain Juppé's recent claim to feel *loyauté* towards M. Balladur and *fidelité* towards Jacques Chirac is a smooth example of a similarly honourable *ménagement*). Aron's lucidity stemmed from being a luminous product of an educational system in which the '*cracks*' could expect to be recruited to the service of the Republic, whether as professors or functionaries, in accordance with the same Napoleonic tradition that, formally at least, had given the Jews equal rights with other citizens.

Alain Finkielkraut is a luminary in a rather different social and intellectual constellation. Like Aron (and like Charles Péguy, the rehabilitated hero of his recent *Le Mécontemporain*) he is an eager political *feuilletonniste*, eloquent in the Cartesian trenchancies through which binary oppositions sustain the machinery of analysis and paradox, but his urgency derives from a renewed sense of being a Jew, rather than Jewish (he makes epigraphic use of Isaac Babel's famous remark, 'If I were to write my autobiography, I would call it "The Story of an Adjective"') or French. Jewishness is the theme which drives its fuse through a text both outspoken and *pudique*; if the writing is incautious, it is artful enough to avoid personal revelation.

Finkielkraut assumes not only his Jewishness but also the mantle of the Parisian *philosophe* to whom life is a text in regular need of *explication*. Whether or not he realises it, he is *français, terriblement français*. Yet, as the son of Polish Jews who repressed their origins in *Yiddishkeit*, the better to sponsor the Francophone brilliance which has seen him prosper as a political analyst, with a regular column in the *Nouvel Obs.*, he has suffered from an increasingly grievous sense of loss. Filial gratitude here takes the form of reproach; awareness of his parents' mortality makes him greedy for what they have chosen to repress, for his sake: accurate memories of the great community to which they once belonged and from which he is forever exiled. His resentment may not be cruel, but it is certainly somewhat cold: he generalises the condition of the Jewish son for whom family *is* religion and indicates sympathy with Portnoy's complaints, though he expresses it with none of Roth's saving, and self-deprecating, humour.

Le Juif Imaginaire was first published in France in 1980, when the author was just thirty. An unapologetic recantation of the facile comradeship which was then beginning to run its course, it is a farewell to youth by a *soixante-huitard* in the process of realising that his revolutionary *prises de position*, in the long aftermath of that theatrical event, were little more than sincere impostures (in his larky *Petit fictionnaire illustre* (1981), Finkielkraut defines *Gauchemar* as 'rêve qui cherche à angoisser mais s'y prend de travers'). Looking back in ruefulness, he recognises that he was never *that* bonded with his comrades. When they chorussed 'Nous sommes tous des Juifs allemande,' he felt like saying, 'You can't become a Jew or a dago just like that. . . . German Jews? With your French-looking faces? What gives you the right to reap the rewards? You haven't paid your dues.' What rewards? A certain right to outrageousness, a credit balance of rights to reply of the kind on which Menachem Begin was to draw with reckless effrontery, when, in 1982, he launched Israel's first aggressive war?

'How many identities we [the *enragés*] assumed', Finkielkraut exclaims. 'Colonized natives with Frantz Fanon, American blacks with Malcolm X . . . guerrillas with Che, partisan strategists with Giap and Ho Chi Minh . . . terrorized by our insignificance, we are the silly and complex-laden generation united by slogans greedily claiming every uprising of the twentieth century as our own.' The renunciation of such spurious mutability has impelled Jews born after 1945 to seek an 'authenticity' (Sartre's term again) whose roots they now find to be atrophied or dead. Unable to believe in the God of their fathers or to invest their emotional piety unreservedly in Israel, they discover themselves to be atheists in search of a synagogue, at least in the sense of a place of common recognition.

An Anglo-Jew, who knows of the Holocaust but does not

know it, is unlikely to experience the same crisis of identity. Anglo-Jewry still lives in somewhat privileged immunity from Continental concerns; if vandalism and assault are not unknown, and casual spite quite frequent, there has been almost no *programmatic* anti-Semitism in Britain. Disraeli correctly predicted that tolerance would procure a Jewish conservatism, a ready and deep allegiance even to things such as cricket, which Sartre might regard as numbingly inauthentic. Finkielkraut is merciless towards French Jews who take on local colour, those 'Israélites' whose wine-loving fastidiousness was affronted by the kaftaned tea-drinkers and side-locked refugees who, as they fled the Nazis, claimed kinship with them. When he sneers at the cultivation of those who write elegant French – would he be a truer Jew if he wrote less well? – or who 'live persecution at a comfortable remove', is he booking his own place in the pillory?

'I am a Jew,' he says, 'yet the figure designated by this statement can be located nowhere. ... A fundamental chasm exists between myself and the history of my people ... the Holocaust has no heirs. ... Among the peoples that constitute our generation, it is given to none to say: I am the child of Auschwitz.' (In this, he distinguishes himself from Wiesel who was, precisely the child of Auschwitz.) 'As an imaginary Jew,' Finkielkraut goes on, 'I have long lived my faithfulness ... in a kind of appropriation. ... In the noun that ... designated my identity, nothing defines or belongs to me. ... If Judaism has a central injunction, it should not be thought of as a matter of identity, but of memory; not to mimic persecution nor make theatre of the Holocaust, but to honour its victims.' Finkielkraut's book *Remembering in Vain*, on the perversities of the Klaus Barbie trial, insists on the vigilance needed to avoid such theatrical *détournements*. The variety and vigour of the world of the dead – so often alleged to have been sick-unto-death even before Hitler – haunts the author's imagination and fuels his fury: 'It was a vibrant, multi-faceted and creative culture the Nazis killed.'

In 1948, Arthur Koestler, once a militant Zionist, declared that the foundation of the state of Israel gave the Jews a clear choice: either to go there or to embrace assimilation. Finkielkraut denies both the obligation of the former and the possibility of the latter, which was based, he asserts, on a 'dreadful misunderstanding'. Genocide, he maintains, 'was not imposed on the Jews *in spite of* their effort to assimilate, but *in response* to this very attempt. The more they hid their Jewishness, the more terrifying they became to others.' If this is so, could it be that Disraeli's role-modelling service to Anglo-Jewry lay in combining unequivocal patriotism with an unabashed flaunting of inescapable origins?

As for assimilation, if it has been known to disconcert the natives, it hardly amounts to a sufficient cause for so complex a tragedy as the Holocaust, although the argument is congenial to some orthodox polemicists. It may be remembered that, in *In Bluebeard's Castle*, George Steiner claimed, with equal assurance, that it was the Jews' cardinal part in foisting unattainable Absolutes on the world – their damnably demanding morality – which provoked their mass murder. The search for adequate explanations is, I suspect, just another aspect of our attempt to rescue the rationality of the world in which Reason itself became a refugee. Both Steiner and Finkielkraut seek an appropriately *Jewish* cause, however understandable or even flattering, for Gentile crimes. Personally, I do not feel the vocation.

Today, Finkielkraut suggests, Jews find themselves in a new situation, which may have old consequences: they are now liable to be envied for their persistent sense of identity. Like it or not, they seem to be exempt from the blurred individualism of the lonely crowd of *consommateurs* created by a society increasingly denied cohesion; the disbandment of factory 'work forces' and of military service, like the seclusion of the television viewer, works against the bonding once found in war, in work and in the theatre.

Can Jews hope to recover and sustain their ancient solidarity, without abiding faith in the God whose covenant they were required to keep? Finkielkraut wants the 'recovery of ritual' to serve as a linking formula, but can reproduced courtesies stand in for a vital relationship with a Jehovah whose silence at Auschwitz seems like a denial more final and less forgivable than St Peter's? Merely formal piety is also a kind of assimilation, an 'acting like'. Even if such mimetic revival supplies a kind of 'memory-theatre' (in the Frances Yatesian sense), can it possibly furnish a dynamic for thought, let alone a specific against another genocidal spasm? 'The future of the Jews cannot be foreseen', Finkielkraut tell us, but meanwhile we have a duty to remember. Memory, however, is also a *mother*; perhaps this implies a duty to the Muses. Then again, in the light of Camus's Sisyphus, should not being *happy* play its part in how we should imagine ourselves and our children, even if it turns out that Genet uttered the grim truth when he said, 'Nous ne sortirons jamais de ce bordel'?

Riders Towards the Dawn

I am somewhat puzzled as how best to deal with Rabbi
Friedlander's new book. To start with, I think it fairest to adopt
a piecemeal approach. Since the book itself contains no single
or developed argument, but proves to be a collection of observations, on the whole laudatory, concerning religious
approaches to the post-Auschwitz world, it is impossible to
undertake any single, overall criticism of it. I propose, therefore,
to examine a few representative elements, and the attitude to
them taken by Albert Friedlander, rather in the style of a biopsy.
In that way, my own position will be clear enough for my
conclusions to be understood and judged in the light of what
may be taken to be my own preconceptions, one of which is
that no human experience should inhibit us from pointing out
falsehoods, absurdities and non-sequiturs (not all preconceptions are mistaken).

Let me begin by saying that I respect the geniality of Friedlander's purpose; I doubt neither the honesty of his calling nor the
humanity of his hopes. However, he affects to be engaged in,
for want of a better term, philosophical speculation; he cites
impressive authorities and believes himself to have substantial
intellectual allies and sources. It is exclusively with his philosophical assumptions and arguments that I wish to engage. I do

Review of Albert H. Friedlander, *Riders towards the Dawn*, in the
Jewish Quarterly, 1993.

not know Rabbi Freidlander personally and I have no desire to
demean him; on the contrary, it is by taking their arguments
and assumptions seriously that we establish our intellectual
respect for those whom we question.

I shall concentrate on the points which immediately excited
my doubt or my amazement. My criticisms are not, to the best
of my belief, of passages malevolently torn out of context.

Let me begin with a simple instance of divergence. In his
introduction, we read:

> 'Are we only to turn to the religious establishment at a time
> when we know that religion has failed in countless ways? Who
> else should instruct us?
>
> Today, people flee across a darkened landscape and have no
> time to give or to receive instruction. Nevertheless, one may begin
> to discern a group that I have called the Riders Towards The
> Dawn: those who come out of darkness and have not forgotten
> it, but who also know that dawn lies ahead, and that they must
> journey towards it.

In his supposed zeal to be fair to everyone, the non-religious
as well as the religious, Friedlander manages at once to overstate
his case and to fudge it. The overstatement is in the diagnosis
no less than in the putative cure. *Do* people flee across a
darkened landscape? Of course, some people may, but whom
do you know who is in that condition now? The image of the
world in a state of such panic that there is no time to teach
or to learn is, for most readers, entirely melodramatic. An
immense amount of 'people's' time is spent in watching vacuous
television or in trying to make more or some money. Leisure-
time today, whether because people work less hard or because,
in painful cases, they have no work at all, allows great opportunities for learning; the problem is not a lack of time but
an appetite for crassness, sponsored by the kind of society
which Mrs Thatcher made and the ennobled Lord Jakobovits
endorsed. It is wholly exaggerated (especially for those who
live in Western Europe) to pretend to inhabit some particularly hazardous present when in fact part of our – the post-
Holocaust Jews' – imaginative, intellectual and, in some
cases, religious crisis derives from the fact that we have reversed
the old Dantesque notion of hell: we do not look back on
happy times while unhappy; most of us look back on unhappy

times (endured by others) while in a state of luxurious security.

It is true, of course, that there are those, like Friedlander and Elie Wiesel, whose reading of the world is dignified and marked forever by personal experience. It is not for those fortunate enough to have suffered almost nothing (except a fright) to reject their sense of what the world means, but nor is it for them, or anyone else, to insist that inadequate arguments can be validated by virtue of their (or anyone else's) sufferings. It may be admirably modest of Rabbi Friedlander to say that he has many teachers, but maturity requires a critical response to what one is taught. It is suggested by the unanswered question 'Who else should instruct us?' that, in the present penury of philosophers, only religion can lead the way. Honouring a certain ecumenical latitude, Friedlander seems to think it tactless to claim that Judaism alone is right, and so we are left with hints that Francis of Assisi and other worthies, from other camps, have their contributions to make to some omnium gatherum of spiritual wisdom, consolation or 'knowledge'. However, no secular philosopher of the smallest competence, alive or dead, is seriously considered, although the cant requires that Kant be mentioned. A succession of variously blinkered rabbis turn out to be the only people whose ideas deserve respectful attention. This kind of deference is comely in its way, but as a method it has a very blunt edge. Finally, it serves only to show how limited is the author's idea of an idea: piety and lack of trenchancy are dull intellectual companions.

To say that 'What can I know?' is 'answered by metaphysics' is an absurdly tendentious statement; to claim (in Kant's shadow) that ethics answer 'What shall I do?' and religion 'To what can my hope aspire?' is equally void of modern intelligence. Of course, in his usual fudging way, Friedlander tells us that the 'Dawn-Riders' (a recruiting phrase with a great deal less charm for me than it has for him) 'are not strict followers of philosophical injunctions', as if it were meritorious to ignore logic or as if philosophy were indeed composed of 'injunctions'. The claim that Primo Levi 'is also a poet' (*is* he?) once again suggests, datedly, that poetry is able to transcend the prosaic world of reality and gives us privileged answers. To speak, with reference to Eugen Taeubler, of historical writing as having 'narrow borders' is equally bizarre; here too poetry is supposed to offer an opportunity for a higher expression of the historian's truth. Does it? Can it? Friedlander must be for broad intellectual acres indeed if he supposes that historical writing lacks scope. The truth, I suspect, is that he cannot endure the idea that secular 'disciplines' could possibly, and under any circumstances, offer sufficient means for the investigation and understanding of the human condition (he sees 'anthropology' as answering the question 'What is the human being?', one which is, in any case, unlikely to be posed fruitfully, if it is ever posed at all).

Friedlander concludes his introduction with this:

> The murders of our time were born in the Holocaust, when human beings were expendable. But viewing human beings as expendable preceded Auschwitz; the land enclosures of an earlier time, the use of famine in Ireland, the discovery that economic problems are solved if you value land or products more than the human being, all of these preceded Auschwitz but became part of it.

This paragraph manages to be both perfunctory and repetitive before showing itself to lack historical sense. It is, in the derogatory sense that the French use the word, an amalgam. It is also painfully inelegant: what can it mean for murders to be born? The question is not casual, or trivial; the misuse of language betrays the frivolity, however solemn, of the author. In his effort to give Auschwitz some kind of aetiological pedigree, he then analogises land enclosures with the expendability of human beings. It may be that the enclosures were cruel or unjust, but they were not exterminatory (some argue that they led to the mass movement to the cities which created the industrial revolution and that the rural masses actually had a higher standard of living as factory fodder than as haymakers). The waffling synopsis of *idées reçues* is not a promising method in a teacher, or a pupil. There is no explanation of how famine was 'used' in Ireland, but the suggestion is that it was an implement of policy, whereas it is truer to say (as Cecil Woodham-Smith's book makes painfully clear) that the English authorities did not know what to do and were swamped by the fact of crop failures and their own inadequacy: it was not in their *interests*, nor in their metaphysical scheme, that the Irish peasants should die, though this can have been small comfort to the starving. Friedlander wants to create a category of common experience in which the extermination of human beings is regarded as natural or desirable, but he has chosen ineptly. He does not mention modern warfare which, from the American Civil War onward veered towards the tactics which became overt at Verdun, where the mincing machine was set in motion, by both sides, each calculating that the enemy would suffer unsustainable losses. After the war, Siegfried Sassoon (a brave anti-war campaigner) wrote of taking part in a victory parade where he wished that the troops would turn and kill the civilian crowds which cheered their passage. If one wants to understand the residue of violence which marked the 1930s and stained the 1940s with the infamy of the camps, it is worth looking at European history, although no causal link between the Great War and 'Auschwitz' is necessarily established. It is also worth looking at the tradition that 'religion' conveys knowledge and supplies warrants for the destruction of heretics, but to do this would, of course, require Friedlander to look at his own credentials and to challenge, with less than ecumenical amiability, the record and purpose of other 'faiths'. The only path along which he cares to ride towards the Dawn appears to be the Rotten Row of *bien-pensant* platitude.

A little further on, we are treated to this summary of the problems facing Jews and Christians as we enter the twenty-first century: 'Myth can be subsumed by faith, which is so highly sensitive to the truths of its mythology that it can move away from the keen razor-edge of the connections between the events of history.' Can anyone make sense of this observation? What does it mean for connections to have a razor-edge and how do we know what connections there are, of any kind, between the events of history? (The notion of an 'event' is itself problematical.) To speak of the 'truths' of the mythology of a faith is at once to uncouple what we mean by truth from any notion of verifiable content and to say that speculations, conjectures and dogmas are in some sense true. To claim that they are valuable, or tell us something about the spiritual life (how rarely one sees any instances of that form of existence!), might have some metaphorical validity, but to speak of the truth of mythology is simply to seduce the reader into believing that one 'truth' is as good and as unchallengeable – and, of course, as unverifiable – as another. It is to abandon philosophy for wishfulness; such a departure is. not forbidden, but it should be acknowledged for what it is.

Next case, a little further down the page:

We listen to them (Christian as well as Jewish victims, observers, historians) and their answers are not always our answers. Twentieth-century humanity cannot be healed fully; we remain flawed and maimed as we enter the new century. But they do not bring instant healing.

Once again, and not by chance, the reader can scarcely believe that Friedlander is using a language he understands and in which he can hope to make us understand anything. What does 'but', in the last sentence, have to do with what precedes it? If 'They' refers to the 'answers' of the Christian and Jewish people mentioned above, what is the sense of the adversative? What would it be for us to be 'healed' and what conceivable cure is available for our flaws? (I know: the Talmud.) The oratorical blather blinds us to distinctions between worthwhile treatments of human failings and the eternally vacuous promises of 'faith'. When Friedlander goes on to display noble tolerance of the secular contribution and to say that 'the progressive Jew and the secularist are just as much part of the people of Israel as the Jew living in the fastness of Mea Sh'arim', one realises that actually he is smuggling religious fundamentalism into the arena of intellectual and social respectability under the guise of allowing non-orthodox Jews a voice in the debate. This is the tolerance of self-deception, if not of deceit itself.

The high regard in which Elie Wiesel stands has been earned in a way which few of us would dare to disparage. However, does Wiesel's experience mean that he is a great writer whose parables must be accepted without criticism? To speak of him as 'the greatest of the messengers in our time' is to abandon all notion of literature as a domain with important intrinsic values. For the truth is, Wiesel's novels and stories, unlike the scrupulous accounts of Primo Levi, are often wilfully tendentious. What unsentimental sense can we attach to the story of the little boy at the Seder, immediately before the Holocaust, who 'knows' that this was Elijah entering . . . sitting in Elijah's seat, drinking his wine?

Afterwards, he sees the stranger freely getting into one of the freight trains heading East, towards the death camps. And then he knows that this was Elijah; for, three days later, did not this Elijah, as in the Bible, ascend to heaven in a fiery chariot so that all that remained was ashes, and memory, and the knowledge of the fiery chariot?

With all humility, and profoundly aware of the shallowness of my own easy experience, I have to ask what sort of writing this is, what its purpose or its humane content is. To my mind, it is, however involuntarily, a reading which will do nothing to stimulate any worthwhile reflection. It concedes all practical action to the killers and finds empty consolation in a fabricated reading which is more embarrassing than impressive. If a frightened child could be in the least comforted by what he allegedly believed, that is one thing, but to suggest that this story is 'not fiction . . . (but) reality in its ultimate form' is to renounce all attempts to see the world as a real place at all. Wiesel's parables touch on the vulgar more than the sublime; his concerns are noble, their expression is often melodramatic and devoid of that modesty which great issues demand of those who are not themselves great.

Wiesel provides another supposedly salutary or illuminating text from his novel *Night*. Here Friedlander offers the interpretation of Dorothée Soelle, 'one of the great radical theologians of our time', of the passage in which Wiesel writes of the hanging of a child:

> Behind me I heard (a) man asking: 'Where is God now?' And I heard a voice within me answer him: 'Where is He? Here He is. He is hanging here on the gallows . . .'
> That night, the soup tasted of corpses.

Before we see what the great radical theologian makes of this passage, is it impertinent to remark that the narrator's internal voice says something which, if I dare to say so, sounds like an afterthought, conceived as a literary trope, but utterly improbable (and callously smart) in the actual circumstances which Wiesel suffered? As for the last *sentence*, it is so devoid of sensible content, so wilfully scandalous that one can only assume that its author has no sense of literary taste whatever. It is not a report of what anything vile tasted like; it is an unpalatable sentence taken from horror fiction and more likely to reduce than dignify, or worthily commemorate, what it requires us to take uncritically.

Yes, from time to time it is worth remembering that even writers such as Wiesel are not only witnesses of fact but the creators of the clothing in which they present it. What is defective in *Night* is not the character of the author but the character of his authorship. And now we have the view of the 'important Christian scholar':

> God ... hangs upon the gallows of Auschwitz and waits so that 'the beginning movement towards redemption commences from the direction of the world'. Redemption does nor come to man from without or from above. God wants to use man to work upon the completion of his Creation. Precisely for that reason, God also has to suffer with man.

According to what precision? Wait! Further down we are told:

> The decisive sentence that God 'hangs here, on the gallows' has two meanings. First, it is a statement about God. God is no hangman – nor an all powerful spectator (which would be the same thing) ... 'God' – whatever humanity makes of this term – is on the side of the suffering. God takes the part of the sacrifice. He is hanged ... Everyone, every single one of the six million was God's beloved son, God ... is not in heaven. He hangs there ...

We are promised that Wiesel has thus created a breakthrough in Christian thinking. It may be a breakthrough, but is it thought? The pious intrusion of Christian mythology into a historical crime may comfort the Christians, but what does it tell us about God or religion? It is hardly different, though Friedlander elects to ignore the fact, from the insolence of the cross being raised over Auschwitz. As for giving a meaning to the murder of a child, or saving the face of God on earth, well, it is for everyone to decide on his or her view of the merits of that trick. If it does any good to remove from the concept of 'God' any recognisable meaning, we are left with a Cheshire cat theology in which a sympathetic frown replaces Lewis Carroll's smile. Is this what is meant by new thinking about God, or anything else?

By the time we are told that a Rabbi who was previously unable to believe that God was active in the world had his faith in Jehovah restored by the Israeli victory in the 1967 war, and this view is not laughed to scorn, we must recognise that Friedlander is depending on the infantilisation of the human intellect (for which, in the United Kingdom, Lord Jakobovits and his protégés must carry much blame) and the loss of nerve which follows the various intimidations, crass and supposedly sublime, which have been our soft lot in a period of remarkable peace and recourse to superstitious clannishness in all too many domains.

There are few things more touchingly dispiriting than a second-rate philosophical work written with earnest goodwill, deference for the intelligence of putative 'masters', and an absolute lack of wit or edge. From the first pages of *Riders Towards The Dawn* one fears, from the style and the ecumenical amiability of the text that nothing dangerous or original is likely to be said; one can wait only for banal conclusions frowningly reached. The introduction begins with the most hackneyed of quotations (Grey of Falloden's remark about the lamps going out, in 1914). Although affectations of high cultural awareness lead, eventually, to the inclusion of some lines of Celan (so difficult as hardly to chime with the carillons of platitudes that clang around them), the possibly unwarranted impression left by this eclectic ramble is that it cannot require much capacity or excite much appetite for thought to be a modern rabbi.

The decline in the state of public philosophy since the time when Falloden spoke his only memorable words is manifest and alarming. It has become precipitous in recent years: what alert intelligence of the order of, say, Bertrand Russell, serves to chastise the charlatan or discomfit the dogmatist? The respect offered to public pundits and opinion-pedlars – provided they say what we want to hear and give an impression of careful conceit – has never been greater than in our mediatised times. I use the word 'careful' with deliberation: to 'care' has become the central quality required of those who hope for a mass audience or a Peace Prize. On the face of it, Friedlander's prose honours this demand with its perpetually rumpled forehead, its unassuming solemnity. The author has all the gravity of the modest scholar who imagines that there must be some connection between scratching his head and purposeful cerebration.

Was the Jewish religious leader always expected to be full of pessimistic hopes and unsmiling humours? Not all of those called upon to guide the perplexed can be expected to have the genius of Maimonides or the nerve of Nachmanides. It is now many years since the rabbinate preached convincingly to any audience but the convinced; prophets are rarely found among the salaried. If Jonathan Sacks has intellectual qualities, and unparochial generosities (as his remarks about Bosnia showed),

even the present Chief Rabbi is obliged, by pastoral circumstance, not to preach anything which might excite suspicions of
dispassionate cogitation.

Who can believe that, had we never known the events of this
century (if the twentieth century had been as 'progressive' as
seemed likely at its outset), the trend towards the secularisation
of the Jews would not have brought us, by now, to the point
where, while we might look to rabbis to marry and bury us (out
of antique piety), we should hardly expect them to be justifying
the ways of God to man? The moral disaster of the Holocaust –
I mean the disaster to morals – lies in the realisation of the
horror at the centre of 'civilisation', the enchantment of mass
murder in many eyes and minds. The triumph of unreason has
been unreasonably assessed, by orthodox opinion, in the
interests of atavistic regression. Solidarity with the dead is too
easily assimilated to immobilism and complacency. To some
unadmitted degree, certain orthodox rabbis' blaming of secularisation for the Holocaust is a kind of gloating.

Millions of murders can be counted but never accounted for;
in this the term 'Holocaust' symbolises the collapse of a
metaphysical and moral system and its substitution by statistics.
What the Holocaust was and what it can be said to mean have
nothing in common; that, in sum, is the horror. The tragedy is
that all those people were done to death; our imaginative
meagreness, our loss of confidence in man and mind, our sense
of loss are, in the light of those murders, the petty incon-
veniences for which, if we dare, we are left at liberty to pity
ourselves. What we have lost, one might say, is not only all
those people, whose names and characters recede from us even
as we bend our brows in the effort still to see them, or something
of them, clearly, our loss is also – and this we are tempted to
confuse with regret for those who were once alive – of the
rudiments of a system which seemed to reconcile our history
with the notion of God implicit in it. This is a naïve reading, I
daresay, of the world before 1941 (to choose the obvious
caesura), but its naïveté can be redeemed, if it matters, by
observing to what degree the existence of God, His place in the
world, was a matter of solemn or even skittish debate within
literature and even philosophy before the 1939 war. If 'progressive' opinion was, in many ways, anti-religious or atheist, God
was part of the pattern of language in which Eliot and Kafka
and even James Joyce chose to work. The ideas of justice,

including capital punishment, on which 'civilised' states affected to base their moral institutions presupposed (however 'hypocritically') that the soul existed and that God was merciful. We should never underestimate the significance (or even, in some sense, the 'sincerity') of cant.

The silence of God during and after 'Auschwitz' (to employ the honoured synecdoche) is also our silence *and our silencing*: it is the discovery that His saying nothing was hardly distinguishable from our having nothing to say to Him. God has fallen out of all but the most bigoted or the most credulous or the most superficial of human reckonings. The abandonment of the Jews, by God and by man, is emblematic of the general fear that we are on our own.

There was something irreparable, for all mankind (we are tempted to think), in the abandonment of the Jews by a God in Whom, under who knows how many cruel and humiliating regimes, they had retained the lineaments of what could still, hopefully, be called mutual confidence: the covenant was the Jews' one consolation and strength. According to one reading of Jewish history, favoured by certain ultra-orthodox minds, the great rupture of the nineteenth century (in particular), which prompted the deployment of Jewish intelligence in secular schemes such as, obviously enough, economics, psychology, physics and other germane fields, *bref* the apostasy of the intellectuals, was responsible for the catastrophe that struck, in particular, at those on whom they – the infidel, apostatic system-builders – had turned their backs. Friedlander is too amiable to endorse such crass anathemas, or even, I daresay, to entertain them, but he has chosen to concentrate his attention on 'Riders Towards The Dawn' who show no sign whatever of engaging with modern thought, of allowing for the existence of modes of theological consideration of the order, say, of Wittgenstein's suggestive, if self-parodyingly allusive and discontinuous, remarks on religion, who have packed themselves the lightest possible breakfasts, so to say, in terms of anything that might challenge the platitudes and tautologies on which their mental diet is to be nourished.

It might be said that to lament the *Shoah*'s effect on something so marginal (so demoralising perhaps) to Judaism as 'modern' philosophy is a kind of flippancy. Perhaps to regret the quality of the mourners, and the level of their discourse, is indeed a way of avoiding any direct view of the pit from which there can be no resurrection. However, it could be argued, if we were to apply the full rigour of our perceptions (of experiences, I cannot speak), the smallest show of optimism, any furtive attempt to find sunshine in the days to come, any piety reconstructed from the exploded shambles of prelapsarian Judaism (or any other 'Faith'), is also bound to be a straight-faced fraud, an unseemly joke, a deliberate falsifying of terms of reference, of evidence, of reason, of probability, of what 'the presence of God' ever was meant to mean at a time when it meant something. One has only to look at the un-naïve arguments of Nachmanides, and his criticisms of Christianity, to see how lamely and, it could be said, dishonestly it is now habitual to conduct religious debates and to confront the fundamental questions of 'theology' (it is, as even Hyam Maccoby points out, improper to suppose that Judaism, in its days of engaged intellectual courage, actually had a theology). The retreat from those affectations of privileged authority typical of Sephardic rabbis, even in the years of anguish and persecution, is signalled by the accommodating genialities of our modern Men of God, even as they seek to enforce their rigour on a community which, at the orthodox limit of prescriptive hybris, is supposed to find virtue in arranged marriages, enforced endogamy and who knows what other *a priori* duties.

Friedlander, although elastic in his rigidities, makes one ask whether there can ever be a worthy response to the catastrophe by anyone who still sits within the boundaries of the old thought. How can anyone now hope to sustain the great tradition of continuity on which the rabbinate, at any level of orthodoxy or putative *aggiornamento*, is bound to base its cogitations?

What would it be, one keeps wanting to ask Albert Friedlander, to respond duly, in his terms, to the Holocaust? Then again – and here we interrogate ourselves and our betters – what would it be, in Wittgensteinian terms, to say something *deep* in the light of these things? Can one imagine anything more historically vulgar, more morally shallow, than the views of that rabbi, courteously esteemed here as a *thinker*, whose faith in God was revived by Israel's victory in 1967? What kind of crass credulities will not serve the ends of religious leaders if this is the level of their recruiting sermons?

The loss of intellectual nerve among Jews, betokened by the kind of nonsense to which we are expected to listen with a tolerant sense of 'community', may well be due not only to the central trauma of the *Shoah* but also to the collapse of alternative scientific or pseudo-scientific logics, in particular Marxism. With the discrediting of explanatory and prescriptive secular systems, the worldly and outgoing confidence of the apostate has increasingly been replaced by a slightly shamefaced, introverted nostalgia for *Yiddishkeit*, of which a significant, if trivial, instance might be that ay-ay-aying parody of schnookdom at which both Howard Jacobson and Clive Sinclair play when in their plain-man clothes: both are competent and homegrown users of the English language who caper in kaftan and bells the better to remind us all that there's something we can't get away from, however well we think we can pass for what we aren't. Eh, boys?

Friedlander's text wholly lacks literary artifice or any sense of the ambiguities to which 'modernism' has alerted us. For simple instance, it does not occur to him to admit the degree to which the Holocaust is not seen as regrettable, shameful, unrepeatable, whether in the eyes of the sadistic, of the ideologically crass or – most alarmingly of all perhaps – the shameful (for whom the elimination of all evidence for the shame they should feel is an unconfessed temptation). Friedlander's account of motive, argument, even of hope itself, is naïve to the point of monotony: whatever ground it covers is immediately rendered flat.

The Party's Over

Why should François Furet's magnificent new book appear unimportant to English eyes? *Le Passé d'une illusion: essai sur l'idée communiste au XXe siècle* made a great impact in France, when it was published earlier this year [1995], at roughly the same time as David Pryce-Jones's *The War That Never Was*, a diligent and well-researched account of the implosion of the Soviet Union. By contrast, Furet's 570-page essay deals not at all with recent politics or politicians. It is a rueful meditation on the claims of Marxism – and of the Soviet Union, its supposed objective correlative – on the consciousness not of its own citizens but of those in the West, especially French intellectuals, who were for so long bewitched and stultified by its myth.

In an inversion of the Platonic case, those inside the Communist cave were soon alert to the truth to which they were chained; only those who lived in broad daylight gave credence to the flamboyant fabrications which they swore they could see projected on its walls. Perjury was the art-form which united Eluard, Sartre, de Beauvoir, Vailland, and countless others. Since Furet himself was in the Party from 1944 to 1956, his indictment of western Marxists' ostentatious bad faith marries confessional rage to unblinkered assessment. His earlier desentimalisations of the French Revolution make him particularly alert to the quasi-paternal pride – one of our boys! – which French intellectuals, especially admirers of Robespierre, could take in the incorruptible rigour of Stalin (our own A. J.P. Taylor had the ferocious flippancy to call the murdering despot 'endearing').

Furet traces the dutiful docility of the French Communist Party with regard to the Soviet leadership down the decades from the Congress at Tours, in 1920, when the French socialist 'family' first divided into *frères ennemis* and the PCF was officially founded. The Communists aped Moscow from then until their last Secretary-General, Georges Marchais, concluded – on the eve of the eclipse of the Soviet empire – that the achievement of the People's Republics had been *'globalement positif'*.

Between 1920 and 1990, the influence of the PCF permeated French social and intellectual life; the vocabulary of Marxism was so inescapable that, for egregious instance, Jean-Paul Sartre imagined that it was literally impossible not to 'think Marx', as Isaac Deutscher also maintained. Only Raymond Aron, once Sartre's *petit camarade* at the Ecole Normale Supérieure, disdained what he called 'the Opiate of the Intellectuals', but he was proved right at the price of being regarded as a reactionary renegade. Even today, Paul Veyne, once his *protégé*, offers an interestingly disillusioned portrait of Aron in his *Le Quotidien et L'Intéressant*, where he attacks the great man for being so wedded to law and order. Veyne (a professor of ancient history) is also the author of an essay, *Les Grecs, ont-ils cru à leurs mythes?*, which is germane to an understanding of how intelligent men both do and do not believe in ideas which later seem manifestly incredible.

Furet is most revealing of himself when he tells how he read Koestler's *Darkness at Noon* without being disillusioned at the systematic humiliation of Rubashov, the doomed old Bolshevik. On the contrary, he thought how wonderful it was to serve a transcendental cause. What could be more liberating than to believe that there was something more important than one's own innocence or guilt? From such a view, it was a short step to holding that other people's innocence or guilt was a matter of mere bourgeois concern. The PCF was full of demanding and sinister *apparatchiks*, from Laurent Casanova, the intellectuals' drill-sergeant, to the literary paladin Louis Aragon who, with his cloying passion for his wife Elsa, supplied a paradigm of the loyal Party marriage. The tutelage of the PCF offered both a rigid guide to the perplexed and the prospect of an applauded career to many artists, from Picasso all the way down to those who depended on it for good notices. Its displeasure was brutal;

eviction could drive men to despair and suicide. Sadists and masochists could all be served.

The Party's reputation derived from being *le parti des fusillés*: it lived on the capital of its dead, the Resistance men and hostages who were the chosen targets of the Gestapo and the Milice. Many of them, in fact, had been foreigners, Jews and Spaniards, but they supplied posthumously naturalised evidence that the Moscow-driven PCF – wantonly deferential to the Germans in 1940 – was always more patriotic than French politicians of the Right, many of whom were compromised by Vichy or could be accused – de Gaulle *en tête* – of Fascism (the providential Other). The PCF peddled a morality which was both Manichean and perverse; the working class was flattered into obsequiousness to its leaders, while the intellectuals savoured the sweet pain of a conformity which dignified malice and certified self-importance. The Soviet Union became the City of God and the perversity of speaking well of it was a spiritual exercise that built proletarian muscle.

The apparent irrelevance of *Le Passé d'une Illusion* to England depends on the plausible assumption that the French Left was more thoroughly infatuated with Communism – after all, the PCF won a quarter of French votes in the 1950s – than the intelligentsia or workers of this country. In London, even in the 1930s, it required conspicuous credulity seriously to imagine that the future was to be forged and reaped by the hammer and sickle. There had been no British 'popular front' nor had the Left ever threatened the overwhelming conservative majority in 1930s parliaments. In France, on the other hand, the pre-war *bourgeoisie* was so thoroughly rattled that the slogan *'plutôt Hitler que Blum'* put the Jew and the Red under the same bed.

As far as the English working class was concerned, did not Marx and Engels concede, very early, that it was probably lost to the International cause? The British worker had been irremediably corrupted by his eager, if in fact meagre, participation in the profits and vanities of global domination. England remained apparently immune to the Marxist bacillus, except in the cleverest circles, well into the imperial sunset. Or did it? The degree to which the 1945 Labour government foundered on the attempt to extend democracy at home, while sustaining empire abroad, has given Corelli Barnett voluminous opportunities for irony, but its ideological contradictions have been less gloatingly examined. However, here too the Soviet example had its mimetic effect, whatever the Labour Party's insular moderation. In 1945, the Attlee government's vegetarian version of Stalin's bloody recipe for 'socialism in one country' was to offer the welfare state to electors at home, while limiting itself to the provision of British 'justice', and markets, to the empire. (Orwell's early experience, as a colonial policeman, of the difference between Whitehall-talk and distant practice may have had as much to do with his discovery of double-speak as his later exposure to Stalinist duplicities in Catalonia.) If the 1945 government was embarrassed by Britain's colonial possessions and pretensions, when did it ever suggest to the electorate that it was time to renounce their dividends? Answer: not until there were none. The Labour Party never trumpeted its allegiance to British hegemonic illusions, but it always shared them (the fatuous world-governing prescriptions of H.G. Wells and G.B. Shaw were equally underwritten by the imperial reach which they affected to deplore). Aneurin Bevan was converted, in opposition, to the nuclear deterrent because it kept Britain at the top table; his very British socialism was always a sentiment without a doctrine.

Is it a coincidence that Labour found the nerve, and the votes, to abandon Clause 4 only in the wake of Gorbachev's liquidation of the Soviet Union? The hard and soft Left had always been in uneasy balance, and had different agenda; as the present Tory party proves, broad churches are full of narrow sects biding their time. If some of Attlee's legates gloried in the global conceits of empire and Britain's fraying status as a world power, the Other Labour remained attached to the myth of revolution, of which Clause 4 was the ineradicable promise. While Ernie Bevin was the plain man's plain man and the best British bulldog Labour could breed, Sir Stafford Cripps was the Socialists' serious ascetic, principled enough to be blind to the horrors of Stalinism and eager for everyone in England to have an equal share of joylessness. (The British capacity for believing that lawyers are fair and wise is the long tribute the wigless pay to horse-hair.)

The existence of the Soviet Union weighed importantly in the counsels of the Labour Party. It fostered the notion that the mixed economy was a temporary compromise, which would be succeeded by something like the perfection which the Webbs had 'observed' in the USSR. The class system against which

Labour affected to preach was so crucial to its ideological line that, even in government, it had an interest in maintaining class antagonisms, not least in the work-place. The restrictive practices of the unions were the best guarantee that capitalism would never work, or work efficiently, in Britain. The hard Left's resistance to *In Place of Strife* indicates the degree to which the Marxist model retained its millenary charm: the immediate future of the United Kingdom was of small importance to those who wished to keep its ruinous 'contradictions' in place ahead of The Revolution. Whatever the manifestos said, harmony of the classes – and the attendant withering away of union power and class divisions – was an appalling, heretical prospect: Wilson had to fail in order for Marxism to succeed.

In short, if the British Left rarely spoke about ideology, it was never exempt from the sentimental callousness of which Furet writes so well. For petty instance, I remember so influential a Trades Unionist as Alan Sapper (at the time secretary-general of my union, the ACCT) telling me, long after the exposé of the Gulag, that the Soviet Union was still the working man's best and brightest hope. As for 'intellectuals', when I asked a famously evangelical English playwright of the 1960s to sign a petition for the release of political prisoners, he declined on the ground that, though not a member of the Party, he felt he must honour his 'loyalty to the Soviet Union'.

The English are fortunate that most of their sins have been of omission, but – as Anthony Blunt slyly proved – their temptations were not always so different from those which took fellow-travellers to the Potemkin villages where *bien-pensant* tourists, often writers, saw only what suited them (and their hosts). The Soviet lure was particularly seductive to those who, lacking what they took to be their due of success or influence, fancied a secret, new aristocracy in whose ermine they could hope one day to emerge coped with power. Here we verge on unfashionable topics, most obviously the conscious *perversity* of Blunt and others (Burgess being the camp version) in their two-faced enthusiasm for both of the circles in which they operated, the red and the blue. Alan Bennett made a convenient comedy of this vice in *An Englishman Abroad*; when in doubt, we can always be twee, and popular.

Just as accounts of anti-Semitism tend to ignore the *pleasure* of persecuting others, so attempts to understand Communists flinch from acknowledging the joys of conspiracy, deceit and seduction. When Anthony Blunt spoke of his conscience, he was having the last laugh. What is attractive about spying, as about all duplicities, is that it loads the rift with ore: every action becomes succulent and significant. For Philby, treachery was the sweetest kind of adultery; for Blunt and Burgess, the queerest of perversities. Humourlessness blinds theorists, Left and Right, to the ubiquity of the pleasure-principle even in the grimmest solemnities. In his account of the purges within the Russian armed forces, John Ericson alludes to the 'grinning judges' who officiated, in full knowledge of their iniquity, over the condemnation of quotas of innocent 'spies' and wreckers. The lead came from the top, where – as Pryce-Jones recalls – Bertrand Russell's blood ran cold when he heard the 'guffaw' which Lenin uttered at the thought of executing hostages from the 'obstructive' Kulaks. True believers, on the other hand, are excited and seduced by dictatorial ruthlessness; Godfathers always attract a following.

Furet's title reflects, and throws back at us, Freud's *The Future of an Illusion*, in which Vladimir Nabokov's 'Viennese witch-doctor' analysed religious creeds in terms of the fears and hopes engendered in infant minds by the coercive benevolence of fathers. Freud's 1927 reading of religion as 'infantile fear, awe, and passivity carried over into adult life' (Peter Gay's phrase) affected to be *tendenzlos*, un-tendentious. However, he was clearly disdainful of the theological 'illusion' which, for him, supplied mankind with a rationale for prejudice and, in the most principled cases, for massacre (Hitler was the most sincere modern politician, a positive idealist by comparison with Stalin). When the Nazis burned Freud's books, he observed, unpresciently, that things had improved, since a few hundred years earlier they would also have burned him. He did not live to learn how naïvely optimistic he had been in assuming that the Middle Ages were over.

There is an interesting coincidence between Freud and Marx with regard to religion. It is signalled, as so often in Marxist 'logic', by the fact that *The Future of an Illusion* was banned in the Soviet Union, although (unless it was because) Freud's reading of religion as superstition seemed consistent with Marx's. Freud's 'narcissism of small differences' operates here, as well, perhaps, as a warranted Russian apprehension that Freud was reading Communism as the Godless religion which Hannah Arendt and others later declared it to be.

Another tactfully neglected topic comes up here: the importance – not to say centrality – of 'the Jews', i.e. some Jews, in the
nineteenth/twentieth-century assault on antique pieties and distinctions. The spectre of Jewish particularity and the urge to be
done with its limitations converged in the common desire of
both Marx and Freud to disarm God as totem or ideal; modern
French history, and anti-Semitism, dates from Napoleon's conditional emancipation of the Jews, who were to trade their
communal identity for the individuality of citizens. The lure,
and propriety, of assimilation began at that point. Subsequently,
Jews of greater or smaller genius – starting, say, with Heine –
sought to efface their supposed, or feared, particularity. Some
of the greatest of them proposed universalising logics by which
humanity might (and should) live according to a single, 'scientific' truth. Truth must be true for everyone, Karl Popper
maintained: how can science endure parochial truths? The
positivist moralisation of reality – whereby 'is' entails 'should' –
was implicit in the programme to eliminate 'metaphysics';
philosophers proposed to make Science the impersonal and law-
giving arbiter of correct conduct. To be on the side of inevitabil-
ities was a guarantee of rectitude; conformity to 'a certain kind
of necessity' was a panacea for alienations of all kinds. Jewish
intellectuals were not alone in this kind of argument, but it is
unduly reticent not to remark the frequent urgency of their part
in promoting universally valid (and thus unarguable) solutions
to present discontents.

Freud, like Marx, was obsessed with proving that his ideas
were neither transitory nor parochial: by his keenness to have
Jung second his theories, he tried to detach the tag of purely
Jewish manufacture from psychoanalysis. Both he and Marx
were 'Jews' for whom the stereotype – clannish, cringing and
compromising – served as a point of urgent departure on the
way to a common prospect, and a common character, for all
humanity. It required only (only!) the renunciation of the
implausible and divisive pieties of 'religion' to procure an
undifferentiated world in which, by pure coincidence, they
themselves would be as indistinguishable as everyone else. The
Holocaust was Hitler's refutation of their argument: the 'doctors' plot' (and his 'anti-Zionism') was Stalin's.

The final, paradoxical form taken by the illusion that Jewish
identity was a matter of choice was the assertion by Parisian
students, in May 1968, 'nous sommes tous des Juifs allemands';

Jewishness was thus 'inherited', in safe circumstances, by 'revolutionaries' who used it to bait the Right and blessed themselves with the sweet halo of victimisation. Such impertinence has its *locus classicus* in the tag-line of one of those (American) Jewish stories which are not for Gentile ears: the rabbi is telling his congregation that, whatever their riches or achievements, they are nothing in the eyes of God. The old black janitor happens to be clearing up at the back and is so affected by the rabbi's sermon that he calls out, 'You'se right, rabbi, we'ze *nothin'*!' The rabbi looks up and says, 'So now look who wants to be nothing!' In *The Imaginary Jew*, Alain Finkielkraut has written well, if belatedly, on the succession of impostures on which the *soixante-huitard* generation preened itself; the art form of our time is parody, of which Marxist jargon – oh peace, oh democracy! – was the wildest and most widely practised version.

What is left of the red millennium in the light of the collapse of the Russian prototype? The idea of revolution has had one substantial meaning behind all the variant readings: it implies a turning-around of, above all, *debts*. Their revocation was a constant theme of ancient 'revolutions'. Indebtedness is implicit in conservative societies; as Jacques Derrida points out, in *Specters of Marx*, inheritance is only its purportedly happy instance. Literally or metaphorically, the past makes demands on any society which cannot rouse itself to be quit of the dead. The greatness of their past weighs so irksomely on modern Greeks that they are diminished by the inability to match it. It could be said that Britain's recent celebration of 1945 was a covert way of seeking finally to be done with the fathers and grandfathers whose courage and stoicism are so admirable that we cannot wait to bury them.

Marxism's 'scientific' claims have been thoroughly blown away, but what about 'science' itself? One of the 'self-evident' ideas which determined the programme of the Enlightenment was that of human consciousness originating, at birth, as a *tabula rasa*. However naïve it now seems, Locke's argument for universal suffrage derives in great part from it. In the light of Crick and Watson's uncorked genius, it could be claimed that democratic theory is based on a fallacy (on Freud's view, so is Chartres Cathedral). Who can say what role 'science' might soon once again take in warranting another totalitarian theory? The internet culture promises that the confusion of information into new, supposedly universalising theories is more likely to accelerate than abate in the near future. How soon will some nascent Rightism maintain that, if the new-born have innate, genetically-programmed distinguishing marks, it follows – with a brand-new inevitability – that the fetish of universal education, health care and, finally, suffrage involves a waste of economic resources and distorts human prospects?

In *The State We Are In*, the applauded Will Hutton urges, most genially and concernedly, that we should (must?) be more like the Germans and the Japanese, who are quite shamelessly practical in grading their young, almost from birth, in terms of the economic imperative of fostering their talents, provided they can be proved already to have them. The 'necessity' to conform to the future's scientifically pre-determined standards for survival makes democracy a mutable concept. All kinds of corporatism, and corporationism, may soon be declared more truly democratic – or at least more utilitarian – than mere individualism. One kind of 'scientific' blueprint *peut en cacher un autre*; indeed one ideology not only can, but almost certainly will, hide – and presently give birth to – another. The merit of Derrida's insufferably indispensable *Specters of Marx* lies in its tortuously maieutic necromancy in declaring, as Furet's lucidity does not, that we are never fully done with the dead. The Party may be over, but can we be quit of the mess? Rough beasts do not always need to shamble as far as Bethlehem to be born. If events in the Balkans suggest anything, apart from the abiding shiftiness of man, it is that when the masses are denied a chance to look forward to the future, they will once again look forward to the past.

Loving Garbo

In heaven, they say, there is neither marriage nor giving in marriage, though the elect will have to wait and see whether they still have appetites for the *foie gras* to the sound of trumpets which was Sydney Smith's alleged conception of bliss. What of hell? Its torments will almost certainly include doing will-she-won't-she time with Greta Garbo, whose sulky shade will – on the evidence of Hugo Vickers' account – give *foie gras* the allure of dog food. As for the trumpets, what a monotonous fanfare she will oblige them to sound! Luckless egotists will be condemned to the second-fiddling part of Cecil Beaton and the perpetual re-enactment of a romance so anguished and yet so puerile as to lend Barbara Cartland an aura of Stendhalian grittiness.

The puerility of Garbo and her long-time follower was literal: each, by turns, played the boyish role. Cecil regularly and roguishly wrote 'Dear Sir' letters to a surly Madame who seldom replied. If their protracted transatlantic affair had been nobody's business – or pleasure – but their own, how welcome they would have been to each other! However, Beaton found it as hard to conceal his feelings as Garbo did to have any. Since exhibitionism was his way of life, just as self-effacement was her perverse form of Narcissism, he could not resist publishing

---

Review of Hugo Vickers, *Loving Garbo: the story of Greta Garbo, Cecil Beaton, Mercedes de Acosta*, in the *Spectator*, 1993.

his diary of their improbable *chatouillements*, though he should have guessed that it would lead to his being added to Greta's garbage.

Cecil Beaton's reputation, like flaky pastry, does not keep very well. His datedly posed and lit photographs of a royal family which still had iconic significance are the work of a Mr Toady who worked sedulously for the social advancement which began in the 1920s, when he was a small star, slowly shooting upwards, in the firmament of Brian Howard. He was, in a sense, the Good Fairy to Brian's bad, eternally *disponible* to the extent, so he reported, of it being 'quite usual . . . never to put on ordinary clothes for a week or ten days at a stretch': his early life consisted of a whirl of fancy-dress party-going. Where Brian's mordant malice kept him panderingly alert to the blinkered perversity of the *Beau Monde*, Cecil was – like Evelyn Waugh, who bullied him at school – an *arriviste* who was emulously eager to get there.

He was also hard-working and, like so many bogus talents, deeply sincere: he had a great many feelings. Although primarily homosexual, his desire for Garbo (or for a famous connection) was sufficiently ardent for him to prove a satisfactory lover, on the relatively few occasions when she consented not to be alone. Garbo either hid her face, and person, like a blanketed police suspect or displayed a penchant for get-'em-off nudity. Her off-screen performances gave the impression that she had better things to do than to act, but it is clear that acting was all she could do. Unwisely, she preferred her own repetitive scripts to other people's; her self-styled scenes were of stultifying monotony and, with no Lubitsch to cry 'cut', they went on for *decades*.

It is not difficult to withhold sympathy from Beaton, but he has been so gloatingly mauled by Waugh *père et fils*, that it smacks of pleonastic plagiarism to join in the derision. Why deny him a shaft of the flattering light which he threw with such ennobling skill on his egregious sitters? He may have fallen in love with an *idea* of Garbo, and with that God's-gift-to-photographers profile, but he did go through the long and finally lacerating simulacrum of a passion for someone who, like Proust's Odette (whom Garbo was born to play, and probably never heard of), was not of his *genre*. Cecil was a naïve and sentimental lover, who was at first amazed by the success of his suit; not yet an A-list celebrity, he was unlikely casting for Armand to Garbo's Marguerite Gautier, a part in which she had languished with such tubercular artistry that the camera caught her beautiful cough.

It remains a mystery why she abandoned the unreal life of the movies for the even less real pent-housed vacuousness of the early retirement to which she removed herself. If she hated Hollywood, she does not seem to have relished New York, where she carried on a sequence of three-sided relationships, in which Mercedes de Acosta, a go-get-'em Lesbian who, in her earlier years, rarely went fishing without a catch, and Georges Schlee, the allegedly sinister husband of the legendary dress-designer Valentina, were repertorial players. After various indis-cretions (of *course* published by Cecil in his gabby diaries), Mercedes was finally labelled NOT WANTED ON VOYAGE by the peregrinating Garbo for whom Georges was *cicisbeo*, travel agent and Russian Orthodox Svengali, though he failed to re-start her career. Playing the triangle was Garbo's only lifelong art.

She may or may not have granted Schlee sexual favours (she was not hot for sex, but the Nordic tradition did not make heat a requirement); certainly she liked to play Georges off against Cecil. After Schlee's death, Garbo and Valentina – who only then dared to vent her hatred of her husband's love for the star – continued to live in the same apartment block; it was an economy to be able to cut each other dead without having to leave the building.

Throughout her life, Garbo found an avid market for her demanding cruelties; only the very occasional acquaintance had the nerve to tell her what a mean-spirited tightwad she was (she had managed her finances, at least, with enriching worldliness). The late Count Friedrich Ledebur was her companion on a 'camel trip' when 'Garbo refused to pay her share or to sign the photos their guides produced: "I'm invited, I don't pay." Ledebur was furious: "You're invited? By someone with a tenth of your money." He made it clear that if she didn't do both things, she would be left in the desert. She did both.' Pity, really.

Hugo Vickers seems thoroughly at home with the nobs and (more often) snobs of the *entre deux guerres* for whom the 1939 war was a an irritatingly loud interruption of their self-indul-gences. In the world he depicts, first-nighting is an act of dedication and the Windsors pass for good company. Since Cecil was shrewd enough to take copies of the *billets doux* Madame destroyed, his letters and diaries are at the heart of an affair as substantial as a macaroon. But then what is more spiritually uplifting than to read about a bunch of spoiled, weepy, greedy, spiteful people who, between gushes of self-pity, give each other the hell which they so richly deserve? Sir Cecil was to discover that Loving Garbo was like loving Eurydice: he needed only to look back and there was nothing there.

Aspects of Garnett

The man I was going to see, at an address deep in the Quercyois landscape, was born when Queen Victoria still had another nine years to reign. He knew D.H. Lawrence, before the first world war, and rejected – reluctantly – a seductive overture from Frieda. He played at sea captains with Joseph Conrad – a laundry basket for a ship, sheets for a sail – and he was recruited by H.G. Wells for a barnyard variety of badminton invented by 'the Don Juan of the intellectuals'. He test-drove a speedboat designed by T.E. Lawrence at a time when the latter was seeking to forget Arabia and bury himself in the lower ranks of the RAF. David Garnett had been at Hamspray, Lytton Strachey's country home, when Dora Carrington died after shooting herself; she was heart-broken at Lytton's death and beyond the consolation of her husband, Ralph Partridge, or of any of her occasional lovers, who included Gerald Brenan, Mark Gertler and Garnett himself.

Garnett was also at Charleston Farm, in Sussex, another of Bloomsbury's epicentres, at Christmas 1918, when Angelica Bell, who was to be his second wife, was born. Angelica (from whom Garnett eventually separated after she had given him four daughters) was later to write a bitter account of the deceptive frankness with which the founding fathers, and mothers, of Bloomsbury conducted their own lives and manipulated those of their offspring. She was raised, in repressive tolerance, as the legitimate sister of Julian and Quentin Bell, although her father was the bisexual Duncan Grant who had long been Vanessa Bell's lover. The rigged kindness of her parents left her more with a feeling of having been deprived of her identity than with any abiding sense of liberation.

The complaisance with which the senior Bloomsberries regarded their various liaisons depended on a morality which valued durable friendship above divisive passions. Lytton Strachey may have piped the view, at one famous international conference, that the most important thing in life was 'Passion', but he and his friends generally arranged for it to be subordinate to civility. If Angelica's retrospective reproaches were warranted, the children of what Leon Edel called 'The Lions' were more confused, and bruised, than they were emancipated by their elders' code of behaviour. It has been suggested that David Garnett's 'decision' to marry the infant daughter of Duncan and Vanessa was not purely 'romantic'; it might also have been an unconscious act of appropriating spite, since he had recently been rejected by Vanessa. In her memoirs, Angelica certainly gives the impression that, in retrospect, she feels that – like Simone de Beauvoir in another context – she had been 'had'.

When I was invited to see him, David Garnett was eighty-seven. If he belonged to a legendary group, he was not himself a legend. His name crops up frequently in chronicles of Bloomsbury, but he was never one of the central figures. Nor did he, like E. M. Forster, make a distinct reputation to rival Virginia or Lytton. He could console himself, if consolation was required, with sweeping minor triumphs such as *Lady into Fox*, which sold with suspect facility; as it turned out, his novel *Aspects of Love* was not to be famous until after his death. One of the reasons for his lack of centrality, among the Bloomsbury Olympians, was that he had not been at Cambridge with Leonard Woolf or Strachey or Maynard Keynes; he went to Imperial College, as Wells did, and he was never an Apostle or a homosexual (for all Bertrand Russell's flagrant dissent, the two things were, for a while, more or less indistinguishable).

If Garnett lacked the pale blue pedigree of Cambridge, his parents were well-placed sponsors when he entered the London literary world. Edward, his father, was a trenchant editor and discoverer of promising writers; his mother, Constance, was the translator and populariser of the great Russian novelists (Vladimir Nabokov, not untypically, had little esteem for her versions, especially of Tolstoy, but their readability cannot be questioned). Content to spend much of his life as an unobtrusive reader for Jonathan Cape, Edward Garnett was too much of a gentleman to seek to enrich himself through his acumen. However, he had the wit to recommend the young, unknown Somerset Maugham to Fisher Unwin and he was the first sponsor of the 'provincial genius' of D. H. Lawrence.

The Garnetts, like the Bloomsberries, were part of a self-regarding, yet modest élite, content to live in cottages and flats rather than town houses or country estates. They might be proud, but – at once respectable and aloof from convention – they abstained from being grand. Long before Lytton satirised Victorian propriety, David Garnett's father often paraded about the place negligently naked, in a practical rejection of prudishness. His son followed his example and, in his last book, *Great Friends*, printed a photograph of himself monkeying about, with naked agility, at the first-floor window of a bedroom which, we are encouraged to assume, was neither his own nor unoccupied.

What the Dreyfus case had been to France the Boer War was, in some respects, for England; like the Suez affair, just over half a century later, it divided families and ruptured the ideological solidarity, and the competent reputation, of the ruling class. Edward Garnett was opposed to the war; David followed his example by proclaiming himself a pacifist in 1914, as did Russell and others of the Cambridge connection. Summoned before a War Office board, when conscription was introduced, Lytton Strachey was famously to respond, when asked what he would do if he saw a German soldier attempting to rape his sister, 'I should seek to interpose my person', an answer which, if carefully analysed, may have been a little bit naughtier even than at first supposed.

David was a slightly uneasy pacifist; the early influence of Joseph Conrad – for whom Russell expressed a rare admiration and in whose honour he named his son – gave Garnett the feeling that, if he had acted rationally, he had perhaps also (shades of *Lord Jim*!) betrayed his manhood. However moral it was to abstain from bloodshed, might it not merit the scorn of the great novelist to absent oneself from the supreme test?

David was only six years old when he first went to France. Constance suffered from arthritis and it was believed that the dry air of Montpellier might ease her condition. It did, with the result that she and her son remained in the Hérault for six months, during which David was sent to a local 'dame school'.

He emerged bilingual and never lost his familiarity with the French language, though he was not at home in its literary tradition.

My visit to him was the consequence of an improbable coincidence. We had recently been in Taos, New Mexico, on a pilgrimage to see the notorious 'obscene' paintings of D. H. Lawrence, which were banned by Joynson-Hicks, otherwise known as 'Jix', when he was Home Secretary in 1929. Since the banning order has never been rescinded, the paintings remain under the threat of destruction if they are ever brought back to England. We had paid a dollar each to discover that they were of an almost cloying cosiness. The collection is the property of Saki Karavas, the owner of the La Fonda hotel in the main square of Taos; it is displayed in his office, where there are so many books, as well as pictures, that the windows are blocked out by the piles of volumes. A set of colour prints of heroes of the Greek revolution, including Byron, also hung on the walls. We happened to own several of the same set (we now have one more, which used to be Saki's and which he pressed on us).

Saki is remarkable for many reasons, not least his Greek zeal for art and literature (he has sent me many volumes of Cavafy, Ritsos and Seferis), but also for his refusal to allow the guests whom he befriends – and he befriends many – to pay their bills. Over the lunch Saki insisted on buying, he told us that David Garnett – who I did not know was still alive – had recently stayed with him. He had spent much of his time trying to persuade a stunning American girl to accompany him back to his cottage in the Lot. 'The stupid girl wouldn't go,' Saki said, 'even though I asked her what she had to lose. Ah, that David! He is still a lover.' He gave me Garnett's address, no more than thirty miles south-east of our house in the Dordogne, but I should never have approached him if, on our return, I had not been told, by a mutual friend, that he had spoken enthusiastically about a little book on Somerset Maugham which I had recently published.

When I did make contact, I accepted his invitation to lunch with a certain duplicity (he preferred to stay on home ground, rather than come to us). I might be approaching him piously, but how soon would I be tempted to become a publishing scoundrel? How much could I get out of him that he had not already divulged to other curious visitors? What was the young Lawrence to him today? Would he be glad to reveal, yet again, that Virginia was a bitch or that Vanessa had the warmer heart? How happy would he be to remember Carrington's androgynous/gynandrous attractions? Could I – never mind should I – persuade him to tell me, the last in a long queue, what he thought of Gertler or Lady Ottoline?

What suburban writer has never dreamed of belonging to just such an élite of the intelligent and the talented as Bloomsbury? (Even D. H. Lawrence, who called them 'beetles', fancied creating a pantisocracy of congenial spirits.) But then again, have we not all agreed that Bloomsbury was self-indulgent and over-rated? The Cambridge of my post-war day was instructed by the scrupulousness of Dr Leavis; he was the canonising censor for whom Bloomsbury's metropolitan eclecticism was anathema. I cannot say that I ever heard Leavis lecture, but the echoes of his sternness licensed a disdain which, no doubt, would have turned to devotion if, for instance, Morgan Forster had invited one to a glass of his sherry, however execrable Simon Raven reports it to have been. Forster was still in residence in King's when I was at St John's in the early 1950s, but I neither met him nor saw Wittgenstein before he died; we lived in the monumental shadow of giants it was too late to know.

To Frank Leavis, Bloomsbury lived on in the Sunday (and weekly) journalism which he regarded as so nugatory that he could never dismiss it frequently enough. Bloomsbury's unworthy levity lay in its lack of rigour; it viewed literature as an art rather than a morality. Leavis saw the group as a congeries of slack-wristed, elastic-sided intelligences, apt to mutual back-scratching and log-rolling.

I drove towards the Lot on a heavy day which followed a period of intense heat. My instructions were clear. David Garnett had been a pilot in his younger days; he owned an old German plane which he navigated for himself long before established air-strips and air-traffic controllers reduced pioneers to bus-drivers. He was also a countryman, alert to twists and turns, like the fox into which his lady heroine was transformed. Wittgenstein's pupil and my professor, John Wisdom, used her mutation to illustrate the difficulties of precise definition: at what point, he used to ask us at 9 a.m. in a Mill Lane lecture room, would one be inclined to say 'By Jove, now she's *definitely* a fox?'.

The steep, castellated town of Montcuq was my first marker.

From there I drove to the *château* of Charry, whose owners were Garnett's benevolent landlords. The luminous grey stone towers of the unfrowning bastion belong to the Penrose family; Sir Roland, Picasso's friend and biographer, was alleged to manacle the women whose favours he was enjoying, but he left Garnett in unfettered liberty. I skirted the *château* and found the lane blocked by a very large *remorque*, mountainous with baled hay. The field-workers were young and muscular and might have been posed by Poussin (the light gleamed on their half-naked bodies) or by Millais in illustration of *Aspects of Love*. By another coincidence, Garnett's novel was the first book I had reviewed, forty years ago, in the *Cambridge Review*; I had taken an early opportunity to advertise myself as no respecter of reputations. I now hoped that its author would not have been aware of my *engagé* rigour (nor was he). In fact, I still think the book to be a piece of tosh, rendered even toshier – if that is possible – by the current Lloyd Webber musical. What could be more naïve than a certain kind of wished for sophistication?

The bucolic scene (the trailer was being hauled by oxen) reminded me that Garnett was a field-worker during his period of conscientious objection during the Great War. He and others of like mind had had to be *employed*, although they had wanted to form a co-operative. The government accepted, *du bout des lèvres*, the objectors' right not to be conscripted, but it refused to allow them to be their own bosses or organise their own working hours. Perhaps it was at that time that 'Bunny' learned to endure the very simple life he continued to live in old age.

The cottage, with its weathered shutters and plank door, was the kind of place where, in a Grimm fairy story, someone rather good would almost certainly have been unjustly exiled. Adjacent to it was another, of much the same style, where guests could stay. When Garnett came down the path towards me, he was slightly bowed, very sanguine, with gleaming argent hair. He trod the pebbles cautiously, but without the aid of the third leg which Oedipus might have predicted. He wore beige canvas trousers and a blue shirt which matched those lady-killing eyes.

He seemed glad of my small gift of a bottle of Château Coutet 1975 and took me inside for a glass of the local red, which he poured from a silver-stoppered decanter. The cottage had a rammed earth floor and a double bed for one. There was a pine dining-table and cane chairs. Only the many books and the paintings – by Vanessa and Duncan Grant and their daughter – dispelled the illusion of artless rusticity.

'Bunny', as acquaintances were quick to call him, though I never did, had his daughter, Fanny, staying with him; if he seemed to accept solitude with grateful grace, she was there to make sure that he was not without help, if he needed it. He still cooked his own food and piloted his own Renault 4, somewhat in the Saint-Exupéry tradition of a wing and a prayer. If his exile was without regrets, and his life seemed full of happy landings, 'Bunny's' contented style was the result of decision as well as of good fortune. His radiance was dimmed, though he disdained an old man's tears, when he spoke of his first wife, Ray, who died of cancer after months of agony. Her sister, Frances, was and remains the most long-lived of all the original Bloomsberries; she married Ralph Partridge, after Carrington's death, and continues to publish her pointedly accurate diaries.

In the cruel light of his first wife's illness, 'Bunny' was less afraid of death than of pain. He had no use either for religion or for its advocates. He was a lifelong rationalist; clerics – of any order – gave him the creeps. 'We are all animals,' he said, 'we live and we die and that is all there is to it. Some people will believe anything, because they want to believe that there's something more. There isn't.' He was no less trenchant on other topics. D. H. Lawrence? 'He was a genius all right, if being a genius means changing the world, because he certainly did that, didn't he? We wouldn't be the same if he hadn't lived, even if a lot of his ideas were completely wrong.' Ezra Pound? 'Total fraud!' T. S. Eliot? 'Never knew 'im.'

Despite his Jesuitry, Gerard Manley Hopkins was Garnett's favourite poet. With an old man's youthfulness, he had an abiding scorn for Robert Bridges, who had, all those years ago, both pirated Hopkins' style and, for a long time, withheld his manuscripts because they were 'unsuitable'. 'Bunny' also admired D. H. L.'s poetry; he pointed out that so far from Lawrence's life having been shortened, as some venerators claim, by the harassments he endured so unphlegmatically, it was probably prolonged by them: D.H.L. suffered from 'what they call "indolent tuberculosis" – the only effective treatment for which, in those days, was large doses of adrenalin. Since rage releases adrenalin in massive quantities, every time his persecutors infuriated him, they probably gave him a fresh lease of life.'

Lawrence's regular exasperations may have been a specific against his sickness, but that did not entail that his diatribes lacked sense. His notorious description of Bloomsbury and its 'beetles' – a species unhappily exempt, it seems, from his rare capacity for empathy with the insect world – first appeared in a letter to the young Garnett, warning him expressly against the homosexuality of his friend Francis Birrell and, by implication, against the seductions of Strachey and Keynes.

The mature 'Bunny' regarded homosexuality with uncensorious distaste, although he was not, by all reports, a complete stranger to it. 'In my opinion, it's always a *pis aller*,' he said. His now unfashionable view was fortified by a conviction that Lytton's feeling for Carrington was far more heterosexual than is generally conceded by the gay fraternity (the keenest source of her passion was, of course, Lytton's *knees*). Despite Lawrence's warning, Garnett did not distance himself from Birrell, with whom he founded the Nonesuch Press (their edition of Hazlitt – recommended by Mr Maugham – entertained my adolescence, when I often travelled long distances on the Underground while in pursuit of love).

Lawrence's ability to see the mote in other people's eyes gave him no particular insight in his own case. In the days before the Lawrences' marriage, 'Bunny' and another friend, spoken of only as 'Harold', accompanied the couple on a walking trip in Bavaria, where Frieda was a lot more at home than her lover. Garnett failed to cuckold his father's protégé only because Harold already had: 'Frieda didn't yet realise what she'd got, you see – didn't appreciate what a genius Lawrence was. All she wanted was to get away from Weekley; Lawrence was the best way out. She was a lustful woman, you know, and used to getting what she wanted.' After D. H. L. found out about Frieda's roll in the hay with 'Bunny's' friend, he was as outraged as Professor Weekley had been (and his family still is). Both men accused the intruder of being 'no gentleman'. The apostle of the dark gods could turn very prim.

Garnett said that Lawrence's early paintings had been 'quite charming'. Only when he became a phallic propagandist did commitment compromise freshness. 'Bunny' spoke with confidence about painting; he thought Bloomsbury stronger in the visual than in the literary arts (a symptom, maybe, of an undying preference for Vanessa over Virginia, who might be an important writer, but was not, as he put it, 'important to me'). Over lunch – cold, green soup, a wide omelette, lumpy with *cèpes*, salad and a huge hoop of *tarte aux fraises des bois*, baked by Fanny – he deplored the excesses of the 'Eng. lit. industry' and its voracious appetite for reheated cabbage. There had, he said, been thousands of theses on D. H. L., 'nearly all of them either wrong or unnecessary or both'. There was an insatiable craving for 'new subjects for ill-informed research.' John Lehmann, a second-generation Bloomsbery, had recently told him that, as a result of lecturing on his memories, he was now richer than he had ever been as a partner in the Hogarth Press.

The recent biographers, Garnett observed, were ever richer, if more industrious, although he regarded most of them as 'inept and wrong-headed'. When I mentioned P.N. Furbank's biography of E.M. Forster, he was particularly scornful: 'It's *dreadful*,' he said, 'he simply doesn't know what he is talking about.' I introduced Michael Holroyd's name more delicately (Furbank had treated a novel of mine with the kind of honesty which critics display towards those who are unlikely to affect their academic prospects), but 'Bunny' thought Holroyd's brilliantly footnoted biography of Lytton 'almost equally wrong-headed, especially the first volume'. He suspected that Michael had begun in the hope of debunking the great debunker, but had then fallen in love with him, 'though never enough to get him right.'

What about John Woodeson's book about Mark Gertler, which I had found very convincing? 'Haven't read it,' he said. 'Couldn't stand the fellow, I'm afraid.' Why was that? 'The fact is, I rather think he spoiled Carrington.' It was an eccentric reading of the relationship between the besotted painter and a woman who according to the standard account, treated him with a teasing callousness which destroyed his virile confidence and drove him crazy, perhaps suicidal, with uncertainty. 'It was his own fault,' Bunny said, 'he had no technique – put her off the whole business.' His face remained straight and then he smiled. 'Well, he was my rival, you know. I adored Carrington, and then again – he didn't seem to think I was of any account. Same with Koteliansky, Lawrence's friend.' I asked whether Gertler's being a Jew (as was 'Kot') affected his attitude towards him. 'When a Jew annoys one, one calls him a bloody Jew. It goes no further than that.'

I recalled Quentin Bell suggesting that Leonard Woolf might have divided the world into Jews and *goyim*, although I doubt very much whether any middle-class, assimilated Jewish family in the Victorian age would ever use such a term; I never once heard my father, or his older relations, do so, nor can I believe it of so anglicised and cultivated a family as the Woolfs. If 'Bunny' had a certain grudge against 'the Jews', it derived from their monotheistic fervour and the moral obsessions which stem from the idea of a jealous and commanding God. It would be amiable to suppose that Virginia's prejudices were as reasonable.

In general, 'Bunny' disdained racism: his novella, *The Sailor's Return*, is evidence of his contempt for negrophobia, though its image of a Dahomey woman might not appeal either to feminists or to modern black sentiment. The Victorian Englishman came out in him when he maintained that we should 'withhold our technology from Africans, until they learn how to behave themselves.' This view was excited by the recent excesses of Idi Amin, though it was, of course, Europeans like King Leopold I of the Belgians who first practised genocide on African soil: six million Congolese were killed in a 'clearance' on his personal estates.

Garnett insisted that 'progress' was almost wholly a Western product and that we were 'peddling it round the world with shameful shortsightedness.' He preferred the arrogance of a Platonic (Fabian?) élite to corporate greed. To whom should philosopher kings be accountable? 'A Darwinian answer is the most plausible: success determines whether governors continue to govern. Always providing that the rulers can be drawn from any class, I don't care all that much about democratic control,' he said, 'or about the opinions of the masses.'

He deplored the rise of bureaucratic Socialism in England. When I met him, in the last summer of the Callaghan government, it seemed an irreversible phenomenon. He might have been any decent Edwardian squire when he declared that the British working man had lost pride in his calling ('It isn't yet so in France') and he did not hide the slightly surprising fact that he voted Tory in 1945. To maintain civilised standards required decisive qualities; it was not always safe, or natural, to be humane and well-mannered. Complacency subverted values which had constantly to be re-invented and re-stated. Art (including, I assumed, the art of pleasure) was the essence of what made life worth living.

I asked why, if death was indeed the end of everything, it was worth bothering with art. '*Because of that*,' was his emphatic answer. 'Since art is the only lasting thing a man can produce, it's worth the effort to make a contribution to it.' His age disposed him to take a Keatsian view of the relationship between beauty and truth: one of the worst things about his first wife's illness was that he found it impossible to tell her the facts.

After lunch, my host insisted on carrying my chair out onto the grass, along with his own, and we sat and drank some local *marc*. Rain began to patter high in the over-arching trees. Fanny cleared the dishes, like a good – if dated – daughter; one of her sisters, he told me, drowned herself, like her Aunt Virginia. Sir Leslie Stephen's appalled fascination with death was inherited by his daughters: Virginia's beloved brother Thoby died young, of misdiagnosed typhoid, and Julian Bell, his brother-in-law, was killed in the Spanish Civil War. Nor was David Garnett, in his Arcadian old age, exempt from the awareness of death. He had regrets, but he avoided lamentation. He had known some people and not known others; like many men who have had no trouble pleasing women, he was at once sensual and dispassionate. As for his friends, he loved and liked many of the Bloomsberries, but – unlike Virginia's necrophilous father, with his 'Mausoleum Book' – he lit no doleful candles. He thought best of Keynes, whose biographical sketches he preferred to Lytton's and on whose generosity the whole of Bloomsbury could bank, literally and metaphorically.

With regard to the future, education was the key. 'That's the trouble with America, you see. I'm very fond of Americans, but I'm sorry to say that over there they've had a battle between violence and education and violence has won. Education joins people together; violence separates them.'

When I left, after nearly five hours of his company, he asked me to come again. I should gladly have done so, but not many months later the friend who had introduced me to him went over to see him and found him lying dead among his grapevines; naturally.

Jewish Self-Hatred

This is an important and interesting book. Sander Gilman's arguments are perceptive without being either far-fetched or far-pushed. While advancing no monotonously polemical thesis, he avoids blandness or bogus broadmindedness. He does not affect to rise so high above his subject as to be impartial between malice and its objects. Yet his tone is sufficiently judicious for it to be difficult to know whether he is himself a Jew. His reading, as one would expect of a professor of German, is wide and impressive. His examples are drawn both from essential texts (Marx, Heine, Kafka, Freud) and from more *recherché* sources (Moses Kuh, Josef Pfefferkorn, M. G. Saphir, Otto Weininger). Modern authors such as Henry Roth, Philip Roth, the Singer brothers, Jerzy Kosinski, George Steiner and Saul Bellow are also acknowledged. No British writers are cited, which reminds us of dogs that don't bark in the, night. Two remarkable omissions are Wittgenstein and Chomsky.

The analysis of self-hatred begins with a definition: 'Jewish self-hatred [is] interchangeable with Jewish anti-Judaism and Jewish anti-Semitism'. If this delimits the scope of Gilman's study, it is unchallengeable. If it advances a general truth, it is unsatisfactory. The Jew who decides that Judaism is an unappealing religion or that it implies an arbitrary set of rules for

Review of Sander Gilman, *Jewish Self-Hatred: Antisemitism and the hidden language of the Jews* in the *Jewish Quarterly*, 1989.

living may have perfectly good reasons for rejecting it or criticising it. To insist that he is an instance of 'self-hatred' when he is explaining, without stridency or malevolence, his dissent from the religion in which he was raised or his intention to seek a wider society than his 'community', is to employ what we used to call 'persuasive definitions'. Tolerance – of a Gentile son-in-law, for instance – is not necessarily weakness or treachery. The temptation to regard all criticism as unwarranted or caused by cowardice may be understandable, especially in a cruel season, but it is authorised neither by logic nor by honour. Because I concede the possibility that God is not in His heaven (or that Galilee is not inalienably the property of a given sect), it does not follow that I am turned in against myself in some psychic civil war. The fact that I cannot run away from my own shadow does not entail that I must always applaud its shape. Gilman almost certainly would not maintain so totalitarian a view, but his opening premise might seem to imply it. (I will not spend time on the not vacuous question of whether all self-hatred felt by a Jew is Jewish self-hatred.)

The long theme of Gilman's study is 'the hidden language of the Jews'. This language is suspect and magical in the eyes, and ears, of the Gentiles: It is not, however, constant: at times Hebrew is meant, at times Yiddish, at times a fantastic hodge-podge of argots of various origins. At times Jews are feared, and even envied, for knowing the language of God; on other occasions they are despised (and still perhaps feared) for their diabolical codes. The systematlc charge is that they can never master the master-tongue, that of the Christian majority; hence they are natural liars. Even when they become apparently fluent in the public language, they can never 'wholly possess' it. This, supposedly, is 'because they have their own hidden language'. This might be better put as 'because their hidden language possesses them': everything that is not expressed in their naturally malign tongue is deformed by its unadmitted source in the private language. The Jew lives in translation; his role as trader, as the percentage-taking dealer in currency, is the mercantile correlative of this duplicity. If the Jew reveals, by his accent and his grammatical ineptitude, that he is an outsider, he can have no valid claim to belong to the 'reference group', those whose habits and style of living he would like to assume. If he successfully commands the grammar and accent of the majority, he is a dissimulator and deserves ejection. Whatever he does, he can never belong to any group but his own.

The only 'solution', as Herzl and Sartre both maintained, in different ways, is to embrace the difference and proclaim it as a virtue. The Jew is like Alice when she is through the looking glass: he can approach his goal only by walking away from it. Rejection can be defeated by turning it into a form of triumph. The revival of Hebrew as the language of a modern, secular state parades the hidden language and promotes it into the comity of honest tongues. Wittgenstein's rejection of 'private languages' and his insistence on the logical publicity of all languages is, of course, independent of the motives for its advancement; but it could be held, without distortion, to relate to his painful determination to hold nothing back, to make full disclosure, to purge himself of the guilt that (in racial and sexual form) haunted him. Giving away his private fortune, as he did, and all claims to exceptional status, to privilege, the reduction of self to a minimum and of language to what other people say or can understand, make him a crucial case.

The failure to deal with Chomsky is regrettable in two ways. It deprives us of the opportunity to have Gilman confront a particularly vexed case of what, on his terms, must be accounted self-hatred, though it is precisely Chomsky's good opinion of himself which seems to warrant the vigour of his dissent from sectarian allegiance. It also denies us consideration of a theory of language which, with its homogenising ambition, seems to be another attempt – not invalidated on this account – to deny the existence of special cases, of which the Chosen People might be held to be one. As I understand him, Chomsky insists on the inescapably common structural origins of all language and hence, by implication, refuses superiority (or anteriority) to any particular one. This is, of course, in line with scientific insistence on universality. Chomsky, Marx and Freud constitute a set whose theories are based on research, supposedly without preconceived purpose, but whose findings lead them to make claims about the nature of the world or of humanity and to draw ethical conclusions which, except in the eyes of their disciples, are not evidently consequential on them. Gilman's notion of self-hatred, as a means of understanding the motives of those who seek to escape their shadows, seems to be relevant to the study of all three, though it is worth pointing out that 'self-hatred', as an explanation, is liable to be as circular and self-justifying as Marxist or Freudian analysis. In order to escape this charge, Gilman would need to show how he distinguishes between self-hatred and rational self-awareness. Too perfect a scheme of psychological analysis – like the Freudian effort to account for everything obstinately inconvenient in my account of myself in terms of repression – becomes circular and vacuous rather than omni-competent. Gilman never considers whether or how self-hatred attacks other groups or individuals or, indeed, whether it is a necessary part of a great deal of conscientious behaviour. (Is Lady Bountiful a 'self-hating' aristocrat, seeking to persuade those who benefit from her generosity that she is not like the rest of her hateful class?)

The academic penchant of Jews (whoever they may be) can be read as the consequence of the intelligent desire to escape from the world of 'haggling'. The vulgar discourse of Jews, so the charge has run, relates to buying and selling (so, of course, does the vulgar discourse of peasants and of all those to whom the price matters, but who lack the muscle to dictate it). The scholar retreats, or advances, to a dispassionate (ha!) and impersonal world of timeless and objective rigour. 'In logic,' Wittgenstein said, 'there are no surprises.' Nor are there sales tags or practical dividends (at least until academic studies have televisual spin-offs). Thus the Jew can hope to detach himself, in higher education, from his contaminating personality: he ceases to be anyone in particular and becomes the mouthpiece of the general. True is true, no matter who says it. *My* son becomes *the* doctor.

It has always been part of the self-admiring myth of the Jew that, in medicine in particular, the Gentiles have turned, however reluctantly, to Jews for the solution of demanding problems, especially of health. Gilman points out the ambivalence here: it is not always the reputed highmindedness of the Jew that is admired, or hired, but rather his disreputable access to magic formulae and dark secrets. The doctor is not only a scientist, he is also a medicine man. Stalin's paranoid terror, when it seems that the trick is not going to work, is the sourest modern instance. The Jewish doctor, summoned *in extremis*, is judged only by results; he is a mediator with Death and is suspected of consorting with the enemy. (How can I ever know that this prescription is not poison?) Man seeks obstinately to find a scheme for the world which eliminates, or transcends, contingency. Even when an individual cannot himself believe in a world ordered by some inescapable logic, he tends to have a morbid interest in those who cleave to such a belief. (Hence the atheist has high expectations of the moral quality and intellectual resources of the pious.) Hatred of the Jew is bloody evidence of an excessive credulity in his knowledge of the arcane; Hebrew is the language of God, a code in which direct calls can be made to the ruler of the world.

The Greeks asked themselves, with a measure of humour, what language Achilles spoke when he was among the women, an allusion to a period in the hero's adolescence when he was obliged to hide among a group of young girls and pass himself off as one of them, for the sake of sanctuary. The notion that women, among themselves, speak another language continues to fascinate and alarm those of the other sex. The fear may simply be that they mock men, or speak of them with less respect than they deserve; the Gentile conviction that Jews have a private language and mock Christ in it, is not dissimilar. Kingsley Amis has said that it isn't worth talking to women, just as German jurists used to say that Jewish evidence was not worth taking. The suggestion is that both categories will say anything that suits them to get out of trouble. The charge that women 'have no shame' may owe something to their supposed capacity for unlimited orgasms; no natural incapacity puts a term to their pleasures or their demands. The violence often done to women is not infrequently accompanied by telling them to 'shut up', a phrase of ambiguous sense. The garrulity of the Jew, his supposed willingness to 'say anything', announces his affinity with the female. (Otto Weininger's denunciation of both women and Jews was based on this reflexive relation.) *Pilpul*, with its logic-chopping and its ceaseless *bavardage*, was the living proof of Jewish mutability: the disputant never stayed in one place, honoured one definition, stood by his word. Everything was exchangeable for something else in the process of pseudo-legalistic bargaining. The Jew spoke the language of Proteus and his capacity for mimicry made him dangerously polymorphous. You could not be sure whether he meant what he was saying or whether he was what he seemed. His antagonist on the other side of a linguistic barrier which was impenetrable to a Gentile might turn out to be his brother, or his cousin. Treachery was familiar to those who had betrayed God.

The furtive and duplicitous Jews of Christian mythology might not have become so appallingly significant but for the belief, embedded in Christian lore, that the Second Coming depended on their conversion. Johann Caspar Lavater is rightly cited as paradigmatic here: the Jews, he said, had to be weaned away from the rabbis and persuaded to become Christians. Their obstinacy overcome, heaven on earth would follow. This demand to snap out of anachronistic tiresomeness was polemical in 1768, but it became murderous when it was argued that the elimination of the Jews was as good as their conversion, or better. The same end would be achieved and no obstacle would lie between the majority of men and the bliss they craved. The Nazi argument was infantile as well as savage, but Freud would not be surprised at the conjunction. If it is true that Jews have often been persuaded that they were the bone that stuck in the craw of the world, their self-hatred is no more aberrant than the hatred which promoted it. Even Bertrand Russell, on a bad day, said that if it were true that the extermination of the Jews would procure eternal bliss for the rest of mankind, there could be no good reason not to endorse such a programme. Of course he maintained that it was not true, but he could see no flaw in the utilitarianism which supposedly warranted the murder of vexatious impediments to the greater happiness of the greatest number. Even an atheist like Russell flinched from judging God: if He said that something would be true, on bloody conditions, man could have no right or reason to refuse Him. Certain rabbis might have said otherwise: did they not once outvote the Almighty when He was in His most *dirigiste* form?

The strength of Gilman's book lies, as I have indicated, in the generosity of its examples and the plethora of questions it excites. This strength makes any review which fails to match the text in length and resourcefulness seem either skimpy or ungracious. To complain of issues not raised is hardly less carping, but it is clear that self-hatred is not limited to Jews, nor the charge (or fact) of inarticulacy or alienation levelled only against them. The black population of England, as recent surveys shows, is in a critical state of disintegration and despair. The blacks seem to lack an intellectual élite (though Jewish intellectuals are often accused by Jews of 'betrayal' or 'apostasy') which might give some sublime sense to their anguish. The contempt shown by some English Jews (and Americans like Norman Podhorctz) for blacks who cannot 'do what we did' reveals, if nothing else, the danger of self-love as a substitute for self-hatred. A measure of narcissism is perhaps an inevitable ingredient of self-hatred and has always been present in Jews, who, even in the darkest times, tend to believe that they are central to the world's (sometimes insane) logic. There is indeed something majestic in the margin's belief that it belongs in the middle of the page, even if this leads to grotesque readings, especially of world history or of the significance of events in it. Bruno Bettelheim's attempt to provide a rationale for survival in concentration camps, examined rather cursorily by Gilman, is among those efforts to look horror in the face which are at once honourable and addled. I question, with the greatest reluctance, the judgements of anyone who has experienced these things at first hand but it seems to me intolerable to make survival, in such circumstances, into a determinant of moral worth. Bettelheim and others (Terrence des Pres's *The Survivor* comes to mind) cannot resist flirting with the idea that the concentration camp was a kind of severe obstacle race, an assault course from which the worthy graduated and which the weak failed, through their own inadequate characters, to endure. The attempt to 'save the phenomena', as the Greek philosophers put it, leads Bettelheim, as it did Arendt, to maintain the idea of a just world, in which the worthy come through, in the face of all the evidence to the contrary. The victim becomes responsible for his fate, since otherwise fate becomes too strong for us. The idea that individuals or groups ought to be able to resist modern states, and that they have only themselves to blame if they lack the muscle, is so fatuous, so unfair and so finally conceited that it is hard to see how it can be advanced. The determination, however unconscious, to maintain that the world is somehow fashioned for the mortifying edification of the Jews is a perfect instance of narcissistic solemnity. It is matched only by the view that an American's patriotism is to be determined by the degree of his unquestioning allegiance to the State of Israel. To make anti-Semitism, *in any form*, the equivalent of *lèse-majesté*, a crime as heinous and as inexcusable, under any circumstances, as Uzzah's when he touched the Ark of the Covenant, if only to steady it, is to substitute for self-hatred a form of vanity which will procure that exclusion from the rest of humanity from which both Zionism and science, in different ways, were supposed to deliver us.

The Greeks

The Classics used always to exist in a wholly aloof world. For
the Old School, fifth-century Athens was a sublimely peerless
period in which The Good and The Beautiful were – alas,
temporarily – in tandem. In the dusty study of that unalloyed
golden age, Olympian detachment from both cussed politics
and sordid motives was the recommended style: we were
promised that slavery was better, or at least healthier, than the
internal combustion engine. As for sex, in my monastic sixth-
form days it had only an ugly head, which should not be raised,
let alone scratched.

For an academic to propose enlightening, or alarming, analo-
gies between ancient history or literature and contemporary life
was the mark of the opportunist or (much the same disreputable
thing) the populariser. Dead and providentially difficult
languages were there to furnish the intellectual high hurdles
which clever boys (and very few girls) were set to clear on their
way to high office or academic distinction. As Bernard Knox
reminds us, Thomas Gaisford, in a now notorious Christmas
mid-nineteenth century sermon at Christ Church, Oxford, was
candid to the point of shamelessness: 'Nor can I do better,' he
said, '. . . than impress upon you the study of Greek literature,
which not only elevates above the vulgar herd but leads not
infrequently to positions of considerable emolument.'

Review of Paul Cartledge, *The Greeks*, in the *Sunday Times*, 1993.

Nietzsche was the first scholar of undeniable quality to break the mould. He argued that orderly Apollo and disorderly Dionysus were the antagonistic forces by whose exercise the Greek world was pulled (sometimes torn) this way and that. In staid eyes, his hectic brilliance shed a luridly unreliable light on the origins of European culture. The blanched marble view of the ancient Gods persisted, in England, until the turn of the century, when Cambridge's Jane Harrison employed (now dated, still superb) comparative anthropological means to crack the codes of Olympic mythology, to no very wide academic applause. Only recently has the hermetic dryness of Greek studies been lubricated by the structuralists, and their more or less eclectic epigoni; Paul Cartledge is the latest, Anglo-Saxon, instance.

French scholars such as Pierre Vidal-Naquet, Jean-Pierre Vernant and Marcel Detienne – following in the remarkable footsteps of Louis Gernet – have revelled in unpacking the duplicities and vanities of the Glory that was Greece, without denying its fundamental enchantments. Nicole Loraux's feminist readings of Perikles' funeral oration and of Greek tragedy combine impeccable philology with trenchant re-valuations. The fresh air from across the Channel has now so altered the English climate that Cartledge's work is bracingly enthusiastic with inter-disciplinary influences and interests. It is no accident that his bibliography has a heavily Gallic flavour; he is himself a translator from French.

Considering how many books have been entitled *The Greeks* and how few of them can be read today with unpropped lids, it is a relief to see how much broader is the field of Cartledge's interest, and how much more aggressive the plough with which he works it, than would have been likely a generation or two ago, when Peter Green alone struck brave and heterodoxical notes. Green's reward was a long and lamentable (for us) exile from English university life. Luckily, it has not prevented – and perhaps stimulated – a continuing flow of inspiringly unstuffy scholarship from his pen.

In something of the same spirit, if less elegantly, Cartledge combines defiance with trendiness in challenging yesterday's received ideas. (He writes a jargon-ridden, choppy prose, with some very odd phrases in it; what, for instance, is a 'decapitated head'?) His main weapon is Emmanuel Levinas' 'concept of alterity': the idea that we help to define ourselves (whoever 'we' are) by emphasing that we are not, not, *not* something else. The idea is not sparklingly new (Sartre's anti-Semite defined who he was only by preening himself on what he was not); before that, Freud ironised on 'the Narcissism of Small Differences'. The proposition certainly operated in the Greek world where not to be a barbarian, not to be a woman and not to be a slave proved the ideal recipe for citizenship.

Since very few slaves can be expected to attend the Cambridge lectures which his book epitomises, Cartledge understandably addresses the problems of women and 'wogs' (he has a lively, not to say reckless, let-it-all-hang-out attitude to terminology) at greater length than the embarrassing issue of why slavery was rarely regarded as wrong and often – especially by Aristotle – alleged to be 'natural' (you could tell a born slave/barbarian by his servile posture). The Greek use of slaves embarrasses Cartledge but does stop him in his hermeneutic tracks; like it or not, the society which practised slavery provided Europe (good old 'us'!) with its founding fathers in philosophy, drama and literature.

Founding mothers, with the exception of Sappho, are few, although Artemis, Athena, Aphrodite, Hera, Demeter, Helen, Klytemnestra, Medea, Alcestis *et aliae* remind us that the forceful character of the female (mortal or divine) was amply acknowledged, and often dreaded, in a phallocracy in which *anangke* – commonly translated as Necessity, by which the Gods no less than mortals were constrained – was also the word for penis, although this unspeakable truth was not widely advertised in any sixth form I was in. In the modern style of full disclosure, Bernard Williams' magisterial *Shame and Necessity* is an indispensable account of the common (and uncommon) moral ground between the ancient Greeks and ourselves.

Where Cartledge's admirably non-male-chauvinist approach loses me is when he moves from the (deplorable) Greek silencing and political relegation of women, to the suggestion that it is for us to discover 'the true nature and proper place of women'. This is pure cant. It may be that women have been, and often are, ill-used, but it does not follow that they have some God-given or 'natural' place. How can there be a 'discoverable' truth about how people are meant be treated? Even if it were true that kicking a bitch a day would procure the earthly paradise (and that God had offered Certain Guarantees), it would offer no unchallengeable warrant for battering wives. There is no inherent pattern in earthly life which can be followed to an unquestionably golden destination. While alluding to the dangers of 'Aristotelian pseudo-scientific natural determinism', Cartledge allows himself to fall victim to it.

Where did the Greeks get the idea that they were better than everyone else? As François Hartog's book on Herodotus cleverly showed, the Greeks' image of themselves was enormously inflated after the unexpected defeat of the Persians at Salamis in 480 BC (as Peter Green's *The Year of Salamis* reminded us, the Delphic oracle, relying maybe on economic indicators, got that one badly wrong). The works of Herodotus, a marginal Hellene (actually a native of Halikarnassos – the modern Bodrum – in Asia Minor), contributed hugely to the swelling of Greek heads. He enjoyed a breakthrough success when he recited his work at Athens. Paid ten talents and made an honorary citizen for his P.R. work on behalf of the Athenians, he was the first man to prove that History had a market, if you told the right story.

How unarguably Greek were the Greeks? Martin Bernal maintains, in his much disparaged but not quite wholly debunked *Black Athena*, that almost all the Olympian gods and their mythology were imported, principally from Egypt. When they chose to elevate themselves above the rest of the world, the Greeks (like the Jews) may have been less complacent than postulating a much needed morale-boosting definition for themselves. The truth is all very well (the Persians, like the police, required you to tell it), but small countries, embattled against all comers, often need a myth of natural supremacy. Why else, after all, is Britannia still said to rule the waves?

Grossman's Smile

The Smile of the Lamb is the first novel of the author of *See Under: Love*, which won distinguished applause on its appearance in English last year. Grossman is a young Israeli writer fully engaged in the tragic triumph of Zionism. The renaissance and evolution of the Jewish state has altered the character of its inhabitants, creating citizens utterly at odds with the age-old image of the Diaspora Jew, whose badge was sufferance. The 'success' of Israel has been as heartening to one side of the Zionist-Arab equation as it has been mortifying to the other. The irresoluble conflict has generated fears and hatreds which seem beyond rational resolution. It is this snakepit of writhing passions which supplies Grossman with his themes, his urgency and his opportunity.

The greatest of divided loyalties is loyalty to the truth. Only the ideologue and the patriot can suppose that the other side is without honour or grievance. Writing in Hebrew, a citizen of a country surrounded by enemies who demand justice and dream of a bloodbath, Grossman attempts to inhabit the Arab mind with an almost apologetic sense of frustration and shame. He has no illusions about the implacable rage of Arabs within Israel's borders, nor about the futility both of 'humane' and of draconian methods in seeking to appease or repress them. He recognises the savage 'comedy' of mirrored loathing. Going beyond Mercutio, he sees that both sides are already plagued: he prefers to understand rather than to wash his hands of their contagious antagonism.

His book is set in the early 1970s and already – in that now 'historical' period – a sense of incurable futility precludes all 'reasonable' accommodations. *The Smile of the Lamb* is at once sensitive, humane, elegaic and devoid of any optimism, save a vague faith in 'love'. Its sombre, incantatory command of one's attention testifies more to its relevance to world events than to its literary finesse.

An unsympathetic review would certainly harp on the awkwardness which results from rendering a rhetorical unEuropean language such as Hebrew into 'colloquial' English. It would cite a passage like the following and question whether anyone should choose to read on:

> Now a sense of impending loss erupted from his stomach into his throat. He had failed again ... Bitter streams wore channels through his hinterland and, finding each other suddenly, surged through him. It was the same old failure embracing him comfortingly ... There's no need to pretend, your other failures are all here patiently waiting, the loveless life you try to live in your quasi-scientific way, as a diverting sequence of natural misunderstandings, not bothering to fight for anything because there isn't enough reality in you to struggle for, and all you needed was some crazy mixed up Uri to show you how much you lie even to yourself ... A cool jet shot through Katzman. He vaguely remembered something Shosh had once quoted to him ...
>
> It must have been the opening line in a book Katzman had read, too: Happy families are all alike; every unhappy family is unhappy in its own way ...

The passage is scarcely Grossman's happiest, but its earnestness, its artless attempt to crystallise the fluidity of emotional states and its trite allusion are fairly typical of the scope, and the shortcomings, of a narrative for which there may be no adequate translation. It is, of course, precisely the impossibility of rendering the Arab-Israeli issue in diplomatic political or moral terms which makes all 'sensible settlements' inapposite, however desirable. (In what common or reliable language, pray, will that famous conference 'after the war' be expressed?) In order for peace and security to come to the Middle East, the Middle East would have to have different values, religions and concepts of 'peace' and 'security'. Grossman diagrammatises the impasse with remarkable, if inelegant, intuition. Yet for all its humanity, *The Smile of the Lamb* is unmistakably formulaic: it pays homage, I fear, to as bad a book as Graham Greene's *The Honorary Consul*.

It may be unworthily parochial to have problems over envisaging a heroine called Shosh, but you may guess, from the quoted passage, that Katzman is the nasty piece of work (being known by your last name is usually a bad, if virile, symptom) in a triangle involving him, Shosh, and her husband, Uri, the lamb in the menagerie. If the infelicities are admitted, we can come admiringly to the central merit of the story, which impressively concentrates the play of forces (and ironies) in modern Israel. The stimulus of betrayal, the recklessness of perversion (of hopes, ideals and love), the energy of despair are fiercely implicit in what is, in some ways, an anatomy of transgression.

Both sides are united only in looking into the same abyss, though each contrives to ascribe its existence to the dire purposes or cowardice of the other. Uri, the cuckolded good kid, is echoed by the old Arab who takes him hostage, in a crazy attempt to force Israel to retreat from the 'occupied territories'. The senile 'terrorist' Khilmi is the village sage and the village idiot rolled into one old *djellabah*: he is the 'father' of all the local illegitimate children, a derided, sacred figure who loves Uri and yet decides to kill him when he comes to inform him, out of affectionate pity, of the death of his son in a 'security operation'.

The 'poetic' tone of the narrative works against clear perceptions of the characters and even of their emotions. Fantasy, reminiscence, lamentation bedevil the realities. Doubtless this is true to the spirit of the damned, holy land, but it obscures the drive of the story and, by rendering it literary, turns drama into melodrama. The end of the kidnap is predictable not because of any tragic inevitability but, because – having been here before, in other novels rather than in life (lucky us!) – we expect the wry twist.

There is much to be learned here – not least about the village Arabs and their long humiliations, even as Israeli 'citizens' – and much to respect, but there is an excess of grand notions, not least about love in all its aspects, and a lack of grace which can turn even the most 'personal' passages into unleavened claims for significance.

The Politics of
Martin Heidegger

'What a shit God is!' Randolph Churchill was reported to have cried out, when Evelyn Waugh gave him the Bible to read, for the first time, while convalescing in wartime Yugoslavia. The frequent shiftiness of those he chooses to venerate is not the smallest peculiarity of man. When did the indefensible lack defenders? Neither Adolf Hitler nor Joseph Stalin is short of brave admirers today (and each will probably have more tomorrow); the Khmer Rouge, like the SS, impress the credulous with their ruthlessness and their 'sincerity' (a key term among the witless). Man's standard – and conveniently impersonal – warrant for rigour is Logic, from which, as from other dictators, there is no appeal.

Logic appears to render the argument from 'inevitability' irrefutable: what rational man flies in the face of History or Being or market forces? Through the centuries, the pedlars of Destiny have supplied both Church and State with warrants for crusading cruelties for which mere greed or blood-lust might have lacked the energy. Philosophers affect to care only for dispassionate considerations (there is more than a hint of astrological charlatanry in the term), while simultaneously seeking mundane preferment. Anaxagoras was Perikles' house pet; Churchill called on his 'Prof', Lindemann, to verify what he wanted to hear. Did any ruler, however enlightened, ever

Review of Hugo Ott, *Heidegger: A Political Life*, in the *Sunday Times*, 1993.

keep someone to contradict him? Frederick the Great soon got rid of Voltaire.

When Plato had failed disastrously to put his blueprint for a 'Republic' into practice in fourth-century Sicily, he never began to recognise the categorical fatuity of seeking to clap logical moulds on human societies. In modern times, the Soviet use of mass murder as a means of accelerating the earthly paradise found no opposition from intellectuals like Jean-Paul Sartre who prated of freedom and craved bondage; when chiliasts and killers travel together, clear the fast lane. However, if their systems are threatened by the discovery of places like Auschwitz or the Gulag, or their masters fall from power, the omniscient can be relied on to know nothing about them. '*Points de détail*', the French fascist Jean-Marie Le Pen calls concentration camps and gas chambers, which is fairly philosophical of him.

Martin Heidegger never ventured even as far as Le Pen in acknowledging – let alone thinking deeply about – the death camps. His dedication to truth was of a piece with his denial of it. The individual, he was to say, meant nothing; only the (Nazi) state and German nation commanded allegiance. Treachery to friends, honour and the academy itself was thus excused. Yet we are promised, not least by him, that he was a philosopher of the first importance: 'In *Sein Und Zeit*,' he wrote, 'the question of the meaning of Being, for the first time in the history of philosophy, is posed and developed expressly *as a question . . .*' It is part of Heidegger's profundity that he hyphenates words in sign-if-I-cant ways and also adds ponderous em-phasis to ordinary words, thus making them his. He and Hitler were alike in turning language, as did Thomas Mann's Mario the Magician, into mesmerising monologue.

Those to whom precedence is a preoccupation maintain that Heidegger and Ludwig Wittgenstein are first on the grid in the race for the philosophical Grand Prix in our century of copious genius and slaughter. Wittgenstein may have been an egotist, but his methods came to display a systematic modesty to which Heidegger was immune. As an Austrian of Jewish origin, Wittgenstein also fought, without bellicose zeal but with out-standing bravery, in the First World War. Heid-egger – *my* revealing hypen! – skulked as a meteorologist (as Sartre, his verbose disciple, did during the Second), although he later egged the youth of Germany to fight hard for the *Führer*. This qualified as 'obedience to Being'.

Those with no pressing appetite for men who entrench themselves in metaphysical labyrinths to which they alone claim to possess the key, may wonder what urgency demands the rehabilitation of a prompt member of the Nazi party (once it was Being sufficiently successful to deserve his subscription). Heidegger dismissed one of the great scholars of his own Freiburg university as 'the Jew Fraenkel' (who moved to Oxford and inspired some of our foremost classicists there). We know that duplicitous affection and cynical careerism are part of the charm of the academic community, but – among many others – Heidegger betrayed both Husserl, who had been his predecessor, and Jaspers, his respected colleague. The Christian Husserl was 'racially' a Jew; both men had Jewish wives. What can you expect when *Sein* and *Zeit* (Being *and* Time!) call the tune? At his rectoral induction, Heidegger included the *Horst Wessel Lied* on the official programme.

Although he affected to think his quest more significant than his pro-visional answers, Heidegger believed that, by retrieving the pristine truths of which he took 'the Greeks' (especially the pre-Socratics) to be the certifying source, the beginning of 'Aryan' culture could be given a renewed incipience (he specialised in etymological redundancies). Without ever showing a hint of sceptical humour, Heidegger insisted that Greek and German were the only languages in which philosophy could be expressed. His destiny was to replace the morally limited Catholicism to which, as a young academic climber, he had sworn self-advancing allegiance. He advocated a transcendental and primordial Reality which was void of any ethical component – 'Being' preceded the factitious world of Good and Evil – and supplied a licence for men of world-historical significance. As Jean-François Lyotard documents in his 'Heidegger and "the jews"', the philosopher had a particular soft spot for the brownshirted SA (after the 1934 Roehm purge, he lost something of his fervour). Meanwhile, and Logically, '*Sieg Heil!*'

The *Führerprinzip* gave Heidegger an unquestionable authority which the great questioner found so congenial that, in 1933, he chose to become the Hitlerian rector of a once free university. Perhaps he was only honouring the lyrical advice of Mel Brooks, in *The Producers*: 'Don't be stupid, be a smarty/Come and join the Nazi party!' At all events, by 1934, his rectorship – luckily for his later 'cover story' – ended in acrimony and resignation. He returned to the ivory tower from which he emerged in 1945, with affectations of anti-Nazi (mental) activity; he even managed to assume the pose of Martin the martyr. His admirers chose to regard his declaration that Hitler's *Mein Kampf* was 'unreadable' as a courageous recantation, even if the criticism was made public well after the author's demise. By contrast, rightist sympathies had not deterred Thomas Mann from an early and courageous rejection of the Nazis, although he was offered all the laurels which the craven Heidegger so eagerly grasped.

His *Introduction to Metaphysics*, the book of the lectures given by the Herr Professor in 1935, is instinct with tendentious bad faith, for all its show of philological independence. There are moments of insight (he is particularly strong on the Greek sense of light and epiphany), but that its author betrayed his friends was not a social aberration; his conduct was of a piece with his intellectual slyness and bombast. It would, I daresay, not have occurred to him to read his own behaviour or style in ethical terms, but that, of course, is exactly what was wrong with them.

Hugo Ott's self-imposed modesty, in dealing only with Heidegger's 'political' life, does not inhibit him from outlining, somewhat thickly, a damning indictment. Among men of famous intellectual weight in our ignoble time, few can have had less honour or integrity, in the literal sense, than Heidegger (Brecht is *prox. acc.*). He spent pages and pages talking about The One and about the ineffable singularity of Being without suspecting that his own personality was a paste-up of resentments, jealousies, pretensions, lusts, vanities. Like Hitler, he could not endure the competition of any but the dead: his contemporaries are consistently dismissed and derided. The ultimate conceit of the close reader entails setting such high standards that no one alive can rise to them; thus he alone, by being their vigilant custodian, can claim in some sense to have met them.

Professor Ott is a historian, not a philosopher, and his account of Heidegger's political life makes this a book not to be read too soon after a heavy meal. The philosopher's subtle defenders will, of course, find fastidious holes in the quality of Ott's inelegantly damning researches. That these advocates have often been Jews testifies both to their magnanimity and, perhaps, to some perverse appetite for exemption: do they perhaps imagine that Heidegger could do the dirt on Husserl and Jaspers and Fraenkel, among many others, but would really appreciate *them*?

Since I do not claim to have read the *opera omnia*, can it be just to come to a summary verdict that in Heidegger we are dealing with an intermittently insightful psychopath, who would be better excerpted (using a long, sterile spoon) than swallowed *holus bolus*? There are, of course, passages of provocative quality, but then Bertrand Russell once warned, apropos of Hegel, that the worse the logic, the more interesting the results. Russell's disciple, A. J. Ayer, famously declared that Heideggerian existentialism was posited, rockily, on a prolix misreading of the uses of the verb 'to be'; as a contribution to philosophy, his remark may not have been particularly witty, but it was liberatingly brief. And to allow its justice does avoid the risk of wasting a great deal of *Zeit* making a god out of a shit.

Hilberg's Characters

As a historical subject, the Holocaust raises almost insurmountable problems of style (the very use of the word – by Elie Wiesel – was challenged, by Christopher Ricks, as an example of impertinent appropriation). The *Shoah* – to employ Claude Lanzmann's term in his film documentary – also raises questions about the nature of motive, about the meaning of truth, about the myth of human progress. It provokes doubt not only about the innate decency of human beings but also about God. The largely successful attempt to exterminate the European Jews was a protracted crime which has, in truth, been only superficially punished, although it is still widely suggested that 'the Jews' persist in unworthily vindictive feelings towards the now antique murderers (and thieves) whose actions, for one reason and another, were ignored, concealed or even secretly endorsed by the victorious wartime powers. The latest symptom of elegant indifference is to argue that Winston Churchill maintained Britain's belligerent independence in 1941, largely for reasons of personal vanity, when the national interest (of which Mr Alan Clark is the self-recognised arbiter) was for an accommodation with the Nazis. If your silver spoons are long enough, you may, it seems, consider dining with anyone without losing your appetite.

Review of Raul Hilberg, *Perpetrators, Victims, Bystanders*, in the *Sunday Times*, 1993.

The question of style, when it comes to dealing with what the Germans and their allies (and ours) did, is particularly difficult for Jewish writers, who forfeit their credibility if they lose their cool. The facts are the facts and have to be set down in a unopinionated manner. This was the approach adopted by Raul Hilberg over thirty years ago when he broke the terrible silence which had more or less covered the Holocaust. *The Destruction of the European Jews* was, in an admirable sense, pitiless. His dispassionate language was so well-judged that the Holocaust was admitted, belatedly, to academic consciousness; he has been a professor ever since. He showed that the most terrible of crimes was also a series of specific acts, decisions and murders perpetrated by almost a whole nation on what was perceived as the reason for all human – or at least European – misfortune, the Jews. Hilberg's tone resembled that recommended to his peers by W.H. Auden, who coined the phrase 'the necessary murder' to excuse Stalin's ideologically warranted hangmen: he operated like a surgeon, healthily heedless of blood, in the pathology department of our times.

By the end of his labours, Hilberg was finding it difficult to conceal a certain contempt for the docility with which the majority of Jews went to their fate. It could be said that professorial persons have been known to feel much the same contempt for those who commute meekly to factories and offices or who, trusting in the law of the lands in which they live, do what policemen or local authorities tell them, which was also the Jews' big mistake. Should they have known that the Germans and their innumerable helpers were bent on murder? Did anyone think to utter a warning? Neither the BBC nor the Vatican radio ever broadcast a single cry of 'Watch out!' Why bother, when it came to Jews?

The suggestion that the large majority of victims were cowards outraged Jewish opinion. Other historians were able to find many instances of resistance, however futile. The battle of the Warsaw ghetto was only the most conspicuous. Personally, I cannot find it reprehensible that exhausted and bewildered people, mothers with children, men with old parents, accustomed to obeying the laws of the Gentiles, failed, often after days and days in freezing boxcars, to fling themselves with martial recklessness on SS guards and their savage dogs, but others set more demanding standards.

What is certain is that the myth of cowardice – rarely levelled at allied soldiers who surrendered their arms against much less hopeless odds – has been immensely convenient to the European conscience. The accusation that the Jews have subsequently hounded their enemies is delivered, with a shake of more tolerant, Christian heads, quite as if the petty quota of (usually low-ranking) murderers brought to justice more than paid for six million dead Jews (the figure should probably be eight million) and that the presentation of further bills was a sadly Shylockian performance. The European mind cannot confront the extent of European guilt, even now. As the vote in the House of Lords on the War Crimes Bill revealed, Noble Lords – Mayhew *en tête* – have not found it difficult to forgive what, in principle, they would prefer to have forgotten. (Murder is not, in sober truth, a 'war' crime at all, but the perfumes of Arabia have their steady seductions.)

What would it be to respond 'adequately', in moral, literary, social terms to the decision to exterminate millions of people on the grounds of an economico-theologico-racist 'philosophy' which is as laughable, in intellectual terms, as the belief in phlogiston? In what 'appropriate' style would a book be written which told the world what really happened and what it really meant (and who would read it)? Hilberg tells us that the children of the ghettos played at executions and funerals; they prepared themselves for death as happier children, by playing at wars or weddings, ready themselves for life. Post-war Europeans have played a rather different game; unable to register the horror, they have restored their monuments and their cities, which is admirable, and they have found ways of maintaining their moral vanity, their public philosophies of law and religion, which may be less so: even novelists have flinched from including the evidence of systematic inhumanity in their versions of reality, although Auschwitz can have its amusing or salacious side, as Martin Amis and D.M. Thomas have had the courage, if that is what it takes, to reveal. (How clever to find ways of making it less *depressing*!)

The reason that no Jew, and no honest man, can ever confront the Holocaust in its entirety is that language breaks down in the attempt. The effort has been made, but even the bravest voices break, as Celan and Primo Levi and Bruno Bettelheim prove, and only shameless 'revisionists', like Faurisson and Irving, can finish their dismissive sentences without a tremor. Hilberg's new book is not of the magisterial quality of his first; it is a prosopography of the *Shoah*, a series of portraits of those who, as killers, victims or spectators, were more or less involved in what might have made God weep, as Jesus – so they say – once wept.

Perpetrators, Victims, Bystanders is a reduction of a world-historical crux – a scandal in the literal sense of an affront to faith – to its petty components. It is, I am sure, accurate (though perfunctorily written), but its tact is too great, almost too servile, if only to academic niceties. Great questions are perhaps of their nature unanswerable – and pettier ones too, such as why the Bulgarians behaved better than the Roumanians and the Roumanians than the French and the French than the Croats – but they cannot be ducked forever. Hilberg's career is not crowned with his new book, but he has a fundamental place among those who had the nerve and the will to try to spell out the unspeakable truth about an irreparable moral catastrophe which neither God nor man can ever make good.

Dignity and Decadence

'Victorian art and the classical inheritance' is the sub-title of Richard Jenkyns's latest rumination on the way in which ancient Greece and Rome informed and emboldened the Victorian vanity. In *The Victorians and Ancient Greece*, he dealt with the literary legacy and its effect on the manners and supposed morals of the age. Frank Turner, in his *The Greek Inheritance in Victorian Britain*, dealt along the same lines in particular with Mr Gladstone, whose lifelong veneration for Homer did not prevent him from what we now regard as wholesale misreadings of ancient society, its scope and morals. The priggish Gladstone imagined that he could validate his own politics by throwing a Greek light on it and, to do him justice, he probably mitigated his own self-righteousness by playing the diligent pupil sitting at Homer's feet. Attaching classical tags to your political baggage seemed to guarantee the nobility of your destination.

The comedy of western culture in general is that it is founded on texts so alien that their meanings remain elusive and which lend themselves to both fancy and falsification by their interpreters. Neither Hebrew nor Greek is an accessible language; neither ancient Palestine nor ancient Greece had much in common with the world of our own dear queen. Yet Englishmen, especially in Victorian times, have been prompt to assume

Review of Richard Jenkyns, *Dignity and Decadence: Victorian art and the classical inheritance*, in the *Sunday Times*, 1992.

fancy dress and play, in particular, the antique Roman and the antique Greek. A generation earlier, Shelley was convinced of the sublime nature of the Hellenic world and sought to derive his high-minded, not to say addled, idea of sexual and social morality from classical models. Winckelmann, a great classical scholar, founded his aesthetics on the Laocoön and the Apollo Belvedere, although the former now seems ridiculous and the latter, as Jenkyns puts it, is 'noble in conception, but in execution lifeless'; both, of course, were Roman copies of originals which Winckelmann never saw before that Triestine cook stabbed him to death as a result of a homosexual (?) liaison which was, in some sense, also a tribute to Greek practices, though not of a kind which the Victorians elected to venerate.

The erotic, as Jenkyns wittily emphasises, is very much a part of the Victorian ethos. He locates the heartlessness and prudery of which the cant accuses the Victorian age as belonging just as much to the Regency. Dickens's experiences in the blacking factory came before Victoria's accession, even if they were remembered, untranquilly, during her reign. The old story about putting bloomers on piano legs is relegated to legend: the Victorians gloried in majestic nudes, for which there were toothsome opportunities in classical subjects ranging from Pygmalion to the Muses, Ariadne to Andromache (nothing like chains to lend a little spice to the prospect of a naked beauty). Jenkyns refrains from easy mockery and entertains us with erudition and iconographic close-reading, especially of the artful postures in which slave-girls and hapless victims were arranged for the patron's delectation. Even the exaggerations of Sir Lawrence Alma-Tadema OM – whose 'camp' absurdities are once again getting high prices – excite a straight-faced Betjemanesque respect, though Jean-Léon Gérome trumps him for saleable sexiness.

The great antagonist of the classical manner was, of course, Ruskin, who is the only subject to whom Jenkyns ascribes genius. The key book is *The Stones of Venice* in which he attacks the dry formality of Greek building with evangelical urgency, although he is not so foolish as to deny its merits. His enthusiasm is reserved for the Gothic, with its innumerable touches of variety, its evidence of individual contributions from a myriad of nameless craftsmen, its lack of pompous reiteration. The Greeks may be honoured as originators, but 'the medievals win the true glory'.

Ruskin was a demanding, not to say obsessive, advocate of

standards which, in practice, were difficult to meet, not least in a time when there were many more buildings than men of genius to design them. Ruskin's inability to see merit in modern techniques, especially those demonstrated so scintillatingly by Brunel, blinded him to the direction which architecture was bound to take. Today's revulsion, in some quarters, against the use of steel and concrete (and the presumption that the material determines the form) inspires some sympathy with Ruskin in his losing battle, but the surviving instances of Victorian Gothic are surely a magnificent warning against the aesthetic tyranny even of a genius. 'The Gothic Revival,' Jenkyns concludes, 'was too ambitious, too morally impassioned even, to be as durable [as the Greek] for ordinary purposes.'

In fact, as he illustrates with splendid industry, the classical tradition was never obliterated by the Gothic, even at the height of St Pancrasisation. Especially in provincial towns such as Bristol, Liverpool, Newcastle and Norwich, not forgetting Glasgow and Edinburgh, the second rank of British architects – men such as W. B. Gingell and Alexander Thomson – produced solid, and sometimes agreeably larky, variations on Attic themes. Jenkyns sees Thomson as a forerunner of the early, deep-gabled style of Frank Lloyd Wright, although Wright's 'organic' affectations surely had little in common with Thomson's.

Jenkyns has an admirable tolerance for Victorian titans like Lord Leighton and Waterhouse and Watts, of whom he wittily observes that he stood at the point where the artistic establishment and bohemia met 'rather as Regent Street separates Mayfair from Soho without quite having the character of either'. Elsewhere, the style is less refreshing; to speak of 'praising with faint damns' is a little jejune, while the habit of saying things like 'to this subject we must now turn' reminds us dustily of the origins of this book in academic lectures. Nevertheless, it is a pleasure and an education to read. The only place where I detected a failure in astuteness was in the reading of certain 'Gothic' images in which a naked woman is being rescued, or at least approached, by a knight in armour. My disreputable memory reminds me that to engage a woman 'in armour' was Boswell's way of alluding to what is now called 'safe sex'. Was there perhaps a touch of what Byron called 'Attic salt' in the apparently chaste romantic iconography of the distressed maiden and her deliverer?

Iron John and Tin Bob

Sub-titled 'A Book About Men', *Iron John* is the latest what's-wrong-with-us-all, get-in-touch-with-yourself best-selling gospel to sell half a million in the US. Robert Bly is a counsellor who would be king, but in the most republican possible way. If, as Graham Greene argued, no great success is ever wholly unwarranted, Bly must be onto something. He believes that American men have been weakened to fearful, often tearful inadequacy by the assaults of, yes, Feminism. Now hold it, girls, females – whatever you want to call yourselves or us to call you – because Robert has nothing against your gender or against *most* feminism, it's just that we can't take too much more of your often justified criticism. If men go on agreeing to be the Trouble With Everything, they will cease to function and you wouldn't want that, would you, unless you were Andrea Dworkin? Never mind who would want Andrea Dworkin.

So, it's crisis time for the male sex. Men are out of touch with the hair on their chests. They have lost contact with – but here comes Our Hero now – Iron John! Remember the Grimm brothers' emblematic tough-guy who lives at the bottom of a pond, but is willing to help the little prince who's willing to help himself? John is a sort of prototypical hard-hat, but – you've guessed it – he has a heart (and hair).

Bly's book is a meditation which takes the Grimms' story as a text. (I once met a man who claimed that the brothers' fairy stories were fundamental documents in the rise of *Volkisch* ideas and Nazi ideology, but why spoil the party?) Our author's point is that American men have lost their faith in their fathers and hence do not know how to grow up and be fathers themselves. Lacking mentors, they can't hack it through the rites of passage; they don't get a chance to clash their spears against their shields and they have no blood-brothers. Instead of growing up, men will be boys: they stay Peter Punks who cannot take responsibility. They hanker after approval – especially from feminists who more and more wear the unisex pants, have the combination to the slim-line briefcase and set the goddam agenda.

Don't get Robert wrong: he doesn't presume to tell women what they should be or do (so don't hesitate to buy the book, girls), he just wants to save masculinity before we all go the way of Cybele's devotees. If you don't remember what happened to them, or to Narcissus or Tammusz, take Bly's hand: he's no stranger in paradise (a term, he reminds us, because he knows, that originated in a walled garden) and he has comparative mythology at his fingertips. Saturn, Demeter, Pluto, Babylonian seals, the Dordogne caves, Viking legend, Indian ceremonial, they all have their place in the hundred-egg cultural omelette which you are cordially invited to share.

Where Allan Bloom, in *The Closing of the American Mind* (last season's Surprise Best Seller denouncing the Way We Are), adopted a tone of mandarin condescension as he observed the young deafening themselves to high culture by listening to Rock on their walk-persons, Bly blows the whistle in a less huffy way. Indeed, he plays quite merry tunes on it, often of his own composition. Not being a tenured professor, more a wandering guru, he can revel in learning without being a pundit or a poop; he's in favour of juiciness, not aridity, just like Iron John. He also roots for the lower half of the body (ankles as well as genitals), like The Wild Man. Don't we ignore them at our peril? With the Death of Ideology and the End of History, man needs to get in touch with himself again. Bly gives you the numbers to call.

Make no mistake, this man does not come at you *de haut en bas*: he has been down there in the ashes, as he calls them, with the best and the worst of them. He too had a mid-life crisis and he wrote a poem about it which he quotes right next to – and at greater length than – Robert Frost (whom he loves 'because he is able to sustain the tension between men and women, with neither attitude understood as wrong, but different'). Mull on

that one, team, while Bly gives you an earful of his own
Parnassan potage:

> Those great sweeps of snow that stop suddenly six feet from the
>   house . . .
> Thoughts that go so far.
> The boy gets out of high school and reads no more books;
> The son stops calling home.
> The mother puts down her rolling pin and makes no more bread.
> And the wife looks at her husband one night at a party, and
>   loves him no more.
> The energy leaves the wine, and the minister falls leaving the
>   church . . .

I could go on, ladies and gentlemen (the author sure does),
but I think you have the gist: the centaur cannot hold. Something must be done to get the old teacher back in the groove
and all the young ephebes around him. There's no time to
wonder why mother used a rolling pin to make bread with.
Maybe it was the resulting stodge which led men to go out to
buy sliced bread at Safeway, with the consequent decline of the
pot-bellied stove and the rise of the one-parent family. Think
about it.

All right, Bly is bumptious, sententious, overblown and totes
more anthropological samples than a snake-oil salesman. Just
because he has more answers than most of us have questions
doesn't mean he has to endure the torture of a thousand pseudo-
sophisticated sneers. Shouldn't he be given marks for ringing
that tocsin before men find that everything has fallen off
forever? Now can we rise again before we hit bottom or, as Bly
has it, become 'open to ashes'? He gives us examples of men
who have (this is the full list): 'Richard Pryor, John Cassavetes,
James Baldwin, Reshad Field, C. Everett Koop, Woody Allen,
the recent Jimmy Carter, Cesar Chavez, and so on.' What a
touring party to recover the ashes! Who is C. Everett Koop? I
was going to ask you.

Of course, you will recognise many of the obsessions of D.H.
Lawrence, including the sentimentalisation of the ruthless
savage who truly values women by fighting her all the way. Bly
is so in love with everything he has read (and too much that he
has written) that he sings the body eclectic at the top of his
voice. His vital point?

Every man and every woman on this planet is on the road from
the Law to the Legends. Surely every person reading this book is.
The Legends stand for the moist, the swampish, the wild, the
untamed. The Legends are watery, when compared with the
dryness of the Law. It takes twenty years to understand the Laws,
and then a whole lifetime to get from there to the Legends.

Yeah? so meantime gimme a beer.

Vous Autres Français

'*Là-bas*' is how Parisians speak of all locations except Paris: everyone else lives 'down there'. This Gallocentric condescension is common, in particular, to intellectuals who – far more influentially and almost certainly more perniciously than in England – consider themselves an *élite*. Their vanity traces its lineage to Montaigne and Voltaire and Rousseau, but they derive their social and 'moral' centrality from the Revolution, from which, rightly or wrongly, they assume the whole of western socialist theory, and much of its practice, to derive.

Although Simon Schama's *Citizens* has recently been at pains to show how incoherent were the ideas, and how mutually destructive the idealists, of 1789, the conviction has persisted that France's revolutionaries showed the world the way to a Utopia, of which the iniquitous *bourgeoisie* temporarily deprived it. Putting history back on course has been the announced purpose and pride of *les intellos* throughout the present century. France might, through folly or incompetence, have been defeated and humiliated by great wars and small ones, but a certain consolation was to be found in the prospect of predicting and backing winners, even if they wore Stalin's (or Hitler's) colours.

At least since the Franco-Prussian war, Left and Right in

Review of Tony Judt, *Past Imperfect: French Intellectuals 1944–1956*, in the *Sunday Times*, 1993.

France have been united only in their sense of French impotence. After 1944, for every Benoist-Méchin who was disgraced because he overdid his admiration of the Wehrmacht, there were a dozen fellow-travellers unabashedly revelling in the success of the Red Army, at least until it was used to crush the Hungarian uprising of 1956, upon which (though with very few choruses of *mea culpa*), a number of ranking *philosophes* hedged their bets on the USSR as the vessel of human salvation, turning very often to the Third World, whose noble savageries supplied them with another hopeful model in 'People's Liberation Fronts', of which the Khmer Rouge of Pol Pot, a Sorbonne graduate, is only the most uncompromising and latest case.

Few repentant Stalinists were converted to what the French call 'Liberalism', tainted as it is with Anglo-Saxon capitalistic hegemony, with all that entails of blue jeans, fast food and the culture of *le best-seller*. Only with the recent collapse of Communism, and with it a source not only of 'democratic' hope but also of privileged travel – ask the English PEN club committee for local details – and massive print-runs, has a thorough revision of the very concept of Socialism become inescapable. The current *déroute* of the French Socialists, who can expect less than 20 per cent of the vote in the coming elections, is perhaps due less to corruption or ineptitude (France remains a very prosperous country) than to the demoralisation provoked by the collapse of the Soviet system of which the generation of Sartre was tempted to think of themselves as the indulgent uncles, if not the furtive fathers.

Tony Judt concentrates on the period after 1944, when the reputations of Camus (with some justice) and Sartre (with very little) emerged from the Liberation draped in the colours of the Resistance in which the Communist Party had, in many eyes, redeemed the national honour (and its own, after the ignominy of the Hitler-Stalin pact). Even today it continues to be described as '*Le parti des fusillés*' on account of the large number of Communists shot, often as hostages, by the Germans, even though a good number of them were non-French Jews gracelessly abandoned, if not betrayed, to their fate.

The *pur et dur* seriousness of the Communists procured them 25 per cent of the vote immediately after the war and made them the largest political party in France. The future seemed to belong to the 'working class', as Marx predicted. The Communists' record and their powerful prospects attracted the guilty respect of those like Sartre, whose vicarious braying covered an ambiguous wartime record; his Resistance had taken the form of speculative verbosity while keeping warm at the Café Flore. As the recent mordant volume entitled *Une si Douce Occupation* ... reveals, Sartre and Simone de Beauvoir marched away from the guns with some despatch: on the first night of *Les Mouches*, when the allies were about to disembark on the Normandy beaches, he was clinking brave glasses with the occupying nobs and their *collabo* toadies. De Beauvoir needed all her dialectical skill to turn her lover's play into a signal act of intellectual defiance which the Nazis were too witless to perceive. Judt deals unsparingly with Sartre's masochistic vanities and is no less judicious with the Catholic Marxism of Emmanuel Mounier, the editor of *L'Esprit*. Mounier was a kind of pious Kingsley Martin, always finding excuses for Stalin and publishing clever justifications of 1950s show trials like that of Slansky in Czechoslovakia and Rajk in Hungary. Sartre's endorsement of violence – as the logic of those dispossessed of other forms of expression – sprang from a tradition he (like the egregious Althusser) was lasciviously keen to embrace. As a Christian liaison officer, Mounier doubled in the role of chaplain to Socialism, offering tepid consolation to its victims and prompt absolution to their executioners.

Judt's account of the behaviour of those whom Simone de Beauvoir unsarcastically fictionalised as *The Mandarins* is closely documented and often very entertaining. Relating their apparently grotesque foibles to the traditions which they supposed themselves to be honouring, he succeeds in both understanding almost everything and pardoning almost nothing. Merciless but rarely smug (as Paul Johnson was in his opportunistic volume *The Intellectuals*), this is two-thirds of an excellent book. It tails off in the last section, which seems to have been appended at the instance of an American publisher. Instead of pursuing his post-war theme, Judt turns away to deride fellow American academics who whore after the ideas of Derrida and Lacan and Roland Barthes long after they have passed their quote-by date. At the same time, he sneers modishly at Bernard-Henri Lévy who, despite his self-promoting profile, was one of the first to denounce the squeamish mercilessness of Emmanuel Mounier. Roger Vailland who, like his fellow Communist and hated rival Louis Aragon, became the house intellectual of the PCF after being cast out of the ultra-chic Surrealist clique by

André Breton, deserves more than a fleeting reference. As a riveting account of life *pendant ces années-là*, Yves Courrière's recent fat biography of Vailland fills in the gaps in Judt's brisk story with innumerable details of spite and cruelty in the French domestic scene, and not only in matters of editorial nuance.

Past Imperfect remains a very useful survey which breaks new ground in a well-ploughed field (there is a helpful bibliography). Will French philosophers now be disposed to abandon the monologue as the standard form of discourse and start to listen to – even solicit – objections to their ideas? Sartre never deigned to respond to Raymond Aron, who quietly refuted nearly every 'argument' he advanced. Can the Parisian tradition of autistic garrulity yield to one of mutual respect in a thoughtful world whose plans for the future do not run red with other people's blood? In view of the influence of, in particular, Hegel and Heidegger, it is a moot point whether the German army or German philosophy has done more lasting damage to France.

Joseph Losey

Modern biography is, not infrequently, a form of necrophilous social climbing. The author gets on intimate terms with subjects who would have been out of his or her league while they were alive. It is not clear that Edith de Rham's account of Joseph Losey is entirely a work of love (at times one seems to hear the gritting of teeth at one more act of flagrant pettiness or vanity), but she moves gushingly among the celebrities as they unbutton. For all the deliciousness of the incidental gossip, unless Losey was the cinematic genius which his admirers maintain, his long career of ruffled feathers and rumpled bedclothes hardly merits exhumation.

As it happens, I have never read a book in which I have had personal acquaintance with more of the cast. On the whole, Ms de Rham has hit them off pretty well, though with cliché-ridden superficiality; the tape-recorder and the cuttings library are not reliable sources of knowledge or style. The treatment of Losey himself is more profound, if only because the director thought and talked enough about himself to furnish the author with more intelligence than she displays elsewhere (her habit of quoting journalistic critics, of no matter what pliable triviality, feeds one too regular a diet of stale puff-pastry).

The general outline of Losey's career is fairly well known. He

Review of Edith de Rham, *Joseph Losey*, in the *Times Literary Supplement*, 1991.

came from Wisconsin, the same state as the Junior Senator who, supposedly, hounded him from his career in Hollywood (in fact he took off with some alacrity, leaving no great reputation behind him); he had hard times in Europe in the 1950s – like most Europeans – and then made a grand career for himself, thanks largely to the advocacy of the French highbrow magazines, like *Cahiers du Cinéma*, whose dubious contribution to cinematic aesthetics was the elevation of the director to quasi-divinity. The *auteur* theory did much to jack up the *hauteur* of those it promoted, although modesty was rarely their most pressing problem. Craving for veneration and the need to condescend, to give and procure favours and jobs, make directing an 'art' which resembles that of the politician quite as much as that of the 'author' (with its solitary, self-reliant connotations).

Losey's eminence was zealously, even militantly, argued by those who were convinced that he had been an innocent victim. Yet his reputation depended not least on the idea that he was a lifelong Communist whose uncompromising views warranted, and even ennobled, his surly integrity. If he always acted as though he had been the victim of injustice (he told President Giscard d'Estaing that it had made a 'Jew' of him and so qualified him, despite his negligible French, to film Proust), it seems that he never renounced the Stalinist myopia which the brilliance of his eye did nothing to alleviate.

The most interesting (because the least showbiz-chatty) of Ms de Rham's chapters is about the making of *The Assassination of Trotsky*; it is alleged that cryptic pressures were brought to bear, including perhaps very specific threats – of exposure or even violence – if, as late as the 1970s, Joe failed to tread the hard Party line. The outrage with which Nicholas Mosley – the author on whose novel *Accident* was based – greeted the final version of a film supposedly shot from his script certainly suggests a major failure of nerve. Film writers are, of course, regularly (and often gleefully) betrayed by the directors who, until the words are written, lean so heavily on them, but Mosley's eviction was manifestly the result less of artistic differences than of Losey's apprehension that his writer's being the son of Sir Oswald had cast 'progressive' suspicion on him. Thus, when a testing moment came, the man of integrity endorsed guilt by association in a particularly craven way (Nicholas Mosley clearly had not the smallest moral or political affinity with his father). Like the Junior Senator from his home state, Losey was long on accusation (and boozy paranoia) and short on loyalty himself; he hated more easily, and more copiously, than he loved.

The wonder is that many movie-makers were obstinately, even fanatically, faithful to him, although others were disgusted by his tearful bullying, his frequent cowardice (he was hard on minnows but nice to sharks) and his drunken conceit. His treatment of women was savage and patronising, when dependence did not render him supplicatory or puerile. Only Jill Bennett, it seems, achieved a relationship with him which endured – without sexual continuity – from soon after his arrival in London to the eve of his death.

Given her own lack of critical ambition, Ms de Rham's treatment of Losey's life can only be as good as the information she extracted. Dirk Bogarde has, I suspect, been her most voluble witness: he certainly emerges with great credit from his own evidence. In spite of the odd betrayal and the rupture it provoked, Bogarde was a reliable friend as well as a crucial star during Losey's most productive years. The rapport between them was so great that Dirk called Losey's house, to discover how he was, at the very moment of the director's death. 'Knowing Joe as well as I did, it would not have surprised me if, somewhere along the psychic wavelengths, he had summonsed me: and I had obeyed.' The verb 'summonsed', for the more obvious 'summoned', suggests that answering Losey's call could have something of a penal aspect to it, like responding to a sub-poena. However, as *The Servant* and *Accident* established, Bogarde's career prospered hugely under Losey (and Pinter). I did not know that the actor himself directed early scenes of *The Servant*, when Losey was too ill to come to the set. Clearly, he did so with seamless competence.

Greatness should be able to survive being portrayed warts and all, but there are times here when Losey becomes all wart. On any view, his life establishes scant equivalence between morals and aesthetics, unless you think he was a rotten director. Plenty of great artists, it appears, are shits, and Losey was no exception, even if his greatness was the result more of special pleading, much of it by himself, than dispassionate judgement might accept. He was a masterly placer and mover of the camera, but his narrative sense was as unreliable as his sense of humour (the two are closely related in the technique of film editing).

Losey was the maestro-type without ever quite producing the work to justify his self-casting. The frequency with which he wanted to work with those who had worked with or 'belonged to' men of genius suggests a ready belief in fame by association: why else did he cast Monica Vitti in *Modesty Blaise* in which she was given little help by Losey who, it is plausible to think, was torn between a wish to succeed and a desire to destroy Antonioni – an infinitely greater talent – by tarnishing his star? (Bogarde went around saying 'Miss Vitti is a pitti,' but Ms de Rham does not mention the fact.) Typically, Losey took no blame for the disaster of *Modesty Blaise*, but persisted in saying that it was 'ahead of its time' (like Stalinism, I suppose).

Evan Jones, who was the least 'fashionable' and perhaps the most reliable of Losey's screenwriters, is the honest witness who saw that Joe had re-written the script of a comedy without having any idea of what it was to be funny. Evan's reward for long service was to be dumped, although I have no doubt that the only memorable moment in *Modesty Blaise* – when Dirk, pegged out to die of thirst in the desert, croaks 'Champagne, champagne . . .' – came from the writer.

Losey, unlike Chaplin or Welles, was as good only as his collaborators (amongst whom Richard MacDonald, the designer, was steadily outstanding). Directors are nearly all organisers and selectors rather than individual creators. They resemble conductors more often than composers (hence their frequent desire, perhaps, to direct opera even when, like Losey, they have no ear for music). Losey's claims to enduring worth depend, I think, on the first half of *The Servant*, *The Go-Between*, *Mr Klein*(?) and bits of *Eve* (Ms de Rham alludes to the sculpture of Adam and Eve which figures in that film as being 'on a church in Venice', when it is, of course, on the corner of the Doge's Palace). It is a measure of the film industry's unprincely governors that his last film was the forgettable (if you're lucky) *Steaming*, when it might have been based on Pinter's magisterial version of Proust, for which he could obtain no funding.

The Alien Maugham

The selectors generally agree that Somerset Maugham is not among the important authors of this century. The mark of the 'deep' writer, they say, is the subtlety not only of his language but also of his implications, whereas Maugham was famously stigmatised by Edmund Wilson as incapable of saying anything in an original way. Who can deny that his work is often awkward with banality? His platitudes may be devices for making the common reader feel at home, but their regularity makes it seem that the author too is an unsubtle man who, by attention to gossip, has heard, and will supply, any number of amusing, but unsubtle, anecdotes.

The magician reveals the emptiness of his sleeve the better to conceal the aces which he has secreted elsewhere; distracted by his patter, the audience fails to notice his cunning. In that entertaining tradition, Maugham passed himself off as a pedestrian craftsman with tricks as unremarkable as his vocabulary. To have been taken at what seemed to be his own modest valuation has not prevented him from being undersold. Anthony Burgess's droog-like treatment of his Maughamiam butt, in *Earthly Powers*, seemed intended to yank Willie out of the closet, quite as if his self-portraits had been so dishonest that he deserved to be dragged through the literary world on a hurdle.

Maugham's *absit omen* depiction of camp characters (most obviously of Elliot Templeton in *The Razor's Edge*) has indeed excited accusations of dissimulating his own sexual preferences (an appropriate usage in Maugham's bisexual case), quite as if, like Proust in Gide's eyes, he had disingenuously passed himself off for a member of the straight majority. Maugham's fictional treatment of homosexuality was discreet almost to the point of obscurity, whether in 'Macintosh' or in an oddity like 'Salvatore', where an element of risk (though not of the *risqué*) is declared in the opening sentence, 'I wonder if I can do it'; the ending avoids mawkishness, by a whisker, with the 'disclosure' that the challenge lay in writing about 'goodness, just goodness'. In fact, the story is a declaration of love for an idealised Italian fisherman; one may guess that part of the author's pleasure, and purpose, in writing lay in seducing the straight reader into complicity with a passion to which the library public would never overtly admit. The desire to 'turn the weekly trick', in Edmund Wilson's condescending words (Wilson was himself a more or less weekly critical trickster in the *New Yorker*), fails to account for Maugham's stamina or for the sense we have that he means more than he tells, and somehow tells us so.

In the 1950s, when already himself in his eighties, he announced his obsolescence, in some eyes, by declaring that characters like Kingsley Amis' Jim Dixon were 'scum'. He may have been nettled by the speed with which Amis proved his modernity in penning a derisive picture of Maugham himself, as the expatriate littérateur Buckmaster, in *I Like it Here*, a novel which was sponsored by Amis's receipt of the Maugham Award. Maugham perhaps felt that it would not be uncivil for Amis to wait until the end of the meal before he bit the hand that had fed him.

Maugham's character has been assailed no less vigorously than his work; he won few marks from Ted Morgan or from Gore Vidal, whose life-style has not wholly differed from that of his target, although he rarely writes as amusingly (and never as self-deprecatingly). One of the unconfessed reasons why Maugham is an awkward element in the twentieth-century canon may be that he set a rather better example, in important respects, than his putative betters: he never embraced any of the now embarrassing, or disreputable, ideologies which lent teeth and claws to so many Undoubtedly Great Authors. Moderation denied him a claque of supporters, from either Left or Right. He was not duped (or fortified) by Fascism or Communism nor did he confuse his own desires with what everyone else should feel or applaud. Unlike Pound or Eliot or Yeats or Lawrence, he failed to advocate measures or morals which might, coincidentally, serve his own ends or provide a pedestal for his own dignity; he lacked dictatorial grace.

On the mundane level, he did not hurry to pay taxes but, unlike Edmund Wilson, he did not expect artistic persons to be exempt from them; nor did he concoct high-minded 'political' reasons to glorify reluctance to honour the common law, as Wilson did when he was discovered not to have filed returns with the IRS. If Maugham took advantage of whatever loopholes he could find, he never argued that persons of intellectual distinction should have the right to cut their own.

Although never a crusader for a specific camp (such enthusiasm would have been the essence of Edwardian bad form), he was always – like some prosaic Byron – on the side of tolerance. Maugham's apparently disinterested style owed something to his medical training (Evelyn Waugh, with malevolent accuracy, was the one man to call him 'Doctor' while staying at the Villa Mauresque). He was a shrewd diagnostician, but his notes and his prescriptions, such as they were, were written in an ill-advisedly clear hand; it is unwise, in our time, for a writer to be understandable without the help of an interpreter: Joyce's obscurities needed Anthony Burgess, and hence flattered him; Maugham's perspicuity did not, and exasperated him.

There may, however, be more to some of Maugham's stories than – as I fear he might have said – meets the eye. Part of his abiding 'inexplicable' claim on our attention is due to a heavier dosage of duplicity than dismissive readers have cared to perceive. In defence of this view, I should like to look more closely than it is usually assumed to deserve at one of his most famous *nouvelles*. Even a superficially straight up-and-down tale such as *The Alien Corn* offers an unexpected instance of concealed identities and identifications.

In the Great War, Maugham worked for MI5 in Geneva, where he passed himself off as what he, in fact, was (a successful dramatist): what better 'cover story' than the truth, or part of it, what pretence more sweet than to pretend to be what in fact one is, a man of parts? It may be a mistake to suppose, even after his spy-masterly days were over, that Maugham's *alter ego*, Willie Ashenden, was ever wholly *limogé*. In *The Alien Corn*, the first-person narrator never calls himself by his name, but he remains a sort of Ashenden, a discreet, yet diligently reportial, spy in the household of the Blands, whose impostures are, it seems, the story's central concern.

On the face of it, *The Alien Corn* is a longish tale depicting the absurd comedy and finally tragic consequence of an English Jewish family passing itself off as Anglo-Saxon. (The film version, with Dirk Bogarde, failed because, in the squeamishness of the time, it repressed the repression and never mentioned Jews at all.) In the printed text, 'I', the conventional narrator, watches with amiable indifference as the assimilated Jews are torn apart on the reefs which they refuse to mark on their charts. The illusion of dispassionately observant 'naturalism' is maintained. What else can, or need, the story be about but what it tells us? Is Maugham ever more profound than his surface?

Before we meet the Blands, the author treats us to a preambulatory account of an old social acquaintance of his, Ferdy Rabenstein. Ferdy is the brazen instance of what the Blands have no intention of being: an unapologetic Jew without 'English' affectations or cover. To begin with what seems like a digression jars with Maugham's advertised notions of narrative rectitude, but Ferdy Rabenstein eventually justifies his place in the scheme: he turns out to be related to the Blands, although the narrator has known him in a wholly different milieu, ever since 'I' was an impoverished, emergent author beginning to be invited to the country houses of fashionable hostesses.

Unlike his philistine English fellow-guests, the elegant Ferdy was genial, and conspiratorially 'artistic', with the almost unknown young writer. Rabenstein's character and connoisseurship resemble those of Proust's Swann, another worldly Jew, though a less avowedly Jewy one; Ferdy avoids the slur of being suspected of Jewishness by making a proclaimed virtue of it (as Disraeli did). He is said to be the favourite of aristocratic ladies whom he pleasures more pleasurably and treats more affectionately than those who presume themselves entitled to their affections.

The narrator's attitude to Rabenstein carries admiration to the verge of envy: despite the shared tastes which sweeten their complicity, Ferdy has a cosmopolitan assurance which 'I' cannot equal. The author and the Jew are most at one in their outsiders' disdain for those who imagine themselves their betters. Dependent on the patronage of a smug and cold-hearted society, they find furtive satisfaction in amusing those whom they are obliged to humour but cannot respect.

When, after the outbreak of the 1914 war, German names become anathema, Ferdy elects and contrives to survive without changing his, as others did; he retires into tactful privacy until the allied victory licences his return to London society. He has the perennial usefulness of an exquisite who knows the art market. Combining the expertise of an accessible Berenson with the shrewdness, though not the opportunism, of Duveen, he is flamboyant, but not vulgar; bold and passionate, he is also discreet and considerate. Like Swann, Ferdy makes an art of life; to appear to be at home in a demanding society requires more wit, and yields more secret pleasure, than any born member of it is likely to guess. The narrator's irony lances society more keenly than the man who might have been its butt. Can it be that Maugham found himself more on Ferdy's side than he first intended, and if so, why?

He concludes that he has commemorated Ferdy less stylishly than he should. Max Beerbohm, he suggests, would have been his ideal biographer; Aubrey Beardsley should have been the illustrator of his 'barbaric magnificence'. Maugham goes on: 'Thus would have been erected a monument of triple brass and the ephemera imprisoned to succeeding ages in the amber's translucency.' One wonders how, and why, an author who repeatedly advocated simplicity could have written, or left unemended, so cumbrous a sentence (a monument of triple brass and *amber* is as close to a mixed metaphorical abomination as any Rabenstein might wince at). Does Maugham's awkwardness betoken an access of sincerity which doped his usually vigilant determination not to make a pretentious ass of himself?

To my mind, Ferdy may stand for a character of another kind entirely: The Unequivocal Other – socially, artistically and perhaps sexually – whom 'I' would like to emulate. Ferdy's magnificent aplomb as a Jew is enviably unguarded: he dares to be what he is. After the gauche sentence I have quoted, the next paragraph begins (as if in logical sequence) 'Ferdy's conquests were social and his venue was the great world'. We are then hurriedly informed that his independent means were acquired in South Africa (a plausible source of wealth for a Jew, as Barney Barnato and others, somewhat notoriously, proved) and that Ferdy came to England only when he was twenty. This gives him a vestigial affinity with Maugham, who was also not born in Britain, yet made his way in its 'great world'.

It remains slightly odd that Maugham speaks of Ferdy's 'conquests': they are said to be social but are soon revealed also to be sexual. One begins to suspect that Ferdy was not, as Maugham liked always to pretend with his characters, drawn from life (albeit from an amalgamation of models), but that he is a fabrication inspired (and inhabited) by Maugham's own social and sexual ambitions, experiences and fantasies; Ferdy is the *parvenu* as man of sensibility, the *arriviste* as *arbiter elegantiarum*. He supplies an *alter ego* who can be applauded as if he were wholly distinguished from the author: Ferdy is Willie as a witty, heterosexual, rich metic, the part which the Paris-born Maugham did, for a time, play in his Hill Street days, a few dozen yards from Curzon Street, where Ferdy entertains the *beau monde*, even though, like Maugham, he has 'at the bottom of his heart a feeling of ever so faint contempt for the hearty British gentry that surrounded *us*'. My emphasis underlines the affinity between Ferdy and the author of *Our Betters*, a play which flaunts ironic deference to its contemptible subjects.

Mutatis mutandis, Ferdy is a Semitic Gunga Din, an inferior whose qualities of heart and nerve ridicule the condescensions to which he is exposed. Once again, the paragraph paying tribute to him ends with a gauche sentence, as if to signal the author's fear of too close an identification with an outsider: 'Jewish stories were his speciality and I seldom met him anywhere without hearing him tell sooner or later the latest he had heard'. This does not sound or read quite right; its uneasy word order hints at the common foreignness which it seeks to disavow (it could well be a translation from the French).

Maugham's belief that his stories exemplified the classic rules of structure implied by the insistence on a 'beginning, a middle and an end' is, in the case of *The Alien Corn*, belied by his practice. The anecdote in which Lily Langtry visits the Duchess of Somerset appears first in *A Writer's Notebook* (in a note written in 1915) and is here intruded without any significant bearing on the main theme. In fact, it seems improbable that Ferdy Rabenstein – who is alleged to have played a part in engineering Jersey Lily's excursion – would not have guessed that a visit to a once beautiful woman might prove a painful experience for a reigning star, although the 'inadvertent' malice of a (secret) homosexual might have been piqued by procuring her discomfiture. Can it be that Maugham here (and elsewhere) adds an unconfessed aspect of his own character to that of Ferdy? As the story proceeds, he doubles the Blands' fear of exposure as Jews with his own dread of discovery as a homosexual; he too belonged to a despised but, in his view, more amusing and more 'honest' élite than it would be prudent to declare. When it comes to society, deference and disdain are very close.

The long paragraph of eulogy, in which Ferdy's credentials as an honest artistic broker, and supporter of young talent (he sponsors an anonymous Morel as a violinist 'at a rich man's house'), ends with a banal sentence: 'His own musical parties, very small and carefully chosen, were a treat'. Immediately following this bathetic tribute, comes a paragraph which consists of three words: 'He never married.' It is a deliberate, if crude, stylistic switch. You wonder, for a moment, why the phrase is dignified with such isolation and, more importantly, I think, why it is so familiar. The familiarity is due to the fact that it is, or was, a standard obituary formula. To the *avertis*, along with its variant 'He was unmarried', it announces not only the subject's putative celibacy but also his homosexuality. In this curt paragraph, Maugham thus touched on the hidden thrust of his story; then, as Proust often did, he flinches from – or has too much wit for – the full disclosure of his own partiality.

The next paragraph implies that he is soliciting (and endorsing) a tolerance on which he need not depend. He ascribes to Ferdy the indulgent statement '. . . I flatter myself that I have no prejudices, *tous les goûts sont dans la nature*, but I do not think that I could bring myself to marry a Gentile.' The tactful French of the first part of Ferdy's explanation of his bachelorhood contains the remark which is really important to Maugham and which he is seeking to 'sell'; the second part returns the narrator to the side of the majority to which he is telling his tale. Rabenstein soon adds that he could not marry a Jewess either ('our women are so prolific'). Thus we arrive at a situation where being unmarried can be passed off as a symptom of virile fastidiousness; Ferdy disqualifies all women from eligibility, without having to be portrayed as a man who, in fact, dislikes the idea of living with a woman at all. The attack on marriage is made more damaging by being ascribed to a man who is said to love women.

Immediately after this, Ferdy's aristocratic affairs are recounted with almost salacious admiration (as if he had got away with something). The narrator is said to have been present on one occasion at which an antique duchess, having had a cocktail with the author, is offered another by her host (who is improbably late). When she says that she has already had one, Ferdy says 'Ah, I wondered why your eyes were so doubly bright', upon which 'The old raddled woman flushed with pleasure'. Once again, the effect and the language seem forced. 'So doubly bright' is difficult to say; it seems a *written* rather than a spoken phrase. As for 'old raddled woman' it is spiteful, but not witty; it smacks of sincerity. Maugham uses the incident to signal his aversion from aged females but relies on Rabenstein to lend a camouflage of charm to his own distaste.

The next paragraph begins with a brisk passage of time, signified by the author's growing middle-aged and undergoing 'experiences': he is said to fall in love and out of it. The assumption is, in view of the adjacent emphasis on Ferdy's gallantries, that the narrator's affections were also for ladies, if not for duchesses. Is it far-fetched to maintain that the narrator is advancing a different, and more urgent, case from the one which he appears to be diagnosing so dispassionately?

It is only once he is well into the story that Maugham comes to the anecdote which, on his formally declared principles of story-telling, should have been introduced much earlier, that of the Blands, the rich family of crypto-Jews who are doing everything they can to conceal what Ferdy infuriates them by flaunting. They hide the fact that the resident grandmother of the family is, in fact, Ferdy's sister, Hannah. It is part of the comedy which history supplies that the baronet who presides over Tilby, the country estate where much of the action will now take place, has 'anglicised' his name to Adolphus from Adolf. However, the master of Tilby is known as Freddy throughout the story, although his father name's 'Alfred' (*ci-devant* Alfons Bleikogel) is actually more often familiarised into Freddy than is Adolf. One suspects a certain slapdash confusion, but I have reason to suspect that the slip was more Freudian than lazy, as I shall explain later.

Freddy has been to Eton and Oxford and, with the family name blandly anglicised, he is the perfect combination of the genuine and the bogus. He has taken on all the local colour he can contrive, but his contours cannot conceal their foreignness: the accent may be Oxford, but his nose speaks for the race which the tongue denies and, for the moment, derides. The description of Tilby, the family seat, might be that of a grand country house of the period, whether the owners were Jews or

Gentiles, but its nine-hole private golf course and the wilfully British decor recall that legendary mansion where Sir Philip Sassoon (memorably said to resemble 'a purée of white kid gloves') entertained with greater refinement than the refined would care to display (he had tennis courts set at various angles, so that at any time of day his guests could play without either side having the sun in its eyes).

The decision to call the Blands' house Tilby – an unglamor-ous-sounding place name (compare Henry James' Jeevesian relish in naming his Great Good Places) – may be somewhat artful; it is very close to Trilby, the title of the famous novel by George du Maurier which concerns the predatory relationship between Svengali, that quintessentially manipulative impresario, and an innocent young actress whom he promotes to stardom and mesmerises into what we are surely intended to take for sexual subservience. Svengali is the bad Jew whom the altruistic and unpredatory Ferdy mirrors when he helps to 'bring out' George, the eminently 'Anglo-Saxon' heir to the baronetcy. George is described as 'the perfect type of the young English-man' and he is the apple of Freddy Bland's eye; his brother, Harry, looks Jewish as George does not, but – with schematic asymmetry – he is full of the conventional ambitions which Freddy is disappointed not to find in his unblemished son.

When 'I' mentions Ferdy, the Blands are chilly; they accuse Lady Bland's uncle of being 'such a fearful snob'. Muriel, *née* Miriam, is disgusted by his embarrassingly unpatriotic failure to change his name during the war when Freddy was 'running munitions'. Here again Maugham manages both to flatter and to denigrate: if he describes Freddy as a sort of English Walter Rathenau, 'running munitions' also carries an undertone of 'gun-running': Freddy, however gentlemanly, seems to have been one of the hard-faced men who did well out of the war. There is no reason why Maugham should not pillory profiteers, but his expression suggests connivance with prejudices which, in other aspects, he deplores. Perhaps one cannot convincingly deal with vices from which one is wholly immune, nor does an author often feel impelled to do so. On the other hand, the charge of 'anti-Semitism' cannot sensibly be applied to anyone who observes differences between Jews and Gentiles. It has been convenient for those who want to disparage Maugham to accuse him of defects which, in more canonic figures, are regarded as interesting refinements or negligible foibles.

When the narrator, with feline tolerance, informs his hostess that 'it is very difficult in England now not to know Jews', the appalling Muriel/Miriam, Lady Bland, who is – somewhat surprisingly, and probably only because it supplies another comic twist to her corkscrew character – a Roman Catholic, delivers the standard cant: '. . . I think some of them are very nice. They're so artistic. I don't go so far as to say that Freddy and I deliberately avoid them . . . it just happens that we really don't know any of them very well.' Might she not just as well be speaking of homosexuals?

When, a little later, Freddy (whose name is, of course almost an anagram of Ferdy, the uncle by marriage from whom he is determined to distance himself) is talking about his own lord-of-the-manor character, he declares that rural life in England resembles 'the Greek ideal of life', an observation so lacking in the kind of knowledge which Eton and Oxford might have inculcated that it is plausible to think that the ignorance of what the 'Greek ideal of life' might really be is also a reminder of what one 'ideal' Greek practice actually was. 'I could not but smile' is what the narrator tells us, in response. The smile is promptly said to be due to the unworthy thought that an English country gentleman couldn't keep up his place 'without a packet of money safely invested in American bonds', but *un sourire peut en cacher un autre*.

George tells his father that he wants to go to Munich, though not why. Before he goes, 'I' carries a message to the young man, from Ferdy, inviting him to lunch. The family forbids the meeting, but Ferdy is persuasive and 'I' is present. After the meal, which is salted with Jewish stories, Ferdy plays the piano ('three or four little waltzes'). When George is invited to play, he says, 'I only play classical music. I don't think it would interest you.'

Once George and 'I' are in the street, the young man says, 'What a filthy old Jew.' Soon afterwards, he leaves for Munich, supposedly to learn German, but in fact to study the piano. He becomes a Bohemian and is determined to be a professional pianist. His father learns, from a letter, that he wants to take the old family name of Bleikogel. Freddy is outraged; Muriel is mortified, especially in view of the grand coming-of-age party which is planned at Tilby. When George's allowance is stopped, he asks the disreputable Ferdy for money; Freddy is obliged to beg the old Jew not to send it. 'He's had things too easy for him,' he tells the narrator, 'I've been much too indulgent. There's never been a thing he wanted that I haven't given him. I'll learn him.' Is the last an expression even a pompous Jew is likely to have used after having been to Eton and Oxford?

Maugham treats the big scene, after George's reluctant and temporary homecoming for his twenty-first, with summary abruptness.

When Freddy refuses to sponsor his son's return to Munich, George says he will earn money by selling old clothes.

> 'Like a Jew?'
>
> 'Well, aren't I a Jew? . . . We're all Jews, the whole gang of us, and everyone knows it and what the hell's the good of pretending we're not?'
>
> Then a very dreadful thing happened. Freddy burst suddenly into tears. I'm afraid he didn't behave very much like Sir Adolphus Bland, Bart., M.P., and like the good old English gentleman he so much wanted to be, but like an emotional Adolf Bleikogel . . . He cried noisily and with great sobs and pulled his beard and beat his breast and rocked to and fro. Then they all began to cry . . . Of course it was very painful, but to our rough Anglo-Saxon temperaments I am afraid it must seem also a trifle ridiculous . . .

'I' puts hasty distance between himself and the behaviour he reports. He shows little secret sympathy with the outsiders when they become lacrimose and foreign (one cannot but wonder whether so ardent an Anglo-Saxon as Sir Adolphus would have a beard in 1930, but it is a conveniently outlandish thing for him to pull). The narrator does not affect to have been present, but he retails all the stereotypical details with the glee of someone who wants to ingratiate himself by sharing the dry-eyedness of his readers.

However, it is the old Jewess, Ferdy's sister, who speaks sense, albeit in a foreign accent, and advocates giving George a limited chance to prove himself. Once again, Maugham chooses an unashamed character (who has never pretended to be other than she is) to advocate a tolerant, commonsensical solution, which is adopted. Freddy refuses to say goodbye to his son. Maugham comments, 'I permit myself a trite remark. It is strange that men, inhabitants for so short a while of an alien and inhuman world, should go out of their way to cause themselves so much unhappiness.' The triteness is compounded with pomposity, but the largeness of the sentiment rather swamps the occasion which prompts it. Maugham puts on a stiff collar to make a plea for kindness seem like a toffee-nosed generality, but the notion that all of us inhabit an 'alien' world tips his hand somewhat.

I do not, of course, imagine that I am exposing Maugham's real motives, still less disparaging them or their concealment; it is part of a writer's art, not of his dishonesty, that the fuse which drives his narrative can (and perhaps should) be sparkier than he is obliged to disclose. When 'I' happens to be in Munich and visits George, he finds that he has completely come out of the closet, as it were; he revels in the Jewishness he once felt obliged to conceal:

> '. . . You know, I don't like English people. I never really know where I am with you. You're so dull and conventional. You never let yourselves go. There's no freedom in you, freedom of the soul, and you're such funks. There's nothing in the world you're so frightened of as doing the wrong thing. . . .
>
> 'I like the smell of the Ghetto and the sense of life, and the mystery and the dust and the squalor and the romance . . . That's the real thing. All the rest is only pretence.'

Where did Maugham find the passion which informs the banality of George's blatant desire to be what he 'really is'? My answer is that the desire of the Jew to be at one with what he is can be seen to be both alien to Maugham and easily understood by him. The narrator, who appears to be so much at his ease, so manifestly unthreatened by the fears and danger which hound the Blands, is their brother under the skin: always liable to exposure, he too craves unmasked freedom from inhuman bondage. In travesty, as it were, George speaks for the love that dared not speak its name (Wilde had paid a price few dared to risk). To suppose that Willie was merely amusing himself by deriding the Blands and, to some extent, the prejudices which they themselves have internalised is to be too quickly on the bandwagon. Maugham's weekly trick was more subtle and more subversive and more deeply felt than it was prudent for so bland an operator to disclose.

We find a kind of symmetry with the Blands in Maugham's own family. One of his brothers, Henry, was also a writer and a homosexual and lived painfully in that alien world to which Willie referred. He was of an aesthetic temper which left him vulnerable to guilts and disappointments from which his famous brother wilfully insulated himself; Henry's suicide is matched, incongruously, by Willie's obstinate longevity, but his death has something in common with that of George: Henry also wanted to be an artist and realised that he could never be. There is another concealed source of energy among the Maughams. His oldest brother, who became Lord Chancellor (Willie described him as the most odious man he had never met), was the father of Robin, to whose homosexuality Willie stood in much the same relation as Ferdy Rabenstein did to George's Jewishness; Willie was the enabling instance and supplied the wicked uncle who licensed Robin's coming-out parties. And there is more: the Lord Chancellor's first name was Frederick: he is the Freddie whom Willie wanted to expose as a hypocrite and hence the Freudian slip of giving his unlikeable brother a nominal fraternity with a humbug like Adolphus.

I hope that I have made a case for thinking that *The Alien Corn* can be read as a more personal and more complex myth than Maugham's competence is usually assumed to manage. One literally final touch is rather pretty. The disappointed George (whom the Jewish pianist Lea Makart declares can never in a thousand years be an artist) goes into the gun-room at Tilby and 'began to clean the gun that his mother had given him on his twentieth birthday'. Of course, he kills himself 'accidentally'. Maugham's professional conscience requires a wry ending and the last sentence reads: 'One reads of such accidents in the paper often.' Once again, the sentence is both simple and awkward (try saying it aloud) and seems to hint, involuntarily, at a charge of emotion it affects to deny. My final observation is that George's suicide (as we are meant to take it to be) can be seen as a gloss on George V's remark, when told of a so-called gentleman's homosexuality, 'I thought men like that shot themselves.' George Bland is the sacrificial victim of more English prejudices than the anecdote openly declares and he does shoot himself (much good may it do anybody). It is this quality of duplicity in Maugham, covered by his blandness, which will maintain interest in him, despite the disdain with which our betters are pleased to treat him.

The Old Party

The cant proclaims Somerset Maugham more an enigma than a problem: difficult to understand as a man, he can scarcely be said to have created texts to test the exegete. He was intelligent, but he was not an intellectual; he was shrewd, but he was rarely subtle. He was less successful in the pursuit of love than of money, which he announced to be the sixth sense without which you could not enjoy the other five. He added (which was less widely reported) that you should take care not to pay more than twenty shillings in the pound for it. Maugham entertained generously, if exactingly (tennis and bridge were skills worth packing) and exactly (dates of arrival and departure were always stipulated) but he developed no coterie and was sustained by no reliable faction.

The public and the copies it bought supplied his confidence; critics he affected to ignore. Far and away the most famous living writer of his time, he was recognized by crowds wherever he went (and he went very nearly everywhere), but the recognition of those he might have called his 'betters' was denied him. Edmund Wilson (whose work he had recommended to his publishers in America) was famously vituperative, although his own notebooks reveal a dispassionate affinity to Maugham's. Wilson, of course, craved success in the theatre, which he never

Review of Robert Calder, *Willie: The Life of W. Somerset Maugham*, in the *Times Literary Supplement*, 1989.

achieved; his attacks on Maugham's stories can be read as a displacement sideways of his envy for theatrical triumphs which could hardly be winced to insignificance. Much later, Cyril Connolly wondered why so many people disparaged *The Razor's Edge*, after having confessed the pleasure they had taken in it, but a re-reading of that novel suggests that faint praise was no great injustice. However, part of the reason for Maugham's wary reception by reviewers probably lay in his own acerbic tone: they thought they had to prove themselves as sharp as they took him to be.

Robert Calder won the confidence of Alan Searle, who was Maugham's friend, lover and secretary, for some forty years. Although no substantial literary material was made available by Searle (the manuscript of *Looking Back*, which is rumoured to be both more scandalous and better written than the serialised sections, was held by Searle but remains unpublished since his death in 1985), Calder had the benefit of many hours of interview with Maugham's companion, whose trust he has amply honoured. *Willie* will seem indulgent only to those who relished the demolition undertaken by Ted Morgan's 1980 biography, which had the loyal assistance of Maugham's daughter Liza and her husband. Calder is said to have spent fourteen years on the present work: it is unlikely that anyone will discover anything very much more, in the way of Maughamiana, to confound his diligence. All the retrievable evidence is, it would seem, before the court, even if the summing up is likely to remain more interesting than the verdict.

Calder's diligence is sometimes not far from indulgent. There is decided affection (verging on impertinence) in calling this book *Willie*, a name which Maugham preferred to Somerset, but never much liked, and whose place in the current smutty argot pokes posthumous fun at its *pudique* possessor. Making the best of a bad job was very much his way of life; making the best of a prosaic talent was his industrious method. Even Maugham's apologists cannot point to a clinching masterpiece. *Of Human Bondage* is monumental and persuasive, but its literary means are meagre; its hero, Philip Carey, is not only unheroic but, in his bruised wariness, largely uninteresting, if rarely boring. It is a *bildungsroman* constructed on ground and basement level. Philip is humiliated by Mildred, the demon-waitress, before being redeemed by the love, or at least the affection, of a decent girl with whom, in a parody of optimism, the author would have us believe that he will lead a happy, humdrum life. The message of *Of Human Bondage* is that there is no motto in the cracker of life, and rarely much of a bang.

Maugham's life has proved more interesting than his work, though this was the last impression he would have chosen to leave. He hoped to fashion his *oeuvre* into a plausible façade, depicting a persona so verisimilitudinous that no one would inquire whether there was anything behind it. Thus he made first person narration into the antithesis of egotism. When Calder has him say '*Et ego in Arcadia vixit* (sic)', the Latin howler is oddly appropriate; it becomes the trite echo of Rimbaud's '*Je est un autre*'. Maugham was least himself when 'I' came into the story. His art did not conceal art; it concealed him.

Calder is disposed to agree with the conventional wisdom that Maugham's character was blighted by the long dread of exposure and destruction of which Oscar Wilde's fate was the brutal paradigm. The accumulation of money made it easier to dispose of transient trade without scandal, as did an address outside the scope of Scotland Yard.

Biographers are, however, thwarted at their subjects' peril. Ted Morgan reminded us that doubt is not always beneficent. Calder, for all his sympathy, assumes that Willie's caustic evasiveness was the consequence of his homosexuality. But did the sins of the flesh perhaps weigh less on his conscience than those of the spirit? Was he not haunted (it is remarkable how many ghost stories he liked to tell, for all his realistic tendencies) by a sense that he had gathered too many sixpences on earth instead shooting for the moon? Charles Strickland (that other Gauguin) announces Maugham's romantic admiration for a recklessness he could not match, although his foraging expeditions to the East, encouraged by the prospect of both raw material and unpoliced cruising, proved that he never lacked courage or enterprise. (There is, it seems, something in the homosexual temper, or response, which arms certain writers with provocative energy: travelling light and going too far sets them bravely apart from the straight and the narrow.) Willie never went so far that he could not come back; he admired the beachcomber who could throw caution to the winds, but if he could fall for the Edward Barnards, he never fell with them.

Proper caution inhibits Calder from speculative questions.

The limitations and the courtesies of biography coincide here; the term 'critical' is significantly unappended. Psychoanalysis has its ponderous say, in quotation, but no inventive 'reading' is undertaken of the man and his work. Perhaps Calder feels that his earlier study, *William Somerset Maugham and the Quest for Freedom*, covered that side of things; nevertheless, its omission suggests an uneasiness about Maugham's literary importance which affection cannot dispel.

The oddness of Maugham lies in the unobtrusive singularity of his circumstances: he was a rare bird without being a gaudy one. How many writers are of truly Anglo-French culture? Maugham's unquenchable regret over the death of his mother surely owes something to the transplantation which was its consequence. Calder's opening sentence tells us, rather inelegantly, that Willie 'came into the world carrying a passport', by which he seems to mean that he was by nature a travelling man, but the truth is that he felt French before he was English, for all his claim, technically, to have been born on British soil (in the Paris embassy). His beloved mother, in the style of her generation, gave him into the hands of a French nursemaid and his early days were akin to those of Proust, a novelist whom he omitted from his roster of greatness with at least as much perversity as Henry James when he omitted Maugham from his *TLS* list of young authors to watch. Willie too played on the Champs Elysées and teased the stall-holders; he too entertained his *petits camarades* with nervous precociousness.

Show and concealment were in tandem long before the issue of homosexuality presented itself. 'Telling stories' has a nursery sense which no writer ever quite outlives: Maugham deflected and attracted attention by the same means. It is now impossible to know how much of his reported candour was whitewash: was that old gentleman encountered at the Garrick really a quondam bedfellow, or did he merely wish his interlocutor to believe so (or would he have liked it to have been so)? If, in his weekending youth, he was indeed no stranger to the casual homo-eroticism consequent on having to share sheets in Edwardian country-houses, he soon came to acquire the straight face which made a joke of middle-class morality. Hypocrisy, Maugham was privileged to discover, is the name the English attached to the prudence of those who like to have one set of cakes and eat another.

Duplicity was, of course, a staple ingredient of the French

literary models for whom Maugham retained enduring respect (Balzac, Stendhal and Flaubert were abbreviated, *pour mieux sauter*, in his list of the ten best novelists), but if adultery was a compulsory figure, bisexuality (until Barthes's *S/Z*) was less well marked. Any naïve semiotician would certainly notice that Maugham uses the same name, Rose, to denote the two 'real' loves depicted in his fiction: the Tercanbury schoolboy and the delectable heroine of *Cakes And Ale*, to whose real life model, Sue Jones, he proposed marriage before his disastrous engagement to Syrie Wellcome. Maugham was to use Mailer's terms. 'the prisoner of sex', not least because, unable to match Spinoza, he could not escape human bondage through decisive acceptance of its imposed necessities.

Genuine plain-speaking could hardly be the style of a split personality; common sense, in such a case, becomes part of the disguise. Maugham, we are told, never looked in mirrors; appearances, you might say, were too important to him. He sat to Gerald Kelly, in his most stylish days, when a good tailor was at last within his means, but his pose suggests a man who is contriving, with whatever show of Edwardian dignity, to sit on the fence as comfortably as he may. Enstooled by Sutherland, he seems, in creased old age, to accept his absurdity with lofty grace. His irony always found its first and steadiest target in himself, but he was not eager that other should fire at the same bull.

Calder's unaggressive but rather prolonged treatment of the homosexual issue suggests, if nothing definite, a clear instance of over-determination: everything, almost, in Willie's genetic and accidental circumstances pushed him, with whatever reluctance, in that direction. (He had a homosexual brother, just as he has a stammering cousin.) However, had he stayed in France, he might have been less ashamed, just as he might have been easier in his speech. If there is any apt comparison, it could be with André Gide, another 'made' writer, whose 'genius' lay in the compiling of an *oeuvre* rather than in one brilliant flash. Gide made a virtue of outspokenness, where Maugham affected reticence; in his work, Willie discussed almost everything except homosexuality. Only in the passage on El Greco, in *Don Fernando*, did the mask crack, without being dropped, whereas Gide harped endlessly on the subject. In other sexual respects, Calder points out, Maugham was more daring, particularly in his early work (*Mrs Craddock* is an instance) than England was likely to applaud. He often came up against the Lord Chamberlain, whose exigences, no less than the commercial anxieties of theatrical managers, finally impelled him to renounce the stage altogether.

The French literary climate might have suited him better, just as French morality might have liberated him from enforced duplicity. The Revolution banalised aristocratic morals and made them available, above all, to intellectuals. Elegance ceased to be a social virtue and became a literary one, a devolution never available in England, whose aristocrats retained a monopoly on privilege at least until the Great War encouraged a degree of homogenization. It is indicative of Maugham's ambivalence that sections of his work have a prescriptive tone which reads like a translation. *The Summing Up* has no obvious parallel in English but is of a piece with, say, the *Carnets* of de Montherlant. Maugham's acculturation enables him to escape awkwardness, but is it not a little too well-spoken to be wholly at home? (Ferdy Rabenstein, in *The Alien Corn*, contains more of his author than you might think.) Translate a passage of Maugham's prose into French and you are immediately aware of how little, in the way of subtlety or implicit meaning, has failed to make the crossing. His rejection from the established English canon is not merely a matter of merit; in some sense, he was never a proper candidate for admission (after all, he was not even Irish). He did not ask nicely enough or knock forcefully enough. To have a foot in both camps was his natural condition. He was never entirely at home anywhere; his conformity was the measure of his alienation. Observing the very rules he was amused to bend, he had the temperament and the nerve of the classy spy. His cover-story was, like Willie Ashenden's, consistent with the truth, but not with the whole truth. He was a man who put his cards on the table the better to conceal the ace he kept up his sleeve.

If Maugham was a closet Frenchman, he hardly went all the way with republican virtues. Liberty might fascinate him, but fraternity embarrassed and equality unnerved him. (The snob would sooner defer than be taken for a peer; it leaves him with his vanity unshared.) In this regard, Maugham was comfortable with the English ethos; here he never had to choose between the reactionary and the progressive, between Maurras and Jaurès; English writers never presumed to supplant the aristocracy as arbiters of social taste. Middle-class talents might ape the manners and even satirise the habits of their betters, but neither Disraeli nor Trollope, whatever their secret or advertised conceits, supposed that he had replaced those whom it was entertaining to sauce. Maugham's failure to be wholly at home with the English aristocracy was made the opportunity for a recent *exposé* by John Bayley, who repeated a story told him, one assumes, by Anthony Powell. Powell was Maugham's neighbour at a lunch when Maugham remarked that in the Edwardian era the upper classes were in the habit of referring to their offspring by their courtesy titles rather than by their first names. 'They still do', said Powell, upon which the coldest of Maughamian shoulders was turned towards him. Bayley builds an edifice of scorn on this petty instance, as if Powell's knowledge of aristocratic usage revealed Willie as an fraud (impostors are, of course, common in Maugham's work, although their fraudulence has a way of trumping their betters). It may have been that Willie had had enough of being taught to suck eggs by a junior; alternatively, if the style of Powell's autobiography is anything to go by (and it is certainly nothing to stay for), Maugham may simply have wearied of the man. However, it is likely that a sore point was touched: Willie was never entirely easy in the ways of his adopted country; he was, in more respects than one, waiting to be found out. In later life he was convinced that he was about to be bankrupt; he fled to Switzerland in the hope of finding a refuge from taxes which never, owing to his foreign residence, consumed much of his income. In no department of his life was Maugham secure: to be '*bien dans sa peau*' was never his portion.

Denied a reliable identity, a writer finds his natural form in dialogue, which was Maugham's professional strength. (It was when he first heard audiences laughing at his lines that he realised that success was attainable.) Always described as a stammering and reluctant public performer, Maugham was surely more of an actor than anyone cared to notice. Who writes dialogue convincingly without being its eager secret voice, or voices? The outsider is more alert to the quirks and absurdities of local speech than any native. Maugham, like Coward, made his apes more amusing than those whom they parodied until he came to be the model for his models. What parvenu could have better evidence of his arrival?

Maugham's dialogue rarely depended on any aptitude for mimicry. Only in *Liza of Lambeth* did he attempt the phonetic reproduction which Steinbeck, for instance, used in *The Grapes of Wrath*. Conscious that no gentleman speaks other languages without an accent, he never paraded his command of French and German when depicting foregners: a French senator says, 'It's love by blue', a locution which helped to earn Willie the dismissive contempt of René Clair who said that he knew nothing about France. Maugham's dialogue, especially in his plays, flowed with unstammering continuity, but it rarely distinguished one character from another by any individual pattern of speech. Cockneys lacked aitches and toffs were toffee-nosed, but none was identified by a personal vocabulary. Maugham discriminated between theatrical and prosaic dialogue in a very intelligent way. Like an accurate but unshowy *charcutier*, he knew precisely how to weigh his merchandise; if artful generosity could add a slice more than you asked for, he was careful never to give you a surfeit.

His dialogue in the stories is always at the service of the anecdote: sticking to the point is cardinal. Speech carried things forward and is always used to 'break up' the narrative, but it hardly every obtrudes and it is never far away from its author's controlling tone. In the plays, there are memorable lines, but few memorable characters. 'Who will forgive God?' asks the bereaved mother after her only son has been killed in the war; does anyone remember her name? When Maugham is the magician, the rabbits are there to play their part in his stew rather to display any individual bounce. The manipulative domination of the author (typically remarked by D. H. Lawrence) reflects his wilful control of all the ingredients of his imagined world. He passed for an observer of the human scene, an impersonal recorder of case histories, but here again there was a measure of straightfaced imposture: as much as any writer, he made naturalism an opportunity for a self-love that was careful never to speak its name. His use of a multiplicity of voices was an apt way of translating hesitation into fluency; he was the ventriloquist whose artful modesty lay in making a dummy of himself, the better to earn applause for his creations. He postponed *sine die* the question of who and what he really was. When the day did come he collapsed into senile panic, to the glee of those who envied his abilities and coveted his cash. His readers seem not to have been greatly disillusioned. They continued to trust a doctor who prescribed the mixture as before, but always contrived to give it a slightly fresh flavour.

Maugham attempted a variety of forms, but he remained decidedly Maughamian in all of them. He might advertise exotic fruit, but he was an apple who did not fall far from the tree, even if his branch of it had been grafted in the first place.

Henry Moore in Paris

The best criticism of art is better art or, sometimes, simply 'other' art (at the limit, in the paradoxical tradition of the new, discontinuity becomes evidence of a continuing process). The habit of critical immodesty in our time is most clearly illustrated by the intrusion of political considerations – in the form of formulaic programmes or anathemas – into the practice of the arts in general. If this pre/proscriptive performance is chronic in literature, where correct 'values' trump talent (and discount popularity, that 'democratic' way of by-passing critics), it is to be found in the visual arts too, where critical language is particularly gluttonous of any conceptual thickening of its watery discourse, any way in which it can be made to sound more significant and become more imposing. The disposition of the intellectual to participate in the arts, not by gaining practical experience through the process of apprenticeship and eventual mastery, but by summary graduation to magisterial roles (curator/purchaser, arts councillor, journalistic pundit, political adjudicator, sponsoring executive), has been part of a style of appropriation which lacks either the callow honesty of those who, in the tired old phrase, 'know what they like' or the commissioning generosities (and ideologically imposed scenarios) of old-style monarchical or ecclesiastic patrons. This adjudicating role for the critical intelligence has come remarkably late in the history of art; it has been claimed by authorities whose own performances do not begin to rank with those of Vasari, for notable instance, the man who first turned evaluative biography into, if not an art form, certainly a form of artfulness, a way of going straight to the top table if only in order to arrange the seating plan.

The critic's assumption both of a 'right to judge' and of the capacity to judge right might be laughable if it had not also eroded the sense of mystery which led the Greeks not merely to make sculptures of their Gods but also to make gods of (some of) their sculptures: the first 'critics' – one might argue – were also, literally, diviners who, scanning a row of sculptures, were able to detect which images were somehow impregnated with godliness and which remained unanimated lumps of wood, metal or stone. Those who practise today's critico-biblio-bio-graphical fetish, the prying prurience of those who analyse a subject's interest in terms of the variety of sexual performances (especially succulent if, like Eric Gill's, they go too far), have not *sought* to destroy the integrity (the secret cohesion) of the imaginative craftsman whom romantics chose – quite late in the day – to categorise with the title of The Artist; yet the disintegra-tion of respect (literally the 'due way of looking') in *all* domains of human life has something to do with this greedy 'appropria-tion' of art by 'society' and, in particular, by the intellectuals who articulate its now almost wholly parodic – hence intimida-tory, rarely exalting – value-system. The mantic intuition of the ancient (and anonymous) god-diviners is modernised into dip-sticking the artist's reserves of biographical juice; the extraction of his story makes 'him' easier to swallow than the density of his work, just as the price of buying him as the subject for a book remains within the common range when that of his work (clearly enough in the case of Moore or Picasso) puts his stuff beyond most individuals' scope. (We honour a man who can buy a Canaletto as if *he*, not the picture, had divine qualities, and even if he needs an adviser to have it pointed out to him.)

Words replace works, even 'inside' art itself. Once Jack Critic declares himself as good as a master, because he has learnt the routines and jargon of the adjudicator, whether he is a TV executive, the administrator of a trust or an intellectual journal-ist for hire, he *requires* art to furnish a room, a programme or a text; he cannot afford to be silent in his respect or to respect what does not speak quotably to him; he must be a translator or a transporter; he must, by one means or another, obtain a purchase on the work: in this frail sense at least, he still can be said to buy it, or not. The names of the patronising companies who, as they say, helped to make the Moore exhibition possible testify to the glamour they hope to cadge from backing a safe horse: British Steel and British Airways are, in their own esteem, like the Farnesi, except that they sponsor nothing new in the way of art, merely seek to wear Moore like a medal of merit; they have bought shares in a reputation.

Those who cannot be patrons can, as critics, still be patronising. The modern mind seldom separates the contemplation of an accepted master from some commissioned obligation to find a talkative critical position. Verbosity is all the style; the television voice-over (or at least the properly chosen music) must come in to take the curse off any unsettling feeling of awe which the voice of silence might provoke. In our garrulous world, the routine of the professional critic, the sophist of art who is determined to differentiate himself from the gushing publicist, must be to wonder, when cued by commissioned circumstance, what can be said *against* the masterpiece. The critic, today, is as often as not someone who *resents* artistic autonomy, who – when he sees art – wants to be in on the deal.

The 'natural' response to intimidating qualities tends to be murderous; treachery is the most earnest form of piety. We recognise the master in order to know where to concentrate our attack. In the arts, the reigning 'king' announces our target and stands in the way of its attainment; genius renders us superfluous and hence motivates malice; mediocrity is much more congenial. Brutus the critic soon makes his pen his sword in these cases: like John Berger with Picasso, he bends his wit to find disparagements which will relativise the Master and give art a future which, without his displacement, the genius seems already to have pre-empted. To be ahead of one's time is to have the air already of returning from a place which others have yet to explore; the trophies of that leap into the inaccessible spoil the adventure for everyone else and thus render the innovator – that archaeologist of the future – vulnerable to charges of pillage. It is not fair (as if art could ever be fair!) not to have searched and yet already to have found.

Picasso's failure, in Berger's book, lay in a lack of political *serieux*; the feline critic found an ingenious way of making the artist's 'professional' virtuosity into a moral defect; his protean dexterity was held to make him veer, whatever he said or wanted, to the right. His success was in the unreliable light of today, and yesterday; his failure was to invest himself wholly in tomorrow. His actual talent was boundless and a-historical and, for that crucial reason, somehow immature. Genius can arrive so easily at impossible (irrelevant) destinations that it would be well advised, Berger suggested, to use a reliable map and to plan its excursions with a certain solemn and, yes, self-denying purposefulness (there is, for all his air of social deprivation, an end-of-term reporting house-masterliness about Berger's attitude to playful humanity).

For such a critic, Picasso's affectations of 'Communism' could not be anything but casual, a patronising gesture like a wave from an errant limousine, not a vote for the prompter presentation of the future. Berger was not unaware that Picasso's work was capable of such mutations, such stylistic versatility, such authoritative whims, that allegiance to any political attitude would have limited and lamed it, unless (and here was Berger's central demand, like that of any Commissar) the artist took his political commitment so seriously that he channelled polymorphic zest into single-minded enthusiasm and become, as he could, and hence – in the ideologist's view – *should*, a genuine proponent and advancer of the Communist cause.

I simplify an argument which, in the early 1970s, appeared somewhat Calvinistic in its demanding deference to genius, but even a partial account reminds us of how grasping some of the best critics have been, how determined to master the masters. A belated sense of indignation at Berger's subtle plausibilities is, I daresay, the petty measure of how right he once seemed to be; even though the wilful mercilessness of the man (doubled, at times, with his denunciations of the inhumanity of the *bourgeoisie*, quite as if all the world's inhumanities could be laid at their brass-knockered doors) was chilling; it was also peremptory in its conscripting force and exciting in its sado-masochistic solicitation. Berger was eminently against the anthological eminence of Sir Kenneth Clark, who seemed to find merit in everything that was canonical, regardless of the character or political posture of the artist. Permanently Red Berger appeared to be riled by the claim that art was timeless and that we had all the time in the world to look at it (although one might guess that he also wanted, very badly, to be king of the critical castle, if only to announce that it was to be converted into accommodation for worthy workers). To a committed critic, the political agenda for the revision of the world rendered abhorrent the criticism which was hardly to be distinguished from a *catalogue raisonné.* He was exasperated by the pandering tolerance of the connoisseur (Kenneth Clark *en tête*) who tabulated, rearranged, enumerated, but never challenged the great seating plan of world-class artists, never dismissed from the top table anyone who had been there for a long time.

Going to Paris in order to write about the Henry Moore exhibition in the gardens of the Bagatelle was not, I need hardly say, part of my professional life: I am not an art critic and I took no sharp credentials with me. The inscription on the main building of the little *château* around which the exhibition is arranged might have been put there for my advised benefit: *parva sed apta*, which might translate as 'keep it short and stay on the subject'. As for the occasion, the illusion of timelessness could hardly have been more ardently sustained if nature had deliberated on its creation: the sun was hot, but not too hot, and its steady radiance gleamed on the worked simplicity of the artfully arranged sculpture in ample gardens which, remote from public transport, were scarcely peopled during the course of an ambling morning. All around, the Bois de Boulogne was a sumptuous simulacrum of 'nature', planned and unplanned, a vegetarian zoo of shrubs and trees in trimmed and tended liberty, set out to please an urban population which might take it for rustic reality. The undoubted art of Moore was ensconced in what seemed the artlessness of the Bois, although the busy mowers and the general air of calculation promised everything to be under control. The gardens of the Bagatelle were impeccable: the roses were approaching their best (which *is* their best) and the absence of the smallest blackspot was an instructive reproach to merely mortal gardeners. The Yorkshire Moores – the pun may be painful but has a definitive point – had come to a preserve of self-consciously elegant *ancien régime* taste; they squatted down, or reached up, in a setting more suited to the the extravagance of blousy Baroque decoration, although the sculptures, even as temporary tenants, had taken up residence with the sublime assurance of cosmopolitan aristocrats who belonged wherever they happened to be.

The illusion of being in the presence of something eternal, conceived to last as long as the world itself, leads to a sense of depersonalisation: it hardly matters who one is or what one thinks. In such a sweetly pastoral setting, it is no shame to become one of civilisation's sheep, a walk-on in a setting to which one is purely incidental. (Sheep are the most human of

Moore's subjects: they even have 'real' faces.) The trouble taken
in mounting the show, in making sure that a reclining figure
looks 'at home' or that the three-piece Vertebrae are comfortable where they are lodged in the middle of a great swoop of
lawn where three slips and a gulley might just as well (perhaps)
be crouching to a fast bowler, this resolve to make the whole
show 'natural', by removing all signs of effort in its installation,
renders the individual visitor not quite an intruder but certainly
accidental. He may be touched – by the world fame of a British
artist for instance! – but he is not encouraged to touch it (hands
off the money, folks). The exhibits are, in every respect, out of
reach; the wardresses blow a whistle if one crosses the grass to
cop a feel, while we all know that the moment is past when we
might take a Moore home with us, when his prices might have
allowed us to get in ahead of the Getty boys. The priceless work
is there because others have decided to make it available to us;
the show is an act of wilful, limited bounty, not – in particular
– of local pride or reverence; it is the initiative of the international task forces of culture, part of the new world order
which, since the collapse of the USSR, has no specific programme, no lien on any announced or plotted future, no hidden
or declared agenda except, perhaps, to keep doing things, just
as television programmes or newspaper editors have no purpose
beyond getting their show on the road (and if you think that is
easy or leaves them time – as Berger's Picasso should, in his
view, have had time for *seriousness* – well, what do you know
about Pressures?).

Make no mistake, the Moore show is not being disparaged
here, nor should it be, since it is, quite simply, stupendous and
magnificent (adjectives suitable for publicity purposes should
perhaps be six-packed for easy access). The work needs no
words, so what is to be said? The show is not only the work. It
was organised by the Mairie de Paris (which is run by Jacques
Chirac), by the Henry Moore Foundation (whose wealth and
prestige depends on international promotion and ever greater
recognition of H.M.) and by the British Council (which is run
by whoever runs it, in the interests of a culture to which
governments, for the last fifteen years or so, have been swagger-
ingly indifferent, in the sense that there is no sign that Jim
Callaghan ever read a book or looked at a picture or that Mrs
Thatcher could ever be *instructed* by anyone or anything or that
John Major has any notion that there is any way of saying or

looking at anything except in the most trite terms). Art has become (or remains) separate from politics in England not because it is too difficult for politicians but because they do not have money for it and because whatever is not economic is not real to them, as the Pope's divisions were not real to Stalin.

Moore is not only as great as he is, he is also a splendidly convenient totemic figure to both 'Socialists' and Conservatives; his glory even reflects well on those who have no time for politics (no time for time, one might say). He has become for almost everyone what the Beatles were to Sir Alec Douglas-Home, a 'secret weapon' which accrues dividends without demanding investment. In this sense, he resembles North Sea Oil, without requiring the infrastructure; since his work comes in 'editions' of varying numbers, he can both be exported and stay at home; he is, it is true, exhaustible – like oil – but, unlike oil, his price will continue to rise, like his reputation. There is something about his fame which suits all parties; he may have been a rugged individualist, a self-made making-man, the aproned artisan who Did It All Himself, but he is also a Yorkshireman, a man of the people, without side, without intellectual pretensions (although possessed of a damn good mind and a good library to furnish what unaffordable schools and unnecessary universities did not), a man of few words (*parva sed apta*), worthy of a county whose players eschewed showy strokes and the philosophy of six-or-out for that of 'get them in singles', the unflashy provincial attitude of steady-does-it.

Yes, the work is worthy of anything good one says of its creator and, as he might have wished, transcends his personal biography or eulogy (that is exactly what an artist's selfless vanity wants). Its variety never makes it unrecognisable; it has its ponderous skittishnesses, but part of what makes it respectable is that it leaves one in no doubt who did it. As for why – why like this, why both innovatory and pious, why *these* recurrent forms – the intimidating authority of the creator brooks no quibbles, not because he is so grand, not because he would ever snap at you, but because his humility and his pride are indistinguishable, like his imitations and his transcendence. How else should we define mastery but in terms like these?

Moore then is a Yorkshireman of this century making objects which will outlast the century, looking at the world like a connoisseur of divinities, who can contribute to its essential furniture. Where he touches the history of his time, it is tangential indeed: he recognised a subject in both the miners of his native land and in the crowds who slept in the London underground to shelter from the blitz (my generation knew him first from these putative tributes to ordinary people, whose ordinariness – arranged in ranks as etymology would like – rendered them without personality, in his eyes, as if heaped in some common catacomb). It is tempting here to outBerger Berger and to find something callous in the attention bent on those whose particularity asked more of Moore than he could or would grant. There is a photograph in the catalogue of the show at the Galérie Imbert showing H. M. (the majestic initials of this common man have a nice pertinence here) leaning against the entrance of a tube station, sussing the location; one has a sense of detached vigilance which is very close to the heartless-ness necessary to art as to surgery (only loud fools make sincerity an important attribute of skill).

I accuse Moore of no truly reprehensible delinquency – of no correctable offence – when I say that, in the presence of his noble work, I have a certain abiding sense of how convenient it is, in certain arts, to care *only* about art. Integrity is rightly regarded as essential to genius; one should be all of one piece in order that all of one's pieces should cohere, should belong unquestionably to their creator and be *his* images, as we – they say – are made in God's. Moore is a small god, of course, and cannot manage the diversity of The Creator of whom Iris Murdoch once remarked that making heads must have been the most divine part of His work. Strangely enough, Moore's heads are the least interesting of his: they are often perfunctory and the faces have neither memorable features nor emblematic significance. One of the least impressive works at the Bagatelle is that cleft head which has the appearance of some modernised confessional. Moore was not a head-man; he worked best in a manner which denied thought (he would be incapable of the pensive vulgarity of Rodin's Thinker). His reticence was reflected in the lifeless mouths of his creatures, from whom no whisper or cry can ever come, although the wind may speak in their orifices. Come to think of it, Moore was not much of a *tail* man: his mothers are maternal, without any Jocastan hints in their comportment or their anatomy: there is nothing under the recumbent figures' skirts, nothing to be peeked at or even guessed at. The kings and queens are majestic, without ambivalent mortality; no breast excites in Moore, no cleft suggests (however many cleavages and disjunctions we are offered). Moore is at home with the enduring elements; he is the very opposite of the man who makes no bones about things: he makes things about bones. The thing is the thing is the thing, immutable in its inhuman thinginess; there is no temptation in the presence of any of Moore's work, monumental or maquette, to lower one's voice: there is nothing to interrupt, no service in progress, no conversation in train, no sexual solicitation to accept or deny.

In the show at Didier Imbert, 19 Avenue Matignon, Moore's unpretentious house at Much Hadham is painstakingly reproduced; it is a small Pompeian exhibition this, the house Just As it Was when death – like Vesuvius – cried 'Time' to the maker of timeless things. We see in the narrow clutter the domestic evidence of the artist's earnestness, the books, objects and artefacts he liked to find familiar. Even here, the man does not let himself down: his simplicities are never cheap. We see a few books of humanising banality (Herriot's Yorkshireness perhaps commended him), but nothing to surprise by its topicality or shock by its crudeness (no old copies of *Playboy* here); the furniture is that of a small man, some of it nicely crafted, some of it dun and suburban (that dressing table!). A hint of tolerance is given by an embroidered cushion with the phrase 'The Moore The Merrier' and tricked out with a Women's Institute version of a 'typical' sculpture, which a more choleric artist might have hurled at its donor. As for artists, here are Degas, Courbet, Daumier, Ruskin, Cézanne, Picasso, Renoir, Picasso, Vuillard: we are among old friends and hardly any new ones. All that is surprising here is the lack of surprises; Moore reassures as much as he impresses, the essence (you might say) of a National Hero. The anonymous makes up a large part of his inventory: the Cycladic and the pre-Columbian, as well as the casual objects and bones, suggest how encouragingly nameless voices spoke to him out of the silent past (Malraux's *The Voices of Silence* is there on his shelves, of course). What you feel with Moore is that complicity with tradition which T. S. Eliot wanted to render normative, perhaps because he was incapable of true allegiance to it (being an *arriviste* and an impostor); Moore could and did lose himself in the objectivity of his work (he hardly needed his head, it seems, any more than the figures are recognisable by theirs); H. M. had a royal vanity, indistinguishable from his modesty, which needed no crown.

A personal note reveals, unimportantly, why Paris on 16 July 1992, when I saw the works at the Bagatelle and the show at Didier Imbert, 19 Avenue Matignon, was and was not only a place of beauty, of sublime feelings, of pure admiration: Louis-Ferdinand Céline wrote a book called *Bagatelles pour un Massacre*, in which he called gloatingly for all the Jews in the world to have their throats cut, and on 16 July 1942, the Parisian *gendarmerie*, without any incitement from the Germans, rounded up and took away 13,000 Jews (mostly women and children) who were held at the Vélodrome d'Hiver, in appalling conditions, until French train-drivers and the brave *cheminots* so dear to the PCF agreed, without a single demur, to carry them to their deaths at Auschwitz. Fifty years later, to the day, we walked in those lovely gardens and saw those lovely sculptures which important companies like those which, after the war, gladly employed René Bousquet, the prefect who organised the *rafle* of the Vel d'Hiv, had so generously arranged for our delectation, to remind us of the timelessness of art and, in the smallest of unintended parentheses, of our right to forget the horror and even of how right we are to forget it. I am, I fear, a little spoiled, and forever, for aesthetics and it is to the aesthete's world of the inhuman, the durable, the eternally valuable that Moore elected to belong. When I read, in the amiable brochure issued for the Bagatelle show, that in his old age Moore was visited by François Mitterrand and, on being made Commandeur de la Légion d'honneur, repeated three times, 'J'aime Paris', I cannot but think that twice might have been enough. Moore's provincialism was both proud and limiting; his fallen warriors commemorate no known war, express not even the pathetic emotion of the dying Gaul, but are durable exercises, evidence of a culture (one might argue) which was earnest but uninformed. One need not say that Moore lacked genius to see that there were things his genius lacked.

Some Philosophers I Have Not Known

We have the idea that philosophy is an unemotional way of considering human knowledge and testing its reliable logics. Is it not an essentially impersonal attempt to discover abiding truths and their orderly, more or less necessary, connection? The philosophers we are incited to respect are those whose logic is least susceptible to charges of idiosyncrasy and whose arguments are clean of rhetoric. When Russell remarked 'the worse the logic, the more interesting the results,' was he not warning us against looking to him for entertaining theories or pyrotechnic display? Flashiness, we were intended to gather, is not a happy method in philosophy; the brightest are those who are not ashamed to be dull; our passion is best reserved for the dispassionate. Roughly speaking, one gathers, all philosophical objects are colourless.

The philosophers most commonly admired in the British tradition are, unsurprisingly, those whose practice mirrors what the British like to think of as their own sensible and typically unassuming qualities: the absence of what Byron called 'enthusy-musy' is the happiest warrant of worth. David Hume's lack of credulity in the prospect of – and certainly the arguments for – religious salvation, makes him an exemplary figure among those who, while honouring a trenchant prose style, are wary of dogma and averse to mystification. Dr Johnson may have accused Hume of writing like a Frenchman, but Johnson had not read Sartre or Pierre Boutang, say, whose so-called philosophy is, for the most part, indistinguishable from exhortation or autobiography, not to say rant.

On the British side of the channel, we attribute a certain nobility to those who make it their calling deliberately to saw the branches on which they might otherwise hold head-in-the-cloudsy sway. Russell's centrality, in the present century, at least until the advent of Wittgenstein, owes something to the paradox of an aristocrat who disclaimed aristocracy, while never quite renouncing its usefulness in intimidating those who did not share his low opinion of it. Russell was a leveller who made a point of being seen to have come a long way down the mountain in order to be at one with the common man. 'Tommy loves a Lord' said Byron, sarcastically, of Thomas Moore, as if he himself did not. How sweet are grandees who elect not to be grand with us!

When he allotted a whole chapter in his *History of Western Philosophy* (1948) to Byron, we can scarcely doubt that Russell was making both claims and allowances. He was asserting an affinity between himself and that other trouble-making aristo-crat whose moral versatility it would not be unglamorous to associate with his own, while also, of course, allowing that a man whose thoughts were scarcely logical, and were certainly never expressed in any systematic sense, could – by his influence at least – be recruited to the philosophical pantheon, even if, like Monsieur Jourdain in more prosaic circumstances, he did his philosophy without ever being conscious of the fact. Russell was also, I think, and more seriously, alerting us to the importance – even to a supposedly 'logical' and 'scientific' discipline – of the general social and artistic climate, to which a popular poet much more than a cloistered logician is likely to contribute, a fact which Plato acknowledged (much less philos-ophically than Russell) with regard both to Homer and to Aeschylus, whose influence he deplored. Scepticism and the pursuit of 'liberty', the emancipation of philosophy from theol-ogy, owe much to Byronic impudence, even if he lisped in numbers rather than making any conscious contribution to the foundations of mathematics.

Russell shows but does not quite state that, while philosophy may indeed aspire to be an impersonal, even abstract activity, analogous to mathematics by virtue of its chaste renunciation of rhetoric and its systematic publicity, it is often flavoured with personal considerations and prejudices and favouritisms which logic may ignore but practice and style confirm. My amateur purpose here is, in part at least, to consider the kinds of elective or unconscious affinities which draw us to one philosopher and alienate us from another, even though we prefer to suppose that our choices have been made on logical grounds, based almost entirely on the quality of arguments advanced or conclusions unarguably reached, rather than on account of more shifty congenialities, such as Bertrand championing Byron, or Ayer Voltaire. I intend to hint at the sorts of reasons which make philosophy attractive to us, despite and because of its aridities or difficulties and despite or because of its failure or inability to deliver ultimate answers to ultimate questions. Despite our sceptical selves and the modesty of at least certain practitioners, the philosopher's stone is something we still dream of discovering in some secret compartment of our chosen champion's luggage, however modest his case.

By 'systematic publicity' I mean simply that unlike poetry or painting, in which privacy privileges the artist to do as he or she pleases, philosophy passes for a common, accessible enterprise where one philosopher may legitimately question the line taken by another; pleasure is not a principle here nor creativity a password. Anything may be challenged, however fancy the brushwork. Logical errors are not a matter of opinion: they are demonstrable, as errors in poetic expression are not. One may wince at a man's rhyme, but one cannot in honour provide an indubitable correction. Plays may have arguments, but they are not right or wrong. The worst daub in the world cannot be refuted. Nietzsche said, 'You say there can be no argument about matters of taste? All life is an argument about matters of taste!' Philosophy and life, in that event, should be studied in different departments.

In the British tradition which was so plausibly propounded at Cambridge, not least by my old supervisor Renford Bambrough, the editor of *Philosophy*, philosophy is not a form of personal expression. 'Mere autobiography' was the standard dismissive formula for statements beginning, 'I sincerely believe' or 'I have always felt'. Intimate convictions do not override an error nor does a famous signature validate a worthless argument. In philosophy, there may be genius, but there is no privilege. The most eminent contemporary or dead pundit may be challenged, and corrected, by a neophyte. What philosophers do is, so the cant argues, a sort of science, perhaps a godless theology, although it no longer lays claim to queendom. Even in the domestic service to which A. J. Ayer once sought to approximate it, philosophy is a discipline whose recruits seek to dispel the dust of centuries and to create a clean, good place in which arguments may be marshalled and their advocates march in reasonable step. Investigation, not speculation, and the evaluation of evidence, not the fervours of belief, were the best means of creating a world of co-operative intelligence which would allow us to banish superstition and band together in the common pursuit of valid methods, rather than of some ultimate Truth. Yet how rare collaboration and how common jealousy is among philosophers! Russell and Whitehead formed the only significant partnership of which I can think.

To speak of a common pursuit is, of course, to allude to what Frank Leavis imagined that literary criticism could or should be. Luckily, this is not the place to discuss whether there can ever be objective aesthetic standards, or whether to assert or deny that objectivity is anything but an exercise in misapplied zeal (it is not), but it certainly seems more plausible to think that philosophers can reason together than that critics can prove that Conrad is better than H. G. Wells. It is more incontrovertible, if I can be permitted such a phrase, that an argument is flawed, if it is, than that (as Vladimir Nabokov insisted) Wells is better than Conrad or, as Leavis did, that Conrad trumps Wells. Philosophy *is* critical, where art can never wholly be, despite the Leavisite presumptuousness which sought to institute a sort of high court of discriminating taste, in which *ex cathedra* rankings would be, as it were, contingently necessary. Leavis could never quite accept a secondary role, although art always precedes what is said about it: as Descartes pointed out, the ivy cannot rise higher than the tree. Leavis's affectations of intimacy with Wittgenstein, to which Ray Monk alludes in his excellent recent biography, suggest how keenly a literary critic can long to be on equal terms with, so to say, the senior service. Similarly, but by no means identically, when Professor Jerome McGann analogises Byron's discursive method in *Don Juan* with Wittgenstein's in *Philosophical Investigations*, we can guess at a desire to dignify the one by reference to the other, as we can at a personal pantheon in which the two utterly different men feature in the same team. Philosophy still dignifies.

The curiosity is that we are constantly piqued by the question of what sort of thing it is. If philosophy is an art, it systematically denies that association, except in raffish cases which, on the whole, do not command respect; if it is a science, then what does it analyse or discover? We do not need to have been subtle students to remember the later Wittgenstein's somehow comforting, as well as forbidding, notion that it has no specific subject matter and that it leaves everything as it is. On this reading, the philosopher becomes a sort of intellectual unsecret policeman, ceaselessly, and selflessly, on the prowl for logical infringements and, if he belongs to the flying squad, outbreaks of metaphysical hooliganism. Such a philosopher is on the beat to detect people pretending to be philosophers in the freebooting manner of those who, with pious phrases, peddle pie in the sky. There is nothing disreputable in the prevention of fraud (nor need one have something to sell of one's own in order to denounce the fraudulence of others), yet this modest view of the philosopher – as a journeyman rather than a pundit, to use Ayer's famously trenchant dichotomy – does little to explain why we attach such importance to finding a congenial or cogent philosophy, or why – despite delusive infatuations or abrupt disillusion – we are disposed, if we are, to take philosophy seriously, indeed – at least in unvexed moments – to regard its study as the very instance of human seriousness.

Philosophy, at least in the tradition which my generation took to be normative, sought to discourage those who looked to it for metaphysical information, whether about the Ultimate Nature of the Real or about the right way to conduct one's life. Ontology could never be a voyage to the essence of Being; ethics could never tell you what to do. The closing of departments dear to continental philosophers testified to the kind of vindictive modesty to which British practitioners were much disposed in the 1950s. Yet the subject retained the lineaments of the majesty from which it sought to abdicate. Nor did philosophers like Ayer and Russell, his paragon, enact the housekeeper's role with any convincingly meek abrogation of upstairs ambitions. I have no polemic purpose in mentioning this; on the contrary, my interest in both men, and in others I shall mention, almost certainly depends on my subjective suspicion – indistinguishable from hope – that they did not mean what they were saying, or denying. A certain duplicity, which has nothing to do with not telling the truth, seems to me to have been essential to the empressing zeal which they, like anyone who bothers to spend his life in argument, undoubtedly harboured and without which they would scarcely have set to sea or assembled a crew. While denying any divine right to command, they were still captains under the god they questioned.

Since I have called this lecture 'Some philosophers I have not known', it is perhaps time for me to give some uncoy indication of why I chose the title and where I mean to go with it. If my preamble was meant to tease, but not to mystify, we are now far enough along my rambling route for its direction and destination at least to be indicated.

The title itself is, I hope and fear, at once modest and mystifying; it is both personal and impersonal; it is clear and obscure. In this sense, it parodies the titles which philosophers themselves often elect to give to their papers. A close reader might remark that, if there is an element of self-effacing egotism in the phrase 'I have not known', there is also selective deference in speaking of 'Some philosophers': without affecting to belong to their league, I am, after all, daring to nominate my team.

Part of the purpose of my title is to draw ironic attention to the modern fetish for the biographical treatment of those who, like at least some artists and philosophers, have often gone to considerable lengths to make it clear that they wish to be judged by their work and not by its motivation or provenance. These wishes, one can quite plausibly claim, do not become commands merely by being formulated; philosophy itself, with its fetish for analytic procedures, could be accused of sanctioning that unpacking, to use Gilbert Ryle's term, which leads us to investigate psychological no less than logical structures and links. Yet the reduction of a man's ideas to the possible reasons or predispositions for them is an inadmissible operation in logic, however toothsome it may sometimes be in serialised practice. The fetishism of biographical facts can become ludicrous or prurient.

A man wrote to me recently to say that he had known Wittgenstein in wartime Newcastle, where, it seems, they both frequented the same public lavatories. There is, I daresay, no scandal in that, although my correspondent must have thought that he was breaking hot news; what made his letter so comic was that he imagined that this banality should be communicated to some central authority where, like a piece of a lapsed mosaic, it might add a fleck of crucial colour to a fuller picture of Wittgenstein. I replied that what interested me about Wittgenstein was not what he did or did not do in public lavatories, which was, I supposed, what any number of people did in those days and nights. Such high-mindedness was not, perhaps, what I might have displayed if the letter had offered details about T. S. Eliot's hitherto unknown naughty moments with a couple of leathered Fascists in the 1930s, but there it was: my idea of Wittgenstein denied interest in the kind of little-did-we-know beans which W. W. Bartley III was the first to spill. Since Eliot is, I confess, someone against whom I have some animus – being one of the jews he thought underneath the lot – I cannot deny (although I might hope) that I should be in the market for dirt on him, whereas since Wittgenstein has no demonic place in my personal bestiary I prefer to consider his supposedly aberrant behaviour *sub specie aeternitatis*, sub-section *nihil humanum a me alienum puto*, by which time it has become smaller than small potatoes.

The mention of Gilbert Ryle prompts me to remember an occasion when he came to lecture in Cambridge, soon after the publication of *The Concept of Mind* (1949) made his way of talking memorable enough for 'Category Mistakes' to remain a part of my vocabulary whenever intellectual special forces must be summoned to the aid of the civil tongue. Ryle, for those who never saw or heard him, was a rather brave, grave man whose light was most comfortable under a bushel. He would be irked if I told you of an instance I happen to have been told about when he procured a fellowship for a man of whom he disapproved, because his disapproval of injustice was greater. When I attended his visiting celebrity lecture, I saw only a famous don and a dry stick. He treated us to a rather severe disquisition in which that old truth-functional double-act 'p' and 'q' were soon on the stage. Ryle, whose face was straight to the point of rectilinearity, was considering an instance where p and q ceased to have mutually exclusive characteristics and veered towards each other, so to speak. The problem of definition, its place and use in philosophy, was much in the air (John Wisdom, affecting exasperation in one of his early morning lectures, suggested to some persistent tourist that we define 'good' as 'anything that adds up to an even number – if you think that would help!'). Ryle's examination of blurred areas, where p seemed tinged with q, and q with p, led him to speak, without a trace of unseriousness, of the q-ness of p and, by contrast, of the p-ness of q.

It is not mere puerility, or the memory of ancient sniggers, which leads me to mention this typically pre-sexual revolution-ary moment. If we take Ryle's inadvertence – if that is what it was – as an opportunity for facile analysis, it is tempting to suggest that his 'Freudian' flourish at least implied – though it certainly did not entail – a sense of the burden of chastity which weighed on academic philosophers. It requires no large leap to turn this suggestion back on its author by remarking that there is something immature in the notion that those who deal with abstract matters are themselves somehow sublime. What I am hinting at here is twofold: one, philosophy is a subject which may create enormous strains, or even trivial ones, for those who seek constantly to use or fashion a vocabulary divorced from mundane associations; and, two, we – amateurs of the subject – have a tendency to insist on the very aloofness which will sustain our belief that philosophers have an unearthly nobility. We want them to be exempt from vulgarities of which, in another mood, it entertains us, however unworthily, to suspect them. Iris Murdoch, in her novel *The Philosopher's Pupil*, ironises at length on this comedy of expectations, although her fictional philosopher lacks convincing personality or ideas.

This lecture-ramble is trying to attend to two things at once, perhaps because it is easier to do two things badly than one well, but also because the two things may be facets of a single relation, that between the philosopher and his admirer. Thus Ryle's possible Freudian 'error' – there is no evidence that it was a slip – is or was comic, not only because he may not have meant *p*-ness to have the anatomical ring which, to adolescent ears, it did, but also because it was uttered in circumstances, which we – the sniggering audience – wanted to be solemn. Our laughter was a function of our determined belief that Ryle cannot have meant what he said. The sorts of things he meant to say were, we wanted to believe, professorial, pedantic, prim, because these sort of *p*-words were properly associated with the paternal place proper to our needs and hence his duty. Our laughter was at our own expense as much as at G. R.'s. Embarrassment no less than schoolboy derision helped to fund it: we had seen a sort of divinity with his fly unbuttoned. One can well imagine a lecturer, of a different reputation and in another school, whose failure to be outspoken – or even obscene – would come as a dereliction, a failure to inhabit his (or her) assigned role. Imagine, quite simply, a Germaine Greer who omitted to say something shocking. One would be shocked.

Apart from being the editor of *Mind* who, in a *cause célèbre* which, I daresay, is no longer celebrated, refused to review Ernest Gellner's first book, *Words and Things*, Ryle was also the author of a singular little study called *Plato's Progress* (1966). The interest I at least have in this slim volume is due to its stylistic curiosity. Readers of *The Concept of Mind* will not need to be reminded of its author's caustic limpidity. No one could accuse that book of callowness, still less of being slightly embarrassing, even if its central thesis now seems paradoxical to the point, very nearly, of being a kind of impractical joke, but *Plato's Progress*, while never foolish, flirts with themes which are, for want of a happier term, 'psychological'; Ryle hints quite strongly at what he suspects to be Plato's motivation in writing dialogues. If I remember rightly, he suggests that two more or less disreputable appetites fuelled his prolificity. One was his envy of the great dramatists, of whom Aeschylus was his favourite target, and the other was his desire to enrapture what Ryle, in a rather touchingly awkward phrase, called 'sixteen-year-olders'. Now I know nothing and, living a sheltered life, have heard not a word of gossip about Ryle's private life, except for the one instance which, as I have said, suggests a shy, wilfully honourable man. I do not, therefore, incline to the easy, juicy view that Ryle was reading into Plato any desire of his own to emulate Noel Coward or to be the Benjamin Jowett of his generation. It is, however, interesting that a philosopher who refused to send Gellner's perky squib for review, on the grounds that it was largely abusive of other philosophers, and without substantial seriousness, himself wrote a book which, as it were, tested Plato's feet for clay. My interest lies in the implication that Ryle thought that philosophers should not be credited with monolithic and unworldly anatomies and that it was not disreputable at least to hazard plausible guesses about what kept them at it. Such guesses would, of course, vary in each instance and they would not, and could not, damage the force of their arguments. It hardly matters whether Mozart wrote a piece in order to seduce a girl, impress a king, pay a bill or give us intimations of eternity. We have all been promised that a work of art will be as good or bad as it is, whatever that means, regardless of its composer's intentions. Sincerity is not a certificate of virtue among the muses. Plato's philosophical worth cannot be affected by his supposed disappointment at being unable to fill the theatre of Dionysus or make its audience jump out of its skin, as Aeschylus' spectators did, at the discovery of the Furies. If he was jealous or amorous, what difference can it make to the merits of the Theory of Forms? Part of Ryle's claim was, as you will remember, that that theory was by no means held tenaciously by Plato throughout his philosophical progress. He argued for a man's right to modify and abandon aspects of his ideas, an argument which Kolakowski was to dignify in his book in favour of inconsistency. Kolakowski's main thrust was against notions of historical inevitability and the putative 'moral' obligation to align oneself with it. To see that history has no compelling arguments or necessary conclusion is to be spared the pseudo-necessity of siding with, in particular, the kind of inhumanity which, in this century, seeks to make philosophy its accomplice. When it comes to trains of thought, however hectic, philosophers may and should test the links between the carriages, but they should not accept first-class seats, least of all on a gravy-train, as Heidegger did.

Just as Dodds argued that the Greeks were troubled, if not plagued, by the irrational precisely because they were such keen advocates of reason, so Ryle's treatment of the 'case' of Plato argues for a belief, on his part, that philosophers were uncomfortably cornered by expectations of both lifelong consistency and an almost inhuman indifference both to ambition and, to put it plainly, seduction. It does not follow that Ryle was a victim of more or less secret anguish or that he was signalling to us that the supposed otherworldiness of philosophers was a sorry sham. Yet it is not impertinent to suspect a certain impatience with Plato's affectations of impersonality and purity of purpose, if not always of method, which remind one of T. S. Eliot. Eliot, you will recall, deplored the notion of individual talent as against loyalty to a tradition, although his pontifical confidence suggested that, however grey he might be, his eyes were firmly fixed on eminence. Ryle was, no doubt, a competent Platonist, in the Greats tradition, but something irked him in Plato's address and disposed him to 'unpack' his life, in a more or less warranted fashion, if only to make sense of his own feeling that Plato was a more mutable character than his craving for the immutable might seem to indicate.

I am indeed trying to have things both ways, and to do two things at once. This is partly for greedy and impatient reasons, partly because, more nobly, I think that in language and in life two things often do happen at once and that one cannot understand heads without knowing about tails. One of the commonsensical quotations with which we marched into exams was Bishop Butler's 'A thing is what it is and not another thing', to which I am disposed to say now, 'Quite right, my lord bishop, and also, of course, quite wrong: a thing is what it is and also another thing.' The p-ness of q is always there to warn us against too abrupt an assumption of categorical purity. The shameless economy of nature, so offensive to G. B. Shaw, in which one organ serves more than one office, infects and invigorates language too: the richness of speech depends on duplicity, just as drama cannot hold our attention unless at least some of what is happening is, for the moment, puzzling or even unintelligible. André Green, in his *Un Oeil de Trop*, makes the point when he likens tragedy – and *Oedipus Rex* in particular – to the dialogue between his parents which is overheard by a child who both understands (the words) and fails to understand (the significance). André Green suggests that the tragic audience is excited and alarmed by being allowed to spy on the actors, just as the child wishes and does not wish to observe and overhear the sexual secrets of his parents.

One may accept this or not, as one chooses. However, it suggests that there may be reasons beyond logic why certain philosophers become, as they say, familiar to us, while others seem almost inexplicably disagreeable. For some reason, I have never had time for philosophers whose names begin with H, with the exception of Heraclitus, who begins with a rough breathing, one might say, and so escapes sanction. Luckily, this means that Hegel, Husserl and Heidegger are as unpalatable to me as stem ginger; happily, there seem to be good philosophical reasons for not feeling too guilty, but they only lend spurious dignity to prejudice. The charm of Wittgenstein has recently been subjected to more or less venomous challenge. The fury of some of his admirers has been interestingly exaggerated. After all, the 'news', if it is new, that the young Ludwig had homosexual appetites, and may even have been disposed to satisfy them, cannot put his philosophical chastity in question. The rage of the keepers of the flame is understandable only in the light of their idea of W., rather than on Wittgenstein's own behalf. The refusal to accept Wittgenstein's carnal reality, like Jesus' loin-cloth, tells us more about his worshippers than about him. It has a manifest affinity with the quite common notion that members of the royal family propagate their species by loftier means than those available to their subjects. In other words, there is a disposition to play the child's part, at once curious and inhibited, when faced with the sexuality of his parents. It is in this sense, among others, that my title was chosen: the philosophers whom I have known I have also not known, and my respect for their knowledge, my belief in their superior wisdom and impersonal purposes, is at least very like our wilful respect for the parents whom we can never know as they knew each other and who at once excite and inhibit our curiosity. Even if you accept this sketchy analysis, it does not, of course, mean that a given philosopher's ideas become less valuable because a reader approaches him with the hope or fear that he will, in some respects, play the 'pure father', who can have the paternal role without ever having played the two-backed beast. The philosopher as father is more frequent, to say the least, than the philosopher as mother. Hannah Arendt, Simone Weil, Iris Murdoch, Miss Anscombe and Susan Stebbing provide a fairly forlorn quintet of females from whom to cast an ideal mother, which may be put down to the sexism of the profession and its emergence from theology, but suggests, if you like, that those who look to philosophers for ideal parents prefer an asexual genesis of at least that sublime aspect of humanity with which philosophy must or prefers to deal.

In an interesting paper on Addiction to Detective Stories, the psycho-analyst Charles Rycroft proposes, with speculative humour, a theory of why so many people read one mystery after another, although in nearly all cases the books are poorly written, even if they are amusingly constructed. What impels people to repeat the process of bemusement and to seek the solution to more or less factitious puzzles which satisfy them so little that they immediately have recourse to another? Rycroft, being an analyst, offers a not unexpected answer: the addict is drawn to detective stories because, putting himself in the investigator's place, he is warranted to ask questions which normally would be taboo. Crime licenses curiosity of which the analyst's essential instance is curiosity about the primal scene. Rycroft hazards the view, in a fairly light-hearted way, that the victim of the most attractive murder-stories is or stands for the father, as it is in the Oedipus instance where the king himself demands the full investigation which will discover his own guilt.

One may take this or leave it, as one chooses. Rycroft's

speculation is not, however, without relevance to philosophical inquiry and our addiction to it, our unwillingness to let go of the hope and fear that philosophers are, as they say, on to something. It is part of the modern style to observe juxtapositions rather than to assert causal connections. Hence to analogise between detective stories and philosophy is not to reduce one to the other or both to nothing very much. However, it is fair to point out that the philosophical paper is, in many cases, a kind of sublime detective story. We are introduced to a problem, however arid, and then to the suspects, those cases where it seems that an exception to the advertised rule is possible. We are usually given an obvious solution to the crux, which we may be sure will not do, and are then introduced to further suspects before being treated to the clinching argument which reveals whatever the author could have announced to us at the outset. If some academic papers are exercises in prolongation, it is clear that the reader cannot be satisfied with the posing of a problem followed by its author's prompt answer. This may happen in mathematics, but it is does not happen in literary philosophy. The fame and fascination of Wittgenstein's *Tractatus*, which partakes of aspects of both declarative brevity and cryptic extension, derive at least in part from the text's remaining puzzling even after the solution has been offered. Wittgenstein is, by the same token, the philosopher whom we do and do not wish to know. You will remember that Heracleitus, whose gnomic style pre-figures Wittgenstein in some regards, alludes to 'The wise one alone who does not wish and who wishes to be spoken of by the name of Zeus'. The oracle, he says elsewhere, neither 'declares nor conceals' but offers a sign. The comedy of philosophy, one might say, especially in a time of competitive incredulity, is that we both believe and do not believe that the philosopher knows a secret and that we both do and do not wish to be initiated into it. We are drawn to those who seem to endorse our scepticism – I am speaking, of course, of my own preference – but we are unwilling to believe that they have told us all they know when they tell us that they know no more than we do. The modesty of the disclaimer becomes as insufferable to us as the pretentiousness of those who proposed grandiose metaphysical schemes. It needs no psychoanalyst to see that we both do and do not want our fathers to be in the same case as ourselves. We wish them, in a sense, to be better investigators than ourselves and also to agree to be our victims (Plato is the father of philosophy who is killed by every generation unless it prefers to kill Aristotle). Hegel is the Dr Moriarty of modern philosophy, the villain who must be done down, and who rises again in order to horrify and challenge us. We can perhaps take Rycroft's analysis of the detective story addict a little further here. To remark the similarity in anatomy between the philosophical investigation and the search for who killed Roger Akroyd is not wholly impertinent. Just as the addict impersonates the detective, those of us who are drawn to philosophy are drawn to the man who proposes, and seems authorised, to ask ultimate questions. Like the detective, the philosopher often affects puzzlement at the cleverness of answers which do not quite meet the case, perhaps, he suggests ironically, because he lacks the wit to see how they fit with other elements in the puzzle. What is the case of all cases to which all philosophers are drawn and into which all of us, pretty well, wish that we had the licence to inquire? It is, of course, the case of God.

The comedy of modern philosophy is that its modesty and its immodesty are inextricably connected: affectations of incompetence, announced by journeymen like Ayer, never convince us that they do not really know more than they will say, just as a show of certainty, on the part of bishops or politicians, leads us to assume that they know less than they claim. We look for certainty to the sceptic and we badger the dogmatist for confessions of doubt. Yet our desire for a clinching investigation of the ultimate mystery is unabated. We do and do not wish God to be dead; we do and do not wish to have investigators who, themselves above all suspicion, will resolve the primal issue once and for all. We cannot conceive of what a proof of God's existence could be (even if we knew exactly what we meant by the Zeus we seek) nor can we accept that a disproof will ever be final, for what would it be disproving and by what conceivable means? As Pascal saw, we are pitched between one attitude and another and can never be satisfied, not least because what we want is not what we want and never can be, given our natural and linguistic duplicity. We insist on being told lies while maintaining that we want the truth. Our intellectual curiosity mimics that of the child who does and does not want to know what his parents do, or did, in bed. We depute others to tell us what happened in the primal scene even as we avert our eyes from it. I do not, of course, mean to say that philosophical investigation comes down to asking others what they can see through some cosmic key-hole, but I am mundane enough to suspect that our lifelong selection of worthy deputies, whose reports we read as if they might contain the solution of solutions, has something in common with the vacuous addiction to such brave surrogates as 007 or Inspector Morse (how perfect that his very name hints synecdochically at the command of codes!).

Our choice of deputies to report on the cosmic primal scene which we dare not observe for ourselves requires them to have more or less supernatural powers and not to be human-all-too-human, just as – for the faithful – Jesus, although supposedly a man, cannot have sexual desires, or even natural functions, if his divinity is to be sustained. The relation of the pupil to his selected philosopher also has something of this wilful aversion from knowing him as a man, even if not in the Biblical sense: we appoint certain men, and our choices are indeed virtually limited by the canon to males, to be our chaste investigators who, we may hope, will report both that God is dead and that everything remains under control despite His demise. The empty room is, of course, the classic locus for the perfect crime. The Holy of Holies in the temple at Jerusalem was, we are always promised, empty. The life and the death of God are thus indistinguishable on all the available evidence: everything points both ways, just as Heracleitus talked of the road up and the road down being the same road. Our trust in our selected team of philosophers puts them in the father's place, just as Christians believe in the capacity of Jesus to mediate with the Father with Whom, in another regard, He is identical and whom he thus supplants and, in some sense, kills.

The abstract nature of philosophy, the rigour we expect of its practitioners, the lack of partiality to which logic must adhere, can be read as devices for concealing the murderous purposes to which we depute it. I am not sure whether René Girard qualifies as philosopher, but his sense of the capacity of human beings to encode and dissimulate murderous formulae in their social routines is certainly worth a deviation, like a two-star restaurant in the Michelin Guide.

If we had no furtive ambitions, whether for the proof of God's existence or for evidence of his undoubted demise, would we return again and again to the dossiers which grow dusty on our shelves? The selective affinity which we have for this detective inspector or that *commissaire* is not, of course, merely a matter of assuming that he and we, if we had the nerve and commission, would be likely to round up the same suspects. Yet it requires a rare intellect to endure for very long the style of someone, say like Pierre Boutang, who we know will produce findings wholly uncongenial to us. We preserve our illusions of impartiality, if we do, by being determined to make our philosophers men of probity selected on the basis of their dedication to the truth. It is, no doubt, a sign of my natural diffidence that I never called Wisdom John or Ayer Freddie, even when my contemporaries had ventured easily on such intimacies; the reluctance to get too close to other men may have all kinds of explanations, but I suspect that I did not want to discover too much humanity in those whom I deputed, deferentially, to handle the Great Investigation. Just as the French, for all their reported *franchise* in anatomical matters, still refuse, in polite circumstances, to allow that women urinate, so I, and others perhaps, preferred to have a Wittgenstein who went to Betty Grable movies but not, not, not to public lavatories. When I declared, latish in life, to Freddie Ayer that *Language, Truth and Logic* had meant a great deal to me when I first went to Cambridge, he replied that it still brought him in a thousand a year. It was rather as if St Luke had remarked complacently that the Acts of the Apostles was doing well in paperback. We want our philosophers to be serious and, however keen we seem to be to have them confess themselves mundane, we look to them to be sublime for us. We do not know them because we dare not find them to be men very much like ourselves. We ask them to dispel our illusions about everything but themselves; it suits us to whiten their sepulchres and to refuse the dirt on them. They are the fathers who kill the Father and whose sons we can be without the necessity for a primal scene. If we are of a sceptical temper, we look to them to provide evidence for the certainty of our uncertainties. The Italians have a saying, '*E certo, certissimo – ed anzi possibile.*' We ask our philosophers to be no less trenchant but much more decisive; they will, if they are honest, always disappoint us, which is perhaps what we want of them, even as we solicit them once again to set out on their white search for the colour of all colours.

Marcel Proust
as Correspondent

What writer more frequently excites exasperation and indulgence, often at the same time, than Marcel Proust? To open his
letters is as delicious as it is infuriating: he is both a sublime
intelligence and an appalling creep. Implacably shrewd in his
judgement of others, he is sensitive to the point of being a cry-
baby when it comes to himself. *Bref*, an author's author!

His great speciality was always condolences, of which there
are many poignant instances in a volume which takes us from
the end of the *Belle Epoque* into the charnel-house of the Great
War, which comes at a very inconsiderate moment for Proust's
fortunes on the stock exchange. His certainty that he is ruined
does not, of course, inhibit him from inviting Princess Bibesco
to choose between dining at the Ritz and the Crillon, during the
darkest days of 1917, nor from relying on the head waiter at
the Ritz for whatever is in short supply. Like Sartre, if only in
this respect, he always overtipped and was always well taken
care of.

The bulk of these letters concern the publication of the first
volume of *A La Recherche*, beginning with the attempts to find
a publisher. In his usual toadying way, he looked to Gaston
Calmette, the editor of *Le Figaro*, to sponsor him. Calmette had

Review of Marcel Proust, *Selected Letters vol. 3: 1910–1917*, edited
by Philip Kolb, translated and introduced by Terence Kilmartin, in
the *Spectator*, 1992.

printed several of his pieces (sometimes with sub-editorial 'improvements' which affronted but did not enrage their author) and 'Swann' was dedicated to him, although he never acknowledged the tribute nor did much to further Proust's purposes. Meanwhile, Marcel's devious vanity disposed him to open negotiations with another publisher (he was offering to defray all the costs of producing the book), only to find himself caught between two scarcely kindled fires: it was no painful decision for either side to defer to the other, leaving Proust unhoused, so to say.

In the event, the young Bernard Grasset became Proust's 'choice', after André Gide and his crowd at the *Nouvelle Revue Française* rather gleefully declined the honour, apparently on discovering a solecism in a single quite short passage (no one corrected proofs more diligently, or more expensively, than Proust and no one, it seems, suffered more dismayingly from misprints).

Grasset is the recipient of letters which veer from the effusive to the elusive and he responds with deference that becomes, in the end, understandably glacial. Having begun as a white knight, Grasset became the incubus from whom Marcel sought to escape in order to rally to Gide, who realised, after the publication of the first volume, what a signal mistake he had made.

Proust's candid slyness and sincere hypocrisy in dealing with Grasset – now accusing him of false accountancy and then suggesting that, if he will let him out of his contract, he will lose an author but gain a friend – are enough to give long-windedness and self-pity a bad name. If Marcel were not, even now, so adept in commanding the reader's sympathy, who could stomach such a mixture of noble sentiments and base motives? The abiding charm of the bed-ridden recluse who seems, despite everything, to have nerve-endings which respond to the atmosphere in every *salon* and are alert to every *coterie* in Paris, succeeds again and again in procuring forgiveness for the unforgiveable and, by the delicacy of his attunement to all the processes of human affection (and disaffection), contrives to become the one literary companion to whom, despite everything, the reader will do anything not to lose access.

Proust, it seems, knows everybody through knowing himself. His ambition to be loved and to be admired would be insufferable were it not for the exquisite means he adopts for its fulfilment. One might argue that, could he have been cossetted and flattered and become the darling of the *gratin* without writing a masterpiece, he would have contented himself with corresponding with nobs and with the long-suffering Lionel Hauser, who gave him worldly-wise advice on his investments. As it is, he had the protracted wit to make immortality a substitute for life.

The fact remains, however, that the little Marcel was an egregious climber and that it is a sentimentality on the part of his admirers to accuse him of an inner core of moral steel. His support of Dreyfus was, of course, greatly to his credit, and his biographers have drawn greatly on it, but here we find him cosying up to the Action Française crowd – putting out feelers to Maurras through the odious Daudets – and offering covert anti-Semitic sops (especially at the expense of Joseph Reinach – a much more forthright Dreyfusard than Marcel) by way of a *laissez-passer* into dubious, but chic circles.

Proust's duplicity cannot be denied, but it was his curious gift to make it into a source of inspiration; more or less concealing his own sexual and 'racial' components when in society, he declared them with luminous generosity in the work. His letter to Gide about the 'virile homosexual' who finds his type in Charlus is magisterial in its dispassionate veracity. He turns Gide – whose treatment of the homosexual theme was flawed with special pleading – from his judge into his pupil. Marcel's craving for the approval of the NRF crowd becomes sweetly embarrassing because it is manifest that his eloquence, his acuity and (yes) his honesty leave them in a class far below him to which, for reasons that have nothing to do with literary merit, he seeks promotion.

This is Terence Kilmartin's last and admirable translation of Proust. It rarely stumbles into translationese and yet retains a Gallic flavour. The editing, by Philip Kolb, is informative and terse, although a few footnotes have gone awry on p.319 and it is not true, as he says on p.403, that Byron died 'on the beach', though his house was indeed adjacent to the water. This volume is for leisurely addicts; to read it in a hurry would be like being served, in a hot-house, with a meal composed exclusively of plate after plate of the finest cream soup.

Cranston's Rousseau

Rousseau was neither eminently noble nor in the least savage. He was the son of a father whose well-born Genevan family had fallen on hard times. His mother died soon after his birth and he never enjoyed her love; his recommendation of breast-feeding to the upper classes, who usually farmed their infants to wet-nurses, was typical of his tendency to legislate, or at least moralise, in areas where deprivation rather than experience was his warrant. He had no more first-hand contact with the idyllic world of the 'savage' than he did with the angels whose existence, or passions, he doubted.

Rousseau is the epicentre of contradictions which spread out from his life and work in still undormant eddies. He has been described in almost as many ways as Byron, whose 'romanticism' was also seconded by a loudly published private life, lurid with vices which, through the seductions of autobiography, were paraded with a frankness that seemed to change them into virtues. Confession may be good for the soul, but it also advances sales.

Rousseau was profligate with programmes for human improvement. His notion of 'forcing men to be free' – by obliging them to acknowledge the authority of the general will – could be accused of being the precursor of both Stalinism and

Review of Maurice Cranston, *The Noble Savage: Jean-Jacques Rousseau 1754–1762*, in the *Sunday Times*, 1991.

the existentialism of Sartre, for whom good faith was synonymous with taking the side of the 'proletarian', an abstract vessel
of virtue very much in the tradition of Rousseau's savage.
Rousseau's prolific prose (he was wise to abandon verse) has
something of Sartre's compulsive egocentricity, but it was
accomplished without the cocktails of drugs and alcohol which
allowed Sartre to play the literary stakhanovite.

The Man of Letters as prophet and celebrity, social scourge
and socialite, was never so stridently instanced as in the age of
Rousseau and his eventual arch-enemy Voltaire. The sumptuous
decadence of the last half-century of the *ancien régime* was loud
with theories of government and with theological heterodoxies.
The *douceur de vivre* so nostalgically recalled by Talleyrand,
after the Revolution, was a time of uneasy consciences and
radical fancies.

Rousseau's precarious genius secured him powerful admirers
– especially the Maréchal de Luxembourg and his admirable
wife – but fame did not entail fortune, especially in those days
of pirated copyright. When the winds of reaction blew, in a
tempest of intolerance, the resident foreigner, for all his laurels,
was swept away. If neither *La Nouvelle Héloïse* nor *Emile* now
strikes us as inflammatory (if indeed they kindle anything but a
dutiful spark of attention), the first seemed scandalous and the
second heretical to those who still governed France in the name
of the King and the Church.

Although Rousseau's theories of sexuality deplored the adultery which, almost officially, allowed arranged marriages to be
alleviated by complaisance on both sides of the bed, his visions
of felicity horrified those for whom 'nature' was tantamount to
atheism. When, in *The Social Contract*, Rousseau alleged that
Christianity was an unsocial religion (a view taken, with less
hot breath, by Edward Gibbon in his reading of ancient history),
the patience of the Powers That Were finally snapped.

Tipped off by the Luxembourgs, on whose estate he lived,
Rousseau escaped into his native Switzerland in the nick of
time. On the road, his cabriolet crossed the carriage containing
officers on their way to arrest him. Had things turned out
differently, he might have been in the Bastille when the mob
burst into it.

The first volume of Maurice Cranston's almost certainly definitive English biography – *Jean-Jacques: Early Life and Work of
Jean-Jacques Rousseau 1712–1754* – was exquisite with the

twists and turns of the philosopher's youth. Primed by the confessions, Professor Cranston took a sceptical, if sympathetic, view of the author's honesty and he retraced his footsteps (Rousseau was an indefatigable walker) with illuminating freshness. He showed that Jean-Jacques was adept at turning even the most disreputable or humiliating moments of his life into endearing instances of weakness or gaucherie. Who else could have blamed an innocent servant girl for the theft of a scarf, thus ruining her 'character' forever, and yet have expected (and almost procured) our admiration for the forthrightness of his confession?

Such confessions are more engaging in the young than endurable in the middle-aged. In his second volume (of an eventual three), Professor Cranston has a pretty well static subject, at first the ungrateful tenant of Madame d'Epinay and then the happily captive celebrity of the Luxembourgs, at whose table Rousseau meets the Prince de Conti, among other unsavage nobs. Madame la Maréchale conceived a chaste passion for him which resulted in a fervent correspondence. Rousseau became so addicted to her letters that, when she was too ill to write, he solicited blank sheets from her, to which he replied with arch readings of what these sweet nothings might be meant to convey.

The solitude which he so affected to relish – genuine affectation was very much his sort of thing – made him an insatiable correspondent; it is not surprising that Julie and St Preux figure in an almost interminable epistolary novel. Life itself took on an epistolary form once Jean-Jacques was installed at Montmorency, near (but never in) Paris. His passions were best expressed in the absence of their targets; some of his *amitiés amoureuses* were with female fans whom he never met.

Like Byron, he never turned his back without wondering what was going on behind it. The solitary 'exile' was as prompt with suspicious, even paranoid brickbats as he was with sympathy-cadging condolence letters, in which he contrived to be more bereft than the bereaved. He abused his publishers – the often maligned Marc-Michel Rey was his equivalent to Byron's John Murray – and he chided his friends, often to the point of explosive rupture, while doting on patrons tactful enough not to patronise him (even the Prince de Conti could be told off for sending him a present of game). When his old friend Diderot made a passingly ironic reference to 'the man who lives alone in the country', Rousseau broke with him definitively, although Diderot's courageous intellectualism was his model.

As for Voltaire, that spiteful resident of Rousseau's native Geneva was already sour before the publication of the *Letter to M. d'Alembert*, in which Jean-Jacques deplored the idea of building a theatre in Calvin's ideal republic. Since Voltaire was as keen on performing as writing his own dramas, he thenceforth became Rousseau's implacable enemy, not hesitating to reveal – for disgraceful instance – how Jean-Jacques had abandoned his illegitimate children by Thérèse, the housekeeper-mistress whom he presented to the *beau monde* as a mere domestic servant. Yet it was Voltaire who dared to expose the Calas Affair (admittedly after the judicial murder of the innocent Protestant), while Rousseau found reasons not to rock the boat from which the Catholics were soon to pitch him anyway.

Cranston's narrative is admirably perspicuous: he does not intrude himself between the reader and Citizen Rousseau. He alerts us to the continuities between Rousseau and John Locke, whose classic biographer and exegete he is, without festooning the text with interpretations. Where Jean Starobinski, for brilliant example, analyses Rousseau's illness (probably prostatic) in terms of the ambivalence he discovers in all of Jean-Jacques' tangled adventures and ideas, Cranston provides the painful facts. If his agony had psychosomatic origins, Rousseau certainly went through real torments: the regular (and often inept) use of catheters alone accounts for his outbursts of stoic self-pity.

It is typical of Jean- Jacques that he should be depicted on the cover in the Albanian kaftan which he came to adopt as daily wear. If one is reminded of Byron, romantically accoutred in Albanian drag, we learn that Rousseau adopted the costume not in outlandish tribute to brave fellows but because its skirt allowed unromantic recourse to the chamber-pot without the trouble of unbuttoning.

Professor Cranston is impressively at ease among the sources. Although his book is long, its length is a function of the volume of Rousseau's output; there is no shortage of dry wit, despite the want of brevity. If this seems a manifestly English view of Rousseau, no disparagement is implied of the biographer's grasp of France or of French, which is masterly. A reader captivated by Cranston (as he should be) will, however, find rich – if very copious – additional material in Starobinski's scintillating speculations on the same elusive/self-advertising, sane/crazy, snobbish/modest, charlatan/philosopher so vividly depicted here.

Hell and Other People

When war broke out in 1939, the two most brilliant philosophers of their generation were recalled to the French colours as meteorologists. During the subsequent *drôle de guerre*, before the Germans punched through the Ardennes, Jean-Paul Sartre and Raymond Aron reported dutifully on the climatic conditions on the Western front. They had been close friends at the Ecole Normale Supérieure, the élite college for future *lycée* teachers.

Aron graduated first in his philosophy class, while Sartre failed. The next year, Sartre emulated Aron; his runner-up was a nicely brought-up Catholic girl, Simone de Beauvoir. Aron's successful doctoral thesis maintained his lead over his *petit camarade*. Indeed, the precocious brilliance of 'An Introduction to the Philosophy of History' all but stifled Sartre. Aron's master was Max Weber and his erudition in French, German and English sources was always to be greater than his rival's, as was his accessibility to (and respect for) the arguments of others.

Aron was a Jew and a pluralist; Sartre, who included the Schweitzers among his Alsatian relatives, was a believer in the 'totalising' of human experience and, at times, in the Marxist version of totalitarianism which affected to have inside knowledge of what History wanted and where it was going.

Review of Ronald Hayman, *Writing Against; a biography of Sartre* and Robert Colquhoun, *Raymond Aron*, in the *Sunday Times*, 1986.

The friendship between the two *philosophes* was breached by the Occupation. Sartre, who was recently famous for his first novel, *La Nausée*, spent the war years in Paris, with summer excursions to the countryside in search of famous company and fresh eggs. His fragile reputation for 'Resistance' derived from tepid dissidence from the collaborationist literary authorities: they sometimes frowned at his plays, but they never banned them. On the evening of D-day, he was clinking glasses, at the first night of *Les Mouches*, with the charming German officers who staffed the Paris embassy. They seemed wholly to have missed the allegorical challenge of what had happened on stage.

After thought, Aron fled to London in 1940. There he became the inspiration of *La France Libre*, the Gaullist house magazine, of which the General did not always approve. The War Office, on the other hand, sent couriers for the proofs of its military analyses. Sartre said later that Aron's wartime articles offered 'an explanation of our time'. However, the two men's notions of an explanation soon diverged radically.

For the best part of the next four decades, Sartre and Aron continued to wet their fingers and raise them to the prevailing political winds. They took utterly different readings, however, and made diametrically opposing forecasts. Sartre found the east wind decidedly balmy; Aron shivered at it and preferred those that blew exclusively from the West.

When France fell, in 1940, Sartre had spent some time in a German prisoner-of-war camp. There he was exposed, for the first time, to the sight, sound and smell of the working class. He found that other people might be hell, but that they were also mysteriously and irretrievably 'other'. He dreamed all his life of some *rapprochement* between the intellectual and the toiler, even though he confessed that he never really liked the male half of the human race. He retained a long appetite, and appeal, for the other half.

When Sartre involved himself, briefly, in practical post-war politics, it was as the soon-disillusioned founder of a non-Communist leftist party. After it disintegrated under its own weightlessness, he practised protracted *coitus interruptus* with the ultra-Stalinist Communist party, until the Hungarian revolution led to a divorce before marriage.

Sartre continued obstinately, not to say crassly, to argue that Marxism was an inescapable doctrine (rather than a form of sub-language). He never saw that Marx, like the 1930s' philos-

opher Alain, was always 'writing against'; he made sense only
as a critic and an adversary. Ronald Hayman has thus chosen
an appropriate, if awkward, title for his well-balanced and
readable account of Sartre's life and times. He trumps Annie
Cohen-Solal's excellent recent biography in the clarity of his
exegesis. If he keeps us amused with gossip, he almost always
honours his solemn purpose. Respectful, but unintimidated, he
comes to his own sensible conclusions (for small instance, he
rightly praises Sartre's Freud screenplay, which others have
chosen to depreciate).

How important, finally, was Sartre? He marked his era all
right. How many afternoons did Left Bank *habitués* (and
habituées) spend debating existentialism – *was* it a humanism?
– while wearing black corduroys and drinking the *Deux Magots'*
overpriced coffee, in the hope of seeing, or hearing, Sartre and
The Beaver *dans ses oeuvres*? Did it matter that the Master's
philosophy in *L'Etre et le Néant* was famously denounced by
Freddie Ayer as being founded, like Heidegger's, on a misuse of
the verb 'to be'? Sartre retorted, with untypical brevity, that
Ayer was *'un con'*.

Sartre's ideas were capriciously personal and he expressed
them in a mystifying intellectual vocabulary. For all his Tol-
stoyan desire to liberate the masses, few of them can ever have
understood his message. He became a rabid anti-American, but
his fictional trilogy, *Les Chemins de la Liberté* (he never wrote
an intended fourth volume) was a tribute to John Dos Passos
and to Ernest Hemingway: Mathieu, wounded and firing on the
advancing Germans, rings a bell as Robert Jordan come again,
having survived the Spanish Civil War. Sartre's plays remain his
best claim to enduring fame; quite an actor himself, he put
memorable rhetoric in the mouths of men like Pierre Brasseur
and in those of a sequence of the actress-mistresses with whom
he tested, sometimes to near-destruction, his contingent
relationship with Simone de Beauvoir, the 'little judge' to whom
he submitted all his work.

His ignorance of facts was notorious. It is doubtful whether
he ever read many of the books he denounced so fiercely, and
at such length, including Aron's. He loathed the bourgeois idea
of art and devoted long periods (of time and prose) to indicting
Flaubert ('The Idiot of the Family'), Baudelaire and Mallarmé
(into whom Charles Maurras also put the boot, from the right-
wing position). His appreciation of Jean Genet, 'saint and

martyr', was not appreciated by his subject, but he did much to promote Frantz Fanon's anti-colonialist cult of violence.

Sartre had a way of writing about himself when supposedly dealing with others. If he was sometimes his own worst enemy, he always had competition. His facile rhetoric did much to license the rebellious youth whose great moment came in May 1968, although he was somewhat patronised by them. (When he went to speak at a meeting, there was a note on his seat 'Sartre, soyez bref!', an injunction which served notice on his *ex cathedra* verbosity.) After 1968, he slowly lapsed into doddery extremism, unable to endure any voice which did not echo his own. In this way, he bore out Camus' prescient observation, years earlier, that he and his *Temps Modernes* 'family' had a penchant for servility.

Raymond Aron dismissed the events of May 1968 as a 'psychodrama'. He had a knack for coining phrases: he used the phrase 'iron curtain' six months before Churchill went to Fulton, Missouri, and he invented the term 'secular religion' to describe both communism and fascism. His clarity was legendary, his disdain magisterial. If he had mistresses, their names do not figure among his credits; he gave discretion a good name. Aron was the king of the Right Bank, as Sartre was of the Left. Abused, often to a scandalous degree, by those who thought it better to be wrong with Sartre than right with Aron, the author of *The Opium of the Intellectuals*, and a shelf of equally long, trenchant works, argued the case for democratic pluralism without ever claiming to have History on his side or the Masses at his back.

As a columnist (and leader-writer) for *Figaro* and as an academic, at the Sorbonne and the Collège de France, Aron was obsessively hard-working (his elegant brother was a worldly playboy). He defended what deserved defence (Europe) and attacked where attack was provoked: when de Gaulle spoke of the Jews as 'un peuple d'élite, sûr de lui-même et dominateur', his earlier reticence gave way to measured rage. (De Gaulle always claimed that his remark had been meant as a compliment.) How typical it was that, having 'come out', so to say, as a Jew, the last act of Aron's life was to speak in defence of Bertrand de Jouvenel, when Zeev Sternhell denounced him, rather immoderately, as an anti-Semite proto-fascist!

Aron had no creative spark or vivid message: no one ever made love or lit a revolutionary brand under the impression that his views were being honoured. When he died, no thousands followed his coffin, as they did Sartre's, but his greatness shines and continues to instruct. England's lack of a comparable pair of intellectual *frères enemis* is not the least evidence of the sorry state of public philosophy this side of the Channel. As president of France, Giscard d'Estaing spent an hour meditating over Sartre's corpse (and perhaps over the divisions which Sartre so wilfully encouraged among his compatriots). It is hard to imagine any post-war English Prime Minister who could consider that he or she had anything to learn from philosophy.

Flesh and Stone

Man is a soft machine who has succeeded, through intelligence, in converting the world to his use and shelter. His gods have sometimes sponsored his adventures and flattered his vanity – the very idea of a Saviour, however severe in judgement, implies that Man merits salvation – and sometimes they have led to his ruin: the Aztecs deferred to the marauding Spaniards because they were white and came from the sea, which they took to be divine attributes. Who can doubt that metaphysics and societies have intimate and consequential relations? In the history of philosophy, mind and body have been held to interpenetrate in varying degrees; human self-expression, or repression, depends on the accommodations they make with each other. Architectural forms are the solid reflection of humanity's dreams and dreads.

Any historico-aesthetic study of the negotiations between flesh and spirit demands rare virtues of cross-disciplinary nerve. Richard Sennett has the qualifications of a professor of history and of the humanities at New York University and also at University College, London. His range of interest, and of reading, is impressive; and it had better be. His emblematic cases are supplied by societies as far apart as ancient Athens and today's Greenwich Village, imperial Rome and decadent

---

Review of Richard Sennett, *Flesh and Stone: the body and the city in Western civilization*, in the *Sunday Times*, 1994.

Venice, revolutionary Paris and Edwardian London (via a close reading of Forster's *Howard's End*). The articulateness of Sennett's work derives from the motif of the human body. Echoing Michel Foucault, he maintains that the characteristics attributed, down the ages, to man's perishable frame more or less determined the form and styles of his habitat. His proclaimed programme is to understand 'how body-troubles have been expressed in architecture, in urban design and in planning practice'. Thus he perceives Harvey's discovery of the circulation of the blood as blessing the *movement* of traffic, and the creation of green spaces as 'lungs'.

It is typical of contemporary academic (and commercial) practice that Sennett analyses societies in the saleable light of human sexuality rather than in the grimmer terms of responses to the threat of war, although the latter may explain, more plausibly than the fear of women, why – in the dangerous years after 1792 – the French abandoned the bare-breasted Marianne, so liberal with the milk of human kindness, as a republican symbol and substituted the more pertinent talisman of a heroic warrior.

Sennett emphasises how, despite man's rational affectations, even apparently utilitarian structures, such as Roman military camps, were sited in accordance with magic formulae. Equally, in the process of making human life less exposed and more significant, societies often burden themselves with architectural obligations of crippling magnitude and impracticality. Strangely enough, Pharaonic Egypt has no place here, but the Emperor Hadrian's construction of the Pantheon is brilliantly analysed as a prime instance of pious intimidation. In building it, Hadrian recognised the gods in the implicit hope that they would return the compliment. Sennett is strong on Rome, but weak in Latin: he really should not accuse Byron, who had a classical education, of mistranslating Hadrian in taking the Latin word *soles* to suggest 'loneliness in the world'. In fact, Byron knew, as Sennett manifestly does not, that the Latin for lonely is *solus* and that *soles* is properly rendered in Byron's lines as 'wonted'. Given the number of eminent minds who read the manuscript with such a range of majestic competences, it is sad that this pretentious howler should have been suffered to shriek so loudly. *O tempora, o mores*, wouldn't you say so, prof.?

This is a lecture which infuriates as it stimulates. In the course of its sprawl of detail and illustration (from *ooh-là-là* pornographic prints of Marie-Antoinette to dingily illegible town-plans), all kinds of judgements are made in the sphere of literature and aesthetics, of sociology and politics. Some are shrewd – such as the contrasting analyses of Jacques-Louis David's two great 'revolutionary' paintings, the death of Marat and the lesser known *Death of Bara*, and Piero della Francesca's *Flagellation* at Urbino – while others are both wild and glib. The examples taken from ancient Greek society are particularly rich in anachronistic half- or quarter-truths. Oedipus is alleged to have blinded himself 'in order to relieve the plague' and to have sacrificed himself in a way 'which has a civic meaning to its contemporary audience beyond the Freudian story of forbidden lust and guilt'. Forbidden lust had no place in Sophokles' Oedipus; the king trangressed the law against incest by sheer inadvertence and yet he had to be punished, in the same way as the Old Testament's Uzzah who, out of instinctive respect, steadied the ark of the covenant and was struck dead by the Lord, although he acted out of amiable motives.

It is not enough to have read Kenneth Dover on homosexuality and Nicole Loraux's excellent work on Perikles in order to pass for an expert on ancient Athens. Nothing excuses the failure even to notice the crucial significance to the Athenians of the god Dionysos, who impersonated both the male *and* the female principle. Without an awareness of that sly god's subversive centrality to the evolution of democracy, any account of ancient Athenian socio-sexual institutions is Hamlet without the prince. When Maria Daraki's enthralling study of Dionysos' bi-sexual, old-young, human-divine ambivalence is not even mentioned in the scholar's hold-all bibliography, one can be pretty sure that Sennett is busking.

He is on surer ground in medieval France and admirable in recognising the superiority of Muslim city-planning to the haphazardness of the old Paris on which Haussmann inflicted such radical by-pass surgery after the Commune. On landing in Elizabethan England, in order to measure Shakespeare's vision of Venice against the reality of the Serenissima's perilous economic and military situation, he repeats the usual view that Shylock's character owed a lot to Robert Lopez, Elizabeth's personal physician whom she delivered, as Lady Thatcher did Leon Brittan, to those who were baying for blood. However, the innocent Dr Lopez ended on the scaffold, as a traitor, not in Brussels as a commissioner. Sennett tells us that Lopez was lynched, which he was not, and that he was a Jew, which he *had been*: part of what amused the crowd which saw him hanged, drawn and quartered, was that he kept proclaiming himself as good a Christian as they. The fact that Lopez was also a Spaniard, in the age of the Armada, is apparently not relevant to the professor of history.

Does it matter that this often intelligent and always inquisitive text is riddled with dubious assertions and written in illiterate word-processorese? After all, the world is full of meticulous scholars whose desiccated texts are faultless with dusty accuracies. Can't we agree that recklessness brings fresh and juicy life to arid pastures? Almost anything can be defended because it breaks new ground, or ploughs old, more amusingly or more entertainingly than usual, but try to find mould-breaking merit in this:

> There is nowhere to discuss the stimulations of the eye on streets like Second Avenue, no place they can be collectively shaped into a civic narrative, nor, perhaps more consequently, a sanctuary which takes account of the disease-ravaged scene of the East Village.

The vacuous caution of that 'perhaps' is as pretty an instance of academic tosh as anyone could wish to ridicule. Since Professor Sennett has so many tenured friends, he will doubtless rally a posse to hound me for daring to suggest that he learn English before writing any more delightfully irresponsible books. Meanwhile, his intellectual *hubris* makes Oedipus look like a model family man with nothing to be ashamed of.

The Many Sicilies

Picasso called modern art 'a sum of destructions'; one might say the same of Sicily. The biggest and the most majestic of Mediterranean islands, Sicily has suffered invasions, sackings, massacres and depredations of all kinds, from Greeks, Romans, Arabs, Phoenicians, Normans and other forms of passing trade for whom its rich soil and ripe cities were too toothsome to be left in peace. Perhaps its greatest tyranny was homegrown: the Mafia may once have been a sort of native self-defence force but it soon became a means of extortion, intimidation and corruption.

The old invaders did at least erect unforgettable monuments; the indigenous and previously small-time predators, now sleek with international narco-wealth, have sponsored the uncontrolled desecration of what once seemed a coast-line of almost unlimited beauty. Word has it that the Mafia has a corner in cement, which may account for why Sicily is full of cement corners, as well as half-finished hotels and houses, rivers with concrete beds and high-rises of an ugliness to make one never again want to see *The Godfather*, that brilliant sentimentalisation of violence and idleness (crooks are, above all, people who do not want to work).

Modern Sicily is a by-word for peculation, mismanagement and mayhem. Just before we arrived, the local chief of the ruling Christian Democrats was shot to death in Palermo. Who by? The mafioso answer is 'Who is still alive?' For what reason? It was the equivalent of a party political broadcast: the publicity serves as a warning to those who know they are being warned. As a Tourist, all you have to do is keep out of the crossfire and hang onto your handbag: Sicilian motor-cyclists are adept at vrooming past with one hand out-stretched for easy pickings. I kept whatever valuables we had to have with us in the inside pockets of my Australian Adventure waistcoat, which has more (invisible) pockets than a snooker table, with the result that we never had any problems except with a couple of Carabinieri. They flagged us down in the middle of nowhere, although (or perhaps because) I alone of all the motorists we encountered did not overtake on corners, cross double white lines or exceed the speed limit. In Sicily, keeping the law amounts to suspicious behaviour. They checked us out at length and at gun-point, before allowing us to proceed.

So what is the good news? The island may have been despoiled, disfigured and 'developed', but its treasures are sublime and to be found in such profusion, in every corner of what Homer would concede is now a well-roaded place, that the want of charm is compensated by a landscape of dizzying grandeur. One civilisation piled on another yields wonders of syncretism as well as a rare series of architectural multiple pile-ups (the cathedral of Palermo for thumping instance).

We flew into Catania after dark and drove up the coast to Taormina. Etna was a soaring black presence to our left, its flanks pulsing with red-hot seams of lava, as if Vulcan were working nights. By day, you can scarcely see the latent heat of the sleeping giant, although his hot breath clouds the summit. We had not been to Taormina for thirty-seven years. Its vertiginous perch on the mountains – and perhaps its remoteness from the home-patch of the Mafia, which is mainly in the western half of the island – has preserved it from the worst of the cement-merchants, although it has certainly grown its share of carbuncular investments. The coast below it, from Giardini Naxos (founded by Naxiots from the Aegean) up towards Messina, is largely bereft of seductive detail, but the lordly view from the heights of Taormina softens the focus sufficiently to sustain the *fantaisie* that entranced Guy de Maupassant a century ago: the sea at least has not been modernised.

Taormina with its tight streets and amiable climate has been a wintering place, famous for its cosmopolitanism, ever since Goethe sang its praises in 1787, but it was the paintings of Otto Geling, a young Prussian, which first lured the tourists. When accused of overdoing the local colours, Geling advised people to compare his canvases with the real thing, which they did, in enraptured numbers. The place became a particular haven for admirers of young boys, who – clothed only in laurel wreaths – were photographed, with prim prurience, by Wilhelm Von Gloeden. His sepia photographs of pubescent peasant local lads are still on sale in the little bookshop on the Corso Umberto. It is no surprise to discover that Roger Peyrefitte, Truman Capote and Tennessee Williams made Taormina one of their regular staging posts. So too did D. H. Lawrence, who attributed dark godliness to the Sicilian males whose unsmiling virility made him read them for impersonations of the Real Thing. We were touched to find a very decent little restaurant called Da Lorenzo (the name by which Frieda italianised her husband). When I asked what had made them settle on the name, the *padrone* said, 'Lorenzo taught us everything – we are all his children.' It seemed a nice tribute, until he added, 'He's gone to America now. He has a place in New Jersey.' There are Lorenzos and Lorenzos.

We were lucky enough to stay at the San Domenico Palace, the now sumptuous (and amiably staffed) ex-convent in which Monty made his headquarters during his cautious progress from the south coast towards Messina and Palermo. Its courtyards and cloister and especially its tight but comely gardens, where friesia and cineraria were blooming in the privileged climate of early spring, offered ample peace in which to relax between sorties and read the novels of Giovanni Verga and John-Julius Norwich's *The Kingdom in the Sun*, a superbly readable account of the life and times of the Norman King Roger II (locally known as 'Ruggero') who reigned from 1130 to 1154 and instigated some of the island's greatest monuments.

Sicily has a famous literary tradition; men of letters and men at arms have swarmed to share (or appropriate) its wealth and revel in its balmy, intermittently explosive, climate. It was visited by Pythagoras and by Empedocles, who procured a reputation for immortality by the rather drastic means of jumping into the crater of Etna, thus making sure that no one ever saw him dead. Taormina's streets pay tribute to the ancient Greek poet Stesichorus, to Theocritos (whose idyllic shepherd boys and girls prefigure those in Von Gloeden's artful poses) and to Pirandello; Sextus Pompeius, the admiral who ruled Sicily nearly two thousand years ago, and made a rare nuisance of himself to the central authorities in Rome, also gets a street named after him (one man's outlaw is another's local hero). My favourite street name is, however, the Via Miss Mabel Hill, whoever she may have been.

The town offers a haven without demanding too much cultural diligence: the little cathedral is hardly more than a chapel, the thirteenth-century palace of Duke Stefano may be a 'masterpiece of Sicilian Gothic' but the eye can encompass its modest mass almost at a glance as you set out for the endless steps leading up to the acropolis from whose ruined fort you can scan Etna for scorch marks or signs of Empedocles.

Lower down is the Greek theatre, its scoop of stone hewn from the flank of the mountain, with its view of the pathless sea and its bare, ruined choir. One becomes a little blasé about Greek theatres in Sicily, though no one with a taste for the ancient world should miss the one at Syracuse. The obligatory drive through Catania on your way to Syracuse will certainly sharpen the reflexes and summon up the bloodymindedness as you endure the shameless aggression of its motorists. However, the temptation to get through it as quickly as possible should be resisted. Catania was the home of Giovanni Verga, whose little novels of provincial life in the middle of the last century began the tradition of *verismo* (truthfulness) in Italian literature. He was admired (and translated) by D. H. Lawrence. The brisk frankness of his narrative echoes that of Guy de Maupassant, that other keen traveller in Sicilian waters.

Catania's cathedral – one of Roger's less memorable foundations – is eclectically lumpy and its other monuments lack allure, but the smart Via Etnea's wide black pavements of volcanic rock tilt upwards towards Etna, which has twice overwhelmed the place. The imagination can easily restore the opera-loving city where Verga's Narcisa, in his autobiographical *La Peccatrice*, seduced her writer-lover and was then abandoned by him. Verga is properly honoured in the old quarter where he lived when the muse had deserted him (the last decades of his life produced nothing to match his early prolificity). The rake of the narrow streets requires sets of sidelong steps to the front doors, so that each one seems to be reached by mounting a little pulpit.

Catania was also the birthplace, in 1801, of Vincenzo Bellini, who is honoured by some enchantingly pompous public gardens, complete with ornate band-stand and an alley of 'Illustrious Men', beginning with Mazzini and Cavour (of course) and dwindling away to the busts of those who were merely world-famous in Catania. Miss Mabel Hill is not commemorated here. A floral calendar, in which the date is daily revised in live plants, pays tribute to the composer of *Norma*, an opera celebrated in *spaghetti Norma*, Sicily's staple form of pasta, which includes chunks of aubergine fried in olive oil. Below the Bellini gardens is the grand *caffé* where you can find the best cassata on the island. Catania has a dowdy dignity which we found endearing, but it must be said that it is also extremely noisy, especially at night when the Sicilian Vespas regularly murder sleep.

Syracuse was once the greatest city in Sicily and its somewhat glacial baroque cathedral and fading palazzi, adjacent to the Great Harbour, still make claims to elegance, but it is the Greek theatre which encapsulates the city's abiding and most ironic significance. The first performance of Aeschylus' *The Persians* was given here, in 472 BC. In it, the great tragedian celebrated the Athenian victory at Salamis:

> The Greeks, like fishermen
> With a haul of tunny netted and trapped,
> Stabbed, gaffed with snapped-off oars
> And broken spars, smashed, smashed, till all the sea
> Was one vast salty soup of shrieks and cries.

The rise of Athens began at Salamis; it was to be arrested and broken forever in the Great Harbour of Syracuse which you can see, beyond the pine-trees, from the very seats in which the audience first heard Aeschylus' paean to Athens' nautical triumph. It was here, not seventy years after Salamis, that the greatest armada ever to leave Athens met a fate hardly less cataclysmic than that of Xerxes' fleet. Thucydides tells the story in prose as durable as Aeschylus' verse: the Athenians came to extend their empire to the wheat-rich fields of Sicily, but their hopes foundered on the resolution of the Syracusans, who were astutely advised by the Spartan general Gylippus. When their fleet was cut to pieces attempting to get out of the harbour, which had been closed by a great chain, the watching infantry knew that it now had no escape. Seven thousand of them were sent to the salt mines in what is now called the 'Latomia dei Cappuccini'. Many were put to death, although the myth insists that those who were able, for their captors' edification, to recite choruses from Euripides' *Elektra* were spared execution. The best modern account of the Athenian debacle is Peter Green's *Armada from Athens*, but I defy anyone to read Aeschylus or Thucydides, while sitting in the splendid theatre, and not feel his flesh creep.

The geological warps and contortions of Sicily provide Syracuse with an amazing show of quarries and grottos. The most startling is the 'Orecchio di Dionisio' (a term first applied to it by Caravaggio and translated bathetically by the Michelin as 'the ear of Denys', which somehow brings Mr Healey to mind). It is a huge, steep grotto, like some chthonic cathedral, with remarkable acoustics; it is said, fancifully, to have allowed 'Denys' to spy on the conversation of prisoners whom he had consigned to its lower depths. Did he hope they would give him another chorus or two of 'sad Elektra's air'? One wonders how the Athenian Plato felt when he came, a few decades after his city's humiliation, to seek to convert the Syracusan tyrant into a Philosopher King. The failure of his educative mission did not, it seems, dispose Plato to think again about the wisdom of his plans for an Ideal City based on enlightened coercion and massive injections of mathematics.

As you walk the streets of Ortygia – the residential area which the Athenians never managed to penetrate – you come to the Fonte Aretusa, named for a nymph who was pursued thither by the river-god Alpheus who, if I am right, must have chased her all the way from Olympia, in the Peloponnese, where his waters were diverted by Herakles in order to wash out the Augean stables and so gave the Mediterranean its first large dose of untreated sewage. The fountain is remarkable for gushing fresh water, although situated right on the edge of the salt-water harbour. Its stone-ringed basin is frilled with papyrus plants amongst which swans and plump ducks keep the nymph company.

Syracuse was also the birthplace, in 287 BC, of Archimedes, the prototype both of the absent-minded professor and of the mathematician whose ingenuities led him into the armaments business. He was said to have served the tyrant of the city by concentrating the sun's rays in order to set fire to an approaching Roman fleet with an arrangement of mirrors and lenses. He was supposedly doing geometry on the beach when the Romans finally succeeded where the Athenians had failed and penetrated the city's defences. When, at the last moment, he saw a Roman soldier coming at him, he is reported to have cried out 'Don't step on my circles'. The unmathematical squaddy ran him through just the same. Syracuse has a new museum which is absolutely not to be missed. It is painlessly instructive in the archaeology of the island and stuffed with well-arranged, well-explained treasures, including a magnificent vase decorated by Polygnotos, perhaps the greatest of Attic painters. I particularly liked the anonymous one with a trio of prim, cloaked citizens on one side who, when you turn the vase round, are seen as randy satyrs, hot to trot. This and the pre-historic stuff would have pleased D. H. Lawrence, not least the gravestone which celebrates the sexual act in graphic style. The phallic prong and the receptive female groove suggested to me that the classic 'egg and dart' motif may well be a stylisation of the same activity.

The eastern side of Sicily is dominated by Etna to the point where you begin to be the victim of its moods. On the way back from Syracuse, we ran into a thunderous storm which laid a flat cap of sombre cloud on the mountain's brow and all but obscured it. We could see neither flame nor snow, but the unseen menace seemed to turn the air to lead. The next morning, brightness returned and we could make the long circuit round the volcano, which took us into the unsmiling villages of the hinterland, where one can recall the grimness of peasant life in the days when the only traffic you were likely to meet consisted of the wonderfully wrought and brilliantly painted farm-carts, each one a hand-carved polychromatic compendium of folkloric art for which Signor Agnelli's omni-present Fiats now provide no happy substitute. The air of Sicily used to be musky with a mixture of herbs and donkey droppings; it is now toxic with the usual carbon dioxide filth (to which, of course, we made our own busy contribution).

The excellence of the roads is a blessing it is churlish to curse, but modern engineering often gives the illusion of over-flying what once had to be lurched through. However, a detour to a town like Enna, whose site was above the clouds on the day we went there, reminds you of the lengths (and heights) to which Sicilians would go to procure an impregnable position. Enna's Lombard castle offers a view which seems to lay all Sicily at your feet, a climax in cragginess; the acropolis of Athens or the pinnacle of Mont St Michel would lie far below it, mere pimples by comparison with Enna's teetering eminence. We would have stayed longer if I could have persuaded the xenophobic parking-meter to take my *lire*, but even a brief visit is not to be scorned. After our somewhat languorous week in eastern Sicily, we were ready for the archaeologically intense prospects of the western half of the island to which, as the academics say, I shall now be turning.

The drive from Taormina to Agrigento takes you into the heartland of Sicily. Skirting the great decapitated cone of Etna, the Catania-Palermo motorway makes the first part of the journey anodyne, but it becomes more demanding after you turn south at Mulinello to reach Piazza Armerina, whose Roman villa was only just being excavated when we were last in Sicily. Its valley site led to its being covered with a layer of mud during the Dark Ages, which was probably the best possible thing for the purposes of its preservation. It came to light again, when a landlord tried to drill a well, in 1812, but was not fully excavated until the 1950s. Its third- and fourth-century mosaics are so fine, and its décor so magnificent, that it was assumed to be an imperial residence of Maximinianus Herculeus. However, as the guidebook sweetly puts it, 'the hypothesis is now unacceptable, and the scholars try to make theses and hypotheses but always with no grounds'.

Whoever built and maintained the elaborate villa of Casale – some six kilometres outside Piazza, a hill-town capped with a greenly domed baroque *duomo* – was certainly a man of substance. The Roman empire's decline was uneven and, to a degree, overstated: there is no sign here of decadence or of apprehension. Domesticity and the ways of peace are luxuriously depicted. The mosaics are surely the finest in the Roman world and their rural setting enables them to trump even those in the Bardo Museum in Tunis, which may equal them in subtlety, but have neither the matchless variety nor the idyllic seclusion. The villa is now covered with an imperially empurpled plastic roof which protects the floors from the elements. Well-arrranged walkways enable you to look down on a polychromatic strip cartoon of almost every aspect of ancient life and mythology. It is as lavish and vivid an excursion into the often underrated charm of plutocratic Roman taste as you could imagine. The mosaics display scenes of hunting and fishing, of fantasy and daily life, of girls at play (wearing bikinis modest enough to satisfy the moral demands of any bishop) and men in the field, all done with colourful audacity and unhesitatingly artful ingenuousness. The villa de Casale puts provincial

Roman life in its prettiest perspective; it is absolutely unmissable and, if you are lucky with your timing, as we were, you will have the place pretty well to yourself.

Thanks to John-Julius Norwich's marking of our card, in his invaluable *The Kingdom in the Sun*, we went in search of the priory of San Andrea, on the outskirts of Piazza. We came, after making several inquiries, to a delightful structure, brick-arched at ground level, with a first floor arcade supported on delicate pillars. How right John-Julius was, we thought, to draw our attention to such a small gem! We looked and we drove on, only to round a corner and come to a solid, honey-coloured church, almost indistinguishable from a fortress, which was unambiguously labelled Priorate de San Andrea (11th C.). We had been admiring the fifteenth-century church of Santa Maria del Jesu (so, I think, might you and Lord Norwich). There was nothing to be done with the locked, honey-coloured priory except to offer it the small change of our enthusiasm before hitting the road to Gela, which was once the rival (and enemy) of Syracuse as the finest city in Sicily.

Your lungs soon tell you that today Gela lies under a pall of petro-prosperity. We gave it no more than a sniff of appreciation before heading west towards Agrigento, along the coast where the Anglo-Americans began the recapture of Europe from the Nazis and their more or less reluctant allies. It was at this stage, in 1943, that the Americans recruited the Mafia to help them with local intelligence and so, inadvertently, assisted in lending organised crime the lineaments of patriotic respectability. While Patton and Monty mopped up the Germans, Lucky Luciano and friends mopped up the gravy. *Hinc illae lacrimae*, as Terence once observed, which is – more or less – the Latin for 'They cried all the way to the bank'.

How European is Sicily? Industrious northern Italians have a saying, 'After Rome, Africa', which expresses their dismay at the ways of the Mezzogiorno, the incorrigible south. The Moorish, North African, influence on Sicilian architecture is indeed always declaring itself, but the island is as often so like Greece that you can understand why the Athenians (and others) saw their manifest destiny in its wheat-rich conquest. Thanks to the triumphs of the fifth-century Greeks, in war and peace, Zeus became the great god here in pre-Christian times, though the Punic Baal also came to have his shrines, reminders of a lease which the 'Moorish' Qadhafi recently threatened (jokingly?) to revive.

Akragas, today's Agrigento, raised its greatest monument to Zeus, although – unlike others in its unique Valle dei Templi – it has not survived. The extant fifth-century temples, beginning with that of Hera, followed by the shrine attributed to 'Concord', in the centre, and that of Herakles at the far end of the long 'valley' (actually an ample shelf of battlemented rock), are outstanding for their Doric grandeur, their ostentatious expanse and their majestic vanity. Akragas was a town of legendary conceit. The garrulous ancient historian Diodorus Siculus promises that the inhabitants had a pet cemetery and raised mausolea to their champion horses. A system of aqueducts brought water which had been trapped in natural cisterns, between the volcanic rock and the clay beneath it, down from the mountains behind the city to supply the great sprawl of its residential area. That Agrigento was a frequent target for marauders is hardly surprising. Its showy position on a crest overlooking the sea, was at once intimidating and provocative (Paula Rego would be its ideal portraitist). Today's modern city is well above the archaeological area. Despite its lofty frontage, it need not detain you for a moment, unless you are determined to find the house where Goethe spent a few days or cannot resist the sight of one more (mediocre) baroque cathedral or enjoy clotted, clamorous traffic.

Luckily, everything you might want to see is admirably displayed in the valley (and if you want a picnic – advisable in a land of gastronomic limitations – you can buy it in Villagio Mose, a hideous but convenient suburb with, at the far end, the best *panificio* we came across on the island). The pleasure of the Valley of the Temples lies not least in the ease of access; there is no entrance fee, so one is able to visit it in various lights, from dawn to dusk, without officious formality. On a less spectacular site, the other, more or less recumbent, temples would be remarkable in themselves; that of Zeus had gigantic supportive pilasters, of Atlas-like figures, which must have given it a grotesque, intimidating and (happily) unique aspect. One of the figures has been reconstituted in the very fine new museum (designed by the same architect as that in Syracuse and every bit as well-planned), but his megalithic fellows were all cannibalised when the first docks were constructed at Porto Empedocle, the birthplace of Luigi Pirandello, a few kilometres away. Pirandello's house, in a fresh coat of suburban stucco, is preserved among the industrial dereliction of his native village.

Not far along the coast is one of the most impressive natural sites in Sicily, although it is unmentioned in any guidebook. In thrty-seven years we have never forgotten our first sight of the so-called 'Turkish Steps' (in fact, although the Turks invaded Crete and Rhodes and attempted to storm Malta – as Ernle Bradford's terrific book recounts – they never set foot in Sicily). The 'Scala dei Turchi' consist of flights of gigantic 'staircases' which are in fact limestone cliffs. They lead down to a fine beach, although it would be unwise to seek access to it via the staircase unless you are wearing five-league boots. The whole area has an intimidating improbability which reminded me, Turkishly enough, of the heights of Pammukele, in the Anatolian hinterland, where geological similarity has also created a series of lustrously white stepped limestone cliffs with something of the texture of Harris tweed.

You can stop off at the Turkish Steps on your way to Selinunte, yet another unmissable set of Graeco-Sicilian temples. On the day when we arrived, the ruined city was buttoned in a vivid spring outfit of yellow daisies. The empty car-park gives onto a set of three new concrete triliths which must be among the most memorable monstrosities in existence: each one frames a different antique temple, one of which – possibly that of Hera (or perhaps of Aphrodite) – was not there when I last scanned the site in 1955. It was resurrected three years later, with the help of a good deal of speculative concrete. Such restoration properly affronts purists, but the fluted result is massively spectacular, while way beyond it, on the acropolis in the distance, is the monumental skeleton of a sixth-century temple, originally of forty-two columns. In the wind-thrashed landscape, Selinunte was a gigantic and almost deserted city whose ruin began when it clashed with Hannibal's Carthage. Hannibal came across the water from what is now Tunisia, to the aid of its ally, Segesta, but his countrymen were in no hurry to return. Until the Romans evicted them, the Carthaginians remained the masters of western Sicily.

Segesta is further along the same circuit and has survived less well than its former rival. What is left is only – only! – a Doric temple on an incomparable site and in a extraordinary state of repair (equalled only by that at Vassae in the Peloponnese). We dashed up the hill between downpours, but the gods were favourable and we made a blissfully dry and unaccompanied tour among the luxuriant clusters of herbs and flowers above the great gorge with its jumble of rocks and pine-trees. It had taken us thirty-seven years to return to Selinunte but we went back to Segesta (which we missed in 1955) the very next day, after a long morning in Palermo, during which we ran the gaudy gauntlet of obligations to Ruggero II and his many embellishments of the city.

The jewel in his memory's crown is, according to John-Julius, on the first floor of the otherwise unalluring castle which now houses the security-intense Sicilian parliament. What should one say of the 'Palatine chapel'? Even in the usual state of scaffolded renovation, it is a literally golden example of the work of those *other* Greeks, the Byzantines, whose craftsmen Roger brought to Sicily three and a half centuries before Byzantium fell to the Turks. What better proof is there that the 'Renaissance' celebrates the 're-birth' of a genius that never died and which rarely ceased to be honoured in the West, despite the ideological rifts between Rome and Constantinople? The Arabs too, whatever anathemas they might excite, contributed scintillatingly. Their abstract elegance adds a welcome note of gorgeous restraint to the small masterpiece of the king's private chapel: the stalactite ceiling (alas, largely invisible to us) and the mosaic floor prove the harmony which genius – and its attendant luck – can find in a compote of diverse traditions. When the luck and the genius run out, you get Palermo Cathedral.

After the grandiosity of many Sicilian monuments, the small beauty of the Palatine Chapel and that of San Giovanni degli Eremiti offer interludes of modest splendour. San Giovanni, although dilapidated (and deconsecrated) has typically Arabic domes – John-Julius compares them to pomegranates, but they look more like turnips to me – and a peerless little cloister. I am addicted to cloisters, whether on the gargantuan scale of La Certosa, near Pavia, or provincially modest like the one at Moissac, in the Grandes Pyrenées – but the Hermits of St John certainly enjoyed a privileged place for pious promenading. The guidebook being our secular breviary, we had to press on to the (Greek Orthodox) Church of the Martorana where you can see the only extant likeness – assuming it resembles him – of Roger II being crowned by Jesus. The mosaics here are the first executed on the island by Byzantine artists (with local asistants, the Sicilians insist). They must have supplied an unanswerable set of references.

The greatest of Sicily's Byzantine treats had to be left to the next day: Monreale and Cefalù. Which is the greater of the two apsidal images of the Pantocrator? John-Julius is firmly in favour of the humane spirituality of the one at Cefalù, but the setting at Monreale and the sublime sumptuousness of its cathedral command my preference. How typical of man's forked nature that the Norman Roger II (*encore lui*!) should have instituted this spiritual fortress in order to create a rival bishopric to that of Palermo, with whose incumbent he was angrily at odds! If Church and Crown had been capable of Christian comity, Monreale would not be there today to astound the faithful and stun the sceptic. What can be said about what must be seen? The cloister here is less modest – its columns, gartered with mosaic bands, would be to Malvolio's taste – but still remarkable, not least for its columnar fountain, like a frosted *churro* twisted out of marble.

Last came Cefalù, where the Pantocrator in the apse of the cathedral gazes with a promise of reconciling magnanimity on Christian and infidel alike, or so it would be pretty to suppose. The cathedral piazza is edgily sited on a plaform of rock in the centre of the steep port whose lowest houses are part of the sea-wall overlooking the sheltered harbour. During the 1920s, Cefalù was the improbable retreat of Aleister Crowley, the devil-worshipping, self-styled Great Beast 666, who with his acolytes inhabited a local castle he renamed 'The Temple of Theleme' (where you did what you wanted, unless it clashed with what he wanted). Crowley was a literally massive Guru of Evil whose prose style suggests that he had a certain ironic sense of his own absurdity. I used to play soccer in Hyde Park with one of his one-time ephebes. His spindle-shanked nimbleness seemed unimpaired by having kicked around with an over-weight devil.

Cefalù had to be our last call in Sicily, but there are, of course, countless things we failed to see which, in a place less layered and constellated with three-star treasures, would command an early visit. Sicily has suffered indelibly from the cruel privilege of its position and its heritage. Cursed with good fortune and the consequent fortune-hunters, it has been one of the great bones of contention lodged in the throat of the Mediterranean. Its troubles are not – and will probably never be – over, but its lure remains incomparable and irresistible.

Science and Prescience

It is now half a Biblical lifetime since C. P. Snow, as he then was, denounced the traditional British gulf between Science and the Humanities. In his famous, perhaps notorious 1959 lecture, he declared that the Two Cultures – *there* was a post-Disraelian dichotomy to conjure with! – spoke different languages; scientists and humanists were lamentably blind to each other's beauty and foolishly deaf to each other's valuable message. Post-war Britain thus suffered from a sort of cultural apartheid. The cure was to make the Second Law of Thermodynamics as natural a part of civilised wisdom as, say, 'It is a truth universally acknowledged that a single man in possession of a good fortune must be in want of a wife . . .' The devotees of the Austin 7 and of Jane Austen were advised to find common ground.

Since he was a novelist and literary journalist, as well as a *quondam* Civil Servant (influential in organising atomic research during the war), Snow had reason to believe that he qualified for citizenship in both the domains whose fusion – or customs union – he proposed. *Strangers and Brothers*, the sequence of novels which made him famous, advertised the ascent to power of the white-coated New Men who, despite (or because of) their lack of metropolitan or artistic graces, had proved their right to manage post-war Britain; they were the blanched porters of enlightened, scientific standards. This new class of practical pundits had vindicated its claims not only over Hiroshima but also at Bletchley, where Oxbridge wits had cracked the Nazis' secret codes; given the right backing, they could now engage

313

with confidence on the riddle of the universe, even if the grotesque laws about homosexuality had deprived them of the help of Alan Turing, the father of the computer.

Snow insisted that if Britain was to meet the challenge of change, Science rather than the Humanities – in the old sense of a classical, literary education – had to supply an objectively valid, forward-looking philosophy. Education had to be practical. Cambridge, like other universities, needed a constructive shaking. Since he was a man of largely affable self-importance, Snow's 1959 State of the Nation lecture was probably intended to be no more than a genial Jeremiad. Was there not timely prescience in his fear that, unless she geared herself to change course, Britain might become a kind of twentieth-century Venice: a once pivotal power which, with the new currents in world trade, would find herself, like the Serenissima, reduced to the status of a marooned curiosity? Investment in 'Science', Snow suggested, was the only plausible way to remain in the mainstream.

Why should a reasonable warning against incipient obsolescence have excited such reverberating hostility? Thirty-five years ago, England had only just been reminded, in the sullen aftermath of Suez, that her position in the world was rocky. If Winston Churchill was still alive, along with the receding memory of his – and Britain's – finest hour, Harold Macmillan was proving himself a lugubriously parodic successor; gestural inertia had replaced the commanding effortlessness with which Great (and Greats) Men had once held the tiller. However, if the Old Etonian posture of amateur superiority was increasingly tottery, as were the social *mores* which sustained it, it could still be claimed that the Old Guard was on parade and should not hurriedly be changed. On the intellectual front, was not our – and perhaps the world's – most renowned philosopher Bertrand Russell, who had been central to the intellectual and moral revolution in which he had figured argumentatively since early in the century? What was so wrong with sclerosis?

If he had taken Snow's part, Russell might have given it some much needed class, but he was probably too much of an egotist to play the foot-soldier in so pedestrian a cause. Where Russell's idea of higher education was lofty to the point of vertiginous, Snow wanted to raise (and revise) the general efficiency rather than to prime an élite to reach for undiscovered conclusions. Lacking Russell's standing, he was wise to be modest, but modesty did not insure him against Dr Frank Leavis, who was the very type of the one-track – and not particularly broad gauge – mind. As the essential Cambridge literary critic, he regarded the Common Pursuit of true judgment in literature – by which he meant almost exclusively English literature – as an end no less than a means: the holistic purpose of a humane education was to nurture the moral self-sufficiency necessary to resist, if not prevent, the very technological revolution which Snow advocated.

When Leavis preached the virtues of his common pursuit, he left little doubt about who should nominate the quarry or lead the chase. He found his idol in D. H. Lawrence, on account less of his dark gods than of his veneration for Old England. Leavis was not only an open-necked Puritan and purist, he was also an unsmilingly disappointed academic who, like so many who announce their scorn for worldly values and popular success, craved the professorial preferment which he believed that adroit fixers like Snow (though not Snow in person) had unjustly denied him. Only Wittgenstein – with whom he affected to have had a closer relationship than the facts warrant – had the ability to render him somewhat humble. Certainly the great philosopher was alone in daring to express his admiration for Leavis's qualities by imploring him to 'Give up literary criticism!'

When it came to the Two Cultures, Snow's lucubrations were more than matched by Leavis's invective. The universality of science appealed to Leavis no more than dilettante ideas about art and literature which he associated with Bloomsbury or the Sunday journalism of which Cyril Connolly was, in those days, the plumpest and most iniquitous instance (how dare he take reading to be less a spiritual exercise than an occasion for enlightened hedonism?). Had not D. H. Lawrence advised that when you were asked why grass was green, you should not offer a 'scientific' answer about chlorophyll but respond simply 'Because it is'? Perhaps the only writer who achieved a synthesis between standards which both Leavis and Snow might have respected was Primo Levi, but neither the literary nor the scientific pundits of the insular 1950s ever began to acknowledge the significance of so marginal a phenomenon as the Holocaust.

Although Leavis was too busy resenting his enemies, real or imagined, to propound a coherent political ideology, it was clear that, while not a formal Conservative, he regarded traditional English values, and the literary canon which articulated them, as a hermetic system to be preserved rather than expanded: no living novelist merited his admiration, least of all the luckless Snow, whose jejune compositions were judged to be of a piece with his flaccid opinions (of his novels, *The Masters* deserves to be remembered alongside, say, Hugh Walpole's *The Old Ladies*). From the other end of the ground they could never have in common, Leavis out-Jeremiahed Jeremiah with anathemas against a Craven New World in which the grant-aided laboratory might banish the library. What could be less desirable than to replace the fervent particularity of English university life with the cosmopolitan banality of formulaic universalism? The sweetness and light-heartedness which might have federated two cultures never manifested themselves. The only touch of humour came when cuttings with the headline SNOW FALLS HEAVILY were larkily pinned to college noticeboards.

So providentially middlebrow and middle-class an enemy as Snow made Leavis a self-anointed Roland, holding the pass against the *schlock* of the new. By a significant coincidence, it was just as the newly signed Treaty of Rome made the Common Market a six-fold threat to parochial boundaries that Leavis composed himself to speak for England. Proof against continental intrusion and insulated against universal claims, his vestigial spirit, like a frowning Cheshire cat, links today's Tory Euro-Sceptics in a community of negation with those on the Left, like their domestic arch-enemy Denis Skinner who, reportedly, has never owned a passport since it would only entitle him to travel where no good Englishman would choose to go.

As for who won and who lost, Snow was briefly installed as a Science Minister in Harold Wilson's first, 1964 government where he was teamed with Frank Cousins, a Trades Union boss whose knowledge of science was not his first qualification. If Wilson supported the white heat of technological revolution, Cousins was reluctant to stoke the furnace if it meant any alteration in the restrictive practices which made the TGWU the force it was. Snow fell once again. As for Leavis, it no more occurred to him to alter his stance than it would to disparage D. H. Lawrence. If science and the humanities are still unable to find common ground, it is due not least to the first Science graduate to become Prime Minister; matching the middlebrow complacency of Snow with the stiff-neckedness of Leavis, Mrs

Thatcher had little use for reconciliations or mutual respect. If the two cultures are still at all vigorous, they are both now at the mercy of market forces and without any large moral or life-enhancing programme. When William Waldegrave announced that we (still) have no choice but to invest in science, his air of woeful obligation was enough to make you rush out and bury your head in *Pride and Prejudice*.

Not Drowning But Waving

Over a bibulous dinner, I once asked the late Marcello Mastroianni why – unlike certain Anglo-Saxon actors who were vainly concerned with their virile image – he never hesitated to appear on screen as a nervous cuckold, an impotent dupe, or a closet homosexual. Did he not care whether the audience took him 'really' to be any or all of those things? *'Beh,'* he said, *'cinema no è gran' cosa!'* Such impious dismissal of the seventh art clashes loudly with the earnest attitudes embalmed in these three volumes (of a projected four) from *Cahiers du Cinéma*. If the magazine's aggressive notoriety can scarcely be distinguished from that of the *Nouvelle Vague*, whose most famous directors – François Truffaut, Jean-Luc Godard, Claude Chabrol, Jacques Rivette – were at the heart of the enterprise in the 1950s, we have fat evidence here of its subsequent opinionated longevity.

Of those four fundamental musketeers, Truffaut emerged as the most starry, although *prêt-à-tourner* Chabrol has made more films and Godard's affectations of martyrdom have secured for him the allure of a St Just with tinted glasses and a

---

Review of Antoine de Baecque and Serge Toubiana, *François Truffaut* and *Cahiers du Cinéma*: vol. I – *the 1950s, Neo-Realism, Hollywood, New Wave*, ed. Jim Hillier; vol. 2 – *the 1960s, New Wave, Re-evaluating Hollywood*, ed. Jim Hillier; vol. 3 – *1969–1972, The Politics of Representation*, ed Nick Bronne, in the *Times Literary Supplement*, 1996.

safe house in Switzerland. Rivette's *Paris nous appartient* remains a somewhat lonely monument to a directorial career which was perhaps sapped by the energy lavished on often excellent critical forays. For a while, the musketeers were one-for-all and all-for-*auteur*ship, but success and divergent aesthetics turned Godard and Truffaut into bitter enemies. Towards the end of his life, Truffaut – who admired Proust and often wrote letters of purposeful emollience which recall the master – wrote at furious length to Godard denouncing his lack of shame or honour and suggesting that, when he filmed his autobiography, it should be entitled '*Une merde est une merde*'. Godard had the last, ruefully fond, word in his obituary preface to Truffaut's copious correspondence, which was published in 1988.

Truffaut began as a prolific, polemic journalist. He was hailed in 1977 by Henri Langlois, the father of the French Cinemathèque (whom François had championed after his high-handed dismissal by André Malraux), as one of the 'only two great cinema critics of the century'. The other was François Vinneuil. Experts will recognise Vinneuil as the pseudonym of Lucien Rebatet, the vindictive anti-Semitic novelist who, during the Occupation, said of the French cinema, 'Il faut d'abord le désenjuiver.' Truffaut was fascinated by Rebatet's work. In 1952, he helped him to find 'quelques tuyaux' after release from eight years in prison for collaboration. Rebatet fared better than another considerable film and literary critic and advocate of mass murder, Robert Brasillach, who had been executed by a pitiless de Gaulle in 1945, a decision endorsed by Pierre Vidal-Naquet who, nevertheless, admired Brasillach's Greek scholarship. In France, the bad and the beautiful often converge.

Truffaut emerges as an emblematic figure of the period between 1948, when – as a *cinéphile fougueux* and teenager *en fugue* – he first knocked on André Bazin's door in the rue des Beaux Arts (where else?) and his (François') death, from a brain tumour, in November 1984, at the age of fify-two. By then, he had done a prodigious amount of work in a lifetime just a year longer than Balzac, his favourite novelist, had required to compile *La Comédie Humaine*. Like Balzac, François attempted not only to create an *oeuvre* but also to be its manufacturer. Balzac became a printer; Truffaut started his own production company, Films du Carrosse. His enterprise distinguished and distanced him from other *Cahiers* directors: Godard had money of his own and proved adept at coaxing it from others in the good cause of the Left, while the *bon vivant* Chabrol became the happy Hitchockian whose up-and-down life he recounted in *Et pourtant je tourne*.

Like both Sartre and Camus, Truffaut was the son of an absent father: unlike theirs, however, Truffaut's sire was not dead but effaced. Thanks to a private detective, befriended during research for the wearisome Antoine Doinel cycle, François was to discover, when already adult, that he was the son of a Jewish dentist called Roland Lévy. We are promised that he felt relief and consternation: 'Il s'est toujours senti Juif', though he is unlikely to have said as much to Rebatet. Having procured his address, he actually contrived to see his father, without informing him, but only got as far as a long shot. Whatever his motive, he did not disturb the old man's solitary tranquillity. Instead, being already separated from his Jewish wife, Madeleine Morgenstern, Truffaut preferred to spend the evening alone at the cinema, seeing Chaplin in *The Gold Rush*.

As a small child, the fatherless François had been delivered, on the death of his protective grandmother, to his unloving mother, Janine de Montferrand, for whom he represented no more than 'une erreur d'enfance'. His stepfather, the often cuckolded Roland Truffaut, proved a responsible, if scarcely effusive, substitute for the other 'repressed' Roland. In order to supplement the disastrous finances of a ciné-club which he had founded, while pretending to have a job, the truant adolescent went into the business of petty theft. Among his most saleable loot were publicity stills from cinemas (cf. the director in *La Nuit Américaine*). He capped this criminal career by lifting a typewriter from Roland Truffaut's office. Truffaut *père* paid his debts, but had him locked up, as the *code civil* then sanctioned, in a reformatory in Villejuif. The boy wrote, 'without hate or emotion', asking for some jam and his dossiers on Charlie Chaplin and Orson Welles. He was not visited by his parents for two months and never forgave his mother. The skinny youth was again to be incarcerated, this time in a military prison, during an ill-advised, and improbable, period as a trainee *volontaire* in the French army. He was dismissed with ignominy and returned to Paris to be definitively recruited to the cinema.

Truffaut's errant early life supplied very raw material for his breakthrough movie, *Les Quatre Cents Coups*, which was also a homage to Jean Vigo's pre-war *Zéro de Conduite*. Truffaut's curtailed *scolarite* had been somewhat less harshly marked than

Vigo's: when he was thirteen, he received 4 out of the standard 20 for an essay in which he remarked, with provocative tartness, that if France had not been on the quickest way for the Americans to reach Europe (and if Syria had been without petrol (!)), Parisian pavements would still resound to Nazi jackboots, 'car notre résistance était dérisoirement faible'. His scorn for authority was to be mitigated by its acquisition as a patron, but he persistently refused the Légion d'Honneur and was promptly insurgent against officialdom.

Effrontery and seduction were the twin engines of his rise to fame. Marginalised by bastardy and hardened – but never callused – by rejection, Truffaut was an intensely earnest and shrewdly ambitious autodidact. His studies were limited to what interested him passionately: the cinema (he often saw three films a day) and literature (he was also a voracious reader). As an adventurer, he was as tirelessly seductive as he could be prudently courteous; he loved women, from whores to stars, and many of them, from Catherine Deneuve to Fanny Ardant, loved him.

If the *auteur* theory was not his invention, he became both its prophet and its beneficiary. André Bazin took the *enfant sauvage* under his wing and soon gave him access to the columns of *Cahiers du Cinéma*. An idealistic Catholic, Bazin regarded the cinema as 'la pièce maîtresse de la nouvelle éducation'; it was to be a democratic art – the lucky seventh – which would give the liberated masses their right to 'equal access to culture'. He was a visionary who never suspected that television would supply the masses with their equal access to whatever would encourage them to buy junk. As for culture, our executive moguls insist that 'classic serials' and script-edited 'drama' are its innovatory instances. We are still waiting for a *Cahiers de la Télé* and critics with the nerve to break a lance for some purpose other than to secure their own enrolment in the machinery.

It was typical of Bazin's astute naiveté to argue that 'deep focus' was more democratic than montage – the traditional way of assembling film – because (he said) it gave unrigged access within the cinematic frame to previously blurred or relegated characters. For this reason, he maintained that the artful egocentricity of *Citizen Kane* could be assimilated to the cursive, unpremeditated neo-realism of Roberto Rossellini. Rossellini's decline from the great days of *Roma, Città Aperta* and *Paísa*, was systematically denied by those who had decreed his irrevocable sainthood (literally). In the *Cahiers* scheme, even *Stromboli*, a melodramatic compilation of clumsy footage, had to be championed as a masterpiece, although it is worth seeing, just, only for Ingrid Bergman's brave display of emancipation from the Hollywood to which she would return.

Truffaut's critical precociousness climaxed in 1954. At the age of twenty-two, he published the notorious manifesto entitled *Une certaine tendance dans le Cinéma français*. It is an aspect of the frustrating integrity of these three retrospective volumes that Truffaut's *J'accuse*, brandished at 'classic French cinema', does not appear in them: the editors have decided to prioritise (as I fear they might say) what has not previously appeared in English. This is both honourable and laming, not least when reference is made to unreproduced articles (for instance on Joseph Losey) more instructive than those which allude to them.

Truffaut's *tendance* essay was trenchant, insolent and decidedly tendentious: it served demoralising notice on the old guard, the better to supplant it. Its main target was the screenwriting fraternity, Jean Aurenche and Pierre Bost *en tête*; accused of 'médiocrité issue de la guerre', their arrogant triteness was alleged to impose a monotonous, literary manner on whoever directed their slick scripts. Their 'realism', Truffaut asserted, 'veut fatalement que les hommes soient bas, infâmes et veules'. Providentially, however, there was one source of cinema which was victoriously exempt from any such mediocrity and in which optimism and spontaneity were bravely framed: Hollywood. *Eh oui*! Eric Rohmer seconded Truffaut by calling California 'that chosen land'. In the 1950s, America was still enjoying a postwar *état de grâce*. Her hegemony had not yet attracted the systematic vilification to which – for very different reasons – the French, Left and Right, were to subject it in later decades. Even then, Sartre remained an admirer of Faulkner and Dos Passos and went so far as to script *Freud* for an unappreciative John Huston and $25,000.

The *auteur* theory was applied to American directors as much as the result of Truffaut's *goût du paradoxe* as of Bazin's humane earnestness. How sweet it was to detect signs of sly individuality in the production-line work of indented labourers in Hollywood studios! Had not Sartre declared that the French had never been so free as during the Occupation? If the theory that films had authors just as books did had been manifestly true, would any wit have troubled to propose it? As the unflagging reader discovers, *auteurisme* fell into abeyance in the 1970s, when the ultra-left *Cahiers* was under the influence of Barthes, Kristeva, Sollers and Derrida and it became chic to maintain that even books did not have authors, unless they bore the names of Barthes, Kristeva, Sollers or Derrida. By this time, the *goût du paradoxe* meant that even the camera could be accused, at very great length and with unanswerable (and intermittently clever) turgidity, of *bourgeois* partiality.

It is not surprising that, as early as 1965, Jean-Louis Comolli could say 'American cinema basically is not an *auteur* cinema'. The onset of the Vietnam war had encouraged an ideological rupture with the American way of filming. However, even at the outset there had always been a measure of wilfulness in stipulating that for something to be a work of art it had to be the product of a single artistic mind. Since it had been posited that 'cinema' was an art *à part entière*, it was logical that there had to be an artist behind each work: the notion of *un film de* derived less from observed facts than from an *a priori* need for evidence to validate the theory. Truffaut and the others busied themselves in rounding up unusual suspects, of whom Alfred Hitchcock became the enduring (and very grateful) favourite. Imagine anyone taking *Rebecca* or *Under Capricorn* seriously! But then again, how many clever people convinced themselves that the Soviet Union was a workers' paradise?

An American leftist, John Hess, had early pointed out that the *politique des auteurs* was a 'culturally conservative, politically reactionary attempt to remove film from the realm of social and political concern'. As Bazin's *dauphin*, Truffaut did not set out deliberately to make cinema what Bazin had hoped that it would never be, but – despite certain leftward genuflections – François was to become a Right Bank, if never a right wing, figure rather than a universal educator. His ostentatious dandyism as he drove through Paris in that contemporary trophy of success, a Facel Vega, coupled with his marriage to the daughter of Ignace Morgenstern, a rich distributor of the sort of films which were written by those whom he had anathematised, confirmed his careerism in the eyes of those as envious of his ascent as they were doubtful of his *sérieux*. If to accuse him of selling out is absurd, it is perhaps less certain that he never bought in. However, his passion was for creation, not mere success. He once said, though it is not quoted here, that one of his ambitions was to make the first James Bond *défici-taire*. He saw that the huge successes of those like Spielberg, who directed Truffaut, the actor, in *Close Encounters of the Third Kind*, would probably put an end to the kind of cinema which demanded anything but money of its narcotised spectators.

Although Truffaut was unquestionably a dedicated lover of 'serious' cinema, he was neither an innovator nor an ideologue. He maintained that directors should write their own films, but his best movie was, perhaps, *Jules et Jim*, which followed the text and tone of Henri-Pierre Roché's novel with luminous piety (Helen Hessel, the original female in the triangle, lived to congratulate him on his fidelity). If Godard always resembled the dadaist who asserted 'When an artist spits, that's art!', Truffaut believed in considered scripting and diligent pre-production.

In the first decade of *Cahiers*, covered by the first volume, the young contributors were as ruthless as they were inexperienced. Wasting no space on what they did not like, they unhesitatingly applauded both their idols – Rossellini, de Sica (for a while), Minnelli, Nicholas Ray, Howard Hawks – and, as soon as they started shooting their own amateurish films, each other. Truffaut unashamedly promoted a *politique des copains*; rigour and cronyism amounted to much the same thing. Having posited systematic hostility to established screenwriters, Truffaut and his friends fabricated a certain consistency by insisting that *mise en scène* – the visual orchestration of the story, the rhythm of the action, form rather than content – defined the specificity of cinema. The director was the creator of these things and hence the only artist on the block. Had not Orson Welles decreed, 'I believe a work is good to the degree that it expresses the man who created it'? Such an aesthetic might not allow Chartres Cathedral to be good, but it offered the conveniently clinching word from the oracle.

To advance Nicholas Ray and Vincente Minnelli (and later Jerry Lewis) as men of genius required less perception than ingenuity. The pages devoted to a eulogy of Ray's *Party Girl* in volume 2 still make one wonder what film it was that his partisans valued. When I saw *Le Traquenard* again recently, Cyd Charisse's legs were still as long and as beautiful as ever, but her dance numbers sadly lacked Stanley Donen's direction and the story and dialogue could have done with attention from

Bill Goldman. As for Minnelli, *The Bad and the Beautiful* was said to warrant his designation as a 'moralist' who also supposedly transcended the limitations of the musical. Did the *Cahiers* boys ever hear how on one transcendentally moral occasion Vincente decided that the only way to keep some peacocks from straying was to staple them to the set? When he was finally cornered and interviewed, the *copains* discovered that Minnelli was 'a nice man' who did not have much to say; it was then resolved that his mordantly articulate producer, John Houseman, was the real *auteur* behind the *auteur*. Only Hitchcock, Welles and Howard Hawks never lost their halos.

Cahiers du Cinéma, with its evolving fads and *prises de position*, is as closely involved with the socio-intellectual history of France during the *trente glorieuses* – 1945–1975 – as with the movies. When French prosperity and confidence, sustained by the huff and puff of de Gaulle and his barons, served both to revive the vanity of the *bourgeoisie* and to excite the countervailing militancy of Parisian intellectuals, the magazine moved from liberal right to doctrinaire left. The most intelligent of the *Cahiers* editors after Bazin was Eric Rohmer (the *nom de guerre* of Maurice Scherer), a *lycée* teacher whose scepticism about 'poetic' cinema, such as Alain Resnais' *Hiroshima Mon Amour*, was never unduly abrasive. As his *Contes Moraux* showed, Rohmer was always more interested in how things actually were, or might turn out to be, than he was an *inconditionnel* of his contributors' (increasingly tortuous) theories. His stringent tolerance led, of course, to his eviction from the editorial chair.

Although many of the nuances of the struggles to 'correct' the magazine's line in politico-aesthetic matters are thoroughly elucidated in the introductions, there is one gaping lacuna: no allusion is made, in the biography of Truffaut or in the extracts from *Cahiers*, to a cardinal illustration of the charmless face of the *Cahiers* crowd when it came to anyone who was not their *chou-chou*. In 1960, Michelangelo Antonioni was invited to show *L'Avventura* at Cannes. The greatest film of its time and one of the very few cinematic masterpieces to mature without dating (having seen it at least a dozen times, I was recently surprised to discover its comic qualities), it was greeted at the festival with hisses, boos and ridicule. A friend of mine remembers sitting next to Antonioni during the projection; 'il a vécu un véritable Calvaire ... Je n'ai pas vu ni entendu à l'époque que les petite copains de la nouvelle vague l'aient soutenu de la voix ou du geste ... tout dont je suis sûr c'est qu'Antonioni s'est senti très seul ... et j'ai éprouvé physiquement ce que c'était que d'être humilié pendant deux heures de projection'. Some French *cinéastes* did seek, *après coup*, to apologise to Antonioni, but in view of how uncritically Joseph Losey was adulated (for instance by Michel Mourlet, on the basis of *Blind Date*), as the cinema's first 'scientific reseacher', the failure even to deplore the grossness of Antonioni's reception remains an indelible blot on the honour of those ageing *jeunes* who, eight years later, would procure the suspension of the entire Cannes festival on the hastily discovered grounds of its élitism. Antonioni's 1962 *L'Eclisse* was dismissed by Jean Douchet, who greatly preferred Preminger's memorably forgettable *Advise and Consent*. We learn that it was left to André S. Labarthe, a consistently shrewd critic, to salute the 'modernity and grandeur, if not perfection' of Antonioni's work. We could have done with these contributions instead of having the third volume, covering 1969–1972. Few years can have been so long for the remaining subscribers: semioticians, Althusserians, Maoists, deconstructionists, Derridans, Lacaniques and Barthistes force-fed them with more verbiage than can possibly have been good for them.

Try this from Jean-Pierre Oudart:

> The ideal chain of a sutured discourse would be one which articulated into figures which it is no longer appropriate to call shot/reverse shot, but which mark the need – so that the chain can function – for an articulation of the space such that the same portion of space be represented at least twice, in the filmic field and in the imaginary field – with all the variations of angle that the obliqueness of the camera with regard to the place of the subject allows.

I should prefer to attend a day-long retrospective of *The Three Stooges* and Abbot and Costello than go through that kind of stuff again. There are pages and pages of it.

For anyone banal enough to be interested in film-*making*, the most instructive articles are in the second volume. Jean-Louis Comolli, for eminent example, is remorselessly fair in his anatomisation of Lelouch's *Un Homme et une Femme*, especially in the director's slack use of so-called improvisation and in the fake flashbacks, from Anouk's dialogue, which are shot from a point of view which involves seeing the speaker in mid-shot. The result is that we are cut adrift from the narrative line and left in no man's land. The fakery of Lelouch's style of 'improvisation' persists in films such as Mike Leigh's *Secrets and Lies*, which Francis Coppola crowned with laurel at Cannes last year, although *Fargo* was clearly a better film. *Le goût du paradoxe* lives on on the Croisette.

Unfortunately, most of the essays and discussions in these volumes are without practical value except to those involved in 'film studies', where such things as narrative, script, character and pacing are of less interest than the verbose analysis of signifiers. Pretentiousness leads to choice absurdities such as Luc Moullet's attempt to justify Godard's private jokes by asserting that (in ancient Athens) Aristophanes was 'esoteric . . . unintelligible without footnotes'. The real civilisation of our time, we are promised, is represented by the comic strips in *Paris-Soir*.

The translations are as pitilessly accurate in conveying the devious ratiocination of the Maoists as in recalling the early urgency of the *auteur*-theorists who have done so much to arm second- and third-rate directors with their delusions of grandeur. The editing is almost flawless, although 'petit (sic) bourgeoisie' is not pretty. The title 'Seven Men from Now' translated as *Sept Hommes à Debattre* (sic), instead of *à abattre*, says it all for what unfortunate movements like film-studies lead to.

Gore Vidal, Scholar

Before we get down to cases, here is an exercise in the etiquette of reviewing. You are sent a book of essays of very many pages, which you look forward to reading over the summer months, as to a sort of prolonged, even spicy, intellectual buffet. After starting it, you discover, buried among its mountainous 1,200 or so pages, a mousy reference to yourself. Do you consider (a) that you can still read and give a fair account of the book or (b) that honour requires you to disqualify yourself from the critical role or (c) that you will not mention the slight, but grab the opportunity to give as good (or bad) as you've got or gotten?

Now for the supplementary: if, having chosen option (a), you find that your response is, in general one of qualified enthusiasm, should you congratulate yourself on your unfashionable fair-mindedness or suspect yourself of intimidated toadyism? That this piece has been written at all reveals my belief that I can rise above personal pique, but you should perhaps allow for a tincture of bile.

Vidal's greatest merit is moral courage, which I suspect to be sustained by his having had what used to be called 'a good war'. He makes almost nothing of his service in the Pacific (unlike his close enemy Norman Mailer), but his reticence speaks in his volumes, which do not scorn to gore sacred cows, including

---

Review of Gore Vidal, *United States: Essays 1952–1992*, in the *Spectator*, 1995.

(notoriously) his – I think – step-half-sisters the Bouvier girls. Give or take a step, he does seem to be close to a lotta lotta famous people (Louis Auchincloss's stories get a familiar pat on the back, rightly). At times Vidal reminds one of a well-connected Alastair Forbes. A Washington DC insider right from the cradle, he lent his step-half-brother-in-law Jack Kennedy books on Byzantine economics, which – we are told – he may have read in the bath (he had less recondite things to do in bed). Gore says that he liked Jack, but eventually disapproved of his presidency (in the spirit of *ho gegrapha, gegrapha*, however, he has the nerve to reprint an early piece of drool over Camelot).

These essays are copious (an editor would be bold to approach G.V. with a comment more cutting than V.G.) and often intelligent, though some of the 'scholarly' waffle – for instance, about the *nouveau roman* – could be truncated and still be too long. On the whole, however, Vidal fights good fights; with accurate affection, he rescues the novels of Dawn Powell, which I have never read, from what sounds to be unmerited oblivion. His most enduring admiration, however, is for himself. He tells us, more than once, how famous his first novel made him and how he fell from grace with his third, which recounted the unblue adventures of a male prostitute and earned him non-person status in the *New York Times*, for which – understandably enough – he cannot forgive that solemnly sententious organ.

He was a dignified, sometimes savage, defender of a person's right to same-sex sex at a time before Gay Rights became a choral number. His defence of homosexual 'preference' is complex: he argues that adult sexual behaviour is a private matter – although it has been made 'political' – and that, if we were logical, we should favour rather than deplore it, since it avoids baby-booms (this was written pre-AIDS). Secondly, he insists that homosexuality was commonplace in the ancient world, at least until Judaeo-Christianity did its stuffy stuff. To my mind, it is not really decisive whether the ancients approved or not (would we advocate torture or slavery because the Lyceum crowd said it was OK?), but it has been argued – for instance by Professor Peter Green – that homosexuality in Athens was a coterie activity, not a common dish on the sexual menu. If it had been, the comedy of Aristophanes' *Lysistrata* would not have worked, since the females' sex strike would have been rendered futile by male blacklegs. Pejorative references to catamites in the literature, and their habitual political disgrace, suggest that antique hedonism was less flexible than Vidal chooses to argue. More significantly, Laius, the father of Oedipus, was condemned by Zeus for his paederastic tastes (Zeus would not have appreciated the *tu quoque* mention of Ganymede). But then again, so what?

On American politics and politicians, Vidal is amusing and illuminating. His grandfather, he soon tells us, and soon tells us again, was a senator; his father was in FDR's 'sub-cabinet'; he himself has run unsuccessfully, but honourably, for office on a liberal-democratic ticket, sponsored by Eleanor Roosevelt in whose political faith and wisdom he still places a certain boyish credence. When it comes to sending up Nixon, Nelson Rockefeller and Ronald Reagan, he uses both invective and ridicule; he has his applauding *New York Review of Books* gallery and he plays to it very smartly. He also accuses Jack Kennedy of thinking that war was 'fun'. Perhaps he catches his own scent there, since polemic is available by the yard with him. I am lucky, I came to realise, to have been visited only by his teeniest gunboat (at least he didn't call me a 'sissy', yet).

All right, I hear you, I hear you: so what *did* Gore (we're all on first name terms with the *gratin* these days, are we not, Bryan?) say about me, and why? Well, in the process of sneering at Somerset Maugham, he alludes disparagingly to my little biography, which is his right. He then adds that I am the author of the obituary of Vidal, Gore which he alleges may, unless he is assumed bodily into heaven like Elijah, one day appear in the London *Times*. As it happens, he has his leaked facts pettily wrong; it was for the *Sunday Times* that I was asked, one dark afternoon some years ago, to file a piece about him. Why me? Why not? Since I have admired his work (in particular *Kalki* and a number of the essays reprinted here), I agreed to write a paltry thousand words on Vidal's literary story so far, without in the least wishing that it go no further: I remember asking tenderly after his health.

However, Vidal clearly imagines himself the victim of a buried hatchet job (a fear which, sweetly enough, echoes one of Mr Maugham's own). Since he himself is said – truthfully, I trust – to have greeted word of Truman Capote's death with the verdict, 'Good career move', one can understand a certain (unnecessary) apprehension, which seems to have led him first to abuse my modest book – modesty being a charge unlikely to be brought against any of his own – and then, by way of a one-two, to go on to allege that I am someone who claims to have read books which I have not.

This witless charge passes a little beyond the genial malice with which citizens of the Republic of Letters must learn to live. It is, however, quite shrewd, in a silly way, since – like the chant of 'The referee's a wanker' – it is almost certain to have *some* truth in it (Gore's gospel, the Kinsey report, having established that not only referees but nearly all those who abuse them have probably indulged in one or more hand-jobs during their lives). In much the same way, it is statistically improbable that anyone who has been subject to the English higher educational system can swear that he or she *never* referred to a text or author who had not been conned from cover to cover. Though few have the nerve to claim, as did Lawrence of Arabia, to have read all the books in the Bodleian, less flagrant lies are almost *de rigueur* among those seeking to gain academic applause or preferment (bluff is part of intellectual poker). Perhaps it has even been true of Vidal, though the last thing I should like to assert, without evidence, is that he is a man like any other.

In the style of a saint unsure that others will speak well enough of him, he asserts elsewhere that he esteems himself more or less unique in always reading every word of the books he reviews. Although *United States* supplies a demanding test of critical integrity, I have now read every word; but has the author? I hesitate to say that the repetitions, misprints and venial howlers suggest that self-criticism is not among his priorities, if only to avoid another outbreak of hostilities, but truth will be served, in due course.

As for the original *casus belli* (his literary luggage is swanky with Latin tags), would anyone be utterly astounded to hear that it is now twenty-five years since I observed, apropos *Myra Breckinridge*, that 'Gore Vidal has announced that the novel is dead, and now he has sent M.B. to the funeral'? Subsequently, I commented amiably on his work, but if you want your words to remain unremembered among book-chatters, you have only to say nice things about them. In the trudging pursuit of his long grievance (he has many, many more against other people), Vidal goes ironically italic over the use – in my 'twee' Maugham book – of 'constipated' to describe Theodore Dreiser's fiction. Perhaps, despite his etymological affectations, Vidal is not clear that the word means, literally, stuck together or coagulated in a lump; it says nothing of the quality of the mass, only that it is pressed together. Maybe *An American Tragedy* strikes Vidal, whose wit knows little brevity, as a model of airy elegance, but one is not obliged to the pillory for failing to join him in his tastes.

Vidal is a great one for great ones. As befits a man whose grandfather – you will remember – was a US senator (albeit from tricky-sticky Oklahoma, where the waving wheat etc.), he is at ease in lofty company, where his horse can be relied on to be at least as high as the next man's. He writes persuasively well on Henry James, as of a classmate, and he jeers at best-sellers with condescending fairness (finding reluctant skill in Herman Wouk, whose orthodox, marriage-oriented Jewishness does not, *prima facie*, recommend him to the waspish grandee).

Although our author has too much *morgue* for Ezra Pound's 'suburban prejudice', he does not conceal his disdain for Ikey-come-lately presumption in the US socio-literary scene. Well, we can all wince together at the smugnesses of the late Alfred Kazin and Irving Howe and some of the *Commentary* crowd (Midge Decter's queer-bashing gets a deserved bash in response). Why, on the other hand, Vidal insists so querulously on the illiteracy of alluding to 'homosexuals' (he would like us to say 'homosexualists'), I am not clear. He objects to the use of adjectives as nouns, but how seriously deplorable is it? Does he refer to himself as an Americanist?

It is very much Vidal's style to adopt the haughtiness, if not always the charm, of his betters: for instance, he preens himself on honouring the Nabokovian distinction between criticism of his art (which he affects to take in good part) and that of his scholarship. In the latter case, the 'Black Swan of Lake Leman' – hardly an apt designation, since black swans are found only in Australia, which VN never was – announced that he always 'reached for his dictionary'. He did so to better effect than Gore, who – had he reached for Liddell and Scott in due time – might have avoided explaining the etymology of 'pornography' by reference to the Greek words *pornos* (male only) and *graphos*. He would have discovered that *pornos* is rare and that as for *graphos*, my Liddell and Scott tells me that the noun was used once in the sixth and once in the fourth century, both in inscriptions and never in extant literature. Does it matter that pornography in fact derives from *porne(ia)-graphein* (to write about whores or whorish matters)? Not really, but if one elects to parade one's scorn and irony, with regard both to Academe and to Hackademe (a twee locution which I offer Mr Vidal without ascriptive obligation), one had better get things – preferably everything – right, had one not?

Although he has given us improving entertainment with his recensions of the ancient world (the sideshow nature of Xerxes' Greek expedition was splendidly caught in *Creation*) and his *Julian* was a fine, if extensive, gloss on Ammianus Marcellinus, Vidal should beware of speaking in dead tongues. His *oeuvre* is heavy with play on the phrase *e pluribus unum*, but his coinage *e pluribus meum* is Latin which not even the dog (*canis*) would swallow or cough up. He admits to speaking French with André Gide, in his post-war youth, but he pays too bold a tribute to the old master when he attributes to him the invention of the *'acte gratuite'* [sic]. Even when propounding extremely silly notions of freedom, no mandarin Frenchman, however heterodox, would take it upon himself to change the gender of words.

Although its princely author may never believe me, and it is unlikely to deter him from another prolix display of Charlus-like *hauteur*, I did not solicit this volume, nor did I have advance knowledge of its reference to me. If I should not have reviewed it, *meum culpa*, as our author might say. After taking a good deal of pleasure in its *aigre-doux* flavour, I conclude that some people are born bloody-minded; others have Gore thrust upon them.

Revisiting Brideshead;
a Re-Introduction

In the epigraph to his longest (and only first-personal) novel, Evelyn Waugh promises us that 'I am not I; thou art not he or she; they are not they'. It is more than a writer's routine, more or less honest, disclaimer; the author may have been immunising himself against charges of reminiscence, but he was also announcing both the revision of his experience and, more particularly, the representation of himself as someone else: Charles Ryder is more comely, more sane and somewhat duller than egotism might have contrived, just as the retrospective view of the pre-war world is more luxurious, more confident and much more complacent than history could warrant.

Art and vanity are compounded in the cosmetic which the middle-aged author applied to his youth and its circumstances. When he began the novel, Waugh was on indefinite leave from a Commando unit which had found his particular form of belligerence surplus to requirement; it was said that he was barred from further active service partly for fear that his men would take the opportunity to shoot him before turning against the enemy. Literature was the beneficiary of an ostracism which certainly wounded, but at least did not kill, its object. Keeping in step was not Waugh's vocation.

The author was only in his early forties, but felt – and announced himself – an older man. His novel is both a celebration and a lament for a pampered paradise which he now took to be lost forever; nuanced pre-war Britain already seemed doomed to yield to lustreless 'Socialism'. It was goodbye to the durability of the world which had garnished his youthful satires with the characters and social *mores* that he had both mocked and adulated. If he had never belonged, as of right, to the Bright Young Things whose chronicler and, to some degree, propagator he was, Waugh had the social climber's assessing eye for the greasiness of the pole whose summit he was so eager to reach. If high society had not enchanted him, how could he have spoken so ill of it?

In the ten years between *Decline and Fall*, his first novel, and *Scoop*, which appeared in 1938, he revelled in what he deplored and mocked what he craved. *Brideshead Revisited*, on the other hand, was a work of reappraisal; the brevity of youthful wit was replaced by obituary sententiousness. As if on guard against accusations of sympathetic portraiture, Waugh claimed to be interested less in 'character' than in 'the use of language'. Yet his veneration for the English country house, and for its hereditary owners, was as ardent as it was stylish. His use of language was dedicated to an elegiac romance which was also a declaration of faith. At his leisure, and in sumptuously unrationed and unbasic English, he enunciated his belief in a way of life which had been at once grandiose and, in his wishful eyes, responsible: paternalism was axiomatic in a class system where, as he saw it, rank was not negotiable and duties were not a matter of opinion.

Echoing Henry James's veneration for the English country houses of which Poynton is but the most memorable, Brideshead is Waugh's Great Good Place, peopled with iconic aristocrats living in an Old World still corseted in a social grammar as formally structured and as unexceptionally rigorous as the orders of architecture. In fabricating Brideshead, Waugh's new, incantatory style becomes almost pagan with resurrective earnestness. Few re-visitors to the past – that 'other country' of which L. P. Hartley spoke in *The Go-Between*, where they 'do things differently' – have looked astern with quite so undisguised a desire to emigrate permanently to it.

Charles Ryder's Oxford 'romance' with Sebastian Flyte sets the tone of the novel; it is the story of a 'crush' which assumes that Baudelaire's *hypocrite lecteur, mon semblable, mon frère* will understand the homosexual attraction which is never stated and certainly never realised, in any genital sense, although the bibulous hours which the two young men spend together, unspiced by anything so drably middle-class as intellectual interests or political earnestness, surely owe a good deal to the tradition of mutual infatuation which the public-school fraternity once took for granted, though seldom for publication.

Charles's passion for Sebastian's world has, of course, its element of entranced curiosity; his lover gives him the *entrée* to a family whose embrace he craves and from whom – with neat irony – Sebastian dreams only of liberation. For Ryder, the antique Catholicism of Brideshead is founded in a recusant history which dignifies its inhabitants with enviable and radical constancy. It also affords them the strength and the grace, in their creator's eyes (Evelyn Waugh's, I mean), to trump the gross urgency of men such as Rex Mottram, the millionaire *arriviste* who has all the nerve and means lacking in Charles (and in Sebastian) and whose wanton colonial insolence enables Waugh's unheroic hero to favour himself with delusions of gentility.

Rex behaves towards Julia in a way which flagrantly parodies Charles's more timid approach to Sebastian. The unspeakable nature of homosexual desire – Waugh destroyed his own Oxford diaries containing details of undergraduate debauches – gives Ryder's attitude a kind of delicacy absent in Rex's aggressive siege of Julia. In heterosexual courtship, social self-advancement and physical desire need not be distinguished; their confusion is almost required. However, Charles's love for Sebastian can find public expression only in a friendliness which lacks the energy or the warrant to procure the doomed youth's salvation, although Ryder is, in some sense, engaged to him. Instead, Charles is drawn into a relationship with the family, and especially with Lady Marchmain whose embarrassing hope it is that he will be able to 'save' her son. In Waugh's scheme, there can be no redemption this side of the grave; human love, even if sacramentally incorporated in His mysterious scheme, cannot usurp the grace of God.

When Charles first meets Julia, a woman who incarnates everything he craves, it is in a scene of some psychological acuity, whose literary contrivance testifies to Charles's almost reluctant conversion to heterosexual awareness. Having met him (somewhat improbably) at the station, Julia drives him to Brideshead in an open car (hinting at availability?). Charles has been summoned to his friend's bedside, though Sebastian's 'grave injuries' amount only to a cracked bone, incurred when playing croquet:

She so much resembled Sebastian that, sitting beside her in the
gathering dusk, I was confused by the double illusion of familiarity and strangeness. Thus, looking through strong lenses, one may
watch a man approaching from afar, study every detail of his face
and clothes, believe one has only to put out a hand to touch him,
marvel that he does not hear one and look up as one moves, and
then, seeing him with the naked eye, suddenly remember than
one is to him a distant speck, scarcely human. I knew her and she
did not know me. Her dark hair was scarcely longer than
Sebastian's, and it blew back from her forehead as his did; her
eyes on the darkling road were his, but larger; her painted mouth
was less friendly to the world.... Because her sex was the
palpable difference between the familiar and the strange, it
seemed to fill the space between us, so that I felt her to be
especially female, as I had felt of no woman before.

The language is significantly strained ('as I had felt of no woman
before' is an uneasy phrase), but the transfer of sexual interest
could hardly be more clearly, if chastely, declared. Julia *is*
Sebastian and Charles's nascent desire for her is as conveniently
proper as it becomes desperate: the female Flyte is a permitted
object of sexual covetousness and, although the difference
between her and her brother seems 'only' to be one of gender
('he or she' says that epigraph), she appears to offer Charles
another way into the charmed circle to which, with Sebastian,
he can be only tangential. Since Charles is more passive than
Rex Mottram, he appears more fastidious, but Julia is, for both
of them, an occasion for betterment. Although the attraction
between Julia and Charles begins, somewhat obviously, with
affectations of mutual indifference, it offers the middle-class
narrator a future which is irresistibly alluring and whose
frustration will lend the novel its compromised air of moral
tragedy and social comedy: neither the kingdom of God nor the
highest rank in English society (they seem close in Waugh's
scale of things) can be entered as easily as bumptious, or
discreet, climbers may choose to hope.

Waugh's wilful insularity disposed him to affect small interest
in foreign literature, but the passage I have quoted has manifest
affinities with Proust, who revisited his own past in order to
redeem his wasted years and, from their detritus, to contrive a
masterpiece. The dance of the three spires, as they seem to
shuffle their orientations when observed on the road to Martin-

ville, is here matched by the image of the 'strong lenses' and the delusive proximities they create.

Although Waugh attempts no schematic psychology (he can never, in view of God's mysterious presence, pretend to comprehend man), *Brideshead Revisited* is larded with observations about the ways of the world; the asperity of the early Waugh is alloyed with a disconcerting compassion which flirts with sentimentality, whereas Proust preferred, with a show of scientific aloofness, to divine what he believed to be the inflexible rules of mundane existence. Both authors are often derided as insufferably snobbish, yet both combine deference with mercilessness; the shallow conceit of the Duc de Guermantes is matched by that of Lord Marchmain, who returns to the Catholic Church, at literally the last gasp, with something of the reluctant rectitude with which Guermantes honours the social code only when it becomes inescapably incumbent on him to apply it (if the duke can avoid being *formally* apprised of his friend's death, which to his knowledge is only imminent, he is determined – since grief is only one more duty – not to forgo the pleasures of the Ball). Like Marcel, Charles is the witness whose desire finds its fuel in star-struck ambition and for whom art provides the *entrée* to a world endowed with so many delectable treasures that their owners scarcely notice them. The Brideshead family is, for Ryder, at once a work of art and a focus of reverence; it is *his* private chapel in which, in blasphemous veneration, he is inclined to a reverence that they express, more properly, in the place of worship which he can only embellish with his brushes.

It requires no suggestion that Waugh had read – still less that he had copied – Proust for us to observe other similarities between the two works. The most obvious is that each contains a sacred monster, of overbearingly homosexual insolence: the Baron de Charlus is matched by Anthony Blanche. If Charlus' domineering pedigree exempts him from Blanche's marginality, each serves to remind the narrator of the standards which he is failing to meet. Emancipation from shame allows them both a tutorial outspokenness unavailable to more cautious, and more compromising, characters (Bergotte and Mr Samgrass). When Anthony Blanche puts Ryder condignly in his place after it seems that his sketchy career as an artist has culminated in serious acclaim, his ingratiating pitilessness has the sweet accuracy of the criticism which, in a famous *New Statesman* review,

Brian Howard directed towards Osbert Lancaster's *Classical Landscape with Figures*.

Although they were undergraduates together, Waugh looked up, in awe and derision, at the flamboyant Howard, whose provenance may have been tainted (he was born in America) but whose control of his Oxford set seemed as arbitrary as his behaviour was reckless. Although 'the much loved' Hugh Lygon, who died young, is sometimes said – for firm instance by Sir Roy Harrod – to have been the model for Sebastian's personal appearance (the teddy bear, at least, seems certainly to have been his), views differ as to the sources of Sebastian's charismatic personality. Harold Acton is the usual choice, even if Waugh's charmer has none of his *avant-gardiste* aestheticism, but Brian Howard's relations with his mother, who both pampered and manipulated him, through her control of the family purse, echo those of Sebastian with Lady Marchmain; in addition, Brian – like Sebastian – later had a German lover to whom he displayed a similarly selfless and unrewarded devotion. It can be argued that Waugh, like many novelists, made opportunist use, almost in the paste-up style of a collagist, of characteristics and incidents in the lives of his acquaintances, but his Oxford generation's mesmerised fascination with Howard (who, whatever his delinquencies, was an uncompromising and prescient enemy of Fascism) argues for his seminal place in the conception of both Anthony Blanche and Sebastian Flyte.

The Oxford of the 1920s was Waugh's first and foremost Great Good Place. Later, however, he became a frequent and abiding visitor in aristocratic country houses. As Randolph Churchill was to say when he had Evelyn elected to White's, it amused the *gratin* to be observed by a member of the middle class, whose abrasive envy could be sated by the mischievous generosity of affording him a close sight of what he was not encouraged to touch. Even at Oxford, as a Lancing Old Boy member of the incurably unfashionable Hertford College, Waugh both was and was not his equals' equal; neither his provenance nor his income entitled him to insouciance. His satire was an expression of frustration and its mordancy bore testimony to how often besottedness expresses itself in the vocabulary of disillusionment.

The counter-jumper, like the counterfeiter, must be alert to what need never be taken into conscious account by the genuine article. He resembles the convert in choosing deliberately to embrace what others have been born to take for granted; in Brideshead, Charles Ryder takes instruction in aristocratic manners just as Rex Mottram does, in his unsubtle New Worldly way, in the Roman Catholic church. Yet even at the outset of a lifelong infatuation with what he could never be, Waugh recognises how unrequited appetite wishes glamour onto a *jeunesse dorée* which proves, on closer examination, to be flaky with imposture (and frequently plastered). On leaving Oxford, abruptly, Anthony Blanche is likened to an impresario who 'had buttoned his astrakhan collar and taken his fee', leaving the 'disconsolate ladies of the company without a leader'. Waugh's Oxford friends, even the Etonians, are thus metaphorically feminised and, on going down themselves, they are likened to actresses:

> For a few happy hours . . . they had played splendid parts, their own great ancestors, the famous paintings they were thought to resemble; now it was over and in the bleak light of day they must go back to their homes; to the husband who came to London too often, to the lover who lost at cards, and to the child who grew too fast.

When a fastidious writer such as Waugh allows himself a sudden clutch of clichés (splendid . . . great . . . famous; bleak light) and even a solecism – 'came to London' should surely be '*went* to London' – one may guess that he is in the grip of art's archest enemy, sincerity. In mundane truth, it requires the wilfulness of an outsider such as Anthony Blanche to enliven the Christ Church toffs who imagined that he was superfluous to their strength; his departure turned them, as Alice's did with the royalty of Wonderland, into uncourtly cards. In much the same way, in his own creation Waugh doubled for Blanche/ Brian: his determination that there had to be a splendid and valuable world from which he was barred, by his Golder's Green origins, was an essential ingredient of what he wanted to believe was Brideshead's innate merit.

The wished for superiority of the great family puts Charles Ryder in a place from which no true promotion is possible and thus makes his ignoble position natural: however polite Brideshead's welcome may have been, it was not in anyone's gift to confer full membership in its society. Waugh's hero, like Waugh himself, could never be wholly at home in the world to which he came so close; only in the Church could appetite secure election, only with God was the convert indistinguishable, at least in his prospects for salvation, from the well-born.

When the novel was published in the immediate *après-guerre*, Charles Ryder's conversion alienated earlier literary admirers, among them the self-confident Edmund Wilson. Such a denouement may have seemed offensively 'reactionary', in a time of glib and secular progressivism (and wilful blindness to the nature of Communism), but it was undoubtedly in character for someone like Ryder, for whom emulation was the only key to either social or moral redemption.

Whatever the disclaimers, Charles is his author's shadow on the page: he is elongated, or foreshortened, or all but obscured, by the light, or darkness, that falls across him. If his projection is not to be identified with his creator, it would be absurd not to acknowledge the shaping spirit which lies behind him. *Brideshead Revisited* is often alleged to be a masterpiece whose flaw is its salient feature; Waugh's critics usually prefer the heartlessness of the juvenile satires (in which pain is played for laughs). They are affronted by the literally awful snobbery of the revisitation on which Charles conducts us. Yet nothing here is *only* as it seems; the old mercilessness may have been conscripted to the service of veneration, but as Waugh said, when advised to cut down on his drinking in the mess, one does not easily give up the habits of a lifetime.

Waugh's text remains instinct with a subversive, even suburban, accuracy which he could not abjure: like Goya's, his formal portraits sap the very dignity they are calculated to depict. None of the Brideshead family, with the poignant exception of Cordelia (who, like her Shakespearian namesake, is denied her due), has any interesting quality; if Julia is a racy beauty, Lord Marchmain is a poop, Lady Marchmain a blinkered bigot, Sebastian a pretty soak and Bridey a morally rectangular prig. The house itself stands for a world whose human inhabitants cannot live up to it and who, after wartime depredations and, in particular, the desecration of its private chapel, betray its fabric.

Brideshead Revisited is an elegy which has something of Cowper's limited genius; it is the work of a man who both cannot forget and, in a typically British way, is ashamed of his youthful sentiments (not because they were youthful, but because they were sentiments). The prose is highly *worked*, yet it makes no intellectual demands on the reader; unlike *A La Recherche du Temps Perdu*, the text of *Brideshead* is neither allusive nor theoretical, though it is certainly tendentious. Waugh proposes no laws of desire nor does he criticise 'society'; he may mock the Cliveden set (in a carefully contrary skit), but nostalgia always trumps subversion. The social cleavage created by the General Strike, for eminent instance, has none of the intriguing place in Waugh which the Dreyfus Affair furnished for Proust. There is something so childlike in the whole-hearted yearning which centres on the unattainable Brideshead that, finally, Charles Ryder has something in common with Lewis Carroll's Alice. The nannied Englishness of Waugh's vision of paradise reminds us how often the insular genius expresses itself most memorably, and most touchingly, in writing for children.

Your Oscar and Mine

Luckily, most honours are undeserved. If the rewards of this world were always justly allotted, we should know only too exactly where we stood in the social or artistic scheme of things. It is no secret that, in the Great War, even MC's were sometimes handed out on the principle of Buggin's turn. In today's world, where Sir David and Sir Robin and Sir Alistair supposedly merit our deference and where noble lordship is the reward of political failure, if not perjury, there are few honours for whose want it is worth crying oneself to sleep. When J.B. Priestley had whinged his way to the Order of Merit, Rebecca West remarked that his acquisition of it had devalued at a stroke the last remaining honour worth having.

Injustice can pay dividends. Had Achilles received the spoils he thought he deserved, he would not have been angry at Agamemnon's appropriation of the lion's share and without the story of his anger, we should have no *Iliad*. Awards do not have to be fair in order to be either delectable or stimulating. You would have to be a fool to believe that they are the most important things in the artistic world (look at the number of negligible writers who have won the Nobel Prize, never mind the Booker), but only a prig can maintain that they are invariably meaningless.

Review of Anthony Holden, *The Secret History of Hollywood's Academy Awards*, in the *Sunday Times*, 1993.

Inverted snobbery alone would allot Oscars only to movies that no one wants to see. One unquestionable advantage of winning is that you then belong to a smallish club whose members can disparage belonging to it without being accused of sour grapes. It is, of course, rather braver – if perhaps a little strident – to refuse to accept the award, as George C. Scott did for his performance in *Patton*, which most certainly did deserve it, or not to turn up for it in person, as Marlon Brando did (not) for his in *The Godfather*. Brando sent a girl who said she was an Apache, Sacheen Littlefeather, to collect his statuette. The Academy was not amused to discover that the lady was, in fact, an actress primed by Brando to protest against the treatment of American Indians by the film industry. Her performance was apparently quite dignified and she made her point, but she did not get an award for doing so.

The origin of the Oscars, the awards given (in case anyone doesn't know) by the Academy of Motion Picture Arts and Sciences, is not particularly glamorous: the statuettes were the result of a doodle by Cedric Gibbons, MGM's perennial art director, during an early meeting of the Academy committee. Why he elected to represent 'a naked knight plunging a crusader's sword into a reel of film' is one of the many, almost certainly dull, secrets which Anthony Holden elects not to disclose.

The Academy began as a small self-nominating 'group of movie people getting together to give each a pat on the back' in the words of Janet Gaynor (whose back was the first to be patted, in 1928). It was soon appropriated by Louis B. Mayer, the godfather who did not come from Sicily, and turned into what he intended to be a company union for the movie business. By putting his stooges in charge, the MGM boss hoped to limit the financial and artistic claims of the 'creative community'. The rigging of the Awards was just one aspect of the tight ship Mayer meant to run.

In the end, the Academy's claim to speak for all the talents was broken by the creation of the Directors', Writers' and Actors' Guilds. For a while, in the late 1930s, it seemed that Oscar would have a short life, but the Academy was saved, largely by the energetic presidency of Frank Capra, whose desire to win had led him to one of the ceremony's legendary humiliations when the 'Frank' called down to receive the 1932 award was Frank Lloyd, not the bumptious director of *Lady for a Day* who was already down front with his hands out. Ever since then, the full name of the winner has been enunciated, if sometimes incredulously.

Holden's year-by-year narrative has all the readability of an edition of *Spotlight* which has been on steroids. Trying to give an impression of jauntiness as he trudges along his commissioned way, he shakes improbable adjectives in all directions. What can he mean by saying that, after Woody Allen had won for *Annie Hall*, 'the awards were by then deep into their seminal struggle between *The Deer Hunter* and *Coming Home*'? *Seminal*?

Holden, like so many writers about the cinema (and royalty), is torn between wanting to be an insider and the determination to adopt an unintimidated tone. Implying that he has access to a superior scale of values, he derides the Academy for failing to give an Oscar to Billy Wilder's *Some Like it Hot* (which I have always thought one of Billy's worst films) and then, much later, he derides Wilder for 'an overlong acceptance speech' when receiving the Irving Thalberg Award in 1987, during which he went so far as to send a get-well message to his collaborator Izzy Diamond, who died ten days later. If the sentimentality was untypical, it was not ignoble. Diamond, like Charlie Brackett, was an integral part of Wilder's success. Billy recalls that the most enthusiastic response Diamond ever gave to an idea, during a script conference, was to think about it and then say, 'Why not?'

A lot of old cabbage gets into the pot here. The lamentable treatment accorded to Orson Welles is a standard ingredient. Pauline Kael – that one-woman casting vote – is quoted uncritically (of course) when she alleges that Herman Manckiewicz was the real author of *Citizen Kane*, for which he did, in fact, receive a screenplay Oscar, shared with Welles. However, Peter Bogdanovich's intelligent counter-claim, in defence of Welles as *auteur*, remains uncited. Welles's failure to win for Best Director may be ridiculous, it may even be seminal, but it scarcely condemned him to outrageous obscurity. In fact, by the character of Kane, Welles meant to provoke William Randolph Hearst, whose newspapers could make or break a movie, and he certainly meant to make a scandal.

An unquoted legend has it that, at awards' time, Orson found himself by chance in the same elevator as Hearst and, after a few glacial floors, he asked, 'Are you coming to the ceremony tonight, Mr Hearst?' Hearst strode out of the elevator without replying. The great Welles voice was then heard to boom out, 'Charles Foster Kane would have come!' To create a fictional hero that trumped the master of San Simeon was better than any Oscar. Poor Orson: he will just have to settle for immortality.

There are some laughs here, a few of them intentional. The best is when Steven Spielberg is quoted as telling Barbra Streisand that *Yentl* was the best film he had seen since Citizen Kane. It is, of course, possible that Steven had seen Welles's picture that same afternoon, which would make the remark a masterpiece of honest flattery, but otherwise it suggests that Holden has been collecting evidence by sharing frozen yoghurt sundaes with Ms Streisand, which is a most enjoyable experience although not one which always yields unvarnished truths.

The Oscars are not distributed like candy, nor yet with the discrimination associated with the Garter (which has had some duff recipients all right). There are manifest absurdities and injustices, but the Academy is not a court of law; it is a fat electorate of hacks and time-servers and artists and technicians which, today at least, is about as 'democratic' as it can be (and as the British Motion Picture Academy is certainly not). The awards are part popularity contest, part political, part sales-gimmickry, part caucus race: in the end, most deserving parties receive an Oscar, though not always for work which deserves it. I always attribute to Billy Wilder the remark with which he, quite unjustly, credits me: 'Awards are like haemorrhoids – in the end, every ass-hole gets one.' Why not?

The Humanity of
Theodore Zeldin

Admirers of *Middlemarch* will remember the meticulous Casaubon who spent his life assembling material for a masterpiece
which his death aborted. Determination to leave nothing out
consigned him to conspicuous sterility. Theodore Zeldin has
now brought off what Casaubon never managed: he has, I hope,
succeeded in publishing everything he can think to say about
the nature of human relations, their past, their present and their
hopeful future. His book of books bulges with bibliographical
warrants of due study and solemn attention; his prose for all
seasons garnishes a lay sermon based on enough texts to give
Casaubon apprehensions of glibness.

Before he elected to become the world's doctor, Zeldin was –
as he remains – an Oxford academic and a social historian of
France, whose culture and inhabitants he has made his area of
special study. His methods are those of Fernand Braudel:
synchronic, not diachronic, he ranges far and wide in time and
space, not hesitating to walk on air or water in order to pluck
significance and intelligence from all the trees of knowledge
which have gone to seed in our blighted Eden. Starry-eyed
enough to look amiably on astrology, trendy enough to call
ancient Athens 'a protection racket', convinced of 'cosmic
justice' and re-naming God 'the Generator of Diversity', he can

---

Review of Theodore Zeldin *An Intimate History of Humanity*, in the
Sunday Times, 1994.

still spare the time to count the versatile heartbeats of the waterflea; a man of the world, he is no stranger either to the cockatrice's den or to the Senior Combination Room.

Too astute to apply for the chair of Dr Pangloss, Zeldin never goes so far as to say that all is for the best, but he does argue, in a very constructive and companionable way, that our world could, and should, be infinitely better, more cheerful, more fraternal, more optimistic than it is. Well, why not? Man, he tells us, can be remade, not least by becoming more feminine (have I heard that one before? Do I want to hear it again?). In his book (which acknowledges the inexhaustible bounty of the author's wife), love is a much more moveable feast than is dreamt of in our suburban conjugal philosophies: according to that clinching authority the Congolese author Sony Labou Tansi, eroticism is the art of 'cooking love well'; there is, we are promised, 'a menu still to be discovered'. And just think: we haven't even seen the wine list yet.

Zeldin thinks that mankind should make radical moves, but without uprooting itself, of course. Like so many anthropologists, he is fascinated by the habits and inspired by the innate wisdom of non-Western societies. Ever since Margaret Mead was shown by Derek Freeman to have been consummately duped by the Samoans who fed her a sex-pack of traditional stick-it-to-the-researcher lies about their adolescent habits, it has become prudent to remember that a strange observer affects the nature of what he/she has come to see, but reading 'the West' sermons about the superiority of the primitive is still a Rousseau-esque urge which trumps all caution.

A global villager to make Marshall McLuhan look like a shuttered stay-at-home, Zeldin has a mission to make humanity one great big happy family, generous, trusting and, in the most responsible and responsive possible way, promiscuous. Why should the milk of human kindness not be delivered to every doorstep? If you are nice to crocodiles, the satirical Jonathan Miller once told us, they will be nice to you. Zeldin's conclusion, which is a very, very long time in coming, is that 'Searching for what we have in common, despite our differences, provides us with a new starting point'. He does not add 'and *vice versa*', but why did I hear a little voice that did?

Good-heartedness is not in short supply in this massive and informative volume. Its form is, however, a little peculiar: almost every section begins with a Tony Parkerish sociological monologue in which a French woman, whether bright or dim, black or white, Parisian or provincial, pours out her ambitions and disappointments. These more or less identifiable autobiographies do little to incline Zeldin to weigh hopes against practicalities: he prefers to rummage in the marvellously stocked bran-tub of his research for ways in which the new thing can be prescribed in the old language. Patchwork is, for him, the future for *haute culture*.

What curmudgeon will dare to challenge the general proposition that mankind should, with just one more heave, jettison the positivistic passivity which the French tend to call '*fatalité*': the idea that things have to be as they are and there is nothing much to be done about it? (A doleful statistic tells us that one third of Brits like to be told what to do, but it is, of course, our duty to tell them that they must change.)

The collapse of political ideologies – symbolised by the fall of the Berlin Wall – means that we are into a 'new era in human relations'. Just as the generation of *soixante-huitards* – the students who manned and womanned the barricades in Paris in 1968 – are beginning to write their rueful middle-aged apologies, Zeldin applauds the schoolkids who, led by sixteen-year-old Mandarine Martinon, recently helped to 'force a government to surrender four and a half billion francs'. That, like blackmailers, hi-jackers and other idealists for a cause, the children were 'neither grateful nor impressed' is part of their merit, apparently. As a consequence, 'the school has become the children's other home; they accept it as they accept their own home; all they want is to make the best of it.' Does this *conceivably* beg a few more questions than it answers?

Zeldin employs his Memory-Man omniscience in the interests of what his admired Frenchmen call an 'amalgam', though he might not welcome the accusation. His method, like Braudel's, enables him to seem above the fray and unblown by commonplace winds, but it also insures him against contradiction and makes any cavil seem petty. He validates wild conclusions from dubious premises and never doubts his own sagacity. When he asserts that 'No Athenian demeaned himself by being an employee of a fellow-citizen', he seems to say that free men and slaves never worked side by side, which is quite false. Moses Finley (*not* Finlay) might have pointed out that Pheidias himself was paid an artisan's wage for working on the Parthenon. Socrates, it is said here, invented 'dialogue'; no mention is made of the theatre, where both sides of more arguments were put forcefully by Aeschylus (and even Aristophanes) than in the rigged reportage of Plato.

By contrast with ignoble Athens, the Ayatollah's theocratic regime in Iran is, it seems, deserving of admiration, as is Jack Lang, the narcissistic Minister For Playing To The Gallery in France's last Socialist government. The Ayatollah is applauded for giving 'permission for women to appear on television'. He also authorised contraception 'but of course he balanced that by other controls'. These included systematic intimidation of dissentient women, torture and execution of political rivals and opponents and the subjection of a whole, rich and ancient culture to autocratic *fiat*. But then Zeldin is rather sympathetic to bossy figures who want to frogmarch mankind to happiness; he reproaches those who doubt the universal wisdom of Jean-Paul Sartre (who deliberately lied about the Gulag, and many other abuses by 'progressive' regimes). Without a shred of irony, he tells us, in a chapter on 'new kinds of friendship' and fraternity, that 'In Serbia, Croatia and Bulgaria, there are records of brotherhood being renewed each year'. Has he noticed that the regions of France where castles are most common (and I do not mean the pleasure-domes of the Loire) are those where warfare has been most virulent? Annual declarations of fraternity are much less needed where 'brothers' are reliable or treachery rare than are castles in peaceful communities. As for finding 'a way to eliminate the gradations of respect created by money, education and appearance', does this mean that we can soon expect all to be admitted as Fellows of St Anthony's (where Zeldin is a – or is it *the*? – *senior* Fellow), before becoming film-stars and VIP yacht-owners?

A Cloistered Life

I once worked with a film director/producer with small neat feet and a trim red beard and a short, straight nose, who had been to Yale and was not eager to acknowledge his Jewish origins (i.e., his father and mother). A man of marked fastidiousness, he changed his socks three times a day (doesn't everyone?). I worked with him first in London and then I was invited to visit him in California. He and his newest wife, who had money, had just renovated and expanded their house in Beverly Hills. Alan had built a screening room and office for himself in an annexe at the back of the lot. It was a large rectangular room with white walls. Narrow apertures admitted sunshine at clerestory level. No pictures had yet been hung on the walls. At one end there was a dais, with a big, two-doored mahogany cabinet in the middle. It probably concealed the projector for screenings, but it recalled the ark in which the scrolls of the law are kept. 'Alan,' I heard myself say, 'how terrific! You've built yourself a synagogue.'

We may be what we eat; we are also what we live in. However, I do not think that I could be accused of recreating an environment in which my ancestors would feel at home. Synagogues are not my style, but cloisters, I have discovered, are. I cannot find any reason to suspect myself of Christian genes, so perhaps my cloister idealises the ghetto (the nicest ones I have seen are, of course, in Spain, especially in Cordoba, from which I like to imagine that, like the great Maimonides, my Sephardic ancestors were forced to flee).

What is the attraction of a cloister? Go to Cadouin, or

351

Moissac, to the Court of the Lions in Granada (Islamic cloisters are particularly fine), to the Certosa at Pavia, to Monreale in Sicily and they will tell you. A cloister is a place of enclosed refuge in which a fountain burbles and a man may sit at a desk and work in the margin of society without fear of intruders. Whenever I hear the word 'community', I reach for my (conjugal) isolation. Jean-Paul Sartre taught my generation of writers that we should be *engagés*: committed to political purposefulness and scornful of 'art' and *littérature*. The ivory tower was a *bourgeois* form. However, Sartre is likely to be remembered best for saying 'Hell is other people', which is something I can swallow without a glass of water.

On the road between Bordeaux and the Périgord, where we have a farmhouse, you come to a signpost indicating St Michel de Montaigne. Perhaps the greatest of essayists, and a notorious humanist, Montaigne was the son of a converted Sephardic mother, Antoinette de Louppes, whose original name was Lopes. There is, however, nothing synagogual about the tower – limestone, not ivory – to which he retired after serving as a counsellor to the *parlement* of Bordeaux. On the beam above his head was carved (and can still be seen) *Nihil humanum a me alienum puto*. It is, I find, much easier to *think* nothing human alien to oneself than it is to revel in rush-hour traffic or to gaze with admiration at the arm-pits of rock bandsmen or even to look forward to witty ministerial broadcasts from Dr Jack Cunningham. It is not surprising that perhaps the noblest, if scarcely the most practical, manifesto for universal liberation should have been composed by a classical scholar who spent most of his working life in the reading room of the British Museum.

Montaigne spoke Latin with his mother and, though his Greek was inferior, he was always at home in the Classics. I was transported to them, from New York, where I first went to school. Cloistered, so to speak, in the North Devon hotel to which my school was evacuated, I learned what a recent, abusive correspondent called 'useless things' (like the use of *ei* with the optative) while Stalingrad failed to fall, European Jewry was murdered, and the British spent the last of their treasure winning the war, after which – if we are to believe Corelli Barnett, and our eyes – they lost the peace.

Dead languages gained me a scholarship to Charterhouse, where I saw my first cloister, in the Gothic style. It was built to commemorate Carthusians who died in the Boer War. In the days of the empire, the school had sported an 'Army Class', for those less gifted when it came to *ei* with the optative. I disliked my time at Charterhouse more than I can say (though I have said a good deal) and have never joined the OC's. However, I did acquire just about enough useless knowledge to make me nervously independent of those who judge a man by what he can do for them, since I can do practically nothing except take written exams, which is what the author's life involves. *Experto crede.*

My father had always told me that a First in Greats was a passport through life (he had got a Third, at least partly because he took his Finals when suffering from kidney stones). However, good fortune and swotting took me to Cambridge, where – should I be sorry? – I felt no guilt whatsoever in enjoying the cloistered life, although I abandoned the Classics for philosophy. Wittgenstein had recently died, but we – the happy few – touched the hem of his therapeutic positivism and imagined that we should soon cure the world of metaphysics. By the end of my four years of higher education, I still had no practical qualifications. This was the evidence of my superiority. I reminded myself of it when my first paid activity turned out to be writing link material for a Radio Luxembourg series of songs by Doris Day.

Evelyn Waugh once said that the purpose of education was to give a man a decent prose style. How wicked of him! And how true? Due at least in part to the French Revolution, 'writers' have been blessed with special powers in modern society: they are the astrologers who have themselves become stars. Like Petronius, who was the emperor Nero's Melvyn Bragg, the arbiter of taste, certain scribes have done very well playing the Pharisee; they enjoy both fame and fortune, not to mention decorative honours. Such men combine authorship with editorial or executive office, where they can compensate for the lameness of their own achievements by kicking shins.

The Latin poet Horace was a tubby little social climber who had the nerve to say '*odi profanum vulgus, et arceo*': i.e., I hate the crude common people and keep them at a distance. I suspect that if Montaigne had been as honest as Evelyn Waugh (No Admission on Business was inscribed on his gate), he might have incised Horace's words above his head. Is it a scandal to admit that one hates crowds eating fast food from greasy boxes, the proximity of beery men who have had a long day wearing trainers and those who, like Neil Kinnock, elevate their style by saying 'between you and I'?

There is no surer way of maintaining one's generous hopes for humanity than to be well removed from it. It is no necessary part of a belief in democracy to have to agree with the opinions of the majority: it is enough to abide by its decisions. The cloister enables a man to think without politically corrective invigilators scrutinising his thoughts. When John Prescott wishes to re-abolish the 11-plus because he remembers how painful it was to fail it, he imagines that he wants to eliminate childhood suffering, but the *effect* will be (has been) to create a society with no interest in intelligence and no capacity to criticise Mr P. Pleasure, he might note, if it doesn't upset him, is not the absence of pain.

The Tories who want education to create job-qualified graduates are equally crass: most of the qualifications will be obsolete before they are useful and the people lumbered with them will lack the capacity for independent judgment which, when you come down to it, is no small part of what a decent prose style involves. The uselessness of the classical education is, I have come to realise, what is useful about it. Of course, it is even more useful if it enables you to write for a living. A Labour cabinet minister, later one of the Gang of Four (remember them?), once sat next to me at a dinner when, by way of proving his charm, the first thing he said to me was, 'Why do you like money so much?' This might have sounded like a coded way of calling me a bloody Jew, but I knew that a Socialist would never use that code, so I said, 'Probably because it enables me to whistle up a helicopter whenever I want to and get away from c**** like you.' I am not rich and I have never whistled up anything more volatile than a minicab, but you have to tell them, don't you, some of them? And not always with polysyllables.

Not long ago, infuriated by loud traffic and casual callers, we decided to enclose the gravel yard in front of our all-too-accessible house with a wall. By the time we had finished, we had a cloister in which a modest fountain burbles, roses bloom and dangle, and in which, after monastic sessions illuminating my manuscript, I can sit and puzzle over my daily bit of Sophocles, armed with Hugh Lloyd-Jones' crib and Liddell and Scott's immortal dictionary. Truth to tell, I am still a very uncertain Hellenist, but I am, I fear, some kind of a bloody old Carthusian after all.

Reading the Century

To start with a postscript: I conclude that this essay is more a meditation than an argument. Intended as a pacifying polemic, I should prefer it not to excite any synthetic expectations. My interest is in why it is, or at least how it is, that we both do and do not understand our time; there is, I suspect, something *systematic* in this: the future is endurable only if the past can be both digested and – in a sense – excreted, preferably without smell. A fairly unforced reading might say that the creation of the state of Israel, in so far as it was admitted to the world map by a *fiat* on the part of the powers who recognised it (the USA and the USSR *en tête*), was also final notice to Europe's surviving Jews to knock at no other old or new doors. The creation of Israel was, in this light, over-determined: we need not find alternative – still less mutually exclusive – 'reasons', for things being as they are, even if the desire for heroes or villains tempts the ardent to single-mindedness.

If we now judge the twentieth century a human disaster, we are also, *a posteriori*, proud of ourselves precisely for seeing it 'clearly'. *By* having seen it, we exempt ourselves from having been its dupes or even participants in it. We observe the 'Darwinian' savagery of Nazism and the parodic imposture of Communism (in which cynicism was costumed in morality) and – since 'we' have survived – we take ourselves to be wiser and better than those who succumbed to either doctrine, whether as instruments or even as victims: the foolishness of, for instance, those who tried to *sauver les meubles* licenses Hannah Arendt's contempt for their innocent 'sheepishness'. Foresight, she will not allow, is a kind of connivance. *We* would never be so naïve, would we?

For all her condemnation of totalitarianism, Arendt cannot shake off the pat disdain for the malignly unsuspicious *bourgeoisie*. Her manner of thinking owes something to Marx and to the élitist philo-patter of the *entre deux guerres*. By 'élitist' I mean something different from the going cant, which equates élitism simply with favouring the high road; Arendt's posture, like so many ideological attitudes left and right, scorns the crassness of the unenlightened who do not recognise the paramountcy of the very parties she attacks. This is not an assault on Arendt; it merely places her in her humourless time. When it comes to the uses of humour, we should remember Nabokov's claim that what, perhaps *per impossibile*, the torturer can never endure from his victim is *derision*. It is in this light that his prediction of Communism's collapse was based on style: it was not its economic ineptitude which promised its fall but the inevitable revenge of the Russian *language*. Art for art's sake is art for society's sake.

How does it come about that we both can and cannot 'read' the past? How is it, for instance, that so few people cared, as they say, at the time of the Nazis' murders and so many seem to care now? Why it is that the British have taken fifty years before they manage to charge a single old man – *le pauvre!* – with 'war crimes' or to take any action whatever against him – when, as David Cesarani has documented in his *Justice Delayed*, it has been known all along that an SS division, full of guilty men, was recruited to work in the UK almost immediately after the war, at a time when a so-called socialist government withheld work permits from 'Displaced Persons'? The machinery of evasion relies on the notion of 'naïveté' and 'emotionalism'. Diplomacy insists that such questions be answered with a pitying smile and the weary whisper, 'If only it were that simple . . .'

The disreputable is part of what we are. The projected European Union is not simply an economic or supra-national ideal, it is also a means of repressing the past whose diplomatic beauty lies in the fact that it was never conceived in that spirit: the repression even of motives is what we mean by a new start.

The German investment in Europe, leading to the creation of a synthetic European 'identity', is an act of sublime oblivion; the ashing of the ashes becomes an ideal and – the hint of threat can be heard – the only specific against more wars. Timothy Garton Ash's *In Europe's Name* is the lengthy ledger of these often worthy calculations in which each side of the German political equation needs the other: the fiercer the dispute, the surer the cohesion, issuing – at the right moment – in the grand coalition. Who did the wrong thing? Did anyone?

Adenauer's 'reparations' to Israel were at once a noble and a shrewd instance of the economising of morals; payment identified the state of Israel – quite improperly, it could be argued – as the due recipient and hence the qualified discharger of debts. Israel became the place where Jews rightly went and from which they should not seek to come. Considering how much of the German economic miracle was funded by Swiss banks from appropriated Jewish fortunes, we can – with a certain smile – speculate on just how partial Adenauer's nobility was. The cries of amazed outrage at President Clinton's recent support for action by individual Jews and Jewish organisations minded to recover their pre-1945 property in Europe is the measure of how good a deal the Germans made. There are futures in forgiveness, as in anything else; Adenauer acquired his in a modest market. Before imagining 'the Jews' to have been ill-served here, it is worth wondering, for the sake of moral example, and even of hope for another future, whether the moment will, or can, come when Israel considers its debts over the expropriation of the Palestinians, whose assimilation to 'the Arabs', on the part in particular of Golda Meir, shows how important (false) logic is when it comes to the fate of 'peoples'. (Elie Kedourie's view of the Armenians is another instance of how perfectly decent men can persuade themselves into callousness.)

Unless we have some sense of the uses of division, of distinction, even of suspicion, we are unwise to presume that civilised uniformity can be imposed – at the last minute – on a bloody century. Experience does not throw an even light. The paper crown of European homogeneity resembles the chummy cap they crammed on poor Louis XVI, in the brief period between his eviction from power and his execution. There is cruel comedy in the hustle to community on the part of a continent which has so mismanaged hegemony than it now hopes for comity in committees. What sense would 'Europe' make if there were not some deep – for want of a better term – *psychological* need for Germany to launder its linen, and its accounts, in the name of some transcendent and immaculate ideal? Such a question does not argue against political compacts or happy hypocrisies; it asks only how white we want our whitewash to be, and why.

History is full of events, but what else does it contain? Should not other elements be included in its inventory before we are sure that we have got our inheritance 'clear', as the lawyers say? If clarifying is not the same as clarity, it can be a move towards it: investigation does not always secure convictions, but it can make lies less glib. To corrupt Wittgenstein's remark, we are not here to give the accommodators a good time.

Of all the changes in human society and circumstances, the most elusive, when it comes to giving a later account of it or even to speculating on its nature after the event, is a change of motives. To put it less cryptically, if less sweetly, one of our most awkward problems, when looking back, is to grasp the motivational ambience of an epoch. It is as difficult as observing the wind in a photograph from which the bent trees have been cropped.

'Why?' is a question to which there can never be a definitive answer in the case of individual human conduct; it is even more difficult to answer after a system or a civilisation has foundered. Morals can supply a measure, never a mechanics (man might be moral, and Communism a possibility, if it were otherwise). The belief that moralities can stabilise society in a virtuous mould supplies the grim charm of fundamentalism. Since its ideal world is retrojected onto the past, fundamentalist piety hopes to get back to it. The fundamentalist proposes that what he believes to have been so should return as what is. In orthodox schemes, memory has a compact with oblivion. Plato's fundamental reliance on a 'noble lie' – actually 'genealogical lie' would be a better translation – admits, even as it proposes to ignore, the existence of a 'Gödelian' trade-off at the heart of any ideal social project: no system is self-validating, but no orthodoxy can acknowledge what it postulates. This is why a reasoned programme of 'more religion' cannot be a social prescription, as Iris Murdoch, for intelligent instance, proposes in her *Metaphysics as a Guide to Morals*. Maimonides avoided this categorical error.

The orthodox – whether Muslim or Jewish – maintain that the movement of history can be aborted or reversed. Immobilism becomes their cardinal social ambition. In order not to repeat an error (assimilation, say) they would retrieve a time when it has not yet occurred. Even Marx tried to validate his vision of the future by the insistence that a classless, unalienated 'primitive communist' society had worked in an ideal past. The second coming is not a purely Christian notion; man has the idea he can take second chances better than first. To want to live today in an ancient light, and by an immutable code, is another kind of assimilation. This does not 'condemn' it, though it may locate it in a place which embarrasses it: today.

All orthodoxies are content to seem, as if by chance, to exclude alternatives; certainty has a lucky logic, according to which dissent *incidentally* becomes treachery (no man willingly errs, hence to err is to be at fault and becomes a crime). As it happens, few consequences are more implacable than logical consequences; what appeal is there against 'therefore'? The mundane result is that the most callous cruelties are those which can be regarded as 'inevitable' and hence can (*must!*) be executed dutifully, and without remorse. When recruiting killers, the Nazis came to rely more on the dutiful – the 'banal' habitués of routine, the products of disciplined education (and religion) – than on people with personal animus; if crooks trump cranks when it comes to lending method to madness, reasonable men are the more reliable accessories (see Christopher R. Browning's *Ordinary Men*). The notion of 'reason' as *hostile* to the irrational ignores the mediating role of rationalisation: reason, Dodds *almost* argues, in his *The Greeks and the Irrational*, is a function of what it apparently discounts, just as European unity is a warrant of its disunity.

Biography – as against history – suggests that some Nazis were not all that *happy* with what they were doing: Speer is the finest instance of the man who did and did not do what he did and did not do. Only after 'waking up' in 1945, did Rip Van Speer *assume* the responsibility of what had been done (he did this *nobly*, a captain who preened himself on *not* going down with his ship). In his ambivalent self-inculpation, Speer *dignified* himself by recovering his lapsed, civilised personality; he did what he did, he had us think, but only when he was not himself. His infatuation with Hitler had made his crimes *passionels*: 'C'était plus fort que moi' is in almost all instances a credible assertion, but – as Freud failed to see – there are pleasures which last much longer than sex. No single scheme of motives will ever cover the forked creature's duplicities.

Hitler's mesmerising competence need not be doubted even if (and because) it cannot be calibrated. In the appendix to his memoirs, Benoist-Méchin describes Von Paulus's meetings with Hitler, in each of which the beleaguered general begged to be allowed to break out of Stalingrad while he still could (in the first case with most of his material). In each instance Hitler's immutable cruelty (towards his own, losing, side) prevailed. Hatred of one's own people is often part of caring for no one else: when they fail to be as good as they should be, they deserve whatever happens to them.

Hannah Arendt's imputation of cowardice to the Jews she left behind is embarrassingly philosophical in its pitilessness. The 'banality' which she attributed to Eichmann (and, by implication, to all Eichmanns) announced the condescension of an academic whose standing among her peers depended on finding a paradoxical account of Nazi evil. She, at least, was out to avoid the stigma of banality. In view of Arendt's relationship with a less banal – but hardly less emblematic – figure in the Nazi world, Martin Heidegger, the ordinariness of Eichmann was what made him a providential scapegoat. By alleging evil to be 'banal', Arendt averted the world's gaze from the deep thinker who might otherwise have stood in the dock. Hers was an extension of the device which Speer had already used: to associate evil with second-rateness had the 'accidental' result of excusing the officers of malice at the expense of their dupes.

Speer breathed one air between 1931, when he joined the Nazi party, and another in 1945, when he 'came to'. Can we say that he was 'the same man' in both periods? We can and perhaps, legally speaking, we must; but we lend him a certain autonomy, as well as a *mens rea*, when we do this. It suits us to save our world-view by seeing him as a man who should, or could, have known better; in short, as one of us. Does not knowing better always involve having to know what is worse? Choice is what makes man free, and a villain. Since the end of Eden, virtue is a fabrication, which is its merit (and also, maybe, why Wittgenstein equated ethics with aesthetics: the equation too has its beauty).

It is difficult, if not impossible, to draw the *air* of an epoch in the style of the vanished epoch itself: is Marcel Proust alone among novelists in having furnished his world with its own palpable atmosphere? Or is his prose also not manifestly *repro*? (Snobbery always projects, which is why it is always disappointed.) In the present we have no perspective; in due course, we tend to lose access to what was and make it more and more like what is: we come to say of the past what Gertrude Stein said of Oakland: 'There is no there there'.

Hence the survivor, of whatever stripe, makes more sense than the victims; unless we are Marcus Porcius Cato, we always veer to the side of the former, hence the success of *Schindler's List*. It is a film about succeeding; it declares the necessity of being exceptional or chosen by the exceptional. Hitch your wagon to a star and 'Let the dead bury their dead.' Whatever his researched diligence, Edward Gibbon's retrospective wit places ancient Rome in the eighteenth century; Thucydides wrote about Athens' greatness as one who knows it will lose it; Adam may be the first man, but he is not our man.

Today's view of Hitler, and of his views, is distorted by the happy hindsight that he will not prevail. We judge those who fell under his spell in the light of its eventual eclipse; would they still be wrong, had he prevailed? On what moral platform would Archimedes stand? Our own confidence is posited on Hitler's humiliation; we can almost (oh almost!) be grateful to him for his demonstration of what did not work. Since, by definition, we are exempt from his time, we fortunate ones will never see twentieth-century Europe in a contemporary light; we can only descry its shape in the dubious afterglow of our own sententiousness or in the not always reliable brightness of an imagination which, if it is in an aesthetic tradition, trades in a dated currency. We think we can now say, or insist, 'Never again', and mean something new (as if a common moral currency had recently been established). What we mean, in practice, is unlikely to be more than that the irreversible has happened and so *need not* be repeated. History may have lessons, but they are rarely history lessons.

Kenneth Burke's *A Grammar of Motives* was a literary critic's attempt to analyse the grounds on which people are moved to do things (consider how rarely the *ground* is the *subject* of a painting). In view of Burke's rationalising defence of the Moscow show trials, we should watch for a certain perversity in his work (he was most prolific in the 1930s and 1940s). His discursive intensity foreshadowed the ponderous woolliness of deconstructionism. However, Burke had an invaluable sense of the significance of the unsaid; he indicated how it can shape even when it does not speak out in a work of art or in a political creed.

Derrida's *Specters of Marx* protracts Burke's work, on the subject of the Communist manifesto, in suggesting that the dead are not *that* dead, and can sometimes be the more powerful for not being alive. To the question 'Qui fera peur aux riches?' the easy answer, which any Stephen King could supply, is 'ghosts, of course'. Europe is full of them; their denial is part of the plenitude. The EEC (now the European Union) supplied a morally indifferent logic for the future of the murderers' continent. It can never be understood as a merely pragmatic coalition; it was – and remains? – a programme for oblivion.

Kenneth Burke proposed that we look at literature (and its interstitial silences, since pauses are still statements) as 'the dancing of an attitude'. That he was himself an apologist for Stalin – perhaps less out of millennial credulity than because of the scandal of defending the insufferable – underlines the danger of assuming 'neutrality' in any account he (or anyone) offers of anything. Deconstructionists warn that the grammarian too has his secrets; messages are not clear because they have been decoded: there is also the decoding to decode, forever. Hell, Sartre might have said, is other people's *work*.

The central place of attitudinising in sophisticated behaviour (of which writing is only one form) is properly emphasised by Burke: consistency – supposedly an intellectual virtue and the involuntary evidence of rigour – can also (and at the same time) be seen as the cleverest of masks. Keynes and Kolakowski, in praise of inconsistency, buck the tide in denouncing those who think of not changing their minds as evidence of integrity. The Man in the Iron Mask and the Vicar of Bray are sometimes cousins under the skin. A stone-faced Proteus cannot be seen to change and hence is free (Sartre claimed that the French were never so 'free' as during the Occupation).

Around each decade, each century even, there swirls a miasma of purposes, inclinations, assumptions, wishes and suppositions which, once a system or a dynasty or a philosophy has perished, deposits no definite trace. Metaphysics, unlike Wittgenstein's 'philosophy', leaves very little as it is; however, like the shrewdest poison, it can often prove almost undetectable. How surprising is it that the great classical scholar Arnaldo Momigliano could remark that, after studying ancient Greek society for half a century, he still had no idea precisely what the Greeks expected of their gods or their gods of them? 'Beliefs' have no *determining* responsibility for the thoughts or the art, still less for the actions, of those who may later flaunt or repudiate their influence. Hence, ideas can be wrong, but not guilty; the persistence of, for instance, anti-Semitism (however slyly mitigated or unsubtly recycled as anti-Zionism) after 1945 is an instance: it is not that the pre-war sentiment ceased to be *felt*, merely that it ceased to *pay*. Anti-Semitism, in Europe, was never only an 'emotion' (or a simple 'idea'), it was also an opportunity: it issued both tickets and dividends. It is a mistake to suppose that profitable *investment* cannot figure among 'psychological' motives.

Perhaps the most interesting modern case of a man enveloped by a 'logic' onto which later he sought to unload his own (not very great) shame is that of Martin Heidegger. His apologists often share his ambivalence, just as they crave his posthumous applause. It is convenient for them to be delicate towards his 'misreading' of Nazism, quite as if it had offered him a false prospectus which he failed to read thoroughly; there is 'sympathetic' comedy in the Great Reader's misconstruing of a charlatan's small print. There is also, and more importantly, a failure of the intellectual imagination: his friends do not see, or choose not to see, that it was Nazism that read Heidegger, very accurately indeed. His philosophy of Being, divine and immoral, made space for their texts, as if by some malign abdication.

The defence of his 'naïveté' becomes increasingly more plausible as the ambient air of his time dissipates his opportunism. We are left with the airless picture of a *disappointed* professor, who hoped innocently for a healing revision of Germany and found that his doctor was Goebbels. How difficult to imagine that it might be the lure of corruption, blowing in the wind, a whiff of his own furtive predilections, that kindled his 'folly'!

The prospect of a symbiosis of the intellect with power – the *hope* of an overpowering licence for malice and dictation – thrills academics. Association with *force* enables them to trump the artists who have, in their eyes, only one petty attribute – the imagination – to elevate them above their betters. The obsequious hatred of artists is mitigated in Plato, but still manifest: Hitler and Stalin were his idealistic surrogates in our time.

In 1965, Isaac Deutscher (one of our own!) could say, 'Are we going to wait until Marxism and socialism have conquered the world, and then stand there last in the queue, waiting for its return to us? Or shall we save ourselves from our own increasing and terrifying backwardness?' (This was the peroration of a 'serious' lecture given at the London School of Economics.) Deutscher's earnestness is the more droll by virtue of its moral vacuity: it was the imminent 'success' of Marxism and socialism – not their moral grandeur – which required 'us' to buy into them. In this, of course, Deutscher was no worse, and no better, than the French politician who once said, 'I am their leader, I must follow them.' Nothing is less helpful in understanding the case of Heidegger, or the lure of Nazism, than the facile assumption that Jews would never have been Nazis, even if they had been eligible, or that, in the case of Communism, they were incapable of egregious malice and stupidity.

Deutscher stands for no few Jews who, given the opportunity, were recruited to an inhumane totalitarian cause. Malcolm Muggeridge once told me that I had said of Graham Greene that sin began *from* wherever he was but did not, strangely, include him. I am not sure that I said this, or that I was right, but it can as well be said of those like Deutscher who 'sold' Marxism less on the grounds of its worth than because it was bound to prevail. (There is, of course, a certain convergence here: even Jesus spoke of how hard it was to kick against the pricks.)

What makes the case of Deutscher relevant to that of Heidegger? For my purposes, it is that we have only very recently come to see the iniquity in Deutscher's attitude; we have – to make Burke and Yeats converge this time – managed the postponed operation of separating the dancer from the attitude which danced him. The reason for our new perception is that our own temptation, and fear, and hope, no longer blinker us: the collapse of the USSR alters the nature not only of the world but also of vision.

A more benign example of the nimbus of ideas which is both pervasive and invisible is to be found in the pragmatic tradition which accompanies the democratic idea without being a constitutive part of it. As a result of the 'right-Marxist' assumptions that the bottom line is the only one that really counts, American foreign policy is systematically incapable of understanding particularisms which seem absurd to those in Washington where it is assumed that everyone in the world is 'really' motivated by money or by the desire to be American.

In the understanding of why things happened, it is sometimes valuable to look at the *air* which a society breathed. To take a safely distant instance, what can *we* ever know for certain about Alexander the Great's *purpose* in invading Asia? How should we read it accurately? During the heyday of Western imperialism, W. W. Tarn could seriously argue that Alexander's intention was to civilise the Orient and that his forced marriages, between Macedonian males and Persian women (never, of course, *vice versa*), were part of an enlightened attempt to homogenise his empire. Later, a less genial view was taken, for example by Peter Green who, in his biography, argues that Alexander was less concerned with the harmonious blending of cultures than with the creation of a corps of Janissaries. The rootless children of the mixed marriages would owe allegiance only to Alexander himself: as the Emperor Franz-Josef might have said, homogenisation *for me*. What Tarn considered to be Alexander's transcendent scheme was reduced, by Green, to a politico-military expedient. The Nazi experiment of breeding babies expressly for the Führer's élite guard made plausible a reading of ancient history which, until 1939, might have seemed merely fanciful. Today changes yesterday.

Wisdom after the event is a function of the *zeitgeist* of those who pronounce it: we can only ever achieve a parallax view of anything that has happened. History deserves constantly to be rewritten as new motives are deemed plausible or old ones need not be concealed, since the interest involved in repressing them has lapsed; René Girard's *Things Concealed Since the Founda-*

tion of the World is an attempt, of rare intelligence, to demystify 'myth' and most religion in the light of the (human) sacrificial rituals which are both declared and concealed in the 'recipes' that are to be discovered in their books. Girard's marginal status as a *philosophe* testifies to the degree to which his 'unpacking' of the religious scheme is an affront to contemporary devices of concealment; he says more than the world wants to have said, or so his own analysis implies.

It should not be inferred that we cannot know anything of the past because we cannot know everything. However, the persistence – and retrieval – of clues reminds us that no case is ever closed, except legally or (much the same thing) by demanding standards of evidence which limit what we choose to admit as relevant. The *pleasure* to be gained from persecuting people is rarely allowed as an element in anti-Semitism, for instance: we are still categorically Aristotelian enough to discountenance the idea that hedonism, or frivolity, can determine a tragedy.

One of the most solemn dwellers on the significance of the Holocaust happens, to my knowledge, to be a deeply conceited sadist. This does not deny the quality of his comments but renders faintly comic his incapacity to see that malice need not be principled or based on deep, if fallacious, doctrines. He wants the Nazi 'philosophy' to have impressive roots and cannot conceive that his inability to perceive its vulgarity is part of his own need to hide from himself.

The necessity of fiction, as a mode, is that, however unreliable, it is part of what assists our access to knowledge (I make no greater claim). Much of fact *is* fiction, one might say, though not too loudly, which accounts for the strange eminence which the novel, in particular, continues to hold, despite so many lamentable modern instances and despite 'the media' which, in almost all instances, are the *joint* work of editors, executives, advertising people, etc., and hence lack that singlemindedness which is necessary for insight. Generally speaking, there is no such thing as collaborative insight, which is why art is not a science and also why there can be no substitute for it.

Index